CRIME AND THE RISE OF MODERN AMERICA

D1610825

Cast in eye-catching headlines, illuminated by the media glow, American crime captures the public imagination. From sex crimes to political corruption, from hate crimes to terrorism, the way people break the law shapes national identity. But this is not a new phenomenon, nor one limited to the present day.

In his book *Crime and the Rise of Modern America,* Kristofer Allerfeldt studies the crimes, criminals, and law enforcement that contributed to a uniquely American system of crime and punishment from the end of the Civil War to the eve of World War II to understand how the rapidly-changing technology of transportation, media, and incarceration affected the criminal underworld.

In eleven thematic chapters, *Crime and the Rise of Modern America* turns to the outlaws of the iconic West and the illegal distilleries of Prohibition, the turn-of-the-century immigrants, and the conmen who preyed on the people of the Promised Land, to examine how crime and America both changed, defining each other.

Kristofer Allerfeldt is a lecturer at the University of Exeter where he teaches diverse American social and diplomatic history courses.

CRIME AND THE RISE OF MODERN AMERICA

A History from 1865–1941

Kristofer Allerfeldt

Routledge
Taylor & Francis Group

NEW YORK AND LONDON

First published 2011
by Routledge
270 Madison Avenue, New York, NY 10016

Simultaneously published in the UK
by Routledge
2 Park Square, Milton Park, Abingdon, Oxon OX14 4RN

Routledge is an imprint of the Taylor & Francis Group, an informa business

Typeset in Bembo and Stone Sans by
RefineCatch Limited, Bungay, Suffolk
Printed and bound in the United States of America on acid-free paper by
Walsworth Publishing Company, Marceline, MO

Library of Congress Cataloging in Publication Data
A catalog record has been requested for this book

ISBN13: 978–0–415–80044–0 (hbk)
ISBN13: 978–0–415–80045–7 (pbk)
ISBN13: 978–0–203–83032–1 (ebk)

NSF-SFI-COC-C0004285
The SFI label applies to the text stock.

To Matilda and Frederika Allerfeldt, because I love them.

CONTENTS

INTRODUCTION

It is almost unimaginable that an account of contemporary America would not deal with crime. It seems that America is obsessed with crime. Perhaps it commits more crime than any other state—it certainly imprisons more of its population than anywhere else. Americans obsess about crime with their television and in their films. It dominates the newspapers, and forms a recurrent theme in plays. Crime has an entire genre dedicated to itself in novels. It could be argued that so many famous American icons are connected with crime—the western sheriff, the gangster and his moll, Alcatraz, the electric chair, or the hard-boiled detective— that it is perhaps fair to say that crime and criminals could make as a good a definition of modern America and contemporary American-ness as any other.

It seems like the public will never tire of accounts of spectacular crimes like Bernie Madoff's colossal swindles and there is an endless analysis of sensational trials like the O.J. Simpson case. There are also the biographies of major criminals. The lives of Jeffrey Dahmer and Jim Jones, for example, will no doubt provide material for biographers for years to come, and are equally certain to attract huge readerships. Fictional criminals, detectives and prison dramas consistently form one of the most popular genres in the bestsellers lists. But it is not as if contemporary, or recent, criminals are unique in their appeal. A quick scan of Amazon.com would show that the lives of Al Capone and Jesse James are perhaps of even more interest than the criminals of recent years and it will also reveal that the novels of such writers as Edgar Alan Poe, Dashiell Hammett and Raymond Chandler remain perennially popular.

Given this enduring obsession with criminality it is hardly surprising that the history of crime is also a popular genre. There are, for example, countless accounts of the growth of the Mafia, the impact of Prohibition, the horrors of lynching or the reality of the Wild West. Some of these are well-researched and accurate historical works. Others are less rigorous in their methodology and approach.

Whatever their individual value, there is also another problem with the vast majority of these accounts. Few give a summary of crime across a period as a whole. They are often limited in scope, both geographically and temporally. They may examine John Dillinger in the context of the War on Crime in the Mid-West, or Al Capone in relation to years of Prohibition.

Accounts that give a long-term overview, such as those available to, say, the military or immigration historian, are very rare and more often than not limited to purely factual encyclopaedias with little or no analysis or context. There are some very notable exceptions, like Timothy Gilfoyle's *A Pickpocket's Tale* or Charles van Onselen's *The Fox and the Flies*.[1] Both of these extraordinary books focus on an individual criminal—which necessarily limits the time-span—but unusually they use him (in each case it is a male) to explore the wider world in which he moved as well as the wider nature of his criminality. Both are analysed in fascinating depth.

It could be argued that there are a variety of reasons for this void, and two stand out. First, in order to cover this vast subject, such an undertaking would have to either give cursory coverage of all aspects of crime, or it would be edited to an extent whereby it excluded vast amounts of material. Either way it would run the risk of losing its purpose. Second, and perhaps most importantly, it could be asked, why would such a volume be necessary? Surely if there was a necessity for such a book, then someone would have already produced it. Perhaps it has not been done because it cannot be done satisfactorily.

The way in which this volume attempts to overcome these two problems is to take a defined period and a tried and tested structure. The period chosen is that during which America rose from a war-weary and divided second-rate nation, to being the most powerful economic and industrial power in the world. This period, from the end of the Civil War in 1865 through to the bombing of Pearl Harbor in 1941, has been called the birth of Modern America. It covers a wide variety of periods of American history, from Reconstruction, through to the Gilded Age, the Progressive Era, the 1920s and the New Deal. It not only sees the massive expansion of the economy, but also the Federal Government, the population, the territory (both within its own continent and abroad) and, by the end, the military. It also sees a huge expansion in crime.

Just as America became obsessed during this period with a culture of "bigness" in everyday life—from skyscrapers and other engineering projects to accumulations of wealth and food portion sizes—so America began to outdo other nations in crime. Americans swindled each other and foreigners out of more money, with the Credit Mobilier scandal (see Chapter 2) and the Ponzi scheme (see Chapter 1). American murderers killed more. This was the period of the first recorded "serial killer"—H.H. Holmes who stalked and murdered young women at the Chicago's World Fair. Americans fêted their criminals—from Jesse James to Bonnie and Clyde—in a far more overt fashion than, say, France or Britain. During this period America had crime lords, figures like Joe Colisimo, Frank Nitti, and Arnold Rothstein, who ruled whole criminal empires and seemed untouchable. Not only were American criminals more powerful than those of other nations but they were also somehow more sinister, like the Molly Maguires, the Black Hand, and the Mafia (see Chapter 5).

Perhaps more than any other period in any comparable state, Americans incorporated crime into their culture. Young men imitated or joined violent urban gangs like the Plug Uglies and dressed in uniforms which displayed their allegiances. As the twentieth century progressed, these gave way to the "mobs," "outfits" and "syndicates" as gangsters adopted the creed of modernization and collectivized. Nor was such behavior limited to the "criminal classes." By the 1920s, even non-gang members had adopted the patois of the underworld, talking of "heaters," "stools," and "the slammer," and imitated the gangsters' casual misogyny and disregard for the law. Perhaps as a result of this, during these years Americans were encouraged to idolize their policemen and detectives, with papers running articles on characters from the brutal Clubber Williams to the meticulous J. Edgar Hoover and the incorruptible Eliot Ness. Young men wanted to grow up to be fearless sheriffs or granite-jawed FBI G-men who caught, imprisoned, or shot the wrongdoers with a combination of moral certainty and sang-froid.

As if to show the success of these agents, the nation's prison population grew fivefold as a proportion of the population, and prisons became household names. Few Americans would not have recognized Alcatraz, Sing Sing or the Tombs. Further, throughout these years, America was outraged by new types of criminals. There was the crazed Negro cocaine fiend, the White Slaver, the juvenile delinquent, the psychopath, the serial killer and the white-collar criminal. It seemed that each year the threat posed by crime grew ever greater, in its frequency, proximity and ruthlessness. In part, this was no doubt the result of more sophisticated methods of categorization, policing and detection. In part, it was probably down to a growing intolerance of anti-social, malicious or dangerous behavior. It also owed much to the explosion in the news media. Starting with the mass-circulation newspapers in the last decades of the nineteenth century, the hunger for readers created a thirst for ever more sensational, gruesome and extraordinary crimes which sold copy and fed the hyperbole of the headlines.

If crime as a concept became far more widespread in America over these years, it also represents a very good way of interpreting the period. After all, the divisions generally used by historians fit happily with such an interpretation, and it is simple to map crimes directly on to these divisions. The Reconstruction Era, with its cowing of the South's black population back to a state of submissiveness little better than the slavery they had so recently left, is surely one of the most blatant representations of the hate crime. Similarly, the Gilded Age, with its winner-take-all capitalism, its monopolies and swindles, can be explained and illuminated by examining not only the figures who broke the existing laws, but also those who led to its being changed as well as those who got clean away.

When the twentieth century opened and the Progressivism became the dominant force in politics, these disparate Christian, urban reformers brought with them a moralizing, centralizing urge. Few of their actions demonstrate the essence of the era named after them better than their criminalization of what they considered immoral—prostitution, narcotics, gambling and, eventually, booze. Few figures fit the Dollar Decade of the 1920s better than the criminal fraternity. With Capone, Nitti and Rothstein, crime, like most other aspects of American life was syndicated and dominated by the quest for fortune. What could illustrate this better than the corruption in America's national sport, baseball, or the huge fortunes made from rum running? When the seemingly inevitable crash came, the excesses of the 1920s seemed unattainable. Many of those who lost everything lost faith in the law and even those who did not resort to crime respected many of those who did. In the atavistic times of Depression America, the new breed of motorized bandit was glamorized. Figures like John Dillinger and Clyde Barrow were seen as emblematic of a simpler, self-reliant, more individual lifestyle, one which had disappeared with the change of the nation's fortunes.

Of course, these examples are simplified and generalized, but such overviews enable a clear view of how crime both changed America and reflected other changes taking place in American society. Crime can be seen not only as both an exemplar and as a catalyst, but also as an indicator of things to come. It is in this period that so much of contemporary America is shaped. Giants like Lincoln, Wilson and the Roosevelts illuminated the course of America's philosophical and political mission(s), just as figures like Rockefeller, Morgan and Mellon laid the foundations of the hitherto unseen economic power to achieve those goals. This period leaves other legacies, and many of them are tied to crime, and analysis of these not only can help us understand the period of this study, but also the roots of many of the criminal problems of our own times.

Perhaps most notoriously, it is in 1914 that America passes the Harrison Narcotics Act, which, by criminalizing the narcotics trade, has arguably done more to shape contemporary America than any other single piece of legislation. This Act set up the mentality which would dictate contemporary America's relations with many of its neighbors and other nations associated with the drugs trade. It led, for example, to such schemes as the 2009 Merida Initiative, under which the US government pledged $1.6 billion to combat the drugs trade through military and judicial means in Mexico and Central America. Alongside this was the earlier and on-going Plan Columbia, under which America is committed to fighting not only the cocaine trade but also the FARC guerrillas associated with it. It is the huge profits from the drugs trade—which, many would argue, is the result of the continuing of the American campaign against their international trade—which financed, and continues to finance, many of the enemies of the United States from Nicaragua's Contras to Al Qaeda.

Nor is it only abroad that the reverberations of the Harrison Act's prohibitions have been felt. At home, the economic and human costs have been enormous. Founded in 1971 as a part of Nixon's War on Drugs initiative, by 2007, the Drug Enforcement Agency employed over 10,500, nearly half of whom were field agents, and had a budget of more than $2.5 billion. What is more, like alcohol prohibition before it, the criminalization of narcotics has swelled the federal prison population. Since the inception of the War on Drugs, America's prison population has increased tenfold. The importance of drugs in this growth can be seen in the statistics for arrests in 1980. While the arrest rate for all criminal offenses grew by nearly 30 percent over the year, the arrests for drug offenses grew by nearly 130 percent. It was estimated that in 1993 drug offenses led to the imprisonment of 1 million Americans.

Moreover, the effects of the Harrison Act have been seen as making a major contribution to the huge disparity in society due to the creation of a new criminal underclass. The criminalization of non-whites is perhaps most noticeable in narcotics convictions. For example, in 1998, while it was estimated that African Americans made up less than a fifth of all drug users, they constituted over a third of all drugs-related arrests, over half of the nation's drug-related convictions and nearly three-quarters of those in US prison for drugs offenses.[2] Nor is the Harrison Act the only piece of legislation during this period which created a legacy of racial disparity. Since at least 1882, with the first of the Chinese Exclusion Acts, race has formed an overt and essential ingredient in American immigration policy.

The ideal of exclusion by race which this legislation created was reinforced by the creation of the Asiatic Barred zone in 1917 and then the quota Acts of 1921, 1924 and 1929 which made it illegal for increasingly large numbers of immigrants to enter the country, purely as a result of their race. While such practices may be condemned today, they lived on to form the basis of US immigration policy at least until the Hart–Cellar Act of 1964. Arguably vestiges are still detectable in the present-day attitude to Mexican immigrants. The country's Mexican border is fortified and guarded in a way that would probably lead to an international incident if such measures were applied to the Canadian border. There are numbers of reports made about the huge discrepancies between the treatment of those found illegally crossing the southern border, compared with the northern. For example, America established its para-military Border Patrol in 1924 and it has grown ever since, reaching some 18,000 employees with a budget of nearly $2 billion today. In keeping with the perceived "threat," the vast bulk of these resources are employed policing the 2,000-mile-long southern border which is also being closed by means of a physical and electronic barrier. No such measure is contemplated for the northern boundary.

If narcotics and border control form the two most obvious and expensive criminal legacies of the period of this study, another obvious, but more insidious crime is also building, and it too arguably has many of its roots in these formative years of American history. In 1918, America introduced legislation to make passports a requirement for travel into and out of the US. Although technically this legislation was only extended through until 1921, similar laws remained in place in Europe, making US citizens obliged to carry documentation for most foreign travel, and made the production of valid passports a *de facto* part of entry requirements to the US.

What this meant was that individual identity had become subject to criminalization and a new brand of forgery and theft had become possible. In recent years, the near universal dependence on computers and computer networks for data storage, the massive expansion in the use of credit cards and electronic money transfer, combined with the increasing availability and relative ease of long-distance transport, have made identity theft a huge industry. Identity theft is the fastest growing as well as one of the most lucrative of all crimes in present-day America. The Federal Trade Commission estimates that some $50 billion worth of such crimes were reported in 2009, affecting nearly 10 million US citizens. This has grown from around $33 billion and 3 million reported victims in 2003.[3] Given the difficulties of confirming and collating such information, the real figure is probably many times higher, but, most importantly, in spite of the increasing knowledge of the problem and the methods used, as well as ever more sophisticated countermeasures, there is no doubt that it is a criminal phenomenon that will continue to grow.

In some ways, it is difficult to separate "criminal history" from "mainstream" history. Sometimes this is historical fact and is beneficial to the interpretation and analysis of an era or a region. For example, the criminal activity of the Ku Klux Klan in the Reconstruction South *is* in many ways the history of the Reconstruction South. Sometimes it is simply mythology, which has become "history" and owes less to historical fact than to legends which have become accepted as fact in large measure, because criminal subjects have not been subjected to the same rigorous historical scrutiny as other areas of history. For example, the Wild West was not universally wild either geographically or temporally. It was not a term which was applicable to all the region west of the Mississippi, nor was it applicable to any specific time. It is the aim of this book to draw these distinctions clearly and in so doing use criminal history in a more sophisticated fashion.

So, to return to the two essential questions, it seems that there is a genuine void to be filled, and there is a structure which can fulfil this need without drifting into either rather tedious narrative. Having said that, in adopting the tight thematic structure necessary to complete such a task there will be both omissions and repetition. Some are no doubt simple mistakes. Others can be explained. For example, this book does not deal with serial killers as such, nor does it do more than mention domestic violence. Both were very important in the period, but neither fit in with the limitations imposed by the structure. What is more, some figures recur in various chapters. Charles Ponzi was both a swindler and an immigrant and as such makes an appearance in the chapters devoted to both. Overall, this book is intended to enable this exciting period of American history to be studied in a fresh light.

1

THE CRIMES OF THE CENTURY

It will soon be time for another Crime of the Century. This is the same century, but it needs a new crime. It has been weeks since the front page really smoked and the same Bestial Deed, the same Positive Identification, the same Master Mind, the same Little Woman, the same Alleged Confession, and the same Grim Prosecutor brightened the fireside of every home in this great throbbing country.

Charles Merz, "Bigger and Better Murders"[1]

The act which created a stir far beyond this country is so frightful, psychologically so incomprehensible, so singular in its unfoldment that, if Poe or a writer of detective stories wished to unnerve his readers, no better tale could be invented; no harder knot to unravel; no events could follow each other more effectively than life, or rather disease, has here woven them together.

Dr. Maurice Urstein, psychiatric consultant, on the
Leopold and Loeb murder trial[2]

To the father of the modern American newspaper, James Gordon Bennett (senior), public opinion—guided by press reports—constituted a "living Jury of the nation."[3] Undoubtedly, disregarding the characteristic grandiloquence of Bennett, this concept has some validity for the historian, but it needs to be handled with caution and regarded in context. New technologies, such as linotype, and improved transportation encouraged true mass circulation newspapers. In order to compete in this market, ambitious newspapers vied with each other for the increasingly lucrative advertising revenue of a nation wanting to sell ever more of the goods produced by its rapidly expanding industry. The result was that a swift tour through the metropolitan and rural press of the time rather unsurprisingly reveals—then as now—a great deal of hyperbole.

The everyday does not sell papers and this was certainly true of the American newspapers of the nineteenth century. Instead it produced papers that were filled with increasingly dramatic and eye-catching "true" accounts of "horrible" and "terrible" crimes, "dastardly deeds" and scandals. Not only did these tales enliven, distract and inform the progressively more humdrum lives of growing numbers of "decent" American, they also, hopefully, brought them back, time and again to that newspaper for more of the same.

Crime and depravity sold papers and it is no coincidence that it was as this period opened that the lurid magazine, the *National Police Gazette*, was reaching its peak circulation with its wide working-class, male, readership. Under its rather misleading title, the *Gazette* reported the antics of men and women whose behavior was by turns titillating, inspiring and shocking. It used sensationalist language to show the interests, worries and developments in the criminal world. Typical of the style of the tabloid style magazine was its report on the boom town of Chicago in 1866. The headlines promised that it would expose "Chicago. [Where] A Drunken Woman [Was] Ravished, Stripped Naked and Murdered. Three of the Miscreants Arrested. . . . [It would show] Pretty Servant Girls—Their Indiscretions and Crimes. [It would detail] A 'Slaughter of the Innocents.' [As well as] Exciting Scenes in a Fashionable Boarding House." All this in a single article.[4]

By 1865, the hyperbolic language of crime reporting had made this "national jury" familiar with the concept of the "crime of the century." It seems that the actual expression emerged out of the reporting of the murder of Mary Rogers, in 1841, but it is arguably not until the period of this study opens that there was a crime truly worthy of the title "crime of the century."[5] With the assassination of Abraham Lincoln in April, 1865, the press could—and did—beyond doubt report a crime which, even from the perspective of the present day, undoubtedly altered the course of nineteenth-century American history. Nevertheless, it is indicative of the hyperbole of the contemporary press that by July of that year the *New York Times* had already discovered another crime of the century.

In the wake of the publication of details of horrors of the Andersonville prison camp in *Harper's Weekly* of the first week of June 1865, the *Times* claimed that the torture and starvation of Union troops who had the misfortune to be captured and imprisoned by "ruffians" of the defeated Confederacy were unmatched in their cruelty and criminality.[6] Six years later still it was the Confederate leaders who were being held responsible for "the greatest crime of this or any other century." After all, as Senator Oliver P. Morton of Indiana pointed out, it was they who had sanctioned a course of action—secession—which would ultimately leave 400,000 American soldiers dead; 100,000 American women widowed and 300,000 American children orphaned.[7] He seems to have started a trend, since the German invasion of France in 1870 led to the Kaiser and Bismarck being condemned in similar terms.

Few new categories emerged to top the criminal honors throughout the 1870s. Political crime was the strongest contender with the constitutional status of the compromise of 1877 leading the field. Under this agreement, the Republicans took the White House by agreeing to withdraw the Federal troops propping up Republican state governments in South Carolina, Florida, and Louisiana. The compromise comes in for understandable condemnation from black and Democrat papers, which argue that it was a betrayal of the battles of Reconstruction as well as the Democrat Party as whole. There was also hostility among a handful of Republican papers which considered Rutherford B. Hayes' presidency as something less than legitimate because of what they saw as the less than legal agreement. Typical is the reaction of the way in which for several months following the compromise, the *Fort Worth Sentinel* insisted on adding a question mark after every mention of President Hayes' name.[8]

The tone had changed by the end of the decade. In 1889, Henry M. Hunt published *The Crime of the Century*. It was a dramatization of the murder of a renowned Chicago physician, Dr Cronin, by five shadowy Irishmen. By the time the real-life drama had played out, three of the Irishmen had been executed. Another member of the gang received three years for his peripheral part, but their well-connected leader escaped punishment. With the characteristic hyperbole of the period, Hunt proclaimed his account of the apparent miscarriage as: "A Complete and Authentic History of the Greatest of Modern Conspiracies." It was undoubtedly a "thrilling and fascinating" read, a bestseller which added to the genre immediately, but its long-term impact was less clear.[9] Some, like the Russian-born anarchist Sergei Shovitch, saw the Cronin case as a benchmark of official corruption and, along with George Bernard Shaw, compared it with the conviction of the eight Haymarket "martyrs."[10]

Others saw the hyperbole involved as starting an avalanche of "un-American" interest in crime. They argued that it was simply making "some act of vice or crime a special feature and elaborating it, expanding it and exaggerating it, making it a sensation that discolors all other events."[11] Whether this was the result of Hunt's work or simply the result of the dawn of the age of truly mass-circulation newspapers may be contested but what is certain is that crimes, trials, murders, robberies "of the century" all became far more commonplace. A swift search of a basket of newspapers published between 1890 and 1895 lists some 77 "Crimes of the Century." They show clearly what interested the American public, and include a range of crimes from Spanish atrocities in Cuba and Turkish ones in Armenia, through Democrat tariff proposals and the failure to introduce a bimetallic currency. Among this sensationalism are stories relating to the lynching of eleven Italians in New Orleans in 1891 (see Chapter 11).

This last crime is interesting, not only because of its unique scale—it remains the largest number of victims lynched in a single episode at any point in American history—but it also highlights a couple of important themes in American society at the time. First, lynching and lynch law had been epidemic in the South, with groups like the Klan and the Order of the White Camellia punishing "uppity niggers" or running "nigger hunts" as well as intimidating Republican sympathizers. These claimed unrecorded thousands of lives in the Reconstruction era. They were events which by their unfeeling, unpunished inhumanity and brutality as well as the sheer scale of the offenses could plausibly qualify them as the crime of the century, but were very rarely reported as such—if they were reported at all. What is more, this casualization of violence was not just prevalent in the Reconstruction South, it was just as widespread in the new territories of the West.[12] Here in the vast, sparsely populated, poorly policed lands of greed and opportunity, both crime and retribution were frequently exceptionally violent, even by the standards of the time. Unlike the South, where lynching was predominantly aimed at blacks, such violence in the West encompassed all races, from Native Americans—the most obvious racial enemy of the white settlers—to blacks, to Chinese, to other Europeans.

That is not to say that there was not a racial element to frontier violence. In the 1870s and 1880s, anti-Chinese lynchings and shootings in the West claimed over 200 lives in what would certainly be seen today as an organized campaign of ethnic cleansing. However, in the majority of cases of lynching in the West, it was suspicion of such crimes as murder, rape, robbery or claim jumping which led to vigilante punishment and indeed, in the case of the unfortunate Italians, it was ostensibly the murder of the local Irish-American police chief—David Hennessey—which led to their demise. It is probable that the real reason was at least partially racially motivated. Although the nine accused Italians had been acquitted of murdering Hennessey, they, and two others, were harassed, arrested and eventually lynched largely on flimsy evidence which revolved around the fact that, as Sicilians, they were presumed to be members of some sort of "mafia."[13] Not only does this play to national stereotyping but it also shows up one of the greatest fears of America in the 1890s—the threat posed to American institutions and American lives by the massive increase and shift in origin of European immigrants (see Chapter 11).

As if to reinforce this, when President William McKinley's assassination made the headlines in September 1901, the American-born, Leon Csolgosz's Polish-Catholic ancestry went some way to explaining his seemingly senseless and savage act. How could immigrants from nations which had known nothing other than autocracy possibly adapt to the democracy of America? Revolution was the only available course for those opposed to autocrats and many commentators argued that when these wretched terrorists left their home countries they would, and did, bring that violent form of political action with them. This linkage of xenophobia and violence remained, and remains, one of the most important strains of American popular attitudes towards criminal behavior. Immigration restrictionists in the early twentieth century made great play of the criminal tendencies of the foreign-born. Further evidence was provided in the large number of accounts that pointed to the fact that Csolgosz was also associated with the Lithuanian-born Emma

Goldman—the very "High Priestess of Anarchy"—and her lover, the Russian-born Jew, Alexander Berkman.[14]

Fear of radicalism remained one of the chief crime headlines throughout the next decades. When the larger-than-life, former governor of Idaho, Frank Steunenberg, was blown up in 1905 by a bomb rigged to his front gate, radicals were once again held to be responsible for the "Crime of the Century." The Democrat/Populist Steunenberg had come to power on an anti-corporate, labor, ticket in 1896. Once in power he was seen as abandoning his blue-collar principles. His treason against the "working stiff" culminated in the declaration of marshal law in 1899 and backing this betrayal with a plea to President McKinley for federal troops. When a troublesome alliance of the Western Federation of Miners, Socialists and Industrial Workers of the World became implicated in the murder and the subsequent trial, the authorities ranged an equally powerful combination of Pinkerton agents, Idaho state officials and mine-owners which was tacitly backed by the "spiders of Wall Street" and even the White House. Hired guns fought out a vicious small-scale class war in the Rockies as jurors were bought by either side and witnesses perjured themselves in what was in many ways *the trial* of the first decade of the twentieth century.[15]

The case set the scene for similarly high profile and controversial trials over the next years. In 1910, in what was either a bungled warning to scabs or the work of agent provocateurs, the brothers James and John McNamara admitted to the killing of 21 workers in their bombing of the *Los Angeles Times* building. The case of Thomas Mooney's conviction for the San Francisco Preparedness Day bombing in 1916 similarly divided the nation. Depending on their viewpoint, some Americans felt that here was a radical, using violence to object to American patriots raising money for defense. Others saw him as a stooge for the forces devoted to driving America towards entry into a capitalist war in Europe. Either way, ten were killed and 40 injured in the bombing, which served to keep the fear of revolution more than real in the press. What was more, this time it was not merely newspapers which formed opinion. The controversy was further fueled by a Hearst Studios propaganda movie.[16]

Both the McNamara and the Mooney cases conformed to the requirements of a celebrity case. Both created a moral panic. Both were controversial, not only at the time but for some time after. If longevity of the reputation of a crime is the indication of its importance, then the Mooney case was certainly in the top rank. Mooney's name, in particular, remained highly controversial and visible in the press until the end of the period of this study, largely as a result of those who managed first to commute his death sentence to life imprisonment and then gain him a pardon, after 21 years in prison. Both crimes featured innocent victims—not only those killed, but also, to many, those accused. Both featured "perpetrators," who, like Csolgosz, were American-born of Catholic stock, and, like Csolgosz, the press frequently played them up as foreign—in both cases, Irish—and thus more prone to violence.

If the McNamara and Mooney cases harked back to Csolgosz, then the next serious contender for the American crime of the century owed much to the New Orleans lynchings. The conviction and subsequent execution of Nicola Sacco and Bartolomeo Vanzetti for the robbery and murder of a paymaster and his guard in May 1920 in South Braintree, Massachusetts, were without doubt partly to do with the fact that the two were both Italian. It was probably more down to the fact that, in spite of producing convincing alibis and the self-contradictory evidence given by the prosecution at the subsequent trials, both men were armed when they were arrested. However, what almost certainly ensured their demise was the fact that they were both committed anarchists which meant that they lied when arrested, arguably to avoid deportation.

It also made them more than likely guilty in the eyes of an American public generally suspicious of any radicals in the paranoid political climate of post-World War I America. Events like the steel strike, the Seattle General Strike, the Boston police strike and a wave of bombings convinced many Americans that a Bolshevik revolution was about to topple their democracy. Foreigners became suspects as the so-called "Red Scare" allowed the Attorney General, Alexander Mitchell Palmer, to arrest suspected radicals and hold them subject to deportation proceedings. Although the passions of the "Deportation Delirium" largely played themselves out as the deportees were almost all freed, many of the underlying suspicions of foreigners remain potent forces in 1920s America. As Vanzetti said in his final speech of 1927, "My conviction is that I have suffered for things that I am guilty of. I am suffering because I am a radical, and indeed I am a radical; I have suffered because I am an Italian, and indeed I am an Italian."[17]

As the Sacco–Vanzetti case continued, another celebrity victim of America's racial divisions emerged. The charismatic Jamaican, Marcus Garvey's attempts to create economic opportunity and an African homeland for Afro-Americans ran foul of the decade's tribal nature. Although one of the chief architects of the Red Scare, J. Edgar Hoover, initially admitted he could not indict the black leader, after several years of trying, in 1923, the Federal authorities managed to pin 12 counts of mail fraud on him and three of his associates.[18] The ensuing trials made head-lines as details emerged of Garvey's secret agreement with one of the most powerful Klan leaders; of his suspected involvement in the murder of the critic of Garveyism, J.W. Eason; and of the financial irregularities of his Black Star Line.

Garvey was portrayed as a buffoon in many of the hostile commentaries of the time. Much was made of his Napoleonic dress sense. His failure to use the Black Star Line to settle any American blacks in Africa and his presumptuous assumption of the title "President of Africa" were played up by a generally hostile white American press. Although Garvey was vocally opposed to the status quo, in terms of the position of blacks in American society, and attracted the support of many radicals for his comments on white supremacy, unlike Sacco and Vanzetti, it was mockery rather than genuine fear which proved to be the method of his undoing. As one New Mexico paper headlined—"PRESIDENT OF AFRICA GOES

TO JUG FOR SWINDLING: Marcus Garvey Disappears Behind Bars Amid Wailing of Coons."[19] Ultimately it was stereotypical images of blacks as financially naive, gullible and intellectually and emotionally inferior which led to his imprisonment and, later, deportation.

Similarly odious, and more threatening, images informed the perception of the defendants in another of the celebrity crimes of this period—the infamous Scottsboro Boys trials which rumbled on in the background throughout the 1930s. These trials related to the alleged gang rape of two young white women in Scottsboro, Alabama, by nine itinerant, young, black, men in March 1931.[20] Initially in four separate trials, all except one of the defendants was sentenced to death, the only exception being Roy Wright whose youth prohibited capital sentence. However, this was far from the end of the case. What is interesting is that the general flavor of white reporting outside the South tended to be sympathetic to the "boys," whereas in the case of Garvey, a large proportion of the non-black press was hostile. The verdicts attracted pleas for clemency from figures as diverse as Lincoln Steffens, H.G. Wells, Albert Einstein and Thomas Mann. The case inspired novels and plays. There were telegrams, petitions, attacks on US embassies, parades, rallies and a mass march on Washington, DC, in 1933.[21] This national and international protest led to another set of trials, which upheld the guilty verdicts.

These verdicts were reached in spite of growing evidence of the innocence of the "boys." Communist-backed, often Jewish, International Labor defense lawyers produced a compelling case. This included forensic evidence which showed the allegations of rape to be unfounded. They showed one of the "victims," Victoria Price, to have been extremely promiscuous and to have a criminal record for immoral behavior, making her far from the virtuous Southern Belle that local papers described. More importantly, the other girl, Ruby Bates, denied that the rape had taken place at all. Yet the all white Alabama juries repeatedly returned guilty verdicts. Just as with Sacco and Vanzetti, the case demonstrated that the fear of radicalism was essentially tied in with the nature of outsiders in American society.

This was a true, if localized, moral panic. Black itinerants attacked white women and were defended by lawyers from outside the region. Reports, most probably founded in truth, circulated about Communist attempts to bribe witnesses. They certainly tried to portray the "boys" as martyrs. Outside newspaper reports played up the supposed bigotry inherent in the Southern justice system. These views were compounded through what was seen by many in the South as the ill-informed attitudes of the NAACP and Communist Party defenses. Their provocative language and attacks on the virtue of Southern women simply served to alienate many locals who would have made up the juries—men and women who knew that the region's problems were peculiar to the South. To these jurors, white women needed defending from the bestial appetites of young blacks and turning these rapists into martyrs was as fundamentally wrong as it was fundamentally un-American. This situation is perhaps best summed up by a later novelist who has one of the locals explain the situation in words as apposite as Vanzetti's final statement—"Some Nigger raped a white gal, and a bunch of yids are trying to get him off."[22]

Two months after Sacco and Vanzetti were alleged to have committed the robbery for which they were executed, newspapers were investigating another Italian who, they suspected, was committing what was in many ways a far more spectacular crime. The city editor of the *Boston Post* had become interested in the career of a certain Carlo (Charles) Ponzi. This handsome, amiable, charismatic, intelligent and irrepressible immigrant had arrived in Boston in 1903 with less than two dollars to his name. After a variety of unsuccessful clerical jobs, equally doomed get-rich-quick schemes and scrapes with the law, Ponzi's latest venture, the Securities Exchange Company, took more than $9 million in a little over seven months.[23]

In many ways, this was hardly surprising since the company ran a scheme promising the unfeasibly high interest rate of 50 percent on 90-day investments. Ponzi claimed this incredible return was achieved through playing the unusually strong post-war dollar against a variety of depressed European currencies via postal coupons, although he was never very specific about the detailed mechanics of his alchemy. The mysteries of this system, coupled with the failure of newspapers and government agencies to discover any illegality or liquidity problems, rather perversely excited interest. When added to the knowledge that Ponzi was fighting a million dollar lawsuit, the fraudster's story made spectacular press and the editor of the *Post*, Richard Grozier, knew the value of such a story. His father, Edwin Grozier, had taken over the run-down *Post* in 1891 when the paper had a circulation of less than 20,000.

Grozier proved to be little short of "a newspaper genius," turning it into New England's leading paper with a readership of over 600,000 by the time of his death in 1924. Part of this success was down to publicity stunts, part dogged investigation of stories he knew had public interest. Perhaps his biggest coup was in 1911 when he pursued the Baptist minister, the Reverend Clarence Richeson, for the poisoning of 16-year-old Avis Linell, his pregnant former sweetheart. The *Post*'s lurid and glaring headlines—including at least one reference to the case as the "crime of the century"—drove the investigation, conviction and subsequent execution of Richeson. It also caused some 2,000 hymn-singing New Englanders to wait in the driving rain outside the "Death House" at the state prison for news that the sentence of death in the electric chair had been carried out.[24]

Richard Grozier used this inherited doggedness with regard to Ponzi. By the end of July, the unflappable Italian was being touted for positions from mayor of Boston, through to governor of Massachusetts. To his satisfied customers he was the potent and determined enemy of the money trusts. Where they swindled the public by paying only 5 or so percent, he gave the investor real returns. The "Greatest Italian in History," the man who "invented money"—the amiable fraudster Ponzi was the epitome of the American dream. An adulatory press depicted him as an eccentric mixture of John D. Rockefeller, Robin Hood and Babe Ruth.[25] He was a hero as long as the interest payments continued to be made, which was, as Grozier discovered, as long as he could continue to use new investors' money to pay off the interest for the matured accounts: as long as he could run the swindle known as being able to "rob Peter to pay Paul." As other papers across the nation hyped his financial wizardry, from July 30, the *Post* began to systematically demolish confidence in Ponzi's scheme. Within a fortnight he declared himself bankrupt and was charged with 86 counts of fraud.

To the 17,000 investors, many of whom Ponzi left without their life savings, it was truly the crime of the century and Ponzi's name has gone into the criminal dictionary for this type of fraud. The scheme may have been imitated on a greater scale since, and Ponzi was not the first to use the system, but it was his personal charisma and the precise fit of the crime with the mood of the time that made it headline news. On the other hand his position as criminal of the century did not even last out the next couple of years, let alone the decade. These were years of self-conscious and contested modernity and it seemed that the newspapers could find a spectacular crime to highlight each of these changes. One of the best examples of this is the spate of robberies committed by Celia Cooney in the spring of 1924 which underscored the growing independence and confidence of women. Christened the "Bobbed Haired Bandit" by a breathless media, they used her "stick ups" to show the way in which the sexual, financial, and ethical independence of the "flapper" threatened traditional American values.

In a cynical press driven by circulation figures, the 19-year-old, working-class, Brooklyn girl was everything from a callous vamp who stole for kicks in order to buy fashionable luxuries, to an impoverished mother who stole to pay the instalments on the necessities of life for her growing family in times of inflated prices. The petty crime spree had an air of unreality to Celia as she became the symbol of feminine independence and gun-toting modernity. Nevertheless she jealously guarded her celebrity and was annoyed when another woman was arrested for her crimes, going so far as to write a note to the police telling them they had the wrong girl. Modern girl that she was, Celia would sell her story to the *New York American* shortly after her arrest and lived off her version of the events on her release. The language used to depict it, the glamor and adventure were all reminiscent of the pulp detective stories which both the newspapers and Celia aped to describe the really rather tragic events in which the girl worked her way deeper into trouble, losing her baby and ultimately her freedom.[26]

If Celia Cooney represented one aspect of America's deep divisions and apparent moral collapse in the 1920s, there were far more memorable, and perhaps significant examples. John Scopes' trial could arguably be seen as an even more explicit example of the way in which the media manipulated public opinion and created all the aspects of a moral panic. The young football coach was tried in July 1925 for allegedly teaching evolution in breach of a Klan-backed Tennessee ordinance. The ensuing trial was a blatant attempt to gain publicity for the town of Dayton which had been in decline since the local mining corporation had cut back its operations in the region. Attracting national attention, the so-called "Monkey Trial" became a showdown between Christian fundamentalists and modernists. These were divisions which were played up by the antics, statements and writing of the three central characters: the notorious defense lawyer, Clarence Darrow; the witty, urbane, and widely syndicated journalist, H.L. Mencken, on the one hand, and the rather humorless, fundamentalist, three-time Presidential candidate, and celebrated speaker, William Jennings Bryan.

The trial demonstrated the deep divisions between traditional and modern America, old and new America, small town and metropolitan America of the 1920s which characterized the deeply divided nature of this, the most American of decades. Nevertheless the long-lived celebrity status of the trial does not lie simply in the hyperbole employed by the two fêted lawyers who represented diametrically opposing views—although that was sufficiently outrageous to gain them both death threats. It does not even lie in the unprecedented news copy generated by Mencken and a small army of other journalists who descended on the town for the week of the trial. Rather, its real long-term historical significance lies in the hollow nature of the decision reached. Although Scopes was found guilty and fined, the adverse publicity generated by the trial effectively neutered Christian fundamentalism as a political force in America until Jimmy Carter announced his born-again status nearly 50 years later.

If the arguments put forward by Clarence Darrow and H.L. Mencken spurred a major victory for secularism with the Scopes trial, it is often argued that Darrow had contributed to the tensions of the decade with his defense of the self-confessed thrill-seeking murderers, Nathan Leopold and Richard Loeb a year before. Arguably this trial has more elements which could qualify it as the crime of the twentieth century than any before or since. Revolving around the casual, premeditated and brutal murder of 14-year-old Bobby Franks by two rich, intelligent, and well-educated Jewish teenagers, the case was headline material from the start. When it emerged that Darrow, who vocally and frequently condemned capital punishment as "revolting and horrible," was offered $100,000 to save the youngsters from the death penalty, it became even more fascinating.

Crime, and especially murder, had been good copy throughout the period—as a popular historian would memorably put it, "After Lincoln, the deluge."[27] One survey of New York City newspapers showed that in 1881, crime took up 0.1 of a column inch a month of news space. By 1893, this was up to some six inches. By the time of the Leopold–Loeb trial, it was 165 inches.[28] Sometimes the press led the prosecution and convicted the criminal, regardless of the jury's verdict, as with their near universal hounding of the silent film star, Roscoe, "Fatty," Arbuckle for the rape and murder of the Hollywood starlet, Virginia Rappe in 1921. The comedian was tried three times. Twice this resulted in a hung jury. The third and final trial verdict was acquittal, since as the jury statement said, "There was not enough evidence to connect him in any way with the commission of any crime." Nevertheless as William Randolph Hearst put it, Arbuckle's spectacular fall from grace "sold more newspapers than any event since the sinking of the Lusitania" and the lurid details of his supposed crime set new levels of "Yellow Journalism."[29]

This fast-growing, particularly, almost peculiarly, American fascination with crime was summed up by the then editor of the *New Republic*, Charles Merz, who elegantly argued, with his tongue firmly in cheek, that

> When it comes to focusing the attention of the whole nation searchingly upon a single subject, and giving it a single set of facts on which to test its moral values, it is doubtful whether anything really unifies the country like its murders . . . The Roman Coliseum was a national institution. If we are to have a circus of our own let us develop it with the high purpose and creative effort worthy of a more resourceful nation. Let us have the biggest, jolliest, noisiest, bloodiest murder trials the human imagination can conceive.[30]

The Leopold–Loeb trial lived up to Merz's view of murder as entertainment and more. The two young accused demonstrated no remorse. They clowned and preened and posed for the women in the courtroom. Darrow too gave a virtuoso performance. He veered from weeping for the victim, to weeping for the defendants. He argued for clemency and detailed the inhumane process of hanging, so graphically that the otherwise unemotional Leopold was removed from the court in a screaming panic. He derided the defendants' supposed super-intelligence and called expert witnesses who demonstrated that it was their textbook manias and paranoias which gave them the emotional capacity, and consequent empathy, of 7-year-olds. He got the sentences for the two "poor little rich kids" reduced to life for Bobby's murder, and an additional 99 years each for the kidnapping they faked. In return, incidentally, the murderers' grateful parents reluctantly paid Darrow less than half of his agreed fee.[31]

In many ways, how the press handled it made the Leopold–Loeb case reminiscent of another crime of the century—the murder of the architect and socialite Stanford White by the son of Pittsburgh's "Coke King," Harry Thaw in 1906.[32] That Thaw had carried out the shooting of his wife's lover at Madison Square Roof Gardens was incontestable—it was carried out in front of the entire audience of a musical review.[33] Like the Leopold–Loeb trial, Thaw employed a highly paid defense lawyer, Delphin Delmas—the "Little Napoleon of the West Coast Bar." Delmas skilfully pointed out that the confused morality of the nation's super-wealthy led to actions which the then current medical thinking, including Freudian theory, would explain as the involuntary actions of the insane. Through his use of what one commentator has called Delmas' "carnival of scandal mixed with psychiatric mumbo jumbo," he ensured that after a second trial, Thaw avoided the electric chair, but spent the rest of his life in and out of the headlines and mental institutions.[34] The papers coined a new phrase—*Dementia Americana*.

The press reported the salacious stories of seduction, indulgence and high passion to an enthusiastic readership. It was estimated that 10,000 waited outside the Thaw trial. Both this trial and the Leopold–Loeb trial raised many issues which would continue to form the central problems in terms of the attitudes to crime and punishment throughout the twentieth century. There were cynical lawyers, operating for huge fees, enabling the wealthy to escape the full force of the law. Many held that the "clemency" shown to Thaw and the teenagers was the result of the type of justice only the rich could afford. During the Thaw trial it was alleged that the defense hired, or paid retainers to, so many "alienists" (forensic psychiatrists) that the prosecution could not find sufficient suitably qualified experts to dispute the defense's findings.[35] Similarly rumors spread—in some cases backed by photographic evidence—about Thaw's stay in New York's Tombs prison, where he was "deluged by chickens and ragouts" from exclusive and expensive restaurants, frequently delivered from across the other side of the city.[36] This type of story later circulated about the preferential treatment Leopold and Loeb received at Illinois' Joliet Prison, privileges which included separate cells, meals in the officers' mess, books, desks, gardens and extra visiting rights.

The century's "next" crime incorporated another aspect of modernity—celebrity. It was not so much the celebrity of the perpetrator as the victim—but rather the father of the victim. In kidnapping and murdering 20-month-old Charles A. Lindbergh Junior, Bruno Richard Hauptmann showed all the amoral inhumanity of either Leopold or Loeb. However, there can be little doubt that if the victim had not been the son of such an American icon, the man the *London News-Chronicle* called "the American approximation of the Prince of Wales," it would certainly not have become such a notorious case.[37] In the time between the discovery of the dead baby in 1932 and Hauptmann's arrest in 1934, there were two kidnappings which involved larger ransoms. Brewing magnate, William A. Hamm was released after payment of $100,000 and oil tycoon Charles F. Urschel and banker Arthur Bremer paid twice that for their release. The initial demand for baby Charles was only $50,000.

If the Leopold–Loeb or Scopes trials had been touted as the crime of the century, the Lindbergh trial took this form of crime as mass-entertainment to new levels. The Lindbergh case dominated the news over the period and led to vastly increased sales. For example, 65 telephotos were sent during the first 24 hours of the case. By contrast, the concurrent outbreak of the Sino-Japanese war warranted a mere ten. A survey of Philadelphia and New York papers showed that in the first days of the case their circulation rose by 15–20 percent and when the *New York Daily News* ran the huge front headline "BABY DEAD," its sales jumped by 600,000.[38] The press reported the twists and turns of the increasingly strange case and the hyperbole grew with each report, making the *Montreal Herald* gasp, "What newspapers! What Police! And what a country!"[39] Radio got in on the act, giving lengthy courtroom reports and on the day of Hauptmann's execution in April 1936, Gabriel Heatter broadcast a gruesome live commentary which aimed, unsuccessfully, to gain an electric chair confession or exclusive news of any accomplices. As H.L. Mencken acidly observed, "It was the greatest story since the resurrection."[40]

The success of the newspapers in rousing the nation's ire is demonstrated by the letters the Lindberghs received daily for the first two months of the investigation, totaling 3,000, or the 75,000 phone inquiries the *Chicago Tribune* fielded offering information on the case. The *Bronx Home News* published a letter offering the services of 72-year-old retired schoolmaster, Dr John F., "Jafsie," Condon. Jafsie put himself up as a go-between negotiating with a shadowy character, who may have been the kidnapper himself and who was christened by the press, "Cemetery John." Lindbergh accepted the offer although many felt that Condon was a fraud. He was not alone in profiting from the case. Francis Jamieson earned a Pulitzer Prize for his reports for Associated Press. New Jersey Governor, Harold Hoffman, used his personal investigation into the dubious evidence in the case against Hauptmann as a means to conceal his past misdeeds, gain popularity by cleaning out the police force and put his name forward for Republican presidential nomination.[41]

Hoffman was not alone in his assessment of police incompetence; the media also condemned the police's failures and proposed a variety of solutions, many of which involved using the other experts in criminal behavior—the crime lords. The Hearst press put forward the idea that Al Capone should be released from prison to use his connections to investigate the case. Failing that, Lucky Luciano would do. Ex-Ohio gangster, best-selling author, FBI man, extortioner, bootlegger, and conman, Gaston Bullock Means, was convicted for swindling $104,000 out of the concerned heiress, Mrs Evelyn Walsh McLean, owner of the Hope Diamond, on the grounds that he could use his underworld connections, to find baby Charles. As the *Daily Mirror* told shocked English readers, there was a growing suspicion that "the [Lindbergh] crime illustrates that gangdom in the United States is now virtually in control."[42]

Many Americans did not see the *Mirror's* comments as simple exaggeration. The urban mobs had grown in power over the 1920s and by the beginning of the 1930s the names of some gangsters were as well known as Hollywood stars and their comments, appearance and movements attracted equal interest. The passage of the Volstead Act (see Chapter 7) and the 18th Amendment re-invigorated American gang culture in the 1920s. Prohibition gave organized crime a new and lucrative field for their activities. By 1920, gangland New York had been set back, if not broken, with the smashing of the Eastman gang and their rivals, the Five Pointers. The casual violence on behalf of the political machines which had characterized much of their activity for the second half of the nineteenth century had fallen prey to Progressive reforms and the influence of reformers on public opinion. Prostitution had been significantly reduced by the wartime anti-vice campaigns which centered on the red light areas in San Francisco, New Orleans, and Chicago. Bootlegging, rum running, and speakeasy operations formed new lines of highly profitable activity.

The demand was certainly there. One source claims America distilled, shipped, and drank at least one hundred million gallons of illegal booze each year between 1920 and 1933. In New York alone, the city's 15,000, pre-Prohibition, saloons were replaced by 32,000 speakeasies, and arrests for drunkenness across the nation rose from 34,175 in 1921, to 66,878 in 1929. Those who could supply that demand could make more money, often at less personal risk, than even Ponzi. It has been estimated that Al Capone had a payroll of 1,000 employees, outgoings of $300,000 a month and made over $60 million from his bootlegging activities alone—more than his gambling, prostitution and racketeering activities combined brought in.[43] With this money came sophistication and insulation from prosecution. When it came to putting "Public Enemy Number One," Capone, on trial in October 1931, although sparked by the notorious St Valentine's Day massacre of seven rival gangsters, it was not for murder. The celebrity trial was not even for gangsterism, extortion or an imaginative interpretation of living off immoral earnings. It was initially for tax evasion; the added charges of breaking the Prohibition laws of the Volstead Act were later dropped.

What was more worrying was that not only was the law seen as unenforceable, it was also seen to be ignored in high places. Less than a year after Prohibition became law, federal agents discovered an illegal 130-gallon still on the Texas farm of Senator Morris Sheppard, principal author of the 18th Amendment, prompting the cowboy philosopher, Will Rogers, to quip "Congress voted dry but drinks wet." The link between Prohibition and politicians on the take is clearly illustrated by the case of Pete McDonough's arrest for bootlegging. When the "king of San Francisco's underworld" sold five gallons of whiskey to a federal agent, he thought his connections would secure his freedom. Instead he was sentenced to 15 months in jail, in spite of a pardon petition signed by the city's mayor, both its Congressmen, the district attorney, four police judges, 17 state legislators and a host of other dignitaries.[44] The rot went even higher; it was widely known that President Warren G. Harding drank spirits at his poker nights in the White House. Commentators argued that flouting the law at such a high level was seen as encouraging a general lawlessness in American society. They also claimed that it was indicative of the corruption of the initial years of the "Dollar Decade" that was 1920s America.[45] Corruption was detected at all levels, even in sport—even in the *national* sport. The 1919 World Series final between the seemingly invincible Chicago White Sox and the Cincinnati Reds ended with a victory for the underdogs. Almost immediately accusations of a "fix" emerged and eight White Sox players were accused of taking bribes from professional gamblers to throw the games.

The leading figures of the game, including the irascible and miserly White Sox owner, Charles Comiskey, denied the charges. The public refused to believe the players could have behaved in such a way, but the rumors refused to die. How could heroes, national heroes, taint the national pastime with their blatant greed? In August 1920, Assistant State Attorney, Hartley Replogle, subpoenaed a host of leading baseball figures and a trial which exposed some of the nation's heroes as "a bunch of crooked players and gamblers" dragged on until the end of July 1921.[46] The shock is probably most poignantly demonstrated by the now apocryphal story by the *Chicago Herald* which reported a young fan coming up to one of the leading defendants, "Shoeless Joe Jackson," outside the subsequent Grand Jury hearing and pleading, "Say it ain't so, Joe. Say it ain't so."[47] Although the defendants were eventually found not guilty "of defrauding the public," many nostalgic sports fans felt that the taint of corruption was arguably one of the defining elements of the times.[48]

It certainly seems they had a point. In the first three years of the 1920s, political corruption seemed rife. In Chicago, William Hale, "Big Bill," Thompson, ran the city patronage and graft system during the period in which the windy city emerged as the byword for racketeering.[49] In the state of Illinois, as a whole, the Governor, Lennington Small, became the first sitting governor in the state's history to be jailed. He had embezzled over $700,000. In 1921, in Boston, "Honest Tom" O'Dally admitted he had been salting away $40,000 of public money over his ten years as city treasurer. In North Dakota, the governor was recalled as a result of his implication in a banking scandal. Oklahoma attempted to impeach its governor on charges of corruption. In Texas, Senator Earle Mayfield was investigated for campaign funding and voting irregularities.[50] These were not the only examples, but they laid the scene for what was, arguably, the most defining case of public corruption in American political history—Teapot Dome.

To many Americans what was shocking about the illegal leasing to private companies of the government-owned oil rich land at Teapot Dome, Wyoming, was not simply that these were the US Navy's wartime reserves, and therefore of national, strategic, importance. Nor was it that these "irregularities" were initially explained away to a Senate investigation with little difficulty by Secretary of the Interior, Albert Bacon Fall. It was not even the huge scale of the fraud. The Mammoth Oil and Pan-American Petroleum Companies admitted that between them they stood to make over $100 million from the deal, and Fall himself made over $500,000. What was truly shocking was that so many in the Harding, and from earlier, administrations knew about, lied about and stood to profit from, such an obvious fraud. As the details emerged, it appeared that government was little more than a cosy coterie of "men of large affairs" who would cover their tracks until backstabbing self-interest made them emerge from the shadows and incriminate each other.

When the key players decided to publicly maul each other in a Senate hearing, and later in a series of court cases, the results were spectacular. One witness at the Senate hearing accused a veritable who's who of the American political elite of being "paid for their influence." Oil man, Edward L. Doheny told the investigation that he had "hired" the former secretaries of war, interior and treasury, the former chairman of the Wartime Committee on Public Information, the former Attorney General, as well as Secretary Fall and other leading politicians of both

ie serving and some retired. He was so proud of his connections and so
l of his actions that one commentator claimed his testimony was like
..ng to "a parvenu art collector calling the roll of his Rembrandts and Van
Dykes."[51]

It has been argued that if crime in the 1920s was dominated by the avaricious
corruption and thrill-seeking modernity of the "Dollar Decade," the central
theme of the crimes of the post-Prohibition 1930s was a cruel but elemental
banditry driven by the necessities of the collapsing economy of Depression-era
America. As one paper lamented, "The truth must be faced that the army of
desperate criminals which has been recruited in the last decade is winning its
battle against society."[52] In keeping with this interpretation, the most notable
crimes of this time never got to court, they were perpetrated by outlaws whose
unbridled, cold-blooded, violence meant that they often died with guns blazing.[53]
Ma Barker and her gang, John Dillinger, "Baby Face" Nelson, Bonnie Parker and
Clyde Barrow were all less sophisticated in their methods and their organization
than their Prohibition-era counterparts. Equally famous, they were, nevertheless,
seen as less "successful" and more ruthless, as befitted the times, but this did not
limit their appeal.

John Herbert Dillinger killed ten and wounded seven men in his short career
as a motorized bandit in the Midwest. This made him Public Enemy Number
One in the eyes of the FBI, while his good looks and daring prison breaks made
him a heart-throb in the eyes of an escapist public in the depths of the Great
Depression. Similarly the romance, excitement and mystery of life "on the lam"
meant that Bonnie and Clyde appealed to Americans in spite of their murdering
at least 13 people. Charles Arthur, "Pretty Boy," Floyd, may not have had the
romantic appeal of Dillinger or Barrow, but his daring and unfeeling disregard for
the law made him a household name. While the truth may have been far removed,
several of these motorized bandits claimed that they targeted "only corporations"
for their robberies, or kidnapped only "moneyed men." Legend had it that these
criminals released "ordinary" people caught in the banks they raided. In popular
mythology, it was claimed that the code of honor by which they lived was so
strong that they would rather die than see one of their fellow gang members put
in danger.

These desperadoes enjoyed a status based on a tradition of outlaw villain/hero
rather than the half-legitimate stardom of Capone and other gangsters of the
previous decade. They self-consciously styled themselves on the famous names of
the Wild West, rather than the "sophisticated" urban mobsters of the last decade.
Public Enemy, Alvin, "Creepy," Karpis admitted that he based his image on "the
great bandits of the old West, the James brothers, the Dalton boys and all the rest
of them."[54] Nevertheless, they were celebrities and their exploits took on a status
which was arguably far greater than the actual threat they represented. A part of
this notoriety at least was the result of a prevailing cult of the hoodlum. In an age
of limited prospects and even more limited employment, when authority figures

were seen to have failed the "working stiff," the mobster with his seeming disregard for personal safety, his flashy wealth, and his obvious success with women was an understandable hero for fiction.

This was perhaps most apparent in film, where a new genre emerged in 1931 with Edward G. Robinson's portrayal of Rico, the ambitious, Capone-esque gangster in *Little Caesar*. Within a year, Hollywood had produced over 50 mobster films, including James Cagney's lead role as the vicious, misogynistic, gangland hooligan in the box office hit, *Public Enemy*. While most of these films carried a message that criminals would eventually be caught, or more often die in a shootout, few could deny the influence of the fast-talking, tough-guy, self-reliant criminal on American popular aspirations. A film critic at the time explained the phenomenon with reference to the hero in *The Public Enemy*:

> When Cagney gets down off a truck or deals at cards, or curses, or slaps his girl, or even when he affords himself, or her, the mockery of sweetness, he is, for the time being, the American hero, whom ordinary men and boys recognize as themselves.[55]

As at least one historian has pointed out, the leading prohibition era gangsters were described in similar terms to the leaders of the "Trusts." One contemporary biography of Al Capone was subtitled, with no apparent irony, *The Biography of a Self-Made Man*.[56] In some ways, the rags-to-riches gangster story was to the pessimism of the pre-New Deal Depression era what the Horatio Alger story was to the buoyant mood of the turn of the century. The response to increasing public tolerance of criminal violence was the Federal government's decision to declare a "war on crime." The *New York Times* reported a stirring declaration that across the nation the criminal would be hunted down, and promised that:

> The detectives of the United States will be like its soldiers . . . They will operate under centralized orders from Washington. They will have at their fingertips a complete international identification bureau. They will use radio, telegraph, telephone, photographs, fingerprints, Bertillon measurements [a system of quantitative recordings of an individual's distinguishing features]—use in fact every science known to criminal detection.[57]

A variety of reasons have been given to justify this sudden and massive increase in Federal law enforcement. It has been seen as the result of the personal ambition and empire-building of the head of the Bureau, the indomitable and ambitious J. Edgar Hoover. Hoover certainly garnered increasing power and publicity as the result of the policy. Although initially charged with a "Mobile Detachment" of Joseph B. Keenan's Criminal Division of the Justice Department, it was in his role as the chief "G-Man" that he soon became the face of the War on Crime.[58] Alternatively, it has been portrayed as the outcome of agencies within the

administration vying to be seen to "do something" to fight the
.[59] Another historian sees it as a "masculine" response to the "femi-
ptance of criminal behavior in the 1920s.[60] For many commentators,
then and now, it was the logical progression of the growth of Federal police
powers which had resulted from the Lindbergh case.

Whatever the underlying reasons, there can be little doubt that the catalyst for
this huge increase in federal policing was one single, and in many ways not particularly remarkable, crime—the so-called "Kansas City Massacre." In its repercussions, perhaps it too deserves to be seen as a contender for the title of Crime of
the Century. The facts were simple, and brutal. On June 17, 1933, seven policemen
and Federal agents were transporting the safe-breaker, mobster and, they hoped,
informant, Frank "Jelly" Nash. They were ambushed outside Central Station,
Kansas City, by three machine gun-toting gangsters who opened fire on the car
they were in. Three policemen and one agent died, two others were wounded and
one survived only by feigning death. Jelly was also killed—perhaps deliberately,
perhaps because the attempt to "spring him" was bodged.[61]

This bloody crime had several consequences. First, in launching the war on
crime it added to the move set in place by the so-called "Lindbergh Law" and
federalized criminality in America.[62] It achieved this, both in terms of actual law
enforcement, and in the public's perception of who should be responsible for
enforcement. It was no longer possible for criminals to cross state borders in order
to evade the law. Alongside this, the war on crime, while limited in its objectives,
created a public perception that crime was not only unacceptable but, perhaps
more importantly, surmountable. The contrast with their image before the advent
of the high profile campaign could not have been starker. The prevailing mood
was summed up by an article that with glum resignation told the American public
in 1932 that:

> For the first time in modern history, we are confronted with [criminal]
> organizations directed by men of personality, courage and genius, who are
> above the law . . . How is it that nobody, from the highest to the lowest,
> apparently, is safe in the United States?[63]

It seemed that some of this was the result of poor policing. The law enforcement
agencies were seen as corrupt, inefficient and incompetent. It seemed that when
reports hit the headlines of police activities, it was invariably to show how they
had been outwitted by criminals. For example, shortly before the Kansas Massacre,
in August, 1933, near Chicago, kidnappers Basil, "The Owl," Banghart and
Charles, "Ice Wagon," Connors shot their way out of their hideout. They did this
even through they were surrounded by a cordon of some 300 armed law enforcement agents. By the end of the War on Crime in 1936, the police forces, especially
the FBI, were seen as modern, effective and efficient. To prove it, Hoover touted
the fact that Ma Barker, John Dillinger, Alvin Karpis, Pretty Boy Floyd, Baby Face

Nelson, and Machine Gun Kelly, as well as the bulk of their gang members, had all been either killed or imprisoned.

The Kansas City Massacre in many ways sparked the growth of the modern relationship between the media and the police force in America. It was now the armed federal agent, the "G-Man," who was the incorruptible hero of Hollywood. The highly publicized *G-Men* had inspired seven more FBI-worshiping films by the end of its debut year, 1935. Through these, the American cinema goers were shown that the rule of the jungle, which was so much a part of the Depression-era thinking, had been replaced by a visible, honest, optimistic and fair return to the rule of law through the New Deal's FBI. J. Edgar Hoover, Melvin Purvis, Eliot Ness and the "Untouchables" became household figures as "The Director" manipulated news through his control of the relevant information. He not only gave interviews to the papers and radio, he also put his name to ghost-written "front line reports" in the *American Magazine*, wrote forewords to books and was photographed with film stars. The Kansas City Massacre created the first true celebrity "cops," a national crime fighting force led by a man who would serve under eight presidents and whose influence on America was as profound as it was contentious.[64]

If the War on Crime won over a large section of the American public to the idea that, given the will and the resources, victory over law breakers was inevitable, this optimism was short-lived. The increased pressure on criminality also had the effect that racketeering and violent criminal activity stratified. While the named "Public Enemies," the rural bandits of the Mid-West and smaller urban hoodlums, were—in the public mind, at least—either eliminated or controlled, the large-scale metropolitan operations moved on from the localized business models of Capone and federalized, forming local monopolies within national agreements. According to a report by Chicago Committee on Crime, this emerging criminal network was an underworld which was organized to the extent that:

> [It] has its own language; it has its own laws; its own history; its traditions and customs; its own methods and techniques; its highly specialized machinery for attack upon persons and particularly upon property; its own highly specialized modes of defense. These professional criminals have interurban, interstate, and sometimes international connections.[65]

The fear of this nebulous "Syndicate" was another manifestation of an ongoing threat in American history. The lynching of the 11 Italians in New Orleans in 1890 had drawn on fears of an Italian "Mafia." Fears of violent criminal organizations went back even further than that. The Mafia had been preceded by an equally terrifying, imported, feudal, band of brigands known as the Camorra. From the advent of large-scale southern Italian immigration in the 1880s the popular press had worked up a real fear of the nebulous and insidious "Black

Chapter 10). This part mythical organization was thought to terrorize
munities across the nation, running protection rackets, prostitution
orrupting politicians. Nor were organized crime groups limited to the
Italians. Since the 1850s, Chinese communities had been plagued by the brutal
activities of the Tongs as they dealt opium and shipped white slaves. Although
Irish workers had formed the Molly Maguires ostensibly to protect their interests
in the Pennsylvania anthracite coalfields in the 1860s, they too became seen as a
violent criminal organization, by both local bosses and concerned citizens across
the nation.

When New York District Attorney, Thomas E. Dewey, decided to take on the
city's billion-dollar-a-year rackets in 1935 by going for Arthur "Dutch" Schultz,
he chose to prosecute him for tax evasion. Dewey started a series of events which
ended up with the exposure of the true power and ruthlessness of the American
crime syndicate. Schultz, the boss of the Harlem and Bronx numbers betting—a
form of lottery—was so incensed by what he regarded as a legally sanctioned
assault that he immediately ordered a contract killing on the DA. The contract
was vetoed by the two other leading local crime lords—Louis "Lepke" Buchalter
and Salvatore "Lucky" Luciano. Furious, Schultz vowed to kill Dewey himself;
sooner than risk the exposure this would bring, Buchalter and Luciano ordered a
contract on their fellow mobster. Dutch was killed within days of the decision.
While it made the headlines, until 1940, the death of Schultz was popularly
regarded as just another gangland killing, a result, no doubt, of a "turf" dispute.
But when another hitman, Abe, "Kid Twist," Reles, was arrested, he became a
government witness and implicated seven of the top New York crime operatives,
including Buchalter. The trials which followed resulted in all of them going to the
electric chair and leading to another mobster getting an 80-year sentence. What
was more frightening was the way in which Reles exposed an arm of the organization which was responsible for over 1,000 deaths. The press dubbed it Murder
Inc. and the revelations at the following trials shocked the nation.[66]

What was unique about Murder Inc. was not its brutality, which was truly
inhuman. It was not its efficiency, which was equally callous, including as it did
Reles' pride in his own ability to kill, with an ice pick through the right ear, so
precisely that many of his victims were thought to have died of a "natural" cere-
bral haemorrhage. It was not even the number of its victims. It was the ruthlessly
business-like nature of the organization. Founded in 1931, the theory behind the
operation was simple. Paid an annual $12,000 retainer, a bank of killers were ready
with just a phone call to carry out executions anywhere within the United States.
When the contract was carried out, they would immediately return home.
Whenever possible, the contracts were carried out by persons close to the victim.
This seeming cruelty had the virtue of avoiding unnecessary risk of panic or
failure. As with the contract on Schultz, the decisions to "wipe out" elements
which could harm the Syndicate as a whole were taken with merciless, cold, prac-
ticality which both made for efficiency and insulated the bosses from the crime.

These murders were simply the fulfilment of a contract made between retained hit-men and the crime bosses. To the Syndicate, the murders were banal business decisions.[67]

The way in which the "Combination," as they called themselves, behaved made it appear that Murder Inc. was simply the "law enforcement" division of the criminal corporation which ruled much of inner-city America. Both the Kansas City Massacre and the elimination of Dutch Schultz marked an aspect of modern America which shocked and continues to shock both Americans and foreigners. In many ways the issues raised were indicative of the most long-lived of America's moral panics, that of the constant re-emergence of a violent criminal underworld, not only amoral, but unstoppable by their brutal disregard for the laws of the land. There is something peculiarly American in this problem which the years of the 1930s threw into sharp focus.

There was little new in this, since it drew on aspects of American culture as deep-rooted as the frontier and as ineffable and unstoppable as urbanization, but it was this decade that cultural commentators tend to reflect on as the start of a new stage of violent crime.[68] These times highlighted an apparent inability to stem violent crime without being forced to accept a correspondingly increased level of lethal violence within law enforcement. This is a conundrum whose resolution has remained at the forefront of American public policy ever since, and not least in the continued metaphor of "wars," no longer simply on crime, but on terror or drugs.

CRIME AND THE WEST

Only a few of us could pick out a photograph of even the most prominent African Americans or industrialists [of the late nineteenth century]—let alone a labor organizer or women's activist—but most Americans have heard of [and would presumably recognize photographs of] Jesse James or Geronimo.

Heather Cox Richardson[1]

When the history of the late nineteenth and early twentieth centuries in America is written about, taught or in other ways examined, one of the elements which almost always forms at least a part of the study is the expansion of the nation into the untamed wilderness of the West. The huge territorial growth, the massive increase in economic potential, the draw on public imagination—the subject is almost too big to form a single section. The history of the West *is* the history of America at this time, and as such over the years it has been distorted, revised, and rewritten. Having said that, themes remain prominent and stubbornly unresolved throughout these reinterpretations and it is on two of these that this section will be based—namely, those of violence and lawlessness, and exploitation and greed.

Perhaps the first, and perhaps most enduring, element which comes to mind when looking at this region is the role of violence. It is difficult to even consider the West without violence. It is almost a truism that violence was vital to the conquest of the West and it goes without saying that it was central to subordination and exploitation of the area. Violence took a variety of forms: there was interpersonal violence, state-sponsored violence, and racial violence. The popular depiction of the West is wrapped, soaked, and steeped in violence. This was not only the case at the time, but also in the way in which it has been seen since, because without violence the West would not have been wild.[2] In the popular imagination, violence was the very fuel and essence of the West.

This violence was not always considered detrimental. To many interpreters, academic and popular, violence played out the struggles of the West, the fight between good and evil; right and wrong; just and unjust; strong and weak with violent and Manichean clarity. It is always tempting to have a simple explanation for why regions evolve the way they do, why history is portrayed the way it is, and true to this simplification, popular literature, mythology, folklore, and commercial films have rarely shied away from simplifying the evolution of the American West. Here was a place where opportunity was unfettered by convention and a man carved out his own image and destiny, on one side of the law or the other—with the ubiquitous six-shooter always at the ready to reinforce his decisions.

It is during the period of this study that the West developed its legendary image, which more often than not ended with the familiar denouement that real, humdrum, life lacked. It has become the cliché of dime novels that the novel/comic/film frontier West was lawless and violent, but consistently exciting, heroic and decisive. In a hushed narrow street, the slighted father/brother/sheriff in a white hat faced down his nemesis, the hired gun/bandit/bad man in the black hat. A fascinated crowd of on-lookers, too cowardly to take on the wrong-doers themselves, willed the lawman's victory. A cultural critic memorably and snappily summed up the brutal simplicity of this West presented to cinema goers claiming that "The two most successful creations of American movies are the gangster and the Westerner: men with guns."[3] While this naive vision has been questioned—and largely refuted—by modern, killjoy, historians, it remains the case that crime in one form or another was absolutely central to the conquest of the West.

Having said that, in order to square the two interpretations, perhaps it is a far wider interpretation of crime that is needed than simply the traditional view of the horse thief, rustler, bank robber, cardsharp, outlaw or gunslinger. In this case it is no overstatement to claim that the historical debate rages. The mythology of Western individuality, the historic right to bear arms and the whole image of the frontier become mingled and confused in the Wild West insuring that it remains a live issue and a highly emotive subject to many Americans today.

The revision of the West extends to its very existence, or at least its unique status. Some commentators argue that it is impossible to separate the Wild West—either geographically or historically—from the rest of the nation, in terms of American criminality, especially violent criminality. They point out that there was nothing unique about the West, arguing that violence was equally endemic in the gang-ridden slums of the metropolitan areas of the eastern seaboard and the Reconstruction and Jim Crow South. The ubiquitous gangs of New York—the infamous Dead Rabbits, Whyos, Bowery Boys or Plug Uglies—were virtual armies. They were equally happy to rent themselves out, or defend their home turfs with a casual, cut-throat, violence that matched or exceeded any of the viciousness attributed to the James Gang or any other Western desperadoes. Nor were they alone in their unfussy use of violence. There can be no doubt that the Ku Klux Klan and other white supremacist organizations terrorized and killed argued that it was this violent and cruel environment that formed America. They argued that the very savagery of the West was what differentiated and empowered "Americans" and enabled the ever-expanding Republic to absorb and contain the diversity of peoples entering the nation. It has frequently been claimed that this was as a result partly of the access to, and necessity of, firearms in the frontier regions compared with "civilization," but this, the very essence of the Western myth, has been hotly debated—most notably by the unfortunate Michael Bellesiles.[6]

There seems little doubt there was logic to the perception of violence. Guns are the very essence of frontier culture—necessary for hunting, as well as defense from human and animal predators—and where there are guns, they will be used. Surely, this was so. Given the prevalence of mass-produced, available, cheap, efficient, hand guns and ammunition resulting from the Civil War, as well as the isolation and the consequent necessity of self-defense, guns were an everyday item in the West of the last quarter of the nineteenth century. Add in the fact that most of the Americans arriving and staying in the West were young and male, often bored and, of necessity, adventurous and the situation becomes more volatile. Stir in readily available alcohol; good prospects for making money and/or decent wages (and few places to spend them), add an unnatural competition for scarce women, and the cocktail swiftly, it is argued, becomes lethal. Yet the recorded crime rates in the communities of the West in the 1870s, 1880s, and 1890s were actually no higher, overall, than those in comparable Eastern regions.

If this seems unlikely, then it is perhaps worth investigating one of the most iconic of violent Western towns, the infamous frontier settlement, Dodge City. In its heyday as a raucous boom town in the decade of the 1870s, the cattle town averaged only one and a half deaths by deliberate violence each year.[7] On the other hand, the historians Roger McGrath and Richard White refute this relatively benign interpretation of the West with evidence from Bodie, a mining settlement in California which they describe as being a real "shooters' town." Between 1877 and 1883, they demonstrate that the town was dominated by the activities of a group of violent hooligans known as "Bodie's Badmen." In these six years there were 44 shooting incidents. Twenty-nine of these resulted in killings. To reinforce the normality of this violence, they point out that in spite of this abnormal rate of violent death, only one man was convicted of murder during this period. In order to show how such figures compare with other regions, at other times they equate these shootings to a murder rate of 116 per 100,000 of population. By way of comparison, they use the illustration of Miami, which in 1980 achieved a record-breaking tally of 32.7 homicides per 100,000 of population.[8]

Although these two sets of statistics indicate the contested nature of violence in the "Wild West," they also point to an important caveat in the study of the subject—the West was by no means homogeneous, either geographically or historically. Many of the assumptions which underlie the stereotypical image of the violent West might well be true of regions of the West at *certain times* and for *certain groups* but they cannot be held to be true of the entire region throughout the entire period of this study. For the sake of this argument it may be constructive and informative to compare Dodge with Bodie, over similar periods. They were both frontier towns with more or less transient inhabitants seeking quick money. They also had similar populations—although one was a mining town and the other a cattle town—in terms of size, ethnicity, and social structure. However, the results would be starkly different if these figures were to be compared with, say, Salt Lake City, with its predominantly Mormon population seeking to establish a homogeneous, religious colony, or the pacifist Mennonite farmers who settled in North Newton, Kansas.

The statistics themselves also benefit from further investigation. The figures for deaths in Bodie were largely from within the group of hooligans themselves. Not only were these men more prone to use violence to get their way and to respond violently to any provocation, they were also less likely to be protected by whatever law keepers existed. Also, the seemingly low murder count for the decade in Dodge City was partly the result of a reaction to the fatal shooting of between 16 and 19 men in the first three years of the decade which led to stringent law enforcement for the remaining years of the 1870s.

By 1875, contrary to popular belief now and then, like many other frontier towns, Dodge's newly formed municipal government had outlawed the wearing of guns by private citizens and clearly indicated its intention to enforce the legislation. In the second half of the 1870s, Dodge City had a deputy US, a city and an assistant city marshal; two constables; a county sheriff and an undersheriff, as well as deputy sheriffs and policemen as circumstances required. Although such a small army cost the city nearly $3,000 a year, such expense was seen as vital by the majority of the town, since the image of law and order was seen as essential for trade, property values and expansion.[9] What is more, the very fact that the abnormally high figures warranted reporting, and were made available, would suggest that they were out of the normal range and that such brutality was a worrying deviation from the normal state of things.

If the image of the West as a place of a permanent succession of gunfights, blood feuds and murders is less than ubiquitous in reality, that does not mean that murder and bloodshed were not commonplace or widespread—it is just that the victims may be less visible and less recorded. Leaving aside domestic violence, which—in as much as it was related to criminal behavior—will be dealt with in a later chapter, most of those who met with violent deaths in the West during this period did so as a result of their race, not, as Hollywood would have us believe, their morality—or lack of it. By 1892, the vast majority of Plains Indians were reduced to virtual beggars, reliant on government handouts on reservations. In some measure this was the result of famous military campaigns, of varying success. More importantly it was the result of simple demographic pressures, disease and also, and more important for this study, massacre.

This final category is not only highly emotive, it is also interesting from the perspective of crime. To those seeking to justify the actions of the troopers who caused the deaths of some one hundred and fifty Lakota killed at Wounded Knee in 1890, it was ostensibly a tragic mistake. According to many other interpreters, then and since, it was a massacre. To yet others, it may be, at best, a rather one-sided military engagement undertaken by uniformed soldiers, which essentially concluded a lengthy war of expansion and extermination. What is clearly shown in these confrontations is, as the historian Richard White has argued, that the region was not settled through the heroic actions of individuals—trappers, miners, farmers or sod-house pioneers—but by dogged and persistent federal government intervention. Violence, criminal or otherwise, was overwhelmingly within their hands, which although abhorrent to modern sensibilities, goes some way to explaining why the killing of women and children at Wounded Knee apparently broke no contemporary laws.[10]

That was not the case with the massacre of 108 Apaches at Camp Grant in the Arizona Territory in 1871. Over a hundred of these victims were women and children. Some 29 of the surviving children were sold into slavery in spite of the 13th Amendment's prohibition of enslavement. What is interesting about the Camp Grant atrocity was that it attracted the condemnation of the eponymous president, who condemned it as murder. Within a year, 100 of the 150, predominantly Papago Indian and Mexican civilian perpetrators of the massacre were put on trial. The jury swiftly delivered the verdict "not guilty," since it was deemed they had acted out of self-defense. They had been driven to it by the Apaches' constant raiding of American settlers.[11]

Nor was this tit-for-tat violence limited to settler on aboriginal violence. It was frequently and famously the other way around, with perceived settler violations causing such figures as Sitting Bull, Geronimo and Chief Joseph to fight back. The reasoning behind such outbursts of violence is clearly summed up in an interview with Mexican gang leader Tiburcio Vasquez, who claimed he was driven to a life of crime as a result of his mistreatment by incomers in California:

> "Now, Vasquez . . . Do you like the robber life?"

> "No, not at all. Of course a man would not like to be hunted all the time like a dog . . . I was obliged to . . . When I tried to settle down anywhere and tried to get a living, they drove me out. They [the "Anglos"] wouldn't give me any peace."[12]

The violence against the aboriginal populations was not the only form of racial violence in the developing West. Although less numerous, other distinct ethnic groups suffered violent assaults of varying severity. Jews and blacks were often victims of this less constrained society, but it was the Chinese population in particular, and Asians in general—although such national/racial distinctions were rarely observed at the time—who were, relative to their numbers, most frequently attacked. This could take the form of individual beatings, shootings or other assaults for supposed claim jumping in the mines of Colorado and California. It could also be a full-blown attempt at the ethnic cleansing, as in the case when the Chinese population of Tacoma in 1885 was violently expelled from the city. It might lead to minor injury, as with the stoning of Japanese residents in the wake of the San Francisco earthquake in 1906, or it may become a massacre, as with the Chinese miners at Rock Springs, Wyoming, in 1885. Whatever form it took, the perpetrators were rarely punished. It was the exception that the death of a "Chinaman" would lead to a prosecution. Not least, because in many cases, Chinese and other Asians, who were neither free, white, nor entitled to citizenship, could not testify against a white man in court. Perhaps it is these events which should be considered when telling the story of the "lawless" West.[13]

If violence was one sign of the lawlessness of frontier life, property crime was another, and the two were closely linked. While much has been made of the community of the West and the absence of lockable space in many of the mining camps and early settlements, the armed robberies of the Wild West have become legendary. Unlike the popular interpretations of violence—which were more often than not personalized, they were seen as motivated by individual slight— much of the folklore of robbery revolved around its being perpetrated against the corporation, the bank or the state. Targeting these anonymous, remote, faceless, and frequently hated victims meant that the crimes were often seen as "justifiable." The result is that sympathetic accounts have judged that the outlaw bandits of the Wild West were some of the purest forms of Eric Hobsbawm's mythological "Social Bandits": slighted men driven to banditry in search of social redress. These legendary figures were heroes fighting for their communities who maintained that they stole only from the rich; broke only laws which they considered discriminatory; and were guided by specific codes of honor.[14]

The contested nature of Western communities lent itself to a positive view of these folklore heroes. These were not stable societies established in uninhabited lands, they were fluid communities placed in regions which already had an indigenous population and this was frequently one of the causes of, and excuses for, violence. Incoming "white" populations persecuted and drove out many of the resident populations who in turn, having become dispossessed in their own lands, often turned to crime. For example, in the early 1850s, Southern California was plagued by a wave of Mexican-American banditry which cost 44 lives in Los Angeles County alone. The early 1860s saw a similar war in Texas. In the late 1880s, the Apache Kid and his band of renegade Indians raided ranches, robbed trains and kidnapped women in New Mexico and Arizona. In the early 1890s, part-black, part-Native American, Crawford, "Cherokee Bill," Goldsby and his gang of mixed blood ruffians terrorized and robbed their way around Oklahoma. In all these cases, accusations of racial oppression were used to defend what was, to others, simply thuggery and property crime and this would remain a justification for the actions of bandits like Gregorio Cortez and Pancho Villa well into the twentieth century.[15]

If race played a major role for the image of some of these historically ambiguous figures, then politics was equally important for others. It is the "Anglo" versions of these figures that have done most to propagate this curious mix of lawlessness, heroism and self-interest that is so much a part of Western mythology. Cole, James, Robert and John Younger, and Frank and Jesse James had ridden with the Confederate guerrilla William, "Bloody Bill," Anderson as members of Quantrill's Raiders in their murderous exploits on the Middle Border of Kansas–Missouri. To those who supported them, they were a brave brotherhood of guerillas fighting against huge odds. Later, favorable, accounts would make much of the fraternal aspects. One claimed that all the Raiders swore an oath that—"In the name of God and the Devil [to swear] never to betray a comrade [but to] suffer the most horrible death, rather than reveal a single secret of this organization or a single word of this my oath."[16]

On the other hand, there were those who did not see the Raiders' deeds in such romantic terms. They claimed that they bayoneted farmers who refused them shelter or supplies. They stressed how the Raiders had burned the homes of suspected Union sympathizers. They told stories of how the guerillas had casually murdered Federal prisoners and generally ensured themselves a legacy which meant that when the war ended they could not be expect to be included in the general amnesty. Far from it, when these rebels tried to surrender in Lexington, Missouri, they claimed Union troopers opened fire, in spite of their white flag. In one version of his life story, Jesse James alleged that Federal troopers wounded his mother and several other members of his family and killed his 8-year-old brother.[17] In another account, it was Pinkerton detective agents, hired by an irate railroad, who committed the murders.[18] Whoever committed the atrocities, popular myth maintained that the barbarism of the irregular war in the region made it inevitable that the James brothers would join up with a number of his former guerrilla comrades and go back to war with the most apparent signs of Northern colonialism and oppression in the West. These happened to be the conveniently wealthy Yankee-owned banks and the railroads.

In this region which had felt the full brutality of the partisan Civil War, the James–Younger Gang constructed a self-serving approach to Reconstruction. They undertook the violent robbery of selected wealthy individuals and national businesses. In so doing they met with growing popular support. Graduating from simple bank robberies in the late 1860s, the gang captured the public imagination and local sympathy as they mounted increasingly audacious raids. The nerve of the gang in robbing spectators in broad daylight at the huge Kansas City fair in September 1872 was considered so "high handed, so diabolically daring and so utterly in contempt of fear that [the public were] . . . bound to admire it and revere its perpetrators for the enormity of their outlawry."[19] They managed to rob trains, an activity which while potentially far more lucrative, presented much faster, less controllable and therefore potentially far less predictable and more dangerous targets than stagecoaches, groups of horsemen or individual riders.

As they perfected this spectacular but hazardous work, they altered their tactics from placing objects on the track and wrecking the target train, to the far more hazardous and sophisticated technique of halting the locomotive and boarding the carriages in order to loot the passengers. They achieved this by using kidnapped railway workers to appeal to the engineers, or by utilizing the existing signaling. In part, this was self-serving since frightened passengers would often hand over more booty, and guards could often open the onboard safe faster, with greater ease and with less waste. It also had the happy coincidence that it caused less casualties. There is little in their bloody history to suggest that this consideration was the result of common humanity, it was more likely their seeming compassion was the result of trying to protect their growing local popularity. Such an approach also added to their Robin Hood image, something Jesse James made full of when he bragged to the newspapers that "We rob the rich and give to the poor."[20] To James, and many who would follow in his footsteps, the rich were the corporate businesses, the poor were the local workingmen.

This lines up well with one of the most distinctive features of Eric Hobsbawm's theories of social banditry—the way in which neighborhoods protect, conceal and provide for outlaws they perceive as being members of their community. As if to prove Hobsbawm's hypothesis, the James–Younger Gang continued their career of bank and train robberies with notable successes in the early 1870s. This remained the case as long as they operated in the regions where the local population had a large component of smallholding farmers of Southern extraction. These were also regions with residents who felt themselves aggrieved, especially with the banks and railroads—the most overt signs of outside investment and industrial commerce. When they moved to the more aspirational and affluent wheat belt of Minnesota, the population was neither Southern, nor subsistence.

In this area of the West, the banks and railroads—at least at this point in time—were seen by the majority of farmers as representing the future of the region. They supplied the means to finance and produce the goods which would make their fortunes. They would provide the means to ship out the grain and ship in the machinery, spares and other goods necessary to life on the prairie. Banks and railroads linked these farmers to the outside world. The result was that the locals were hostile to the outlaws and the James–Younger Gang was less successful in this area. Nothing illustrates this better than the gang's bungled robbery of the First National Bank of Northfield in 1876, after which the gang could find nowhere to hide and the locals mobilized the largest posse in the state's history. The end result was the death of two of the outlaws and the capture of most of the rest of the gang. Frank and Jesse James, who survived the raid, continued their careers until Jesse's death in 1882. They did so in large measure having learned not to operate too far from their base of popular support.

The career of that other outlaw legend, Billy the Kid, shows this image of bandit as folk hero equally clearly. Although he lacked James' overt political motivation and, apparently, his charisma, he gained popular support and ultimately mythical status through what were portrayed in some circles as his attempts to create an "economically and politically just society" in the emerging West.[21] Billy's involvement in the openly violent and mobile struggle to break the monopoly for lucrative military beef contracts in New Mexico Territory's Lincoln County seems so quintessentially Western it would appear almost entirely unrelated to the rest of the nation. Closer scrutiny shows it as a struggle against the demons of Gilded Age America—corrupt, cruel and anonymous, rapacious big business. Hardly one who would seek Jesse James' resurgent South, the ex-slave and self-proclaimed outlaw, Nat Love (AKA "Deadwood Dick") nevertheless claimed, Billy the Kid and Jesse James simply targeted "the great trusts, corporations and brokers, who for years have been robbing the people of this country."[22]

The Social Bandit outlaw tells us much about not only the times they lived in, but also the way in which that time has been interpreted. There is something which is appealing about these figures at the most basic, human, level, and it did not take long for the legends to develop. Even in their lifetime they were eulogized. One account called the James brothers "brilliant, bold, indefatigable Roughriders." Another said they were "brave . . . generous . . . gallant . . . honorable . . . men."[23] In other accounts, James went beyond the human, and could not be killed. The *National Police Gazette* reported a story which claimed that he survived George Sheperd's bullet and was nursed back to health by his brothers and was continuing his career of banditry in another region of the country.[24]

After Jesse's death, the legends grew more and more impressive. In plays, magazine and newspaper articles and eventually film, James became more and more benevolent. The dashing young outlaw selected only the evil and wealthy—often seen as one and the same—and redistributed their wealth and rectified other inequalities. Implausible incidents like James' paying off the mortgage of a fellow Confederate soldier's widow were repeated so frequently that they became seen as truth.[25] To many who wanted to believe in such interpretations, James and other outlaws were characters who harked back to times when it was possible to be an individual, before the West became populated by extractive corporations and agri-businesses. To these romantics, the brutality of the outlaw gangs was simply an expression of their freedom of action, after all, these were times before Westerners were wage slaves. This is clearly demonstrated by the so-called "king of the outlaws" Bill Doolin who was recalled by one commentator as being a "naturally . . . kindhearted, sympathetic man . . . nice and polite . . . [and] well-behaved, quiet and friendly." One US Marshall called the Doolin–Dalton Gang "four of as fine fellows as I know." They must have also had mean streaks, because in their extended robbing spree across the Mid-West in the early 1890s, the gang killed at least nine men and wounded many others.[26]

The utopianism Nat Love ascribed to Billy the Kid was taken as a distinctively Western trait in American thought. Romantics, idealists and dreamers would see the outlaws as role models. They have added to the perception that the West has been, and continues to be, seen as somehow different from the rest of the nation: more individual, more tolerant and more radical. Although this contention is debatable—especially given the solidly conservative core of the largest state in the area, California—this difference would be used in this period as a justification for the "direct action" by such individuals as the Mooney brothers and groups like the Industrial Workers of the World. Deliberate distortion in memoires, newspapers and novels, from the 1870s onwards, was made all the more romantic by the fact that, even then, there was a fear that the old frontier regions were shrinking. Like the whole era, the whole region changed beyond recognition, a process of romanticization took over. One newspaper reported that citizens of Boise, Idaho, were complaining in 1881 that it was 12 years since the city had seen a gunfight.[27] Bandits became folk heroes and in turn triggered a series of other Western outlaws, more or less brutal; more or less successful; more or less memorable. The Robin Hood aspect of the outlaw myth inspired and, to an extent, protected figures as diverse and historically distant from Jesse James as Bonny and Clyde, John Dillinger, and Baby Face Nelson.[28]

Nevertheless, while Jesse James, Billy the Kid and a host of lesser outlaws, bandits, lawmen and vigilantes have an indubitable appeal and are of significant value to historians, telling them a great deal about social and moral conditions of the time, they also mask, distort and detract from far more prevalent, far larger-scale, but arguably less glamorous, crimes. In the West, as elsewhere, throughout history crimes related to acquisition far outweigh the importance and significance of crimes related simply to violence. In this respect, the West is once again almost indistinguishable from the rest of the nation. In fact, the region can, in many ways, be seen as a model for the course of criminal activity in the nation as a whole. It has become a truism that the West was won not with the six-shooter, but with the shovel. It is prosaic—but sadly true—that industry, the corporation and the love of money were more important to the settling of the arid, inhospitable spaces of the West than the legendary drive for individualism, or any amount of escapism.

In the final analysis, well-financed, large-scale operations were more significant to the breeding of the cattle; to providing the irrigation; to the quarrying and mining of minerals than the efforts of the isolated smallholder or placer miner. These banks, corporations, agglomerations and monopolies were, in the greater scale of things, the real drivers for the exploitation of the region. The wealthy and well resourced could acquire, extract and maintain, but ultimately this was all dependent on being able to ship the treasures of the region for marketing, consumption, processing or to be exported. The huge scale of the region, and its isolation, represented the most significant obstacle. Maritime routes were slow and costly and relied on harsh, expensive transport to the coast. Transport on inland waterways was limited by the desert nature of much of the region. Overland transport was restricted to the speed of the horse, at best, and that left people and goods at the mercy of hostile natives and the weather. Technology, however, had an answer.

The American trans-continental railroad was the largest single engineering venture of the nineteenth century or any time up to then. This mammoth undertaking did more to alter the American economy than any other single engineering feat before or since. Its 3,500 miles consumed more materials; covered a greater distance; triggered more industries; inspired more patents; and required more laborers than anything engineers had ever embarked on. It was to inspire the Trans-Siberian and Trans-Canadian railroads as well as that other great engineering project of the age, the Panama Canal. It altered the landscape with its trestle bridges, tunnels and grading. It bisected the nation, altering the trade routes from the north to south rivers which had dominated transport before its completion and replacing them with manmade east to west links. Where a railroad went through it, a town prospered: where it bypassed it, the town stagnated. It brought in millions of settlers, supplied their settlements and took out the spoils of what amounted to a new continent. It was the first, the best capitalized and the most visible of the nation's new industrial big businesses and like them it symbolized this era of American history, and—most importantly for this study—it provided a whole new level of criminal opportunity.[29]

Aware of its huge potential, the federal government sponsored the venture, granting some 21 million acres of "free land" which the recipients—the Union Pacific and Central Pacific railroads—would be able to exploit, use as collateral or sell as they saw fit. The scale of investment was vast. The Union Pacific, charged with constructing the railroad east to west, raised some $68 million. Eleven million dollars were raised through stock sales, $27 million came from government loans and $30 million in bonds. The Central Pacific, starting from California and working east, raised $90 million.[30] Even as the rails were being laid, it became obvious that the opportunities for fraud, bribery, chicanery and embezzlement were too great to be resisted.

Subsidized by the mile, the government grants were weighted to allow for the difficulty of terrain. The contractors extended routes taking indirect courses or even looping them around in circles. They paid surveyors to falsify their reports, claiming that the less valuable flat land was actually lucrative mountain grade. When the project neared completion, in order to keep it going that little bit longer, the two companies ran the two lines side by side rather than meeting. They used cheaper materials—like cotton wood sleepers which rotted out before the line was even finished—and yet charged the government for the genuine product. They withheld payments from subcontractors, cut wages to the bare minimum. They cut corners on safety, endangering workers, and provided only the most basic living conditions. The work was often shoddy and incomplete, the result of haste and greed, and it was arguably greed—criminal or otherwise—which was to really make the project memorable and notable.

Aware that the building cost would be huge and the returns would be less than certain, the railroad bosses were forced to adopt risky practices from the outset. To encourage investors, the bonds were sold at up to 40 percent discount and then the already discounted stock was further devalued by being deliberately watered to an extent where the face value of the stock was almost unrelated to the companies' real assets. The vastly over-valued bonds were then used to pay contractors and suppliers, where possible at par value. Even after this sleight of hand, the leverage of the companies was, in financial terms, near suicidal. In the initial boom that followed the completion of the venture, the companies could just make their interest payments and as competitors emerged the situation got worse.

A large part of the problem lay with the behavior of those at the top. On September 4, 1872, the *New York Sun* announced it had uncovered the "King of Frauds." The paper alleged that over $70 million of government aid had been given to the Union Pacific to build a railroad which actually cost only a little over $50 million. Over the next weeks ever more incriminating stories emerged of the scale of the swindle. The claims set in motion the most famous fraud investigation of the nineteenth century. For six months, Luke Poland's Congressional Committee investigated the activities of the now notorious Credit Mobilier. What emerged from the inquiry was that this mysterious corporation had been established to embezzle funds, to hide money and to enable bribery, fraud, graft and corruption on a scale never before even contemplated.[31]

Through this entity, Thomas Durant—the flamboyant, tyrannical, and supremely corrupt former driving force behind the Union Pacific—and his colleagues had orchestrated the systematic buying of votes in Congress. In the words of Oakes Ames, one of the founders of the syndicate and their representative in Congress, company stock was "placed where it will do most good for us." This blatant purchase of the influence of officials had extended from the vice-president and would even implicate his replacement. It would work its way up through a future president, senators and representatives and back down to town clerks.

The investigations resulted in no prosecutions, but the scandal did almost incalculable damage to the US economy, its political system and the reputation of capital. By the end of the investigation, the image of corporate business had been irrevocably damaged, the Grant administration and the Republican Party were tarnished beyond redemption, the resultant banking crisis threw the economy into depression for decades to come and the railroad business became a bye-word for dirty dealings, corruption and sharp practice.[32] While the majority of these shenanigans took place in the East, and largely in the capital, the West had its own, home-grown version, which while arguably less dramatic, through its slow-burning nature ultimately had far more impact in the region.

The owners of the Central Pacific (CP), were four ruthless California merchants. The company had been the brainchild of a visionary and driven engineer, but he would die before the project was completed. While evangelizing about the necessity and virtue of a transcontinental railroad, these men managed to gather huge personal wealth. To the more pragmatic observers, this was the price that had to be paid in order to get the scheme completed. To others, it was simply the result of fraud. What fed these critics' suspicions was the opaque nature of the extraordinarily secretive company's accounts. These were made all the more suspicious by the convenient loss or destruction of anything which could prove incriminating. Those figures that did come out, hinted at the vast scale of the padding of contract costs, graft and other sharp practices, which seemed to dwarf even the excesses of the Credit Mobilier.

At the most conservative estimate, in the first five years of its existence, the Central Pacific Railroad received an estimated $140 million in federal loans, land grants and subsidies. Some put the figure at closer to $240 million. Whichever figure was nearer to the truth, the four directors, or "Associates," as they rather sinisterly became known, billed their construction division, the Contract and Finance Company, for $90 million worth of work. The actual building costs have been estimated to have cost a little over $32 million. Not only did they bank these enormous sums while the railroad was being constructed, but once the railroad was constructed, they had a monopoly on the goods and passengers who traveled on their route. The Central Pacific declared a net profit of $2.5 million for the financial year of 1870. By 1873, that figure was up to $6.5 million. By 1884, they had netted $52.5 million.[33]

In view of these huge profits, it did not take long for questions to be asked about the rates which the CP set. In many quarters they were seen as criminally inflated. This view was given substance by an uncharacteristically indiscreet order by one of the Associates that the carriage charges for customers must be "all the traffic will bear." In practice, this meant that customers—most importantly small traders, farmers and manufacturers—would often be required to produce their accounts in order to get a contract with the CP and its burgeoning subsidiaries— most importantly the Southern Pacific. After scrutinizing the books, the company could work out their rates which would maximize their own profits. These and other monopolistic practices were made all the more galling when smaller shippers realized that large companies were able to negotiate significant "rebates," commensurate with the scale of their contracts and their financial clout.

Far from being the boon to the West which the Associates had promised, within years of its beginning to trade, the CP and its subsidiaries were increasingly seen as criminal corporations. Alongside the companies which ran the emerging storage and elevator companies they were seen as exploitative and uncompetitive. Congressional and local commissions, unions, farmers' organizations and a host of other interested parties attempted to break the monopoly of the railroads. They tried to reduce the power of the railroad lobbyists. They sought to root out corruption, but as one historian put it "Everyone was a kept lobbyist for the railroad. Such political corruption and bribery were perhaps never witnessed in an American Commonwealth as occurred in California [and the rest of the West] during these years."[34]

The railroad was central to the criminal history of the West. The railroad companies are the target of much of the frustration of the little man. Like the huge ranchers, the large mining companies, and the vast logging companies, the railroads were the antithesis of the American Dream. They stifled competition. They controlled the law. They used strong-arm tactics. In short, they negated the power of the individual and inspired the "justified" violence which is seen as so much a part of Western history. Nothing demonstrates this more clearly than the mythology which has emerged around the famous shoot-out at Mussel Slough in May 1880.

The incident stemmed from settlers who moved on to disused land owned by the Associates' Southern Pacific Railroad and started to cultivate it. When they sought to negotiate the purchase of the land, they discovered that the price of $2.50 per acre they had originally been quoted had been significantly raised. Angry at what they saw as the railroad's deception, a group of farmers met with a US Marshall who had been given the task of evicting the illegal residents and installing two new purchasers—who also both happened to be excellent shots. In the middle of the heated row which developed, a spooked horse knocked the Marshall to the ground. A melee ensued and shots were fired. This tragic clash between settlers and the "hired guns" of the Southern Pacific Railroad left seven dead—the two of the purchasers and five of the farmers.

In newspaper reports and fictionalized and dramatized accounts, the rather one-sided contest has been seen as a central part of the Western legend of individuality.[35] In many ways the incident harks back to the founding myths of America. At Mussel Slough, farmers stood up to the might of the ruthless corporation with a suicidal resolve. The similarities of this incident to Minute Men's response to the forces of tyranny at Lexington has been noted by many commentators. Both stemmed from accidental shots. Both have been seen as indicative of the heroic love of liberty inherent in the American spirit. Just like the agents of King George, the Marshall, his men and the railroad were seen as holding themselves above the law. In this reading the settlers had no alternative but to resort to violence. What is often forgotten is that these Western martyr-farmers were actually squatters on land which had been repeatedly proved in court to be the property of the railroad. There is no doubt that crimes were committed at Mussel Slough, but as with so much of Western history in this period, it is less easy to establish the true nature of the crimes and who were the *real* criminals.

3

HATE CRIME

When men feel that the safety of their homes and the protection of their wives and daughters from a fate worse than death are involved, they don't stop to reason; they cannot be held in restraint until the law may take its course; they seize the villain who committed the most revolting of all crimes and they put him to death.

Atlanta Journal, April 27, 1899

"Such barbarity we have not heard of even among the cannibals. It was the crime of the century," said Mrs Ida B. Wells Barnett at Quinn Chapel. "We must reach the capitalists of the North not by talking anarchy and powder, but by showing them the outrages perpetrated on our people in the South and pointing out to them the dangers of investing their money in a country where these things exist. That is our work, together with education of the world through pamphlets and other literature."

Ida B. Wells[1]

Both of the above quotes relate to the burning at the stake of Sam Holt (AKA Hose) in Cowetta County, Georgia, in May 1899. Before he was chained to the stake and doused with gasoline, he had his fingers, hands, genitals and ears cut off. The skin on his face was then peeled off. He was then set alight. As contemporary descriptions reported, his body was then smashed, his heart and liver were removed and his head cut off. The shards of bone and chopped up pieces of his heart and liver were then sold to the crowd of some 2,000 who had gathered to witness the occasion. His crime? He had thrown an axe at, and accidently killed, his boss in an argument over wages he was owed in April 1899. By the time the posse had caught him a month later, his crime had been exaggerated to include blinding his boss' son and raping his wife in sight of her dead husband's body. Perhaps more important was that the victim, Holt, was black. The boss was white.[2]

The best starting place in any discussion of the issue of hate crime must be a simple definition, and it can be summed up as "criminal activity motivated by prejudice."[3] Although the expression itself must be seen as an anachronism in late nineteenth- and early twentieth-century America, in many instances those misdeeds covered by this modern phrase would certainly have been outlawed by the Bill of Rights, the Thirteenth, Fourteenth and Fifteenth Amendments, as well as legislation within individual states.[4] Having said that, in many ways, this period can be seen as the apogee of American hate crime. This was the time when blacks suffered the greatest annual number of lynchings in American history. As the sociologist, James Elbert Cutler, said in 1905, "Our country's national crime is lynching."[5]

Nor were such atrocities limited to "negroes." Between 1888 and 1948, "whites" made up over a quarter of all those lynched. Also when the *Chicago Tribune* began its annual register of reported lynchings in 1882, it discovered that there had been more white victims that year than blacks and that trend continued for the next two years.[6] During this period, the Plains Indian population was reduced by over 60 percent and at least a part of this decline was the result of massacres, if not policies of deliberate genocide. Mexicans, Irish, Italians, Germans, Jews, Chinese, and no doubt others, were murdered purely because they belonged to minority nationalities or races. During these years a simple mistake, like straying into the wrong region of a segregated lakeside Chicago beach, could lead to a race riot in which hundreds were killed or injured and millions of dollars' worth of property wrecked.[7] Nor was such behavior limited to racial hate. Religion, sexual persuasion, political beliefs or economic conditions could, and did, spark violence. These years were a mixture of tension and hatred contrasted with reform and integration.

It is almost a truism to say that during this period, bigotry motivated a great deal of the crime across the nation. Few regions would not have had some form of prejudice which incited either collective or interpersonal violence, and it may be argued that there was little new or indeed uniquely American in this. What was unique was that from its birth, America had set itself up as the beacon of liberty; the "last great hope" and the world's asylum. In many ways these great aspirations were given fillips during this period. This was the time when slavery was abolished. It saw blacks—in some areas briefly—and white women—permanently—get the vote. These years saw the Statue of Liberty erected with Emma Lazarus' inspirational and hopeful words giving added poignancy to the millions arriving in New York.

At least in the second half of the period, America loudly vaunted its modernity and claimed that the logic of rational progress governed. This was the time of the Square Deal and of the New Deal. With this in mind, what is telling about hate crime in this period is not so much that it existed, but that it existed largely unchecked—and indeed in many important cases, flourished and expanded. Why is it the case that this period saw the ideals of the Emancipation Proclamation and the Gettysburg Address give way to what was essentially a race war on the American plains? How could the horror that has been called the Negro Holocaust take place in a nation which was at the forefront of racially inclusive democracy? What was it that caused the mix and match prejudice of the Klan in the 1920s to attract at its peak nearly 10 percent of the nation's adult male population to become members? It is these questions and other similar paradoxes which make the issue of hate crime so vital to understanding America during this crucial period of its history.

Just as hate crime has diverse targets, so it also takes a variety of forms. These may include such overt actions as criminal damage or desecration as well as crimes against the person. Included under these crimes against the person are such nebulous and often difficult to prove crimes as exclusion politically, geographically or economically, and such blatant crimes as murder, lynching, torture and assault. Hate crime may be seen in actions of inter-personal violence or it may take the form of violence against the whole community. It may lead to prosecutions, condemnations or it may go unpunished. In some cases, it may even be condoned and encouraged by the authorities. Having said that, there are some ways in such crimes can be categorized and explained in this period in particular.

Most of what would now be considered the hate crime which took place during this period was neither commented on, nor was it punished, since it often drew on prejudices which were either tolerated or unnoticed. That is not to say that this was the case throughout the period, all over America. Hate crime and the attitudes that engendered it were often limited by region and time, and were by no means constant in either dimension. For example, the comprehensive campaign of intimidation and persecution of blacks in the Reconstruction Era in many of the former Confederate States excited considerable condemnation in areas of the North. In spite of the Fourteenth and Fifteenth Amendments, this opprobrium had largely died out by 1877 when the so-called Jim Crow laws started to effectively exclude "negroes" from Reconstruction's advances in education, political representation and legal redress. In fact, it could be argued that their situation had been made considerably worse since many of the segregationist laws introduced in the period even excluded them physically from regions of the communities in which they lived.

However, outside this well-publicized and generally accepted—if sometimes contested—communal "lawbreaking" existed another widespread level of racial exclusion which was less obvious, but often no less institutionalized. Across other regions of the nation—most notably the Mid-West and the West—similar levels of exclusion either had tacit legal sanction, or were considered too unremarkable to attract comment. Typical of this community-sanctioned discrimination were the so-called Sundown Towns, where violence, custom and, occasionally, law kept out Chinese, Jews, Japanese, blacks or other so-called undesirables. In 1930, the southern California town of Hawthorne was not atypical, with its prominent sign informing black incomers: "Nigger, don't let the sun set on you in Hawthorne."[8]

It was not uncommon for exclusion to target one group in particular, and leave others. Usually this was the group whose presence represented the greatest racial, economic or political threat to the region's other residents. This meant that Texan towns might exclude Mexicans but ignore Irish, Jews or Italians. On the other hand, Asians were the target of prejudice in Washington State where in Seattle and Tacoma there was an attempt to forcibly cleanse themselves of Chinese in the mid-1880s. California ran a long-term policy of Chinese exclusion areas within the state from the 1850s which eventually resulted in a radical change to federal policy which managed to get Chinese immigration all but halted from 1882 until 1943.[9]

Frequently, what was acceptable in one region at a given time was frowned on in another: one man's undesirable infiltrator was another man's victim of bigotry. The behavior of the American Federation of Labor clearly shows this. When West Coast agricultural laborers formed the Japanese-Mexican Labor Association in 1903 and sought affiliation with the AF of L, they found themselves denied entry until they agreed to exclude Chinese and Japanese workers from their own membership. Yet less than a year later the Federation denounced the formation of the largely East Coast United Hebrew Trades Organization for "destroying the solidarity of organized labor by functioning along 'race' lines."[10]

Much of the hate crime in this period evolved from similar economic fears, but in searching for the root causes of hate crime such simple explanations often muddy the waters rather than clarifying the situation. Most notably it is often argued that during this period—a time of continuing agricultural monoculture in the Deep South—race violence frequently grew out of a collapse in the cotton price. It is considered that this resulted from a mixture of white racial insecurity combined with a general rage brought about by general economic impotence. Such reasoning only goes some of the way to explaining the massive upsurge in lynching during this period. While there was almost certainly a correlation between the market price for cotton and lynching, any such monocausal explanation rests on a number of less visible assumptions—most of which were just as peculiar to the region as "King Cotton."

Not the least of these was that it is also true that where local authorities chose to actively prosecute vigilante movements, the instances of lynching dramatically declined. What is more, such explanations ignore context. Cotton's market value had fluctuated in the pre-bellum South, without upsurges in racial tension or increases in violence. This was largely because the institution of slavery had restricted the fears necessary for such behavior. The fear that the emancipation of some 7 million slaves would lead to anarchy among the bestial former slave population was ingrained in the Southern white psyche. Formerly blacks had been controlled, cowed and contained. With the abolition of slavery, the black population was, at least in theory, competing with whites for the resources of the region and the result was the evolution of a more empowered and sinister vision of the "negro" in the uneasy mind of the Southern white racist.[11]

Judging by available figures, such fears were rife. The period has been dubbed the "Black Holocaust," with some justification. It is estimated that in the years 1889–1918 two people were lynched every week and there can be little doubt that the vast majority of recorded crimes which fit the category of "hate crimes" were perpetrated in the Deep South, by white males, on black male victims. It has been calculated that, between 1880 and 1930, nearly 3,000 Americans were lynched in the Southern states, compared with a mere 200 odd in the North and 150 or so in the West, and nearly 80 percent of the victims across the nation were black and the vast majority of the perpetrators, white.[12] In many eyes, lynching was a Southern phenomenon. Perhaps no one put this view better than the NAACP's unlikely, white-looking, leader—Walter White. To him the moral climate—not only the racism, but the prurience, religious fanaticism and stultifying dullness—of the Deep South made such events inevitable. As he put it:

> Most lynchings take place in small towns and rural regions where the natives know practically nothing of what is going on outside their own immediate neighborhoods. Newspapers, books, magazines, theatres, visitors and other vehicles for the transmission of information and ideas are usually as strange among them as dry-point etchings. But those who live in so sterile an atmosphere usually esteem their own perspicacity in about the same degree as they are isolated from the world of ideas.[13]

Given this, he charged that federal intervention was the only way to prevent lynching.[14]

However, in a national context, Walter White gave a skewed picture. Such a view discounted the suffering of non-black individuals and the consistency of motives and responses to these horrific events outside the South. For instance the hanging, mutilating and then burning alive of the black school teacher, David Wyatt, in 1903, in Belleville, Illinois, had all the hallmarks of a Deep South lynching. It was sparked by Wyatt's disagreeing with and then fatally shooting his, white, boss—so it seemed to ignore that vital Southern prerequisite for harmonious race relations—"race etiquette"—as black subservience was so often euphemistically called. What was more, it was carried out by a mob—over 2,000 men, women and children watched and took part in the atrocity. Sadly, and in common with so many similar events which took place in the South, while it attracted the President, Theodore Roosevelt's, genuine disgust—and a great deal of characteristic bluster—and in spite of photographic and other evidence, it resulted in no arrests, let alone prosecutions. However, what was more unusual was that, unlike its often equally horrific Southern counterparts, the incident made the front page of the *New York Times* the following day.[15]

It is also worth noting that not all the victims of such violence were black. In California, it was estimated that there were some 350 racially motivated lynchings between 1850 and 1935 and a high proportion of these would have involved

Asian, Mexican, aboriginal American or southern European victims. In the American Southwest as whole, during the same period, Mexican victims outnumbered blacks. These victims are often ignored. Since blacks made up the overwhelming majority of the victims of lynching, it was, understandably, black-based research which provided most of the statistics. For example, the black Tuskegee Institute recorded some 121 whites lynched between 1898 and 1908. Recent research claims that at least 50 of those were Mexican and claims that Mexican lynchings nationwide exceeded those of blacks per head of population throughout the period, sometimes by almost ten times.[16] It is also worth noting that the largest mass lynching in American history took place in 1891 in New Orleans and the victims were 11 Italians (see Chapter 11).

Not that all mob hate crime was always so targeted or allowed to take place without resistance. During this period, America suffered some of the worst race riots in its history. If the Civil War and emancipation sparked lynching, World War I's "Great Migration" north of over 500,000 rural Southern blacks in search of industrial work, left a legacy which took the form of riots. That was not to say that race riots had not taken place before America's entry into the European war. In 1906, for example, attempts to disenfranchise blacks and accusations of the rape of 12 white women in a week, led to four days of rioting in Atlanta, Georgia, and the deaths of at least ten blacks and two whites, not to mention hundreds being injured and considerable damage to property. What was new was the frequency and location of the violence—between 1917 and 1921, the nation suffered what amounted to a pandemic of rioting.

In July 1917, in East St Louis, Illinois—the first and most bloody of these riots—the shocking violence led to the death of anywhere between 40 and 200 blacks and left over 1,000 wounded. It caused the burning and looting of a vast swathe of the city. The resulting destruction made an estimated 6,000 homeless while spurring the exodus of a further 10,000, largely black, residents.[17] The mutiny of black soldiers in Houston later that year kept up the tension which then reached breaking point in the Red Summer of 1919 when even the nation's most apparently cosmopolitan cities like Chicago, Washington, DC, and New York were rocked by riots. It seemed that, as one Arkansas sheriff put it, the whole nation was out to "hunt Mr Nigger in his lair" and they were willing to scour over 20 locations from Arizona to Virginia.[18] Even these outbursts of violence were not the end. In 1921, in a final burst of bloodshed, the seemingly integrated boom city of Tulsa, Oklahoma, exploded into race violence. As one report had it, this was the zenith of modern race war since, "machine-guns were brought into use; eight aeroplanes [sic] were employed to spy on the movements of the Negroes and according to some were used in bombing the colored section. All that was lacking to make the scene a replica of modern 'Christian' warfare was poison gas."[19] What was the cause of this devastation? Apparently, it was the result of a black bellhop treading on the foot of a white woman in an elevator.

It is naïve to think that the perpetrators of racially motivated hate crime were always whites. Race was sometimes secondary to the feelings of security, entitle-

ment or membership which such acts of violence expressed. This was demonstrated in the Washington State lumber region, where the city of Bellingham in
1907 saw a mob of 400 to 500, driven on by the Asiatic Exclusion League, set
alight to the living quarters of 250 "Hindoos." The rioters then drove the Indians
beyond the city limits. What makes this violence notable in an area that saw plenty
of anti-Asian violence is that this mob contained not only whites, and several
blacks, but also other Asians—a number of Filipinos.[20] Nevertheless, while this
attack was notable as an exceptional incident in the period of non-white-inspired
racial violence, it had precursors. The race war which raged over the Plains States
throughout the early part of the period of this work saw atrocities committed on,
and by, both sides. As Colonel Henry Carrington reported in 1866, the cruelty
and barbarism exhibited in the treatment of captured US cavalry troopers by
Cheyenne braves displayed levels of hatred paralleling the worst excesses of any
Southern lynching or race riot.[21]

As had been, and would continue to be, the case, this event and many other
similar, if smaller, incidents were reported at length, in gruesome detail, stoking the
fears and inevitable reprisals. This link between inflammatory literature and speech
and violence played out all too frequently during the period. While some material
detailed the inhuman actions and growing threat posed by one or other group,
there was a whole other section of incendiary material which relied on cloaking
itself in innocuous and acceptable language. Such an approach broadened its appeal
and blunted prospective opposition. Most infamously, in the years immediately
after the end of the Civil War, the Klan and other "Lost Cause" organizations fed
a constant stream of anti-black, anti-Republican, anti-carpetbagger literature and
rhetoric which would effectively re-establish the old hierarchies in the defeated
South. The Klan's constitution, or "Prescript," espoused seemingly patriotic virtues
including "the inalienable right of self-preservation of the people against the exercise of arbitrary and unlicensed power" but was, in truth, practicing a widespread
campaign of terror which relied on, and maintained, black superstition, Klan
brutality and the increasing lawlessness of the Reconstruction South to reinstate
its own version of "Constitutional liberty, and a government of equitable laws."[22]
In the mid-1910s, the organization would re-emerge and thrive until the last
decade of this study, this time utilizing all the available forms of marketing and
mass media, from radio, to newsprint, to—most famously—film.[23]

When David Wark Griffith released his groundbreaking Reconstruction epic
Birth of Nation, he not only famously gained the approval of President Woodrow
Wilson and sparked a revived Klan, but also led to one of the most notorious,
controversial and influential hate crimes in the history of the South. When the
Jewish businessman, Leo Frank, was lynched in Georgia in 1915, it showed the
power of these new media. Fury in the region stemmed from the fact that although
found guilty by a Grand Jury of raping and murdering his 12-year-old employee,
Mary Phagan, Frank's sentence had been commuted by Georgia's governor to life
imprisonment. Within weeks Frank was dragged from jail, driven over 100 miles

to be tried by a kangaroo court, beaten and hanged by a group calling themselves the Knights of Mary Phagan. These vigilantes were driven on by local newspaper accounts—especially the violently anti-Catholic and anti-Semitic writing of the local populist, Tom Watson. They also, in all probability, took their cue for the aggressive defense of Southern womanhood from Griffith's masterpiece which was at the time creating controversy across the nation. As in so many instances before, although many of the perpetrators of Frank's lynching had themselves photographed alongside their victim, none were ever brought to trial.[24]

The impact of Frank's lynching goes further than simply illustrating that color was not the only "otherness" that might inspire such crimes. In many ways it had the typical hallmarks of a Southern lynching, not least the sexual nature of the crime for which Frank was murdered. During his trial it was insinuated that Frank was a philanderer and a pervert who enjoyed oral sex—a crime carrying a 20-year prison sentence in Georgia. In 1910s Georgia, with its prurience, class consciousness and latent anti-Semitism, this alone could have led to his ostracism, and possibly a lot more. Race and sex and hate crime were inextricably linked. Jews, Armenians, Japanese, Chinese in particular, and many other "non-whites" in general, were regarded as sexually predatory—either as pimps, sex-fiends, or procurers. As inferior races it was held that all these groups had less self-control, but it was black males, in particular, who were regarded as the most bestial in their sexual appetite for *white* women.

This tie was accepted by even some of the most liberal in American society. The Chicago reformer, feminist and NAACP member, Jane Addams, saw lynching primarily as degrading to all and ineffective as a means of controlling

> the bestial in man ... which leads him to rape and pillage ... [b]rutality begets brutality; and proceeding on the theory that the negro is undeveloped, and therefore must be treated in this primitive fashion, is to forget that the immature pay little attention to statements, but quickly imitate what they see.[25]

The feminist, reformer and first woman US Senator, Rebecca Latimer Felton, was even more blunt: "If it will save one white woman, I say lynch a thousand black men."[26] There was remarkably little ambivalence about the subject. As South Carolina's Senator, "Pitchfork," Ben Tillman, explained, the Southern "Negro" was a "demon" who maintained

> The white women of the South ... in a state of siege ... [He was simply waiting] for the opportunity [when he] seizes her; she is choked or beaten into insensibility and ravished, her body prostituted, her purity destroyed, her chastity taken from her.

Given this behavior, he asked: "Shall men ... demand for [the demon] the right to have a fair trial and be punished in the regular course of justice?"[27]

It seems that few did. In 1892, the worst year for lynching in American history, in the case of 60 out of the 161 blacks listed as lynched by the anti-lynching campaigner, Ida B. Wells, in that year, either rape, attempted rape, or insulting women was given as the reason for the "retribution." Unlike the women mentioned above, Wells condemned the idea that rape was the actual motivation for lynching. Rather, she saw the utilization of the violently sexually predatory nature of blacks as "that old thread-bare lie" used by Southerner racists to stave off Northern condemnation of their brutality. After all, she argued, how could Northerners denounce Southern actions to defend the virtue of their women?[28] Whether the rapes took place or not, Wells' work is backed up by a modern survey of lynching which lists 241 lynchings recorded in Arkansas, between 1860 and 1936. It cites that 56 were the result of black crimes on white women.

In an age when miscegenation was a crime in many Southern states—and Arkansas was one—rape or attempted rape, were loose terms and any unauthorized contact between white women and black men could provoke a violent response from the white community. Some victims of lynching were murdered for less serious crimes, indicative of the prurience of Arkansas society in this period. One of these "criminals," Dan Reynolds, "jilted a girl" in 1889, and another, Robert Hicks, met his fate in 1921 for "writing to a white girl." Often such violence erupted simply as an expression of community outrage. One black male, Robert Donelly, who was lynched in Arkansas in 1892 for rape, suffered his fate at the hands of an entirely black mob.[29] However, according to the Tuskegee Institute records, nearly a half of all black lynchings resulted from accusations of either murder or assault and only a quarter were the result of either rape or attempted rape.[30]

This is not to say that sexual misdemeanors did not play a very important role in hate crime as a whole. The racial element of many hate crimes ensured that it would reach the headlines. Less publicized were the crimes against sexual deviants in local communities. Heterosexual promiscuity could lead to ostracism or worse. The 1889 lynching of Cattle Kate (Ella Watson) in Wyoming—most probably in order to take over her homestead—was justified in local papers by reason not only of her cattle rustling, but also her promiscuity.[31] Sodomy and other "deviant" practices could also spark hate crime and no doubt did. Although the details remain murky, the increasing influence of the thinking of such figures as Krafft-Ebbing and Freud did much to introduce a less punitive and more clinical approach to handling sex crime in the 1920s and 1930s, but there remained a stubborn tie between race and deviant sexuality.

This was especially true in the South which saw such "modern" developments as contraception and sexually explicit night clubs, films and novels as indicative of the corruption of European and Northern American society by the influence of immigrants, socialists and blacks. It is not coincidence that in the trial of the "Yankee Jew," Leo Frank, the prosecution spent some time dwelling on his predilection for oral sex.[32] The trial essentially came down to whether the other suspect, and prime prosecution witness, Jim Conley, was lying. Conley, a poorly educated African American, was the janitor in Frank's pencil factory. His evidence that he had seen Frank having sex with Mary Phagan as well as other women workers, and his implications that these incidents had involved oral sex, did much to convince the jury of Frank's immorality, and hence his guilt.

The tensions involved can be seen in the summation by Frank's defense lawyer, Ruben R. Arnold, when he argued:

> Why go further than this black wretch there by the elevator shaft [Conley], fired with liquor, fired with lust and crazed for money? Why negroes rob and ravish every day in the most peculiar and shocking way. But Frank's race don't kill. They are not a violent race. Some of them may be immoral, but they don't go further than that.[33]

The Knights of Mary Phagan clearly did not see things that way, but they had no love for the "Negro" either for, as one historian claims, they made up a significant number of the original 34 men who climbed the landmark at Stone Mountain, lit a burning cross and proclaimed the re-vivified Klan in November 1915.[34]

While the Klan is perhaps the most persistent and best known of the hate groups in the period, they were by no means unique. Throughout the 1870s, when the railroads which had employed the Chinese laborers had largely been completed, Dennis Kearney's San Francisco-based California Workingmen's Party rallied disaffected laborers and artisans. It did this with its combination of violent anti-capitalism, anti-Chinese rhetoric and sinister threats of "hemp is the battle cry." What is more, like the Klan, although the Workingman's Party often resorted to the power of the mob and frequently and publicly threatened violence, the organization and its leader never operated outside existing laws. Far from it, they sent 50 delegates out of the total 152 to the California Legislature in 1878. They also had the law changed in their favor. Kearney's party was also the impetus driving the initial move to gain federal exclusion of Chinese immigrants from 1882 onward.[35] Nor were such political parties restricted to racial motivation. The anti-Catholic, American Protection Association, at the peak of its power in 1896, claimed to have two and a half million members and control some 20 members of Congress who stood on a platform based on rural disaffection alloyed with sectarianism.[36]

What all of these organizations demonstrate is that, then as now, while the motives behind hate crime could be harnessed for political benefit, hate crime often fed off political belief. For example, there is little doubt that action taken against the radical anarchists in the Industrial Workers of the World (IWW) from the organization's foundation in 1905 had elements of what could be termed hate crime. The IWW represented many of the untouchable classes of American labor. It contained hoboes, seasonal and itinerant workers, women workers, socialists, communists and other "rabble rousers," with articles of faith which included the equality of race and sex, the brotherhood of workers, pacifism and anti-capitalism. The IWW also used controversially subversive techniques to achieve its more equal society with its corruption of Salvation Army songs, its use of flying pickets and its loud, gleeful and mischievous shouts for direct action and sabotage. It was pretty well inevitable that it was only a question of time before the "Wobblies" became targets of hate crime.

This was especially the case in the conservative, conformist, small communities of the American Far West where the Wobblies concentrated their attempts to organize seasonal farm laborers, lumber workers and fish canners in the 1900s and 1910s. Their initial tactic of holding "Free Speech" fights resulted in regional polarization and more often than not led to their imprisonment and torture. These controversial events were held on the street corners of the region's small towns where speaker after speaker declaimed workers' rights and demanded better hours and working conditions. As each speaker was in turn arrested, another mounted the soapbox and the process continued, filling the local jails with rowdy, and costly, radicals while the authorities debated the best way to rid themselves of this plague.

The result was that in the early years of the 1910s, the IWW members were subjected to more or less constant brutality and ostracism. They might be tarred and feathered, subjected to neck-tie parties—in which the victim was dangled on a rope just long enough to allow his feet to reach the ground and prevent strangulation. With depressing regularity, the suspected radicals were simply beaten and manhandled beyond the city limits with warnings not to return on pain of further, rougher, treatment. Sometimes—as in November 1916, at Everett, in Washington State—the IWW and other radical unions fought back and there were brief eruptions of what amounted to virtual civil war. The most violent and costly of these flared up in 1914 in the coal mining region of Ludlow, Colorado, where more than 50 died in a guerilla/race/class war between company men, strikers, strike-breakers and militia.[37] Most of the time the authorities expelled the troublesome radicals—with a greater or lesser degree of violence, ironically citing public order as their excuse to rid themselves of the disruptive elements.

Just as racial tension grew during the years of the Great War, so the persecution of non-conformists became more pronounced. America's efforts to supply first the lucrative needs of the Entente and then their own war effort, led to a clamp down on "un-American" organizations. The IWW's opposition to what they saw as a "capitalist civil war" ensured that they would be a prime target. In these years of heightened patriotism, itinerant strangers were arrested simply on suspicion of being members of the IWW, even though the organization was not illegal. Exaggerated fears of sabotage, especially in industries related to the war, combined with accusations of labor agitation, anti-American propaganda and overt internationalism added to the already tense situation. In the minds of American patriots, the IWW, fifth columnists and un-Americanism became synonymous. It was only a question of time before the constant brutality this engendered escalated into causing deaths. On April 5, 1918, in the Southern Illinois coalmining town of Collinsville, it did just that.

German-born Robert Prager was taken from the jail, in which he had sought sanctuary, and hanged from a tree. Hours earlier, he had been stripped and wrapped in the Stars and Stripes. He was then forced to march down the main street of the town ahead of a taunting, drunken, mob before being taken into protective custody in the town's jail. The reasons behind his lynching are a little confused. Some sources claim it was his German origin. Others cite his uncompromising socialist leanings. Another group say both were important, but that it was his looks which led to his demise. A rather peculiar, loner of a man, he was stunted, blind in one eye and with a shambling walk, and these traits, combined with his outspoken socialism, did for him. As one commentator said, he looked like a spy to the miners and to the 200-odd witnesses who hanged him and in a nation alive with patriotism, that was probably enough to seal Prager's fate.

Perhaps because Prager was white, perhaps because the authorities hoped it would halt an unwanted escalation of patriotic violence, the incident led to 12 men facing a grand jury on charges of murder. Such wishes were lost on the ultra-patriotic jury. In less than 25 minutes they unanimously acquitted all the defendants, and then left the court to a band playing "Stars and Stripes Forever."[38] Although Prager's murderers escaped punishment, in the final six months of the Great War, no further lynchings of German-Americans followed.

That is not to say that the super-patriotism unleashed by the war years ended with Prager's death. Although Woodrow Wilson and other members of his administration did attempt to rein in the worst of the excess by repeatedly condemning the practices of "One Hundred Percent" Americans, the bigotry of these homefront heroes had one final murderous flourish. Such instincts sparked a final radical lynching in November 1919. The violence flared when members of the newly formed American Legion marched in an Armistice Day parade in the small Washington State logging town of Centralia. Full of patriotic fervor they stormed what they saw as the unpatriotic IWW in their union hall. The Wobblies defended their position and in the shooting which ensued, the Legionnaires suffered heavy casualties. By way of reprisal, that night a furious mob beat, castrated and hanged the Wobbly, Wesley Everest.

Revolting as this display of brutality was, it is notable chiefly for the increased rarity of such events. Even though over 10,000 radicals were hounded and rounded up in the Palmer Raids of the Red Scare of 1919–1920, the consequent failure to implement draconian measures and deport troublesome radicals can be seen as defining the limits of the state's intervention and, perhaps by extension, its defense of the radical opinion. Although some 250 radicals were deported to war-torn Russia, in the final analysis, mob rule was actually curtailed when the vast majority of radicals rounded up in the Raids were set free. This must, along with other measures, account for some of the de-escalation of anti-radical mob violence in the subsequent years. However the same cannot be said of hate crimes aimed against racial targets. Far from it. Not only did the racial tensions in America seem to escalate over the same period, with riots taking place across the nation, but also, while the worst of the Negro Holocaust seemed to have passed, lynchings were still to remain all too common.

In the years from the turn of the twentieth century to the end of the Great War, one estimate claimed that some 3,500 people had died in lynchings. Of these crimes, only 12 cases had been prosecuted and a mere 37 people convicted for participation. Between 1918 and 1938, over 580 people were lynched. Of these, less than 50 were "non-Negro," a figure which would include all other races.[39] Interestingly, in every year of that period, with the exceptions—for some reason—of 1931 and 1932, at least one bill was introduced to pass a federal anti-lynching law. Between 1937 and 1939, there were over 60 bills introduced. Only two of all of these bills ever reached a vote, in 1922 and 1937, and both of those were stymied by the threat of being talked out in the Senate by Southern filibusters.[40] In end of the period of this study, it appeared that lynching, although indisputably homicide, did not contravene the Fourteenth Amendment's outlawing of the "taking of life without due process of law." Several Supreme Courts upheld this principle since the Constitution applied only to the action of the "State," not the individual citizen.[41]

This was not the only stumbling block. The arguments against a federal anti-lynching law were well rehearsed. White Southern newspaper editors—arguably the mouthpiece of those Southerners most often seen as defending lynching—repeatedly argued lynching was the response of the outraged community to heinous crimes. As Ida Bell had pointed out as early as 1892, newspapers like the Memphis *Commercial* held that lynching was an essential check on the criminal urges of the South's black population since "Nothing but the most prompt, speedy and extreme punishment [could] hold in check the horrible and bestial propensities of the Negro race."[42] It seemed that little had changed in the minds of the lynch mob. Many similar papers held that lynching was, if undesirable, still frequently defensible. For example, when Leo Frank had been lynched, the *Atlanta Georgian* had reported that

> Among [local] men there was evident a grim and terrible satisfaction. "They did a good job," was the comment, spoken in many tones, but with an inflection that was always the same. "A good job."[43]

Such a fatalistic view was even detectable in academia. While "deploring the practice of lynching," the sociologist James E. Cutler's (1905) study of lynching admitted that a federal law was a long way away since in the regions of the South lynching was most prevalent:

> [T]he people consider themselves a law unto themselves . . . [and since it is them who] make the laws; therefore they can unmake them. Since they say

what a judge can do, they entertain the idea that they may do this thing themselves.[44]

A review of his work in the *New York Times* agreed, ending with the rather solipsistic argument that "In the South it is a question with which the South alone can properly deal."[45]

The advocates of a federal law were less lukewarm in their views. Many black proponents—including the tireless campaigner, Ida Wells—saw the practice as essentially community-sponsored murder. Yet others defined it as community-*sanctioned* murder. Communists held there to be a class element to lynching and wanted the inclusion of labor dispute violence, as well as—in the wake of their involvement in the Scottsboro Boys' trial—what they now called "legally sanctioned" lynching. To some, the lynch mob was a crowd infected by a collective blood lust, victims of a disease, caused by as much the prevailing environment as individual events. Plays and books, popular music and art by both black and white artists directly confronted the issue of lynching, condemning the brutality of the perpetrators and the complicity through inaction of the black communities.[46]

Spearheading the move was the National Association for the Advancement of Colored People (NAACP). To them, lynching was quite simply the ultimate racial crime. Using his pale skin and sandy-haired appearance to gain access, the organization's controversial leader, Walter White, toured the country, interviewing those who had participated in lynchings and publishing his findings in mainstream journals. Under White, the leadership gradually abandoned its concentration solely on higher-minded social science methods of persuasion and combined its traditional statistical arguments with a rhetoric of shock which they utilized to great effect. The campaign was to be taken to Main Street, to stun the American public into action, perhaps most famously, with their flying a large black flag reading "A Man Was Lynched Today" outside its headquarters at 69 Fifth Avenue in New York City each time a lynching took place. From the late 1920s, their accounts stressed the barbarity of lynching with graphic and disturbing photographs. By the 1930s, they concentrated their efforts on publicizing the lynchings in Southern communities where such savagery was often if not officially sanctioned, then at least left unpunished. They made America question how such barbarity could be taking place in the world's leading economic power.[47]

Walter White was determined that the one of the prevailing cultural traits which fed lynching was the widespread belief in a scientific racism. This held that the Negro was simply, biologically, inferior. With this in mind he sought out sympathetic academics who would refute this view.[48] Throughout the 1920s and 1930s, a group of prominent Southern social scientists, with the euphemistic name of the Commission on Interracial Cooperation (CIC), ran a detailed survey of the root causes of lynching. They concluded, in their 1931 report, that the lynching in the South was the result of a toxic mix of poverty, cultural isolation and a culture which accepted higher levels of violence than many other regions of America.[49]

Some saw such findings as the main reason that lynch legislation was not passed during the first decades of the twentieth century—since it alienated the South and created a culture of guilty retrenchment. Opponents of this "unique South" argued that it fed fears in the Southern mind that the North sought to destroy its way of life, much as it had tried to do during the post-Civil War Reconstruction. This attitude was best characterized in behavior of a clique of conservative, racist, Southern Senators and summed up in the stance of South Carolina demagogue, Senator and Governor, Coleman Livingstone Blease. Blease was notoriously cited by one of the CIC as claiming that

> Whenever the Constitution comes between me and the virtue of the white women of South Carolina—I say to hell with the Constitution . . . In my South Carolina campaigns you heard me say "when you catch the brute that assaults a white woman, wait until the next morning to notify me."[50]

Abhorrent as such views may have been to a majority of those, both inside and outside Congress, they still found a very small but influential group of supporters and during the debate over the Costigan–Wagner Anti-Lynching Bill at the height of New Deal power, such views were still powerful enough to prevent federal legislation.

Nevertheless, race was not given as the primary motive for the 1935 and 1938 filibusters that defeated the most successful anti-lynching measure to date.[51] It was felt that by passing prosecution of both lynch mobs and the complicit law keepers over to federal authorities—one of the main aims of both the earlier Dyer and the Costigan Bills—the power of local, state, government was being usurped. Such issues had the power to unite a more impressive section of Southern Senators, after all, they had led to civil war in the past. At the end of the day, it was simply a question of the forces which could be mobilized. Southern Democrats, many by right of long service seniority in positions of considerable influence, held a balance of power which could essentially scupper any New Deal measures. As Southern white supremacist, Josiah Bailey of North Carolina, pointed out: "I give you warning, that no administration can survive without [such like-minded Southern racist senators as] us."[52] Supreme politician that he was, FDR knew better than to test this threat and some see the failure of the Costigan measure essentially as the result of the lukewarm support he and other leading New Dealers gave the measure.

Whatever really lay behind the failure of federal anti-lynching measures, hate crime remained a depressingly familiar feature of American society in the 1930s. As if to demonstrate this, during the time of the Costigan Bill, some of the most horrific lynchings took place in the South, including some 14 in the last eight months of 1935 alone. Nevertheless, if the Civil War and World War I had fueled racial hatred among American communities, the legacy of World War II was essentially one of national integration. The West and South were included in the supreme war effort and although the tensions of hate crime would emerge as Civil Rights became a battleground for blacks, Hispanics, gays and other groups, this national unity can be seen as at least one reason for their final triumph.

4

POLICING AND IMPRISONMENT

It is a truism to say that if crime played any role in the birth of modern America, then it must have been codified, detected and punished, or we would not make the association. Nevertheless it is perhaps a statement worth making. This is a period when the whole business of law-keeping changed over the industrialized world. The forces of law and order were adopting new technologies, rationalizing, and standardizing. Perhaps because of its wild reputation, perhaps because of its fascination with crime and the criminal, this is shown most clearly in America. It is glaringly demonstrated by the central nature of the figures of policing. The roles of American law-keepers in this period are iconic across popular culture—from the legendary posses of the West; to the good "ol boy" Southern sheriff; to San Francisco, Chicago, and New York's Finest; to Eliot Ness' Untouchables. So are the names of Alcatraz, Sing Sing, the Tombs, and San Quentin. It is nearly impossible to imagine the immigrant colonies of Gilded Age New York without picturing the Irish cop on the street corner thwarting the activities of the Italian and Jewish gangs of street kids. Popular images of the gangsters of the 1920s always seem to include a reference to the brutality of the regime in San Quentin or Alcatraz or the incompetence of the local police. The images of the South in this period seem invariably to include a chain gang in the background. Across the period and across the nation, the forces of law and justice were as indicative of the progress of the nation as the prairie sod-house and the skyscrapers of New York and Chicago.

Law enforcement and punishment are both indicative and responsive to the changes in US society over the period of this study. As the population settles across the re-united nation, as the major metropolitan areas emerge and as the country feels the growing influences of secularization—so the law enforcement organizations are required to change accordingly. The marked difference of the West, South, and East of the nation begin to merge and disappear in this period.

This is the period when America begins its love affair with incarceration on a national level and correctional programs are developed on both federal and community levels, dealing with all types of criminals including women, juveniles, and the criminally insane.

During these years law-keeping develops a federal response to many of the most intransigent of the nation's criminals and crimes. Policing becomes a largely urban phenomenon and with notable exceptions, crime becomes more about safety and security than morality and ethics. Policing expands dramatically over this period, both in terms of numbers and impact. It evolves ever more sophisticated responses to seemingly ever more intelligent, diverse, organized, amoral, and ruthless criminals. Yet, at the same time, the reforming zeal which bubbles up at the turn of the century extends even as far as to include those who transgress— beginning the transformation of ideas of exclusion, punishment and retribution into demands for prevention, rehabilitation and understanding.

It is not the intention of this section to be an encyclopedic reference work for the development of law-keeping in the United States from the end of the Civil War to America's entry into World War II. That is well covered in other books—most notably in the work of such scholars as Eric Monkkonen, David Johnson, Richard Wade and Paul Keve.[1] This is not going to be a narrative history of the urban police forces, or the prison reform movement in this period. This is, like the rest of this work, an attempt to fit the history of these years into the development of crime in America, but focusing on law-keeping. It is an attempt to explain how the forces of law and order can help us to understand the years in which America developed as the modern superpower it has become today and how policing and prisons can be used to demonstrate a whole variety of the most central issues of the period.

Although no doubt such a study could, and some might say should, examine a whole host of other strands, this section will simply concentrate on five important themes. It will start with the processes of urbanization and how these altered ideas of criminality, most importantly, its detection, prevention and the punishments it inspired. Second, in these years of supreme corruption and venality, this study will examine the control, accountability and corruption within the forces charged with maintaining the law. The third strand will concentrate on the influence of Progressive thinking and its effect on the rationalization, technology, and philosophy of law enforcement and penology. The fourth part will examine the increasing intervention of the federal government in the law-keeping process and how this reflects the expansion of central government from the end of the American Civil War. Finally, in this, the age of increasing literacy, emerging mass-circulation newspapers, Muckrakers, press barons as well as the advent of radio and film, this study will look at the influence of the media on law-keeping and how crime was viewed. It will examine what was to be expected of the forces of law and order and how they lived up to these expectations.

In probably every survey course taught on America at the turn of the century, there will always be a section on urbanization. It has to be one of the dramatic changes of the period. In 1860 just over 15 percent of Americans lived in urban areas—towns of more than 2,500 people. By 1900, that figure was around 30 percent and by 1920 more Americans lived in urban areas than in rural areas. The United States of 1900 had over 40 cities with more than 100,000 inhabitants and, by 1910, New York would have over 3.5 million residents. Cities were considered wonders of modern technology with their invisible underground sewerage, water, gas and rail systems which powered the new industries and made possible their highly visible towering skyscrapers, street lighting, trams and other wonders of engineering and science.

By 1900, America's cities were the centers of the nation's commerce, finance and industry and, as such, magnets for seemingly ever increasing numbers of immigrants—both from other nations, most notably the various regions of Europe, as well as from other regions of the nation and the surrounding rural areas. It has been estimated that at least 50 percent of America's population had migrated to, or from, another region, or country, in the decade from 1890.[2] These migrants were drawn to the poorer areas of the cities, where they lived with other transients as overcrowded and often exploited residents. Such slums were increasingly seen as reservoirs of disease and poverty and as breeding grounds for immorality and crime. In short, the growing city was seen as much as a mounting problem, a police problem, as well as a wonder of modernity. Cities represented new problems, problems of scale—how could these already huge—and constantly expanding—areas be kept safe? How could all their citizens be kept secure—both physically and morally?

Just as the city attracted mixed views in terms of its overall impact, the city as a breeding ground for the "dangerous classes"—criminal classes—was equally paradoxical. Did the processes of urbanization lead to a more gentle (perhaps, urbane) society, or did they present a series of irresistible opportunities for deviants? Like most interesting historical questions, the answer is complex. Historians seem to have shown that, contrary to popular belief, as the nation underwent its most rapid urbanization between 1860 and 1920, the crime rate in those cities which they have studied, the general trend has been that the numbers arrested per 1,000 of population actually went down. This was largely considered more the result of a shift in policing emphasis than an increased respect for the law. There was far less prosecuting of public disorder offenses and a concentration on violent crime since over the same period, for example, the number of homicide arrests per head of population climbed relentlessly.[3]

Whatever the truth of the situation, what was important was that the city was *perceived* as having a detrimental effect on American society. It was the rapid growth of the population, the consequent instability and constant fear of rioting and civil disorder that inspired the formation of the force. Riots and civil disobedience were seen by some as the natural progression of healthy democracy and anything from food, to abolition, to religion could, and did, spark these violent outbursts in the first century of the Republic's history. To others, this mayhem was simply the action of the mob. This paradox was clearly illustrated in the reaction to an 1888 attempt by the Massachusetts State Legislature to erect a monument to the patriotic actions of those who perished at the hands of the Redcoats in the Boston Massacre of 1770. A Harvard don, Andrew Preston Peabody, attacked the idea of a memorial to an urban mob of "ruffians." He saw their behavior as less than patriotic, and more "harmful and detrimental" to the patriotic cause with their "unlawful and immoral" actions. He defended such a seemingly unpatriotic stance when he argued that the criminal behavior of the crowd had alienated many of those still undecided over issues of loyalty to the British Crown. He argued it made loyalists of many who saw this violence less as revolution and more as free-for-all anarchy.[4]

To Peabody and many of his class, the city was the cradle of "mobocracy." The city was always on the verge of violence and the job of the forces of law and order was to prevent the "dangerous" classes gaining that critical mass and "swarming." As one New York commentator put it—"Let but Law lift its hand from them for a season . . . and, if the opportunity offered, we should see an explosion from this [under]class which might leave this city in ashes and blood."[5] Given such fears, it is no coincidence that the western world's two largest cities in 1900 were the first to develop recognizably modern police forces. London's Metropolitan Police were established in 1829, and with their military-style barracks, uniforms and ranks; their patrolling techniques and salaries, they set the model for the emergence of New York's Municipal Police in 1853.

However, the differences between the two forces continued to reflect that American love of democratic expression—as well as its less savory consequences which had so appalled Peabody, and frightened other commentators. It stemmed in essence from the differences between the two nations. Where Britain's suffrage was severely limited in 1829, the majority of New York natives had the vote in 1853. It has been argued that the efforts to make police conform to American ideals of democracy hamstrung both their efficiency as law-keepers and their autonomy as an institution.

One of the clearest examples of this contrast between the British and American models was over the initial adoption of a uniform. Central to the recognition, authority and prestige of London's Metropolitan Police, this seemingly innocuous development met with opposition in the US. Not only did the inherent American fear of standing armies retard the adoption of uniforms, but also the issue brought with it problems related to subservience and cost which jarred with the prevalent Jacksonian ideals of civil liberty. American critics claimed that the British were used to such distinctions of rank and marks of subservience. By contrast, many Americans saw the rejection of uniform as a point of principle, as one Philadelphia police officer in 1855 said—"I hereby present my resignation, as an American citizen—not wishing to wear anything derogatory to my feelings as an American."[6]

Uniforms, and uniformity also, obviously, gave power to those who oversaw these changes and consequently led to battles for such command. In the case of

New York, in the early 1850s, two rival police forces, with rival political backers—the mayor and the state legislature—engaged in a real war which culminated in a battle on the steps of City Hall in 1857. Ironically, bearing in mind the background of the issues which sparked it, the riot was ended only by the intervention of the military. Given that one of the fundamental reasons for the establishment of a unitary police force was the control of mass urban violence, such behavior by the so-called forces of law and order did not look encouraging. However, by July 1863, after three days of looting and rioting over conscription, New York's police were able to demonstrate considerable dedication, enabling them to contain and—with the help of the military—eventually end, the worst peacetime civil disturbance in US history.

This newfound professionalism was clearly demonstrated in the public reaction to the New York police's actions in the wake of the 1871 Orange Riot. When Police Superintendent James Kelso banned the 1871 Orangemen's March on the grounds of the danger it presented to public order, he met with a barrage of indignation from the New York press. Prominent New York newspapers, including the *Times*, condemned Kelso's action and proclaimed the march as a "struggle for civil rights." Sensing a means to reverse their declining political fortunes, Tammany Hall reversed the decision. Tammany's plan backfired. As the march reached its destination, militia, with police support, opened fire on an unruly mob protesting against the Orangemen. Popular sentiment, however, was with the Orangemen, against the "mob," and Kelso's initial decision was seen as vindicated. Curiously, to the majority of influential New Yorkers, the 62 protesters killed were seen as having died as a result of vacillation on the part of the embattled Tweed Tammany administration, not by overzealous, or panicked, lawmen. The authorities not only had the will to intervene in urban disturbances, they now had the means to control them.[7]

If this tragedy demonstrated anything—other than the unpopularity of the Tweed regime—at a local, and later national, level it showed that there was a new intolerance of Jacksonian democracy as expressed through street violence, as well as an increasing faith in the new police forces. It has been emphasized that Gilded Age police forces were a tangible part of the processes of "impersonalization" and the community breakdown that accompanied this intolerance. The police represented the forces of bureaucratization and centralization which were transforming American society, changes most visible and effective in America's expanding metropolises.[8]

What was more, if their ability to maintain order gained them the support of the "respectable" middle and upper classes, the police at this point also took on social roles peculiar to the less fortunate denizens of the new urban environments of America's rapidly expanding cities. By the 1870s, thousands of homeless drifters drawn to the urban areas were being given overnight shelter and, in many cases, food in the station houses of inner city areas. This not only performed a vital social and humanitarian function, it also kept potential criminals off the street—albeit temporarily. In many instances it also provided vital intelligence about the so-called "dangerous" classes of the city's unfortunates—paupers, tramps, and petty criminals.[9] However, as the twentieth century dawned, it is argued that the emergence of professional urban police forces saw the beginnings of gradual change from this class-based concept of criminality, to a more individual, evidence-based, behavioral one. Perhaps the clearest indication of this came with the incorporation of detection and prevention into police work.

Detective squads (divisions) had been established first in Boston and then the other leading cities from the late 1840s. Since it seemed to go without saying that the "dangerous classes" provided the criminals, anyone wishing to investigate their activities not only needed to understand them, but also to mingle with them. Infiltration and surveillance became a part of police work, not that this met with universal approval. To some, this made distinguishing the police from the criminals increasingly difficult. As one of New York's most successful detectives pointed out, this side of police work required the law-keeper to become as "dishonest, crafty, unscrupulous" as the criminals he tracked. The detective needed to make himself like the "miserable snake [in *Genesis* only], not in paradise, but in the social hell" that was turn-of-the-century urban America.[10]

To others, such proximity enabled understanding of what motivated criminals, and created a fascination with detecting and identifying the individual criminal. In this move away from group criminal identity to individualism, police work again harked back to its urban roots. The city's anonymity, the growing mobility of the population, and the underclass' existence in brutal poverty created mysterious crimes where a body might be unidentifiable; a murder's identity confused, even to an eyewitness; or a criminal may have moved to another district, city or even country. On the other hand, the modern world provided some solutions.

Criminal anthropologists for decades had struggled to identify physical signifiers of criminal tendency, concentrating on aberrations such as lower than average foreheads, eyes set overly close together, or misshapen skulls. Out of these observations came the first workable system of criminal identification. In Paris in the 1880s, Alphonse Bertillon developed a system of identification which relied on a combination of photography, accurate physical measurements and precise notation of any abnormalities.[11] The success of the system quickly led to the identifying of hundreds of multiple offenders in France and Britain in the late 1880s and had been adopted by most urban America police forces by the 1890s. Fingerprinting was soon added to this system of identification, initially complementing it, and eventually replacing it. Once criminals could be identified individually, they could also be photographed for "rogues' galleries" and descriptions published in mass-circulation newspapers or their details sent to other regions of the country, first by telegraph, and later by telephone.

At its most local level, this personalization can also be seen in the regime of the "beat cop." The patrolmen became a sort of "roving magistrate" as one historian has called them. Knowing, and known by, many on his beat, the patrolling policeman's day would be taken up largely with domestic and petty crime. The diary of the beat cop, Stillman S. Wakeman, in the suburbs of Boston for 1895 is instructive. It shows that during the vast majority of his time at work his daily routine was made up of policing domestic violence, enforcing issues of public safety and investigating juvenile offenses and petty larceny. The bureaucratization of the period also meant that he spent a considerable proportion of his time on byelaw enforcement—checking construction permits and dog licenses. When punishment was necessary, arrests were rare, most law was enforced by mediation, implying that his status and authority in the neighborhood seem to have been considerable.[12]

What is curious, given the concerns of the day about urban depravity, is that Wakeman spends remarkably little time on policing morals—on the prevention and punishment of drunkenness, prostitution or gambling, which motivated so much of social reforming during the period. This does not mean that this fear of inner city immorality was unfounded, far from it. The details of the daily activity of New York's most notorious cop, Charley Becker—who would die in the electric chair in 1915—could not be more different. Unlike his Boston equivalent, Becker's day was associated almost entirely with vice, whether that was turning over one of the district's 30,000-odd prostitutes, or collecting protection money from one of the area's hundred or so gambling dens. Also, unlike Wakeman, his reputation and authority stemmed from his having "fists like typewriters" and his willingness to use them, and other weapons, with extreme brutality. In addition to his own physical presence he relied on the knowledge that even with his criminal behavior he still had the backing of his superiors all the way back to "Big Tim" Sullivan's corrupt, ruthless and extremely effective political machine in Tammany Hall.[13]

This concentration on policing as politics dominated the New York police and the model would be adopted by other US cities, large and small, over the next two decades. The result was that elected officials nominated police officers for their own wards—often concentrating not only on selecting, installing and promoting from within their own party but also, frequently their own religion, race, national origin and class. Recurrent—often annual—election and the consequent politicization of many of the higher levels of the police forces led to insecurity of tenure and a discontinuity in policy as well as opportunities for what would become legendary levels of cronyism, corruption and graft. It also significantly reduced the pool from which policemen were drawn. This can be seen in St Louis, Missouri, where over 5 percent of the city's population was black in 1901, yet only two out of some 1200 police officers were non-white. While simple color prejudice may account for this, it is also worth considering that the city Police Department was dominated by the Democrats, and as a rule blacks were almost universally loyal to the Republicans, the party of Lincoln.[14]

Charley Becker was also highly unusual. However, in this era of supreme venality, his oddity lay not in his acquisitive motives and aggressive methods—although even by the standards of the day they were prodigious. It was more in his background; in his getting caught and his being hung out to dry by Tammany. For a start, in a police force dominated from top to bottom by Catholic, Irish-American, bosses and their placemen, Becker stood out, simply because he was of Protestant, German, descent. In this urban environment he was also unusual, he was from a rural—*very* rural—New York State, background. Given these disadvantages and the slender odds of even a well-connected placeman becoming a policeman—he was unusual. At the turn of the twentieth century, it was estimated that every applicant had a one in eight chance of being accepted, and Becker took the route which most outside applicants adopted. He gained his post by paying $300 to Tammany Hall in November 1892. By 1894, having paid out another $300 for uniform and equipment, he was on the beat setting out to regain that capital outlay.[15]

Initially patrolling the Manhattan waterfront, within 18 months he had moved on to the Tenderloin where he would remain until 1912. The busy docks offered a cop a range of opportunities in the shape of moonlighting, bribes, graft and theft, but in the Tenderloin area the pickings were still greater. It was here that Becker discovered he had a real talent for extortion, graft and bribery in this, the most notorious of New York's vice districts. In spite of a serious setback early in his career, when he arrested the date of a famous author for prostitution, he rose through the ranks to lieutenant by a combination of luck, cunning and bravery. He also had an uncanny ability to attract patronage. Importantly, he demonstrated a willingness to provide a totally unquestioning show of fabulously brutal muscle for his superiors' extortion rackets. Becker's demise and notoriety came in 1912 when he was exposed as having had a recalcitrant gambling den owner murdered for his refusal to pay the protection Becker thought his due. His superiors could not protect him since the city was undergoing one of its periodic bursts of reform, and they were worried about their own positions. The resulting scandal and trial showed a very different police force from that in which Wakeman served. This was a department in which the arts of the "take" were prized and the individual made his career through his own wits with no regard to duty, and cared only for the law with regard to avoid being caught.

Even though in 1915 Becker became the only New York cop ever to be executed, his actions would not have been considered unique, or entirely surprising by the majority of the public. Typical of the growing pressures to reform American society in the 1890s, in 1894, New York State Senator, Clarence Lexow presided over the nation's first ever detailed investigation into police corruption. Its target was the activities of the New York City police department. What Lexow exposed was an extraordinarily slick and well-organized machine, which became known simply as the "System." Within this operated a whole list of options for corruption. Local businesses paid protection, which ranged from, at the lowest end, $50 a month for a gambling house or brothel, to $100 for a poolroom. These could rise to up to $300 depending on size and activity and, any failure to pay resulted in a destructive raid followed by a further "registration" fee. The graft was broken down to give the collector, usually a beat cop or detective, around 20 percent of the take; the precinct captain took 35–50 percent and the inspector pocketed the balance. Payoffs for positions were normal, with a menu of costs ranging from the $300 Becker paid to become a beat cop up to $15,000 to become a captain. There were annual payments made by all officers to the local boss, and periodic demands for further campaign funds.[16]

One notoriously brutal casualty of the Lexow Committee was Alexander, "Clubber," Williams. Williams had been Becker's boss and his style of policing had made an impact on the young Becker. Williams was a poacher turned gamekeeper. As a young man he had been a sailor who when drunk on his shore leave would often batter senseless any policemen who crossed his path, simply for entertainment. Working on the assumption that he would be an asset to the force, the NYPD took him on in 1866. Williams controlled his beat with similar violence, famously arguing that, "There is more power in a policeman's [night] stick than in all the US Supreme Court decisions." The result was that he was charged with over 350 incidents of violence and corruption. Over 220 of these were sustained, with Williams often freely admitting his guilt, paying the fines and continuing with his vicious form of policing.[17]

Yet it seemed to work, visible crime in New York's Tenderloin seemed to be contained and Williams rose up through the ranks to become an inspector. However, Clubber's downfall began when the Lexow Committee found and disclosed the extent of his huge personal wealth. Investigations revealed him as having some $300,000 in assets; a substantial house on 10th Street; a 17-room holiday home in exclusive Cos Cob, Connecticut, with a jetty and personal steam yacht on which to travel back and forth to his $3,000 a year police job. When questioned how this added up, he claimed he had made lucky and lucrative investments in northern Japanese real estate. It seemed the committee was powerless to prove otherwise. Nevertheless, the limelight was more than he wished and he retired in 1895, on a full pension, enjoying all the fruits of his corruption until his death in 1917.[18]

Like most Progressive Era reforms, the results of the Lexow Committee were mixed. It may have failed to bring Williams to justice, but it did achieve some other notable reforms. Most importantly, Democratic Tammany's stranglehold on the police was briefly broken and a reforming Republican mayor was elected. In terms of being seen to reform, the most significant changes included the replacement of four of the city's police commissioners. By far the most prominent and most active of these new appointments was to launch the political career of the bombastic future US president, Theodore Roosevelt who was installed as President of the New York City Police Board. This fearless, energetic, publicity-seeking, 36-year-old used the burgeoning mass-circulation press to shame negligent officers and report on the intentions and progress of his clean-up campaign. He personalized the reforms using the huge appetites of a news-hungry populace to report his own midnight adventures in the back alleys of New York's seedier districts as, disguised, he personally policed the policemen.

Roosevelt's actions as police reformer showed both the strengths and weaknesses of the Progressive movement as whole. They were typical top-down, centralizing, "rationalization" measures beloved by this group of middle-class reformers, who were just beginning to make such an impact on American politics that they would lend their name to an entire period—if only in US history survey courses. Among the measures he introduced were some very impressive achievements. Roosevelt managed to sack, transfer, demote or retire the most outrageously incompetent as well as the most openly corrupt officers; he extended police patrols beyond midnight; he stopped the purchases of office—at least overtly; he subjected new recruits to civil service-type testing for entry requirements as well as a physical exam; he gave police officers small arms training and tidied up station houses. On the other hand it was that other patronizing, preachy, moralizing, strand of Progressivism which spelled the end of Roosevelt's police days. In one of the hottest summers of the decade, Roosevelt—partly out of duty, partly out of preference—used the police to strictly enforce Republican-backed "dry Sunday" liquor prohibition legislation. The result was that he personally received death threats and was sent letter bombs. The police suffered a reversal in popularity and it also caused a total reversal of the Republican landslide of 1895 with many of the Tammany rogues returned to office—albeit somewhat chastened and a little more cautious.[19]

What Roosevelt's demise also illustrated was the enduring influence of the political party on tenure of office and the consequent drag this caused on reform. While looking to a European model, which would have placed the police largely above partisan politics, what American urban police continued to operate with was an insecure hierarchy which changed too regularly to allow for major reform. Some indication of the scale of the chaos this created can be seen in San Francisco, where between 1900 and 1911, the city had eight different police chiefs. This was not the only city to suffer in this way—Pittsburgh had a different chief each year for the first six years of the twentieth century; Los Angeles had 25 chiefs in 43 years, while Des Moines had 11 between 1900 and 1917.[20]

Yet as in so many of the social aspects of Progressivism, European influences were still discernible in the thinking of police reformers. For example, based on extensive studies of German and British policing techniques, the young New York polymath, Leonard Felix Fuld, argued that the center of urban policing was the beat cop. Like so many other Progressives, Fuld was an academic who came to his subject with a new, optimistic scientific objectivity. In true Taylorist style, Fuld sought to find the essence of police work and lay out simple, rational, targets for the future of urban policing. He maintained that the patrolman could only be truly effective if police were recruited from well-chosen members of a well-educated pool, well-trained and career-driven, backed by a comprehensive system of discipline and supported in the field by well-maintained records and forensics.[21]

At the opposite end of the police theory spectrum, but still very much a part of the thinking of the times, was the pragmatism of Jacob H. Haager. As one of a growing number of professional, career, police executives, Haager had assumed control of the Louisville police after scandalous exposures of corruption and fraud and spent much of his time improving the image and efficiency of the force. In 1908, while police chief, Haager had introduced three petrol-engined Cadillac police cars to replace horse-drawn wagons. Within a year Haager was converted to the merits of the mechanical alternative. He became positively evangelical about the use of the automobile as a policing tool, arguing at the 1909 International Association of Chiefs of Police (IACP) for its economy, predictability, range, speed, reliability and reduced maintenance costs. By the 1920s, the police car was a common sight on all major cities' streets.[22]

While there is little doubt that the motor would eventually replace the horse for police work, Haager's advocacy of motorized policing not only showed the forward-looking mood which urban Progressivism had at its core, but also the way in which such reforms were quickly adopted by others working in the field. It is indicative that Louisville was among the first forces to recruit policewomen (1921), and then black policewomen (1922). However, while such innovations can be seen as examples of the innovative thinking of that force, it is equally instructive to see that during the Depression, experimenting with equal opportunities was not regarded as desirable. In 1938, the incoming Democrat mayor, in a bid to keep down his costs, sacked the four policewomen in the department—two of whom were black—claiming: "They have no specific duties, and practically do nothing."[23] Nevertheless, urban and metropolitan police forces had been among the first organizations to adopt and adapt many of the technological advances which symbolized America at the turn of the twentieth century. Telegraphy, the telephone and radio transformed communications on the beat. Finger printing, photography and other forensic tools transformed detection and conviction, but urban law-keeping reforms did not simply apply to policing on the street.

In the early years of law enforcement, it had been standard practice to use what amounted to torture to extract a confession. In a speech to the IACP, another leading Progressive police chief condemned such treatments as the "sweat box" in which the suspect was placed in a cell so close to a furnace that heat and thirst brought about confession. Head of the Washington DC police, Richard Sylvester, condemned this and other all too common practices of police brutality on humanitarian grounds. He also pointed out that such treatment would often bring out unreliable and unsubstantiated confessions which might not stand up in court, or even lead the police force into disrepute or leave them open to prosecution. Sylvester's arguments are interesting not only because they show the increasing emphasis placed on the rights of individuals, even if in this case they were suspected criminals, but also how they demonstrate both the growing professionalization of the police, and the increasing litigiousness of American society.[24]

If such litigiousness was an increasing aspect of US society in these years, so was incarceration—and that too was very much affected by the Progressive doctrine. During the period of this study, America's prison system took on not only its modern shape, but also many of its modern objectives. Ripe for reform, riven by controversy, with overarching themes of unfairness, waste, and cruelty, the penal system attracted early attention from proto-Progressives. In order to better understand the nature of the penal system the Progressives inherited, it is necessary to look at its earlier development. In essence, the penal systems of the nineteenth century had been informed by William Penn's Biblical observation in 1682 that "The law was not made for the righteous man, but for the disobedient and ungodly, for sinners, for the unholy and profane, for murderers, for whoremongers, for them that defile themselves with mankind, and for freestealers [*sic*], for liars, for perjured persons and company."[25] The implication was that such types needed to be contained. This sentiment combined with Penn's frequently stated interest in the humane treatment of his fellow man led to Pennsylvania developing a revolutionary penal system in the 1790s which was very swiftly adopted by most other states.

The novelty lay in new forms of classification and segregation. In 1797, Pennsylvania's model prison at Walnut Street began to segregate men and women; to separate debtors from felons and isolate the most dangerous prisoners for 24 hours a day. However, the use of the 12 foot by 8 foot common "night rooms"—where prisoners slept two to a bed in a room of eight—led to inevitable accusations of promiscuity and immorality as well as criminal schooling. When this was combined with serious overcrowding almost immediately after the prison opened, it meant that the rather enlightened regime attracted increasing levels of criticism from reformers and politicians. Things came to a head when, in 1803, a bloody riot and fire were followed by an attempted break-out and more serious riot the next year in New York's Pennsylvania model-based Newgate Prison which had suffered less serious disturbances from its opening in 1798.[26] The result was the building of Auburn Prison in 1819. Here the regime followed many of the old Pennsylvania principles, but differed in using solitary cells at night and the introduction of the notorious lockstep march in exercise yards as well as the maintenance of strict silence in the communal labor areas throughout the day. The result was that throughout the nineteenth century the two systems ran side by side with support for them ebbing and surging. Financial considerations favored the cost advantages of building communal areas, estimated at about 10 percent of the cost per inmate of the individual cells: humanitarian and moral considerations favored the solitary system.[27]

Such controversies represented meat and drink to the social reformers of the late nineteenth century, with the result that it is in prison reform that some of the clearest shoots of early Progressivism can be detected. No one demonstrates this more clearly than Enoch Cobb Wines who, along with Theodore Dwight, in 1867 in true Progressive style published 70 volumes of documents relating to penitentiaries. The *Report on Prisons and Reformatories of the United States and Canada* was the result of their nationwide survey of prisons for the New York Prison Association. While scathing about the condition of the prisons themselves,

Wines and Dwight's findings confirmed the optimism of the social reformers of the period in their fundamental belief in the perfectibility of mankind—even the criminal—given the correct understanding, motivation and administration. It is Wines, who perhaps more clearly, if somewhat less realistically, than many other Progressives, summed up their overwhelming belief in the power of scientific reason to rationalize the most irrational of human behavior. Wines was convinced that "crime . . . follows some fixed law." He maintained that if that law was properly understood, then the scientist could foretell "the months in which there will be, respectively, an increase and decrease in the number of crimes, and will be able to foretell almost the hour of the day, in which certain classes of offenses will be committed" and hopefully prevent them.[28]

In this Wines had a lasting legacy, since arguably the rationalization of penal problems would be perhaps the most enduring of all reforms of the period. This was most apparent in the development of scientific rationales for crime, most obviously in the medicalization approach. The thinking behind it was simple. If vaccination, health programs, and hygiene had conquered or contained many diseases from cholera to rabies to smallpox, why couldn't the same ideas be applied to crime? The psychotherapeutic approach developed out of the work of sociologists, psychiatrists, and psychologists, all of whom were products of the rationalization processes begun by the Progressive reformers like Wines. Various experiments in penology over these years concentrated on processes of "individualized treatment" and "case work." The term "clinical" was also frequently used in phrases such as "clinical method of reformation" or "clinical criminology." By the end of the Progressive Era, the "bad" prisoner would become the "maladjusted prisoner." The onus for aberrant behavior was taken away from the criminal's class and placed firmly on his individual circumstances, although, as will be shown in other chapters, such explanations could never overcome traits put down to ethnicity or nationality. By 1926, 67 prisons employed psychiatrists, and 45 had psychologists. While much of this was later dismissed, the investigations, quantifications, and categorizations form the basis of a large amount of present-day penal science.[29]

What also emerged from Wines' study was a rejection of Penn's concentration on containment and a growing movement towards the ideal of rehabilitation. In Wines' view, prison should aim, through a series of rewards, to reform the criminal and make him suitable for his release into society. The incentives of commutation of sentences for good behavior, probation, and indeterminate sentencing became central planks of the new-style "reformatories" which emerged in the 1870s. The Elmira system, named after the reformatory opened in New York in 1876, drew on Wines' theories. The leading advocate of the system, Elmira's first governor, Zebulon Brockway, installed an impressive library; invited guest lecturers to give speeches; introduced a printing press; did away with the striped uniforms and encouraged sport. There was also a strong moralizing element to the regime which was detectable in so many Progressive reforms. Unsurprisingly the library, lectures and press tended to be overwhelmingly of a Christian and improving nature. Sport was seen as self-improving and using up energies which might otherwise be devoted to less worthy pastimes. Equally unsurprising was that such measures came under fire from critics—some felt the regime too lenient, others that it was hypocritical.

Among these critics was the radical, humanist and Republican, Robert Green Ingersoll. He saw Elmira as merely perpetuating the old brutal, senseless, systems and accused Brockway personally of being a sadist who enjoyed enforcing beatings and what Ingersoll saw as the harsh regime.[30] While Ingersoll was prone to using hyperbole, he does illustrate a couple of other points which make the struggle to find a solution to the penal needs of the nation so relevant to themes of the Progressive Era. One aspect of penal practice which came under specific attack from Ingersoll was the prison labor system. In this he had support from many sections of society. Business objected to the unfair competition such a system provided—cheap, or free, labor and subsidized raw materials. Labor saw it as exploitative. Humanitarians saw it as brutal and immoral. State governments found themselves in an awkward situation. They argued that keeping prisoners working not only enabled them to gain skills, take pride in their work, but it also kept them out of mischief. What was more, prison industries, convict labor and prison self-sufficiency all contributed to reducing the costs of an ever-growing prison population.

From the 1880s, some states bowed to the pressures of this opposition—most notably the highly industrialized areas of New Jersey, New York, and Pennsylvania. In addition, in 1887, Congress outlawed the leasing of federal convicts, but in many areas the practices of producing profitable prison goods and providing lucrative convict labor contracts continued through until the 1920s and beyond.[31] This mixed result was typical of the Progressive reforms across all areas, across the nation. They suffered from the fact although there was a great deal of planning coupled with investigation and diagnosis of problem areas, when it came to implementation and law, overall, the schemes met with only patchy local successes. Nowhere was this clearer than with regard to convict leasing in the South. For the majority of the period of this study America's Southern states had virtually no real prisons, in the modern sense. Those convicted of crimes, of all degrees except capital offenses, were made to work in harsh conditions in a variety of largely extractive or construction jobs, ranging from coal mines to turpentine farms or sawmills. Their labor was contracted out to businesses, either private or corporate.

Such an arrangement was pure Gilded Age business. It was immoral, largely unregulated, but legal, and lucrative to both leasee and leasor. The employer got very cheap labor, and the state—or, more often prison governor, or both—got a financial return for leasing what would otherwise be a liability. For example, in 1868, the Georgia and Alabama Railroad acquired 100 black convicts from the state of Georgia for an unspecified period of time for a total of $2,500. At this time, the Union Pacific Railroad was paying its Chinese workers $1 a day. In Louisiana, the system went a step further. In 1870, the Louisiana State Senate leased the entire State Penitentiary to a Major Samuel James for $5,000 per annum. James then leased out the convicts making close on $500,000 in the first year. Over the next 20 years the Major defaulted on even this piffling rent, closed his books to public scrutiny and allowed the buildings to molder and crumble. Nevertheless, the state still continued with the arrangement, only terminating it on James' death in 1901. The picture that emerges from the situation is that like so many of the ruling elite of the post-Reconstruction South, the Louisiana legislature allowed this steady decline and corruption to continue because they were terrified that they would have to pay for the running of the prison. This bothered them far more than any of James' legal infractions or his total disregard for humanitarian issues.[32]

In many ways, the practice of convict leasing was a microcosm of the Reconstruction and Jim Crow-era Deep South. It indicated and exploited the essence of the sad compromises which led to the virtual re-enslavement of so many of the region's blacks. Its roots can be traced back to the Emancipation Proclamation, because when many former slaves left their previous plantations they were forced to adopt an itinerant lifestyle. This made the convict leasing arrangement extremely effective, since these homeless blacks could be arrested at any point for vagrancy meaning that such a system offered an almost limitless supply of labor. The scheme also presented many whites in the rapidly segregating South with yet another means of intimidating, dominating and hopefully breaking any particularly confident ex-slaves. That was not to say that all blacks objected to the system.

Black Senators at the height of the Republican Reconstruction years in Louisiana upheld the lease of the State Penitentiary to the businessman Major James, again terrified that they may incur expense. Those blacks who did object to the deal did so because James was undercutting the wages of other black laborers, not because of the inherent inhumanity of the system. Yet, perhaps nothing illustrates the extraordinary nature of even the so-called "New South" to many Northern contemporaries better than this cruel exploitation, and perhaps no one summed up the situation better than a Southern delegate to the National Prison Association in 1883. This advocate of the system told the New York social worker Hastings Hart: "Before the war, we owned the Negroes. If a man had a good Negro, he [the plantation owner] could afford to keep him . . . but these convicts, we don't own them. If one dies, get another."[33] It was simple economics.

That is not to say that conditions in penitentiaries outside the South were that much better and, as with so many other areas of social reform, it was Muckrakers who pointed out the shortcomings. It is perhaps worth singling out two in particular. Kate Richards O'Hare's account of her incarceration at the Missouri State penitentiary 1917–1919, drew attention to the particular needs of the growing diversity of the prison population as numbers of inmates grew. A socialist activist and journalist of middle-class background, the 41-year-old mother of four, O'Hare, was sentenced to 14 months under the Espionage Act for protesting against the Draft. As a "non-criminal class" woman in prison, drawing on her relentless picture of the filth, cruelty and disease was particularly effective in her later career as a penal reformer. Her account, based on her prison letters to her husband, contained numerous passages which shocked her contemporary readers and still retain the power to shock today. In one particularly harrowing passage she describes being forced to bathe after a syphilitic Native American woman who emerged from the tub revealing that "from her throat to her feet she was one mass of open sores dripping pus . . . [and then dressed herself in] clothes so stiff from dried pus that they rattled when she walked."[34]

In other passages, she described insane and contagiously ill prisoners being housed with healthy and sane prisoners; the regular beating and torture of inmates—which all formed a part of the daily cruelty and inflexibility of the regime. In common with so many women Progressives of the time, O'Hare extended her criticism to include an attack on the terrible state of education and lack of prospects among the black working classes from which the bulk of prisoners came and the daily horrors these people suffered both inside and outside the prison walls. She argued that until America accepted the need for some form of social safety net, the prison population would continue to grow and more and more women would join their ranks. Yet having told such compelling stories, she remains little known and her works received minor attention at the time. It might have been the fact that she dealt with this invisible section of society or it might have been that she was so outspokenly radical that prevents her work from being as well known as that of Jacob Riis, Upton Sinclair, or Lincoln Steffens.[35]

It could have been O'Hare's status as an outsider—a woman, a radical and a prisoner—which prevented her having the effect of other Muckrakers. On the other hand, Joseph Fuller Fishman's near contemporary account of the way in which America's prisons had become "human dumping ground[s]" went into multiple editions. Fishman was an insider. He had been an independent prisons inspector for Federal, State, and Municipal governments across the continental United States, Alaska and Hawaii. What his 1923 undercover report of some 1500 prisons revealed was a picture of vermin-infested, filthy, crumbling prisons run by corrupt, incompetent, and cruel staff. Prisoners, as a result, turned to anything to alleviate the boredom and inhumanity, especially once convict leasing and productive labor were outlawed. Perhaps most shocking are his passages about drug use in which he describes prisoners "using any substance which [would] give them the desired kick or jolt, [including] cocaine, heroin, opium, yenshee (the residue of smoked opium) and in fact anything they can obtain which has any narcotic effect whatsoever."[36]

As if this was not enough, over the next decades from a variety of influential positions within the penal system, Fishman became one of the most articulate critics of the American prison system, attacking not only the complacency, cruelty, and corruption but also the general disinterest and misunderstandings. Almost all of his criticisms have a resonance today. He broached taboos, including those of homosexuality and male rape in American prisons and the existence—often with pandering to, or fostering by prison governors—of gangs in prison. He even questioned whether prisons had any place in modern societies.[37] What was most worrying was that Fishman's studies demonstrated not only that the prison conditions were appalling, but also that in many cases, rather than reforming or rehabilitating inmates, they encouraged older, hardened, criminals to school younger and less experienced inmates. In Fishman's version, the penitentiary simply spread disease and immorality as well as encouraging addiction and other personal vices, creating state- and federal-sponsored schools for, and pools of, criminality.

Yet in spite of Fishman's statements and others' warnings about the dangers of incarceration, it is over this period that America's prison population undergoes one of its periodic explosions. There can be little doubt that this increase is also largely a legacy of just the same drive for rationalization and modernization which had inspired the investigations of reformers from Penn onwards. In 1880, there were some 20,000 inmates in America's prisons. By 1940, there were over five times as many and, in addition, the proportion incarcerated as a percentage of the population had more than doubled. Not only were more Americans incarcerated but also the size of individual institutions grew. Purpose-built, ultra-secure "Big House" prisons were constructed with modern facilities. These mega-prisons such as San Quentin in California and Sing Sing in New York held on average 2,500 inmates. In 1929, there were two prisons of more than 4,000 inmates; four with more than 3,000 each; six with more than at least 2,000 each, and 18 more with over 1,000 prisoners. This growing size reflected many of the changes which had taken place over the period.

The increased capacity was a result of a variety of inter-related social and economic changes which took place over these years. Among many other causes, swift industrialization offered greater wealth, and increased urbanization put the rich and the poor in closer proximity. Both of these elements increased the opportunity for crime. Coupled with this there can be little doubt that policing methods improved, increasing the numbers apprehended and convicted rate for crimes. Further, affluence and education meant there was an increasing intolerance of anti-social behavior over the period—as well as the means and will to check it. But perhaps it is the political changes which had one of the most lasting impacts. Until the creation of true federal prisons in the Progressive Era, state prisons had housed the vast amount of those convicted and the county jail had detained those awaiting trial. In 1846, the first survey of federal prisoners reported 48 inmates scattered across state prisons in eastern states. The large majority were convicted of offenses against the US Mail or counterfeiting offences. In 1891, Congress created Leavenworth in Kansas to house the growing number of federal prisoners which had risen from a little over 1,000 in 1885, to more than 2,500 in 1895. By 1930, there were over 13,000 federal prisoners housed in 14 prisons.[38]

In some measure, this jump in numbers reflected the climate of the times. Over the first decades of the twentieth century, Congress enacted legislation which vastly increased the federal intervention in citizens' lives and as a result, the prison population. Most notable among these were the Volstead (1919) and Harrison (1914) Acts, which proscribed alcohol and narcotics; and the Mann (1910) and Dyer (1919) Acts made it a federal offense to transport stolen cars or women ("for immoral purposes") across state borders. It is often argued that such federal crimes created the demand for organized federal policing, but it can be argued that the extent of federal policing was far greater, far earlier than this. In his study of the FBI, the historian Rhodri Jeffreys-Jones argues that even before the Civil War the federal government employed detectives, for mail theft and other crimes.[39] Immediately after the war, Lincoln expanded federal police by founding the US Secret Service, a branch of the Treasury, in order to check the burgeoning counterfeiting industry which had resulted from the huge expansion of paper money the costs of war had created.

Although the Federal Marshall's Service had been founded shortly after the birth of the Republic in 1789, Professor Jeffreys-Jones sees the real birth of federal policing as dating from 1871. He claims it emerged as a result of the attempts of the federal government to incorporate Southern blacks into the region's body politic. Since uniformed federal troops could not check the night riding and other terrorist activities of the Ku Klux Klan in the post-Civil War Reconstruction South, the federal government used undercover agents, and this, he argues, should be considered the starting point for modern federal investigation and policing. The more usual date taken for this is the creation of a Justice Department detective force by Teddy Roosevelt in 1908. Whichever date is taken, both events illustrate important points about the growth of federal policing and its significance in American history.

To many in 1870s America, Reconstruction was a second Civil War. Essentially the position of the South in the Union and the position of blacks in the South were being fought over all over again. Headed by two former Confederates, the newly formed Justice Department agents fought hard and with considerable success to break the Klan and other organizations' power in the region, demonstrating, at least during the early 1870s, that federal forces were dedicated to the principles of law and order and black emancipation and equality—at least in the South. Jeffreys-Jones claims that the reason why the role of Justice Department agents is played down or forgotten and the date for its real genesis shifted to 1908 owes much to the contemporary reasons given for the failure of Reconstruction itself. The Justice Department's role associated with the North's investment in enforcing black emancipation which was seen as erroneous by the vast majority of academics, politicians, and other influential, white, groups. In this interpretation, agents supported corrupt and self-serving carpetbaggers and were themselves implicated in the imposition of an alien, brutal, commercial regime on a noble, agricultural, community.

At least part of this assessment of Reconstruction drew on themes inherent in the increasingly popular legend of the Lost Cause. Another, related aspect, which relegated the federal agents to obscurity, relied on the perception of the inter-vening years. From 1872 onward, until the end of his term, President Ulysses S. Grant's administration was mired in financial scandal. The fall from grace of the Justice Department agents was also connected with corruption. In 1873, Hiram Whitley, the Justice Department secret service chief, was accused of fraud and rumors went round about his boss, the Attorney General's, misuse of secret service funds. Perhaps these accusations were simply the result of slurs by powerful enemies the field agents and their bosses had made in their campaigns in the South, but whatever their veracity, the charges stuck and both men were disgraced.

What was more, by the 1880s, the Secret Service was suffering severe budgetary cuts and had had its remit reduced to much the same counterfeiting work it undertook before Reconstruction.[40] Therefore, when Teddy Roosevelt entered the White House in 1901, selling himself as *the* Progressive president committed to cleaning up government, he did not want association with a tainted organiza-tion, like the Justice Department's investigative agents. It would have been hostile to the ethos of his administration. It would run better to simply start anew. The result was that the Secret Service was founded with 34 agents, on Roosevelt's orders, in 1908. It is some indication of the increased importance attached to federal crime that by 1941 the FBI—as it had then become—had some 1600 agents, supported by a staff of nearly 2,700 and a budget of close to $15 million.[41]

5

CONMEN, SWINDLERS, AND DUPES

> Are we going to bow our heads after the election; bow in shame that the intelligent, patriotic people of this State did not have the sense or the courage to avert this disgrace? Shall Kansans be greeted by a gibing baaa, the cry of the billy goat, when they walk the streets of other States?
>
> William Allen White, on the repercussions of John R. Brinkley winning the Kansas Governship[1]

Having spent three years as a medical student and after a relatively unsuccessful career as a snake-oil salesman, in 1917, the young John Romulus (or Richard) Brinkley discovered the secret of eternal youth. For a mere $750 he would implant goat testicles to reinvigorate the fading virility and restore the libido of his aging male clientele. Brinkley explained his breakthrough:

> So far as I know, I was the first man that ever did this operation of taking the goat testicle and putting it in the man's testicle. The glands of a three weeks old male goat are laid upon the non-functioning glands of a man, within twenty minutes of the time they are removed from the goat. In some cases I open the human gland and lay the tissue of the goat within the human gland . . . I find that after being properly connected these goat glands do actually feed, grow into, and become absorbed by the human glands, and the man is renewed in his physical and mental vigor.[2]

If he was willing to pay $5,000, the patient could turbo-charge his miracle cure using the far more potent human gonads harvested from death row prisoners. As he refined the process in over 16,000 operations, "Doctor" Brinkley rose to be one of the richest surgeons in America with houses, cars, and yachts to match his status. Over these years he learned to take setbacks in his stride, even turning them to his advantage. For instance, when the American Medical Association refused to publish his findings, he set up one of the nation's first pirate radio stations to pass on the message about his miracle cures. His persistence paid off and he became seen as a pillar of Mid-Western society and was even persuaded to run for the governorship of Kansas in 1930. On the other hand, his claims to a simple mission to "do all the good . . . in all the ways that he could" were not seen in that way by all. Doubters labeled him the "most daring and dangerous" charlatan in the Union. For over two decades, the nation's leading "quackbuster," Morris Fishbean, chased Brinkley, but the good doctor always remained ahead of his nemesis. Bankrupt, he died, scheming new ways of making money in 1942.

Brinkley's story has fascinated Americans. During his lifetime, he was the subject of massive newspaper coverage and over the years since his death his reputation has been kept alive by numerous investigations of his career and biographical accounts of his life. In 2002 alone, two American university presses published separate scholarly biographies of the "doctor."[3] Much of this fascination lies with the very American-ness of Brinkley. It is almost impossible to imagine the story of John Brinkley taking place in any nation other than America. Somehow it is equally difficult to place Brinkley's adventures anywhere other than the Mid-West, although arguably it could be either in the frontier period or in the agricultural depression of the 1920s and 1930s. His career drew on what had become uniquely American traditions of traveling shows based on the sales pitches associated with carnival, vaudeville and the traveling evangelists. To contemporary and more recent commentators, the man's persistence, his use of advertising, his ambition, the scale of his operation, and his pure *chutzpah*, are simply *so* American.

That is not to say that this phenomenon was new in the 1920s. As early as 1850, Edgar Allen Poe maintained that "diddling" was the very definition of humanity:

> Had Plato but hit upon this, he would have been spared the affront of the picked chicken. Very pertinently it was demanded of Plato, why a picked chicken, which was clearly "a biped without feathers," was not, according to his own definition, a man? But I am not to be bothered by any similar query. Man is an animal that diddles, and there is no animal that diddles but man. It will take an entire hen-coop of picked chickens to get over that. What constitutes the essence, the nare, the principle of diddling is, in fact, peculiar to the class of creatures that wear coats and pantaloons. A crow thieves; a fox cheats; a weasel outwits; a man diddles. To diddle is his destiny. "Man was made to mourn," says the poet. But not so—he was made to diddle. This is his aim—his object—his end. And for this reason when a man's diddled we say he's "done."[4]

Others saw the "conman" less as a universal human trait, and more as a distinctly American phenomenon. The very word apparently originates from a New Yorker,

William Thompson, who would walk up to a stranger and ask if he or she had the "confidence" in him to leave their watch with him. Supposing Thompson to be an acquaintance they already knew, many agreed. He would of course never return it.[5] One of the first truly American novelists—Herman Melville—in his final novel, describes the antics of a shadowy figure who attempts to gain the trust of a series of passengers on a Mississippi steamboat in the pre-Civil War South.[6]

The Mississippi is also a setting used by Mark Twain for his memorable, if comically implausible rogue, the Compte de St-Germain in *Huckleberry Finn*. There is nothing new in this. Other writers described other peculiarly American fraudsters. James Fenimore Cooper details the activities of the unscrupulous land agents in the Michigan Land Boom of the 1830s. A decade later, Charles Dickens drew on his own observations of the Mid-West to show how Martin Chuzzlewit is "had" by the Eden Land Corporation. In the 1830s and 1840s, the Southern humorists, Augustus Baldwin Longstreet and Johnson Jones Hooper between them detail a whole rogues' gallery of swindlers from the Wall Street broker to the counterfeiter.[7]

The conman was almost a source of pride to his countrymen, his virtues were *so* American—the very virtues that made possible the conquest of a continent and gave birth to the supremacy of American economic power. The conman displayed those *All-American* traits of ingenuity, audacity, ambition, self-reliance, originality, and even, in some peculiar way—in his radical, redistributive approach to wealth—democracy. If these traits represented the nation, they can also be seen to represent the times. In their simplest terms it is not difficult to detect in the various scams, swindles and cons, the stereotypical images of these years. It is possible to see the lawlessness of Reconstruction; the greed of the Gilded Age; the reform zeal of the Progressive Era; money as God in the 1920s and the desperation and atavism of the Depression. What is more, many of the great events of the times had connections to shady dealings. The greatest engineering feat—the construction of the trans-continental railroad—was mired in a scandal which went all the way to the vice-president.

The settling of the West included the swindling of Indians out of their lands and the ripping off of farmers by land agents, rail companies, and others. The changes of the times nurtured and expanded that native cunning which Poe, Melville, and Twain had detected. Industrialization offered new possibilities for financial fraud and product adulteration. The huge immigration represented a seemingly never-ending stream of unimaginably innocent and gullible targets for shysters, as well as providing some of the most successful and original of conmen. Urbanization offered not only almost unlimited victims, but a new level of anonymity. Hand in hand with these developments came new technologies— trains, telegraphy, telephony, radio, and cars—speeding up communications and offering new possibilities to those who were imaginative enough to see them before others. Fraud in the years after the Civil War became, if anything, even more American.

Ease, reliability, and affordability of trans-Atlantic transport is perhaps a good starting point to try to understand this boom in the confidence trick. With a crossing time measurable in days rather than weeks, undertaken by ships big enough to master almost any seas and shipping lines charging as little six dollars for the crossing, America became the magnet for Europeans not only for the legitimate emigrant but also those on the run. In America the person perceived as the "failure" could start again, often doing those same things which had got him, or her, into trouble in the first place. America offered anonymity as well as huge possibility. This was the land of opportunity, space and growth. The conman had plenty of targets in the urban areas as well as the space to disappear in the huge expanses outside them when the scam was played out, or the pressure became too much. Some certainly arrived with this in mind. Perhaps one of the best examples of these adventurers was a young Scotsman calling himself "Lord Glencairn."

What is interesting about Glencairn—or Gordon-Gordon, as he sometimes called himself—is the way in which he played not only on the greed and gullibility of Americans, but also on the snobberies of his victims in "classless" America. The self-styled "laird" had left London in something of a hurry after having defrauded jewelers in 1868. He is recorded as having arrived in Minneapolis in 1870. Within two years, he had exhausted the opportunities for extending his credit and partying in Minnesota and skipped town to arrive in New York. Here, he was soon working a scam on the railway magnate Jay Gould; knowing that Gould was unsurpassed in both his greed and lack of scruples, the conman played the part of the gullible nobleman abroad. Claiming that he represented the Campbell family he told Gould that he required large areas of land on which to re-settle his over-crowded tenants from the "old country." His act was so successful he quickly got Gould to give him $1 million of negotiable stock as a loan while he waited until his funds came through from Europe. Having got the bonds he immediately sold them. When Gould sued him, he reeled off a list of high-placed courtiers in England and Europe who would stand for him. When this successfully got him posted bail, he fled to Canada where after having defrauded more investors in several other ventures he committed suicide in 1874.[8]

That is not to suggest that Americans were always the victims in these trans-Atlantic scams, far from it. In New York, in 1882, when Oscar Wilde was giving his famous lecture tour across the United States, the celebrity poet and aesthete fell victim to a card sharp, the so-called King of the Bunco Men, Joseph, "Hungry Joe," Lewis. In a single night of cards, the Irishman—who one of New York's chief detectives unsympathetically referred to as "not so sharp"—lost $6,500 to Hungry Joe.[9] Nor was it always the Europeans who made up the victims—nor were they necessarily innocent. In another, rather satisfying case of divine justice, a wealthy American in London, Oscar Hartzell, fell victim to a pretty young Englishwoman, a certain Mrs Nina St John Montague. Posing as an aristocrat who had fallen on hard times who found herself forced to earn her living as a psychic, Nina fleeced Hartzell for $50,000 worth of hush money over a five-year period. The real irony was that she was making him continue to pay her in order that she would not disclose the incredibly lucrative inheritance scam he was running to what has been estimated were his 700,000 or so victims.[10]

It was not only the ease of trans-oceanic transport which aided the development of America as the capital of swindles in this period, nor was it only the snobbery. The sheer size and space of North America which had so aided Lord Glencairn would be used by a variety of conmen during the period. Glencairn had moved on when he felt threatened—from London to Minnesota; from Minneapolis, to New York, to Canada. Each move had given him a fresh start, a new story, new friends and new victims. He was by no means the first to exploit this. As soon as a new link developed, someone was there to exploit it. In some cases the actual transport system itself provided the basis for the scam. It was estimated that the so-called King of the Steamship Grifters, George Devol, managed to take over $2 million in his career as a card sharp, moving around on the Rio Grande Steamship Line on the Mississippi in the 1870s and 1880s. Inadvertently, it was Devol himself who ended at least one lucrative form of this mobile gambling when, having fleeced a railroad director out of over $1,000, he found himself the victim of byelaws the executive put in place which banned gambling on most trains in the region.[11]

If Devol found himself without a venue for his scams, there is little doubt that many forms of the new mass transportation remained valuable means for hatching, setting up, and carrying out of all sorts of swindles. In the early days of the long distance transport, as Melville and Twain had pointed out, the opportunities were far better than in the static world which had gone before. This was even truer of the ever-larger stations, liners, trains, and ferries of the late nineteenth and early twentieth centuries. Not that it was all crowds. The Pullman carriage, dining car, ships' cabin or waiting room afforded cosy, restricted, and relatively private spaces. These were areas of a type which had not existed before, they created a new form of intimacy and presented new dangers. In these situations people were in unfamiliar environments, surrounded by strangers—sometimes great numbers of them; sometimes foreign and often of the opposite sex.

These were places where connections could be made. Sharing the hours and days of tedium and discomfort inherent in such travel, friendships could be manufactured and these became settings where confidences could be played upon. "Chance" meetings could be arranged and scams could be played through. These opportunities worried the authorities. The larger and more efficient the transport system, the more the problems it seemed to bring with it. As one report into steerage conditions on board trans-oceanic steamships put it, the author was

> certain of the great importance to the public of reforms which will protect young and old steerage passengers from the wiles of money sharks, the swindles of traveling gamblers, and . . . it is probably true that definitely organized agencies, planned for the especial purpose of preying on the ignorant, are doing more harm to-day than they ever did before.[12]

When these unfortunates got to the Promised Land, their opportunities to be fleeced seemed to simply increase. The period resounds with stories of immigrants "fresh off the boat" being conned in almost every way. The most widely known was the selling of famous buildings or other structures. The gullibility of newly arrived hopefuls became the stuff of urban myth. In these stories, the Brooklyn Bridge, Grant's Tomb, the Statue of Liberty and countless other landmarks were sold time and time again to unsuspecting foreign investors. One Italian immigrant was not only meant to have been talked into buying the information kiosk at New York's Grand Central Station, but also he was persuaded to pay upfront to have it converted into a fruit stall. The most notorious dupe was the Polish immigrant George Sokolowski who was sold Cleveland's Brookside Park, zoo and lagoon for a knock-down $1,500 in 1925. Ashamed and alien, it is probable that unlike Mr Sokolowski—who complained vigorously about his experience—the overwhelming majority of these events went unnoted.[13]

First, the network of railroads, and then the increasing number of tracks and then paved roads and the vast expansion of car ownership, gave Americans in 1940 a level of mobility—internationally, nationally, regionally, and locally—which would have been unimaginable in 1865. As early as 1920, it was estimated that over a half of Americans lived in the environs of a different city from that in which they had been born. These people may have been members of the 14 percent of Americans who had been born in another nation. They might have been migrants who had gone west for land and opportunity which was so much a part of the national history from the hopeful prairie settlers of the 1870s, to the desperate dustbowl "Okies" of the 1930s. They might have been blacks who moved north in the massive and on-going migrations which transformed the nation.

Whatever their reasons, Americans were more transient in this period than ever before, and this represented opportunity to some. One individual who jumped at this opportunity was the Austrian-born Sigmund Engel. When the self-styled movie mogul proposed walking down the aisle for the final time in 1949 at the age of 73, the blushing bride was to have been what some estimates put at his 200th wife. One account reckoned that his trans-continental mega-bigamy had netted over $6 million for the man the press called the "love pirate." His downfall had been his failure to move on after having completed a successful swindle. Engel was very much a product of his age. His career could not have happened in anything but an urban environment and this was the age of urbanization. In order for Engel's scam to work, he needed to keep moving, and, ideally, over the long distances only a continent could offer. Remaining in Chicago after swindling the widow Resada Corrigan, he simply moved to another district of the city where he was recognized by his next potential "victim." Instead of obediently handing over all her assets as all his previous women had, Genevieve Parro entrapped him, ending nearly 50 years of lucrative, multiply married bliss.[14]

When urbanization is assessed as a topic in US survey courses of the Gilded Age, it is invariably coupled with industrialization. The two phenomena are almost inseparable: essentially symbiotic. Equally inseparable are the phenomena of crime and urbanization. A large measure of this was down to the perception, running in the thinking of urban commentators from Vienna to London, to Boston and New York, that the city was simply a cesspool of greed, speculation and dangerous anonymity. Gone was the idealized parish, a place where everyone recognized each other, societies which regulated themselves and shared a common moral vision for their communities. In their place were new, modern, cities, places where, these critics argued, money had replaced morality. For them, during these years—more than any other comparable period in its history—US society was changing, and it all came back to anonymity and greed. No one represented this change better than the conman. The ease with which either Melville's anti-hero, George Devol, or Sigmund Engel, had moved on across the country from the scene of their scams was replicated, over smaller distances, within the city. It seemed in these places no one fully understood their surroundings, or knew their neighbors, nor, it appeared, did the urban public seem to have a limit to their greed, and there were plenty of anecdotes to illustrate the potential for criminality in this disconnectedness.

Take the example of the Yonkers district of New York—in many ways a typical district of New York City. The area had grown up from being a small farming village in the early nineteenth century to become a recently incorporated city of nearly 50,000 residents in 1900. Many of these inhabitants were recent immigrants from Ireland, Italy, and Eastern Europe. As a result, in 1931, in order to cope with its ever-expanding population, the city began a road-widening scheme which had carved away the side of a hill next to the existing road on the city border. On the Friday night after work started residents started to walk out to the scene to see the workings. Seeing crowds form, a team of four conmen printed up and sold shares in the works, claiming they were the initial workings of a gold mine. By the end of the weekend when the workmen returned and explained the true nature of the diggings, the swindlers had disappeared. They had netted over $135,000.[15] Nor was this the first time that Yonkers residents had been gulled into buying shares in a gold mine. Nearly ten years before the road-widening scheme, a Russian conman, Vasily Cherniak, claiming to be a prospector, had sold at least $200,000, perhaps even $500,000, worth of shares in Salzbury Farm, otherwise known as the Iridium Platinum Gold Company, Inc.[16]

What both of these Yonkers scams played on was the willingness of ordinary people to believe extraordinary tales, something which was particularly prevalent in this land of opportunity where expectations were built up by advertising, reportage, and downright lies. It was not without reason that these early years of the twentieth century earned the name "The Golden Age of Flimflam" (fraud). It was during these years that Joseph, "Kid Yellow," Weil, perhaps America's most successful dedicated conman, began his 40 years as a swindler. He would make at least an $8 million fortune, playing scams on around 2000 individuals. When asked how he made so much money without ever having had a job, he confessed that "Men like myself could not have existed without the victims' covetous, criminal greed."[17] Most Americans had been brought up on tales of rags to riches. The fictional creations of Horatio Alger and the real-life stories of Andrew Carnegie or John D. Rockefeller fed a desire for wealth. As America's wealth grew, so too did a belief that unbelievable riches could be earned not only by hard work, but increasingly by just being in the right place at the right time and spotting the "opportunity" before others. The investors, largely Russian immigrants, who invested in Cherniak's Yonkers gold mine were told that they *should* get a return of $600 for each dollar. In part they believed it because since Cherniak addressed them in Russian and gave them leaflets written in Russian, they felt that they were party to information that others—non-Russians—would not get. They had spotted the opportunity and it appeared that these "opportunities" were rife during this period.[18]

As the historian Edward Balleisen has shown, "vigilance" was the key word for successful investors in the nineteenth century. In America's boom period after the Civil War, the machinery of commerce was so poorly regulated that goods were frequently adulterated, debts were often uncollectable and, perhaps most worryingly, even currency was not necessarily bona fide.[19] Counterfeiting had long been something of an American specialty. In the eighteenth century, the colonies had been so riddled with counterfeiters that in 1773 the business of the colony of Virginia essentially ground to a halt, there was such suspicion of the nature of the currency in circulation.[20] By the nineteenth century it almost seemed that the US currency system was set up in order to aid counterfeiters. As one commentator put it: "The 'bank notes' were bits of paper recognizable as a species by shape, color, size, and engraved work. Any piece of paper which had these appearances came with the prestige of money."[21]

This was especially true of the Civil War period. In 1862, the nation not only had two governments, it also had two currencies and 1400 banks printing their notes. The opportunities for forgery were enormous. There was no shortage of people willing to take the chance on printing their own money and no real method of policing other than at the local level. The result was that in 1862 the *New York Times* claimed that over 80 percent of the currency in circulation that year was counterfeit.[22] As the war dragged on, the problem became more acute. Counterfeiting the Confederate currency—the so-called "Graybacks"—eventually became so intolerable that the Richmond government brought in a team of 262 different clerks to hand counter-sign each note individually.[23]

Part of the reason for the demise of the Confederate currency—its hyperinflation and the poor level of trust in it—was due to the federal policy of, if not actively sponsoring its counterfeiting, then at least turning a blind eye to its faking and subsequent distribution. Such tactics were risky, since the fraudulent production of currency would inevitably sooner or later be turned on the federal "Greenback." Sure enough as the Grayback declined in value, the forgers turned to Washington's currency. By the end of the war, it was estimated that between a half and 80 percent of the "Greenbacks" in circulation were faked.[24] It is a measure of how serious the situation was considered that it merited the formation of the first truly federal police force. In 1864, Lincoln authorized the Treasury Department's "Secret Service." Not only was this agency given almost unchecked powers to operate all over the nation—at least before Appomattox, in areas controlled by Washington—but it also employed some shady characters.

The head of the operation was a Mexican War veteran and prison superintendent whose reputation for recklessness bordered on the insane. His three leading agents were all counterfeiters: two had to be released from jail to work for the government, and one was under arrest for the suspected murder of five men. Their methods were equally suspect. For instance, not only did they use controversial entrapment techniques, but before the war ended, some of the counterfeit money confiscated was deliberately smuggled to federal POWs in Confederate camps in order to get the fake money into circulation in the South. Moreover, there was very little doubt that much of the rest of the counterfeit money discovered was kept by these federal agents.[25]

Currency was a central issue in the United States from the end of the war to the opening of the twentieth century. The federal experience of the Civil War had shown the overwhelming advantages of a unified, national currency. Not only did a unified currency have a universal and unalterable value, it was instantly recognizable and backed by the reserves of a national government. A unified currency— the Greenback—was the symbol of a unified country and it was certainly one of the elements which enabled America's vast industrial growth in the years after the war. The new notes would be decorated with totems of the *national* experience— with *national* leaders and *national* landmarks. It was as important as a symbol as it was a means of trade. Some saw it as a means to write off their ever-mounting debts by inflating its value. To others, the Greenback was a talisman to ward off the specter of a repetition of the bloody internal division which had nearly destroyed the nation and there were few American icons which represented the power of the reunified nation. However, just as the reliance on the paper currencies of the war had offered great possibilities to counterfeiters in wartime, so a unified paper currency was seen as a hugely dangerous step. The growing acceptance of the Greenback was to some degree predicated on a belief that counterfeiting was a thing of the past and in large measure it would become so.

One of the most important ways in which the government aimed to protect the currency from forgery was by federalizing the printing of notes. By 1877, this process was given over to the Bureau of Engraving and Printing. Alongside this, the Treasury counterfeit investigators were given a more formal and standardized operational structure, as well as a considerably increased budget. Investigations became far more scientific and regulated and the results of these reforms were impressive. Many of the leading counterfeiters, wholesalers, money launderers, engravers and plate-makers were arrested. One of the cases which illustrate the effectiveness of this so-called "reign of terror" was a bizarre incident in 1876 involving the kidnapping of Abraham Lincoln's corpse. In this macabre episode, the body of the dead president was to be stolen and ransomed by a gang of counterfeiters in return for the release of an engraver colleague of theirs arrested and held by the federal authorities in Albany Prison on counterfeit charges. The plan backfired and the gang was caught red-handed in the act of removing the body from its crypt, and brought to justice by the Secret Service.[26]

At the other end of the criminal spectrum, away from the "dangerous classes," the zeal for prosecuting counterfeiters hit polite society. Arguing that there must be no ambiguity with regard to mimicry of the currency, the agency also launched a campaign against apparently respectable artists who depicted the federal currency in any detail in their paintings. They famously prosecuted the fashionable still life painter William Michael Harnett for a *trompe d'œil* painting of a five dollar bill. While this sounds ludicrous, it would have echoes in the career of Emanuel Ninger, a German-born counterfeiter. Ninger, alias "Jim the Penman" drew freehand copies of $1, $10 and $100 bills onto coffee-soaked paper which were convincing enough to allow him to live off them for his first 14 years in America. He was eventually caught when one fell into a puddle in a bar, and the color drained away. He was arrested and sentenced to 6 months in prison and a single dollar fine.[27]

Others were more blunt in their attempts but no less successful. James B. Doyle simply bought a genuine plate for a 1861 6 percent war bond from a corrupt Treasury Department official for $33,000 in the 1870s. It proved to be a very good investment. He was arrested in Chicago as what the *National Police Gazette* called a "government defaulter" in June 1880 and was found to be carrying some $250,000 in fake bonds and $300,000 in fake currency. This proved to be only a small part of what he and his gang had made. When he turned state's evidence on the rest of his gang in 1881, he had, by his own admission, printed some $22 million worth of these bonds as well as considerable amounts of other "bonds, certificates and greenbacks."[28] Nor was Doyle alone in getting hold of genuine plates. When the American counterfeiter Robert Armstrong was arrested in Ontario in June 1880, he handed over the plates he had used. These included a genuine "ten dollar plate on the Ontario bank; a five dollar plate on the Canadian Bank of Commerce; a four dollar plate on the Dominion of Canada bank; one and two dollar plates on the Dominion of Canada notes, and two five dollar plates on the United States legal tender."[29]

In keeping with the mood of the times, counterfeiting was becoming more or less industrialized, and Congress was forced to act to limit the potential damage the counterfeiters could have done to what was now a truly national currency. One of the most high profile cases occurred when, in the 1890s, two counterfeiters, Baldwin Bredell and Arthur Taylor—one a chemist, the other an engraver—mastered a technique of transforming lower denomination bills into higher. They achieved this by strategically removing the ink and replacing it with their own print. Since the counterfeits still were printed on Treasury paper, they managed to produce such convincing fake $100 bills that the federal government was obliged to withdraw the entire $26 million worth of the stock of "Monroes" throughout the nation. Legend has it, that when they were caught, they were sentenced to Philadelphia's Moyamensing Prison where they turned their attention to producing $20 bills instead.[30]

What was more, it was not only notes which were forged. Alongside the federalization of notes in 1862 came a similar process for coins and these proved famously tempting to replicate. Spotting a flaw in coinage of the early 1880s, a deaf mute, ex-prospector from New York, Joshua Tatum, managed to transmute the "liberty nickel" five cent coin into the "half eagle" five dollar piece. Using an ingeniously simple, but effective system of plating by simply rubbing gold dust into the coins, Tatum had found a truly alchemic process. For a short period he successfully turned base metal into gold, since the only major difference immediately apparent between the two coins, aside from their value, was that one was nickel and the other gold. Although he escaped imprisonment since he never asked for change, and gold-plating coins was not prohibited as such, his actions led to an emergency meeting of Congress and a subsequent change in the nation's currency.[31]

If the production of counterfeit money, its distribution and laundering motivated massive changes in the law and strategies and organization for its enforcement, it also funded huge changes in the perceived and actual nature of crime. A famous dime novel of the 1890s claimed that Lizzie Borden, the infamous axe-murderer, was innocent. The argument ran that counterfeiters, in attempting to cover their tracks committed the crime.[32] Perhaps more importantly, it has been argued that the Cosa Nostra evolved because Sicilian counterfeiters could not entirely trust the Irish money-pushers they used to distribute their forgeries and thus drew on an ever more secret organization of genuine and adopted family members.[33]

This fixation with counterfeiting can be seen as indicative of many of the changes America went through during this period—from unification, to urbanization, to industrialization, to rationalization—it is also in many ways *so* American that it is perhaps one of the least altered crimes of American history. Not only had some of the first legislation passed in the original colonies been passed to ensure that "this quoine may not be counterfeited . . . [on pain] of capital punishment upon those who shall be found delinquents therein."[34] However, by the late nineteenth century the opportunities for counterfeiting were far greater than ever before in American history. Counterfeiters could now not only forge currency, bonds and certificates, but also in this age of growing bureaucracy they could now forge vital identification documents, from passports to marriage and birth certificates. As people traveled on mass transport and attended massive events like Buffalo Bill's extravaganzas or the World's Fairs, there were increased opportunities for faked passes and tickets.[35] The growing consumer culture led to the counterfeiting of branded products, but as with the traditional conman, there was something which was simply universal to all areas, at all times in America, for as a traveler in the wilds of the frontier had reported in 1824:

> Money was at one time so scarce in Indiana, that racoon skins passed current, being handed from one person to another. But some Yankees forged these notes, by sewing a racoon's tail to a cat's skin, and thus destroyed the currency.[36]

6

BUSINESS AND FINANCIAL CRIME

That some should be rich shows that others may become rich, and hence is just encouragement to industry and enterprise.

Abraham Lincoln to the New York Workingman's Democratic Republican Association, 1864[1]

I see in the near future a crisis approach which unnerves me and cause me to tremble for the safety of my country. Corporations have been enthroned, an era of corruption in high places will follow, and the money power of the country will endeavor to prolong its reign by working upon the prejudices of the people until the wealth is aggregated in a few hands and the Republic destroyed.

Abraham Lincoln on the passage of the National Banking Act, 1863[2]

Arguably nothing demonstrates the changing attitudes to corporate crime better in this, the central period of America's industrial revolution, than the example of the treatment of John Pierpoint Morgan in the last year of his life. In December, 1912, J.P. Morgan was summoned to appear before Congressman Arsene Pujo's Money Trust investigation sub-committee. Seventy-five-year-old Morgan was not a man used to being ordered to do anything. A devout and disciplined man, Morgan believed in honor and order. Without honor and order, his financial empire would collapse. What was more, he did not consider he had done anything for which he needed to answer to Pujo's committee and was extremely uncomfortable in these circumstances. Wishing to end this humiliation as quickly as possible, Morgan arrived a day before the appointed time and made an appointment to see his "persecutors." It is a measure of his status that the committee agreed to see him. Having gained this recognition of his position, Morgan politely asked if he could go home and leave his team of seven lawyers to thrash out the misunderstandings that had resulted in his subpoena. The Pujo Commission's legal counsel, a driven and dapper New York attorney on a mission, Samuel Untermeyer, denied Morgan permission to leave and one of the most famous, if not notorious, cross-examinations of early twentieth-century America got underway.

Under questioning about his involvement in the financial workings of the nation's big business, Morgan denied that he had any power in these matters. In his assessment of his own position, he was simply a facilitator—a bank manager writ, extra, large. This would have come as quite a surprise to those following the inquest. Morgan and high finance were synonymous in the American public's mind. To those involved, and those following the committee's investigations, the name and image of J.P. Morgan would have been as familiar as that of the outgoing President, William Howard Taft. Many would have known that Morgan had bought Carnegie Steel for nearly half a billion dollars, making the takeover the biggest corporate purchase in American history. Some may have known that he had averted a gold crisis in 1895 and had been central to the re-organization of banking that had arguably prevented a severe financial crisis in 1907. What they probably did not know was the real extent of his power and influence in the running of some of the nation's most important corporations.

They were probably not aware that he, and his ten partners in the House of Morgan, held 72 directorships, in 47 of the nation's leading corporations. The capitalization of these enterprises was estimated at some $10 billion—a figure which would amount to some twenty times that total in present-day figures. Together with George F. Baker's First National Bank and Rockefeller's National City Bank, they controlled over $22 billion—which was estimated to be more than the entire real estate value of New England, then America's wealthiest region. Nevertheless, all Americans knew Morgan was wealthy, and they knew he was powerful. Even the elite of American society held the man in awe. Irascible but aloof, Morgan was so powerful on Wall Street that, mixing their Greek and Roman metaphors, his fellow Olympians of finance called him Jupiter—the king of the Roman Gods. For this man to claim that he had no financial muscle was to the average American, at best, disingenuous and laughable—if not a downright lie. Perhaps they felt it was divine justice that Morgan died in 1913, just as the committee published its report.[3]

Whether they saw his demise as holy intervention or not, this public disbelief is central to Morgan's appearance at Pujo's sub-committee. It demonstrates some important aspects of early twentieth-century American life. Such a summons would have been unlikely in the final decades of the nineteenth century. This is not because Morgan was not active, wealthy or powerful during these years—he was certainly all these things. It was more to do with the fact that such power and such wealth would have been seen by many as enviable and desirable. This belief would certainly not be common to all Americans, but it was arguably the opinion of a critical mass of the politically active populace. To believers in the so-called American Dream, the fact that Morgan and his peers had achieved their almost unimaginably huge wealth was a sign of their hard work, thrift, and luck. It meant that it was possible for others to achieve the same spectacular wealth and influence, and there were other real, larger-than-life, living, examples—most famously John D. Rockefeller and Andrew Carnegie.

There was also an entire industry dedicated to propagating this myth. Books, newspapers, journals, and magazines trumpeted the benefits gained by hard-working youths and the achievements of self-made men. Perhaps the most widely read among these were Horatio Alger's rags-to-riches novels. These short books formulaically told of the driven young orphan office boy/stable lad who rose to immense wealth even though he had to support his widowed mother and sickly siblings. Through sheer hard work, the guileless but clever hero became respected and powerful, but never forgot his manners; his humble origins; his friends or his first love, whom he invariably rescued from poverty—if not worse—and married. Perhaps, to the less gullible and more romantic reader, their main value as a parable was that they made their author a considerable fortune into the bargain.[4]

By the turn of the twentieth century, the feel of the nation was perceptibly different. Andrew Carnegie, who was vaunted as "the richest man in the world," proclaimed that the wealthy had an obligation to guide those less fortunate than themselves on the "upward path of progress." Not all his fellow Titans of industry thought or behaved in the same way.[5] The massive industrialization that the nation had undergone in the last four decades of the nineteenth century had not been without its turbulence and upheavals. Financial panics had rocked the nation regularly from the 1870s onwards. These downturns had created immense suffering and seemed to grow worse with each decade, culminating in the terrible slump of the 1890s. There was also increasing violence as the corporations tried to fight these depressions. In times of recession, workers were laid off and/or had their wages cut, or their hours increased for the same pay. Even when the order books were full, factories, workshops, railroads, and other places of work became sweatshops with atrocious conditions and where the safety of the workers took second place to profit. Those who tried to improve working conditions might find themselves prosecuted for union activity. They may be beaten by the police, Pinkerton agents or the militia when they took part in industrial action. Most likely, they would then find themselves replaced by non-union foreigners willing to work for next to nothing and accept the terrible conditions.

As these economic fluctuations became accepted as the norm, there was a growing minority to whom the bosses were less to be regarded as figures to be emulated, than as people to be condemned for their greed, cruelty, and lack of empathy with the common herd. In the light of these changes in perception, many of those who had grown up reading the optimistic gospel of the American Dream started to read the works of an increasingly influential group of pessimistic social critics. The ever-optimistic Theodore Roosevelt called these diverse writers

"Muckrakers," after the figures from John Bunyan's *Pilgrim's Progress* whose minds were so obsessed with their tasks in hand that they could not see the bright future on the horizon. For many children who had grown up modeling themselves on Horatio Alger's heroic life histories, cynicism and disappointment naturally led to Upton Sinclair's condemnation of the exploitation of the Lithuanian immigrant in the meatpacking industry in Chicago, *The Jungle*. They may have been influenced by Ida Tarbell's exposure of the Rockefeller's Standard Oil's sharp practices or Frank Norris' tales of the bribery and bully boy tactics used against San Joaquin Valley wheat producers by Pacific Railroad Trust. Perhaps they had some sympathy with the demands of the American Federation of Labor's demands for an eight-hour day. They may have supported the more radical ideas behind Eugene Debs' American Socialist Party, or even the anarchistic activity of the Industrial Workers of the World.

At the time, very few of these "radicalized" middle classes would have sympathized with Leon Csolgolz's assassination of William McKinley in September 1901. They would more likely have sympathized with his replacement, the unfortunate McKinley's larger than life vice-president, Theodore Roosevelt, who introduced a more equitable rhetoric, if not always delivering the legislation to back such high ideals. Promising the nation a "Square Deal," Roosevelt and a disparate group of reformers, known collectively as the "Progressives," sought to make government, business, and life in America more efficient and through that more equitable. They argued that the prevailing corporate autocracy and lack of competition in big business were irrational and some method had to be found to regulate such inefficiencies out of the system. While his motives with relation to business have been the subject of historical discussion, his legacy is the stuff of American legend. Roosevelt, the cowboy-president, demonstrated a new independence from the leaders of big business when he refused to automatically side with the producers in the potentially crippling anthracite strike. Lacking the guaranteed federal support they had come to take for granted, the mine owners negotiated a settlement. By forcing them to do this, Roosevelt showed that even at the highest level, it seemed that the mood towards business leaders had changed.

This new mood was most clear in the attitude towards the nebulous but ever-present "Trusts"—the huge, "vertically integrated," corporate combinations which although technically within the law, restricted competition, fixed prices and monopolized raw materials in everything from steel to tobacco. When Roosevelt mounted his high profile attack on Standard Oil, he was sending a clear message to all the Trusts. The campaign resulted in the break-up of the Oil Trust which "Trustbuster" Roosevelt and his supporters felt would benefit consumers. They maintained it would reduce the ability of the giant corporation to trample other producers, suppliers, and shippers which had for years forced smaller companies into less than favorable deals with Rockefeller's leviathan. In fact the long-term result was less than successful. Roosevelt's action slew the dragon of the Oil Trust only to be confronted by a Hydra of Standard Oil's constituent parts.

The newly separated parts soon managed to overcome the controls imposed on them and within a few years were trading in ways which were pretty much the same as before. Not only that, but Roosevelt's chosen successor, the legally minded William Howard Taft, in spite of bringing more Trust-busting cases in his single administration than all the combined Presidents before him, would find his administration remembered as one in which corruption and sleaze dominated.

It was these perceived failures which in large measure contributed to Morgan's appearance in the committee room that day in December 1912. The logic was straightforward. It was decided that since financial power was the means that enabled the Trusts to survive and since Morgan *was* banking in the America of the 1900s—Morgan would be the key to the Money Trust, just as Rockefeller had been to the Oil Trust or Carnegie had been to the Steel Trust. Without understanding the workings of the mysterious Money Trust it would be impossible to regulate finance, and that was the real reason for the Pujo Committee—to create laws which would enable government to root out the corruption and dirty dealing which had become so much a part of the image of business.

The Pujo Committee was about defining and hopefully controlling the crime they *knew* to exist in America's financial and business world, but which few knew how to control. Throughout the period of this study it seemed that the law ignored the antics of Wall Street and the corporations, for as one liberal weekly would later famously put it: "If you steal $25, you're a thief. If you steal $250,000, you're an embezzler. If you steal $2,500,000, you're a financier."[6] To govern future behavior and prevent the grossest repetitions of the grossest crimes was, it seemed, the best that could be hoped for. In this constantly changing, perpetually and rapidly evolving world, the law inevitably trailed behind the perceived crimes and regulation followed, rather than prevented, the outcry caused by events.

For the sake of this study, business crime will be divided into four basic headings. First is the simple idea of earning money by illegal business practices, essentially corporate financial swindling. The second section investigates the criminal use of wealth and the way in which the emergence of the corporation destroyed what many saw as the very essence of American society. Third, this study will look at corporate crimes against individuals—investigating such aspects as the criminal treatment of employees and strikers or the mistreatment of both people and products, as well as the environment—and the struggle to install legislation to control such behavior. The final section will address the incorporation of crime and the way in which business models, business practices and business techniques began to be adopted by a range of criminals.

To many Americans, at the end of the Civil War, the idea of financial speculation and corporate business was anathema. As this period opens, the American stock markets are essentially in their infancy. There were perhaps as many as 12 US companies large enough for their shares to be traded in 1865. But this was soon to change. Fueled by war profits and the opportunities of post-war reconstruction, but mostly through the huge money to be made from the rail construction boom and the consequent speculation, the wealth of the nation grew spectacularly in the years following the war and that growth fed even more spectacular expansion over the next half century.

Taking a base year of 1849–1850, industrial production was at over 190 by 1865. By 1880, it was up to 400. At the turn of the twentieth century, it was at nearly 1200 and in 1915 it had reached close to 2000.[7] By 1870, rail and canal corporations had achieved more than half a billion dollars of new investment. The railroads had laid 35,000 miles of new track and, working from a level already expanded by the necessities of war, by 1873, the US had expanded its industrial output by 75 percent. Over the next 30 years, powered by steel production and the railway construction, the US would become the largest industrial producer in the world.

This huge expansion was partly the result of the enthusiastic adoption of cutting edge technologies, like the Bessemer converter. It was partly due to the steady and growing stream of cheap, enthusiastic, and disposable labor pouring in from Asia and Europe. The huge territorial expansion resulting from the incorporation of the West into the Union, drove industrial and consumer demand and allowed for the extraction of huge mineral and agricultural wealth. It was also no doubt a result of an ethos which encouraged the making of money, encouraged ruthless capitalism, and gave rise to some of the most ruthless business geniuses of modern times. Perhaps, above all, it was the availability of capital which acted as the catalyst to release the potential of all of the above elements.

The US banking system had grown hugely during the war. Driven on seemingly endless government money, US banks had learned the ability to raise and lend huge sums. War profit and debt repayment meant that the financiers had huge sums at their disposal in the late 1860s. For example, it is estimated that the New York Stock Exchange held some $10 billion in securities in 1868 and that it was receiving a billion and a half new dollars a year from foreign investors alone. The result was the "Great Bull Market" which "managed with almost lunatic persistency . . . to keep credit easy, prices buoyant and the influx of money at floodtide" until the "Panic" of 1873.[8]

While some welcomed the opportunities of such apparently unlimited credit, others saw this era of speculation as fundamentally wrong. In 1870, the United States was still essentially a rural nation. Over half of the gainfully employed population of the nation was involved in agriculture, while manufacturing, in all its forms, employed less than 20 percent of Americans. While these proportions changed dramatically over the next 20 years—with manufacturing overtaking agriculture by 1890, and farmers playing an increasing, if often reluctant, part in the banking and speculation system—relatively few Americans either understood or sanctioned the huge speculative revolution which was taking place in the nation, centered around the financial capital of New York and the political capital, Washington. There was a feeling that the accumulation of wealth purely through playing the markets, more often than not on credit, was fundamentally wrong. A posse of churches, women's and agrarian groups and many professionals condemned the practices of the speculators, seeing them as immoral, decadent and damaging to the long-term health of the economy.

Perhaps there were no individuals who embodied all the evils of the speculators of this, Mark Twain's "Gilded Age," better than Jay Gould and Jim Fisk. Although vastly different characters, they formed a double act of stellar proportions. Gould was the highly intelligent son of a New York state farmer who made his initial fortune from a wise marriage, then nurtured his insatiable appetite for wealth with shrewd manipulation of railroad stocks. In spite of his soft-spoken manner and restraint, he possessed a ruthlessness which led Henry Adams to quip that he had "not a conception of a moral principle."[9] This absence of conscience was more immediately apparent in "Diamond" Jim Fisk. A former circus showman, Fisk was loud, brash, flamboyant, and exuberant. He was also intelligent, daring, highly immoral and, like Gould, extremely greedy. Both were willing not only to take full advantage of the lax administration of the nascent world of stocks and shares, but also happy to commit overt fraud.

Their partnership began in 1866 with a legendary battle against the equally ruthless Cornelius "Commodore" Vanderbilt for control of the Erie Railroad Company. By 1868, they had ripped off millions from shareholders; printed their own stock certificates; bribed Boss Tweed into signing an injunction against Vanderbilt and still continued to trade even when their dealings came to light. Such leniency simply opened their minds to even greater schemes. By 1869, the pair were targeting the US gold market. Using US President Grant's brother-in-law, Abel Corbin, as a go-between, Gould gained insider information about government plans to sell gold to buy back wartime paper money. This huge undertaking was an effort to halt, or at least check the inflationary tendencies which had been released by the enormous needs of the Union's war effort. Using a team of brokers under Fisk's command, the pair sparked an orgy of speculation creating a huge surge in the price of gold which they successfully rode until on "Black Friday" in September 1869, when the bubble burst. Gould's inside information enabled him to withdraw in time, but he neglected to pass the information to Fisk, who although badly hit, survived. Magnanimously, Gould made up his partner's losses.

The same could not be said of most other investors, or the Grant administration itself. In the resultant fall-out, even though exonerated of any wrong-doing, Grant began his gradual decline from Civil War hero to synonym for corruption. Farmers, manufacturers, and other exporters suffered from the unnatural strength of the US dollar, adding to their hatred of the speculating classes. Nevertheless, after six hours' grilling in front of the House Banking Committee, Congress was unable to punish either Gould or Fisk, who it was rumored personally walked away with up to $10 million, justifying their enemy the Commodore's famous axiom—"What do I care about the law? Hain't I got the power?"[10]

This feeling that the speculator was above the law was perhaps one of the most prevalent sentiments of the Gilded Age. On the other hand, there were those who held that the system would be self-regulating. They maintained that the combinations of companies, through their very size, would lead to new degrees of control and self-regulation, since such men preferred to operate in more settled, stable, and transparent markets. Others, most notably those who felt themselves "Progressive," saw more subtle, less visible, but similarly, fundamentally, dishonest forces were at work. Rather than the brash "bear raiders" like Vanderbilt or Gould who made fortunes using overt intimidation and barely disguised bribes, the new Wall Street was led by a coterie of wealthy men whose power came from agreement, elitism, and exclusion rather than personal feuds, destruction, and power struggles.

This elitism accidentally sparked at least one curious but far-reaching and illustrative consequence. In 1904, a previous insider, Thomas William Lawson, published an exposé of the practices of the Rockefeller Group's Amalgamated Copper. Lawson was a former stock dealer and lieutenant of Rockefeller's. Although he was allegedly worth some $50 million himself, he felt that he had been slighted by members of this super-rich elite. The story goes that when putting forward his plan to build a yacht to compete in the prestigious America's Cup, his proposal was dismissed. The Committee had argued that since he was not, and had not been invited to become, a member of the celebrated and exclusive New York Yacht Club which saw itself as running the competition, he was ineligible to compete. The Club contained some of the leading members of the city's social elite, including J.P. Morgan and, most importantly, Rockefeller's right-hand man, Henry Huttleston—known by many as "Hell Hound"—Rogers. Snubbed and furious, Lawson hit back at this insult. He published his account of what he termed the "Frenzied Finance" of Rockefeller and his cohorts in *Everybody's Magazine*.

He exposed what he called "The System." This, he explained, was a cartel operated and controlled by a small group of the nation's banks and large corporations. In Lawson's judgment, this huge agglomeration of industries, banks, insurance companies and other businesses seemed to have two aims—to increase the wealth of its members and to defraud the public. His book claimed that the leaders of this organization were constantly using the ordinary man's bank deposits for their private advantage, what he termed "dollar-making." They achieved this by speculating, while at the same time shortening the odds by using a combination of watered stocks, insider dealing, and bribing the financial news outlets for exclusive information—while at the same time feeding their competition misinformation. In a passage which does much to demonstrate the climate of the times, he claimed they had

> taken from the millions of our people billions of dollars, and given them over to a score or two of men with power to use and enjoy them as absolutely as though these billions had been earned dollar by dollar by the labor of their bodies and minds.[11]

His exposé was taken seriously, sparking New York Senator William W. Armstrong's overhaul of the life insurance industry, arguably one of the most successful pieces of specific financial regulation of the first decade of the twentieth century.[12] Nevertheless, once again the main culprits, the main beneficiaries, escaped punishment.

Perhaps the failure to bring the perpetrators to justice stemmed from the fundamental and on-going inability of legislation to frame charges in an effective format: laws swift enough to outpace the constantly changing world of business. Perhaps it was due simply to the fact that the financial capitalists were still admired, albeit, less so than before. By the late 1920s, this had changed. Part of this was down to a change in the speculative culture. Although the rationalization processes of the late nineteenth century continued apace, the shareholder pattern diffused, rather than consolidated. The result of this was that while shareholders had influenced corporate decision-making in the early period of industrialization, their influence—and therefore, interest—had waned as the corporations grew. When the seemingly inevitable crash happened in 1929, shareholders who had been rather disinterested when returns were good—when greed was the driver—became far more engaged when they sought to work out where their money had gone.

In March 1933, the Italian immigrant lawyer, Ferdinand Pecora's, investigations for the Senate Banking and Currency Committee began to expose the rottenness of the leaders of the financial world. The Committee exposed Albert Wiggin of Chase who had sold his own stock in the bank, and collected $4 million in profits just as the bank was about to collapse, bankrupting many less fortunate depositors. On discovery of his duplicity, Chase made him retire—but gave him a $100,000 pension. He showed men like Charles, "Sunshine Charlie," Mitchell had lent vast sums of money to his colleagues in the National City Bank, without them having any security in order to save them from ruin, while calling in other debts. What made Mitchell even more despicable in the public's eyes was that he had personally earned over $1 million a year, and yet he paid no federal income tax through fraudulently trading his shares within his family. He was fined a million dollars, but his celebrity lawyer, Max Steuer successfully fought the criminal charges. Nor was he alone. Between 1929 and 1931, the billionaire financier, J.P., "Jack," Morgan Junior, had paid no income tax and received no criminal charges. By contrast, Public Enemy Number One, Al Capone, was sentenced to 11 years for tax evasion.[13]

With the nation reeling from the effects of Depression—which many blamed on Wall Street's dishonesty—the search was on for scapegoats. At the highest level of industry, and the highest level of government, one target stood out—Samuel Insull. Insull's rise and demise are illustrative of many of the forces working in the 1920s and 1930s. A controversial English-born entrepreneur, Insull had begun his career by working for Thomas Edison's agent in London. Moving to the US, he spent some time working for Edison in New York before moving to Chicago where he set up a vast utilities empire. This was achieved through a combination of brilliant marketing, clear strategy, and daring. Most importantly Insull's empire relied on devious and obscure share dealing, under a series of holding companies, the leading one being the huge Middle West Utilities. What singled Insull out was not so much his genius for making money, but his genius for selling not only his products to his customers, but also selling his shares to his consumers. One historian has estimated that at the time of the Crash, Middle West Utilities and Insull's 111 other associated companies had 41 million customers and over a million stock and bond holders, with a capitalization of over $3 billion.[14]

What was also unusual was that Insull had achieved this massive expansion without resorting to the New York banks. Early in his career, the young Insull had personally fallen foul of J.P. Morgan's unpleasant snobbery. The result was that the budding tycoon had borne a grudge against the Wall Street banks, which ironically served him well. Financing himself out of Chicago, his independence of Wall Street had been achieved by using a complex, and some said barely legal, pyramid of financial structures which had lent and borrowed huge sums among themselves. Through what evolved into a staggeringly complex accounting exercise, Insull's empire maintained a uniquely independent structure. It was therefore only with enormous reluctance that in the early Depression years when he needed to raise finance—paradoxically to guarantee the security of the bank which had traditionally backed him—he had agreed to go to John Pierpoint Morgan's son, J.P. Morgan Junior, to overcome what he felt sure was a temporary shortfall in funds.

Vengeful and predatory, the Wall Street bankers sensed a way to gain control of Insull's corporations. While lending the monies required, they forced new accounting practices on him, practices which almost immediately set off the rapid unraveling of his huge utilities empire. But this was no ordinary financial collapse. Because Insull had financed his operations through a wide share base, his demise hit a huge section of the American public, ordinary people whose almost unshakeable belief in him in the 1920s had turned to visceral hatred in the early 1930s. Death threats followed by an assassination attempt, coupled with mounting debts, drove Insull to run. He first went to France, then to Italy, Greece, Romania, and finally, Turkey, from where, in failing health after a heart attack, he was extradited—which required a Congressionally sanctioned change to the structure of US extradition policy. He returned to the US to stand trial on over 20 fraud charges in 1935.

Insull's demise had huge repercussions. In the medium term, in the wake of a famous speech made by Franklin Roosevelt in his 1932 presidential campaign, Insull became the byword for all financial immorality. Part of this was due to Roosevelt's belief—one held by many of those on the left of US political thinking at the time, led by the jurist Felix Frankfurter—that in order to provide any semblance of control, public utilities ought to come under the control of the state. Insull's situation was not helped by the comments of his brother, Martin, who attacked Roosevelt, personally, for these beliefs. In short, the result was that the name "Insull" became associated with all the double dealing, sharp practice, and greed which had caused the crash in the first place. Supreme politician that he was, Roosevelt manipulated this sentiment. When the New Deal attempted to introduce public utilities schemes with the Tennessee Valley Authority and the Rural Electrification Administration, they succeeded where other administrations had failed. In some considerable measure this was because they tapped a ready-made groundswell of support provided by the new utilities "robber baron" whose dishonesty had been brought to justice.[15]

In the longer term, Insull's actions led to a fundamental change in the regulation of corporations. The financial policing body, the Securities and Exchange Commission, was already in place, but in the wake of Insull's trial, through the 1935 Public Utility Holding Company Act, it was given power to regulate utilities companies—whose control had long been one of FDR's most abiding hobby horses. The irony was that although FDR continued to invoke Insull as the very model of the corrupt businessman, one of his most lasting and vaunted pet projects, the Tennessee Valley Authority, used the British National Grid system as its blueprint for the large-scale, unified, distribution of electricity—a system which had been based on Insull's example, and had actually drawn on his expertise as its main advisor.[16]

The Utilities Act nevertheless represented a sea change in attitudes towards the corporation. Gone was the Progressive idea of breaking up the huge Trusts, in came the idea of federal scrutiny of the financial aspects of corporate expansion—at all stages of the company's lifespan. Instead of trying to attack the result of corporate accretions by proving their misdeeds, regulation now required them to show, through an ongoing and regular series of accounts, that they had grown by legitimate means. Not only did this demonstrate the huge expansion of the federal government in all aspects of American life over the New Deal years, it also showed a pragmatic recognition that capitalism has a propensity to favor size and that size, if regulated and contained, can be beneficial. Further, it added to the seemingly unstoppable rise of the corporate accountant.[17]

What seems to have been forgotten when this parable of the evils of hubris has been told in the years since his trial, was that Insull was acquitted of all charges of fraud, embezzlement and false accounting, and walked from the court a free, if ill and broken, man. Some commentators saw this as a sign that the US justice system still worked, in spite of the growing tendency toward trial by media. Others argued that Insull merely escaped just punishment by means of the superior defense provided by his huge personal wealth and it is this inequality that forms the second strand of this section.

During the years of this study while the nation had become increasingly prosperous, the distribution of that wealth had not been even. It has been estimated that in 1860, 29 percent of the wealth of the United States was in the hands of the top 1 percent of the population. By 1890, that single percent possessed over half of the nation's wealth. In certain areas this inequality was even more pronounced.

In Massachusetts, for example, the richest 8 percent of the state owned 83 percent of the wealth in 1861. Twenty years later they owned 90 percent. During these years, legendary fortunes were being made by the top industrialists. In the 1870s, John D. Rockefeller's Standard Oil; Cyrus McCormack's International Harvester; Marshall Field's department stores and Philip Armour's meatpacking empire, had all yielded them fortunes of over $20 million. By 1900, Rockefeller's empire was valued at over $200 million, as were Andrew Carnegie's steel-based riches. Not all the fortunes so characteristic of the age were new, nor were the new ones the largest. The longer-established Vanderbilt and Astor families were estimated to be worth in excess of $300 million.[18]

To a growing number, at all levels of US society, such fortunes were an obscenity, they were against the American ethos. The Progressive journalist, author and political activist, Henry Demarest Lloyd claimed in his *Wealth Against Commonwealth* that one of the fundamental reasons for the American revolution had been to oust King George's courtiers and placemen from their monopolies in the thirteen colonies. By the time of his writing (1894), he argued that the King and his cronies had been replaced by the industrial monopolists. American society was meant to be based on individualism, democracy and the opportunity to create a better life; instead, as Lloyd claimed "that conduct we think right because [it is] called 'trade' is really lying, stealing, murder" and it was being perpetrated every day by the new "industrial Caesars."[19]

While Lloyd may have been using hyperbolic language, the climate was certainly changing with regard to the "Captains of Industry." It would be more than probable that a survey of Americans at the opening of the twentieth century, if it asked who represented the greatest criminal threat to the nation, would get responses which would include at least one of the nation's wealthiest men. At the top of that list would most likely be either Morgan, Rockefeller or the railcar magnate, George Mortimer Pullman, although they would almost certainly have referred to them collectively as the "Trusts." In terms of forging unfair trading advantages, more often than not born of size, the magnates' crimes of greed and corruption were as legendary as their wealth. American corporations seemed dedicated to unfairly getting the advantages of economies of scale. By 1890, it was reckoned that there were over 100 Trusts controlling the markets in everything from whiskey, to nails, to bicycles and—even as the later interrogation of Morgan would they hoped prove—it was suspected, money itself. Yet, as widespread as these restrictive monopolies were in American business, the law seemed to be incapable of reining them in or stopping their spread.

Perhaps the best example of this big business impunity is demonstrated by the activities of Henry Osborne Havemeyer who formed American Sugar Refining in 1887. By 1892, he had amalgamated 17 separate companies into a single Trust which, by one account, controlled 98 percent of the US sugar refining trade. Not one to leave anything to chance, Havemeyer also bought and maintained a protective tariff in order to protect his domestic market from foreign imports. He achieved this by scattering liberal amounts of money about in Congress largely via the supremely venal Senator, Nelson Aldrich. Perhaps more than any other Trust, Havemeyer's empire challenged the Sherman Anti-Trust acts of 1891 which set out that "Every person who shall monopolize or attempt to monopolize . . . any part of the trade or commerce among the several states, or with foreign nations, shall be deemed guilty of a felony."[20]

When taken to court in the *EC Knight Sugar* case, Havemeyer's opponents pursued him all the way to the Supreme Court. The decision went Havemeyer's way. It was decided that it fell beyond the remit of the Sherman legislation. In 1895, his lawyers convinced all the Justices, except one, that since the vast majority of the Trust's business was refining, and the bulk of that activity took place within the state of Pennsylvania, it did not attempt to "control interstate or foreign commerce" which the legislation outlawed. Many spectators were less than convinced that this was the case, and the views of some opponents would prove significant. In the words of Theodore Roosevelt, the decision once again reduced the powers of the federal government to regulate Trusts to "a nullity."[21] Nevertheless, the Trust would remain the symbol of business criminality throughout the first decades of twentieth century. The problem of "bigness" in business became one of the defining historic elements of the Progressive era, exemplified in Roosevelt's epic battle with Standard Oil which continued beyond his presidency to reach its conclusion in 1911.

By the time Roosevelt assumed the presidency in 1901, John D. Rockefeller's Standard Oil had mastered the art of using size to dominate the transport system for oil. In these early days of the oil industry, the rail system was the key. It was not only vital to transport the crude oil, but also essential to move around the coal and the chemicals necessary for the refining, processing, and exporting. Having the power to dominate railroads and then keep their secret deals silent, Standard bullied, cajoled and bribed huge rebates from the railroads to ensure their use of the network. In turn, this enabled the huge Trust to undercut any competitors, drive them into financial problems and then absorb them into the growing behemoth. This was developed into an art, until by 1880 Standard and Rockefeller-owned subsidiaries controlled over 90 percent of the US oil refining capacity.

The fact that Standard could remain in such a position for the next 30 years shows some of the difficulties inherent in regulating big business. Not everyone saw the corporate giants as undesirable, let alone criminal. Aware that business bigness brought with it big money and huge potential revenue, some states fought to attract them. In 1892, Standard took advantage of New Jersey's recently relaxed incorporation laws. When the Governor of New Jersey, Woodrow Wilson, closed down this loophole in 1911, Standard soon found a similarly welcoming regime opened up for them in neighboring Delaware.

What was more, some felt that the benefits provided by Trusts outweighed the disadvantages. Steel magnate, Andrew Carnegie and cigarette baron, James Buchanan Duke argued with considerable justification that large companies increased the availability of their products, through efficient use of resources and the economies of scale. J.P. Morgan was convinced that rationalization through corporate mergers eliminated wasteful duplication through competition, a process he memorably called "cannibal capitalism." Rockefeller argued that his empire stabilized the markets. To these figures and their supporters, the expansion of businesses at the cost of smaller competitors was the expression of the natural order, for as Rockefeller's son—John Junior—told an audience at Brown University:

> The growth of a large business, is merely a survival of the fittest . . . The American Beauty rose can be produced in the splendor and fragrance which bring cheer to its beholder only by sacrificing the early buds which grow up around it. This is not an evil tendency in business. It is merely the working out of a law of nature and a law of God.[22]

On the other hand, there were those who singled out Rockefeller as the representative of all that was rotten in corporate America, but they had only limited success. As early as 1881 in his "Story of a Great Monopoly" the investigative journalist and Populist, Henry Damarest Lloyd, had set the tone. He condemned the authorities for allowing Rockefeller to produce "the greatest, wisest and meanest monopoly known to history" and advised that this "czar of plutocracy will stop only when he *is stopped*."[23] Some nine years later, his warning was translated into action in Ohio—Standard's base of operations. The state attorney general, David K. Watson, filed fraud charges against Standard Oil in 1889. In spite of pressure leveled on his Republican colleagues to get him to drop the case, in 1892, the Ohio Supreme Court ruled against Standard. It was a hollow victory, because Rockefeller merely shifted operations to New Jersey.

Even when Ida Tarbell exhaustively detailed the corrupt, fraudulent, unethical and illegal practices of the company in a 19-part serial in *McClure's* magazine from November 1902 to October 1904 and then in her 1904 book, *The History of the Standard Oil Company*, the results of this exposé, in terms of controlling big business, were less than impressive. Her revelations, no doubt, contributed to the 1911 US Supreme Court judgment that the Standard Oil group was an "unreasonable" monopoly. They were probably influential in the subsequent order to break up the company, but even this lengthy and well-publicized trial fell far short of reining in the huge corporations. Some would argue the decision to break up Standard Oil into 33 constituent parts simply boosted the value of the whole. Rockefeller himself seems to have thought so, and, the story goes, having learned of the Supreme Court's decision, he advised his minister and golfing buddy—if it is possible a man as cold as Rockefeller really had "buddies"—to buy all the stock he could afford in Standard. In spite of the lives ruined; the espionage; the immorality and the corruption, no one in the corporation suffered criminal charges.[24]

Nevertheless, there were some who felt that the Supreme Court judgment changed America. In his summing up of the Standard Oil decision, Associate

Justice, John Marshall Harlan, echoed Lincoln's warning about big business when he argued that:

> All who recall the condition of the country in 1890 will remember that there was everywhere, among the people generally, a deep feeling of unrest. The nation had been rid of human slavery … but the conviction was universal that the country was in real danger from another kind of slavery sought to be fastened on the American people, namely, the slavery that would result from aggregations of capital in the hands of a few individuals and corporations controlling, for their own profit and advantage exclusively, the entire business of the country, including the production and sale of the necessaries of life.[25]

Harlan's assessment tapped a strong current in American thinking at this time. The corporation/big business/Trust, whatever title it went by, was not simply resented for its size, or even its dishonesty or cruelty, but its un-American nature. In the eyes of its opponents, it was through the Trust that immigrant, child, convict and peon labor was exploited in what amounted to wage slavery: a new form of feudalism. Some idea of the widespread outrage at this situation can be found in the variety of legislation—both at a state and federal level—which was passed to regulate business practice. Almost all angles of the workplace were regulated during these years. The importing of cheap, disposable, contract labor was regulated beginning with the 1885 Immigration Act. Congress passed laws regulating child labor in 1916, 1919, 1924 and 1938. Almost all cities had health and safety in the workplace ordinances which governed such aspects as ventilation, fire escapes, and first aid facilities. It is during these years that, after almost relentless pressure, the 8-hour day was finally introduced. However, as with the regulation of Trusts, much of this legislation was either ignored, neutered, or turned on those it was meant to protect.

A tragic event in New York's Greenwich Village a month or so before Harlan's statement, illustrates this iniquity. The Triangle Shirtwaist Company fire of 1911 killed 146, largely young, East European, Jewish and Italian, immigrants. Over one hundred of the victims were young women. The majority of the victims were incinerated as the fire spread, rapidly, in the "fireproof building." The workers were powerless to douse the flames since the fire hoses in the building were not connected to the water supply. Others were crushed by jumping from the ninth-storey windows, or throwing themselves down the elevator shaft rather than facing being burnt to death.

They had been forced to take these drastic measures because the wire-reinforced exit door from the main, loft, workshop had been locked, from the outside. This had been done to prevent petty pilfering and to make sure that the girls did not skulk away from their sewing machines in order to smoke a crafty cigarette in the no smoking building. Ironically, it was probably smoking which led to the fire. What made all these revelations so much worse was that the owners, two Jewish businessmen, Max Blanck and Isaac Harris, escaped with only very minor injuries. Yet, it was a sign of the horror that the incident aroused and the changes afoot in American thinking that, within a month of the fire, Blanck and Harris were arrested. A little under a year later, the two owners were put on trial on six counts of manslaughter. The charges arose from the locked door.

The two were represented at a cost of $40,000 each, by Tammany boss Big Tim Sullivan's attorney, Max D. Steuer—the lawyer who would later represent Samuel Insull. Steuer was also an Italian Jewish immigrant and like roughly half the city's Jewish immigrants of the period, he had himself worked in the garment sweat-shops of New York. His experience and drive proved to be worth the money. Steuer destroyed the defendants' credibility by showing that some of the girls' testimony had been learned by rote. The defense also stressed that the prosecution had failed to prove that the owners knew the exit door was locked at the time in question. The jury acquitted the owners. However, Blanck and Harris lost a subsequent civil suit in 1913, and the plaintiffs won compensation in the amount of $75 per deceased victim. This was not too much of a burden, since it later emerged that the insurance company had already paid the pair about $60,000 more than the reported losses, or about an additional $400 per casualty. In 1913, Blanck was once again arrested for locking the door in his factory during working hours. This time he was less fortunate. He was found guilty. For this, his second offense, Blanck was fined $20.[26]

Perhaps the victims of the fire would have gained no compensation at all had it not been for the relentless pressure of the International Ladies Garment Workers' Union. This was perhaps the start of what can be seen as the golden era of American industrial organization.

By the end of World War I, union membership was, briefly, the highest America would ever experience as a proportion of the nation's working population. But this organization came at a cost. This was an age of frequent industrial violence. During much of the early part of this period there were frequent examples of all-out war between labor and capital. They were frequently fought in the mining areas of the Rockies, but also in the Deep South and industrial East. They broke out in the iron mills of the Mid-West, the textile mills of the North-east and across the railroads of the nation as well as in plantations and ranches of the South and West. The armies were composed of strikers and their supporters. Often portrayed in the press—if not in reality—they and the scabs brought in to replace them were immigrants from Europe and Asia. They were ranged against Pinkerton agents and other hired guns. The strikers may have been the result of the organizing actions of the Knights of Labor or the American Federation of Labor. They may have been organized by the Anarchists or even the Industrial Workers of the World. Issues could range from pay, conditions, hours, safety or simply the struggle to gain an effective political voice.

One of the most notorious events occurred in 1914, near Ludlow, Colorado, where a tented village of striking mine workers was attacked by state militia and mine guards. They were acting on the orders of the Rockefeller-owned Colorado Fuel and Iron Company (the CFI) against whom the miners were striking for better conditions, increased pay, and union recognition. Twenty miners and their families were killed, predominantly women and children burned to death in the ensuing fire. They included an extended family of 13 who were deliberately suffocated by means of a blanket, while they hid in a pit. The violence escalated over the next ten days, and some 70 on both sides were killed or injured before federal troops moved in and restored order. It is difficult to quantify such actions of bosses as criminal, according to the laws of the time, although in this case there was a highly publicized federal inquiry. In the course of this investigation John D. Rockefeller (Junior) himself felt obliged to justify the actions of his hirelings saying that, "While this loss of life is profoundly to be regretted, it is unjust in the extreme to lay it at the door of the defenders of law and property, who were in no slightest way responsible for it." [27]

As if to back Rockefeller's judgment, the State of Colorado court marshaled ten militia officers and 12 privates and found them innocent of any wrong-doing. More unusually the cases of 332 miners arrested for murder dragged on for the next six years, until they were all quashed. What was more, popular opinion was mobilized by a national speaking tour of women survivors of the massacre and the *New York Times*, *Harper's Weekly* and even the *Wall Street Journal* ran stories hostile to Rockefeller for some time after peace in the region had been re-established. The US Commission on Industrial Relations investigated the massacre for two years and when it reported, it condemned the CFI's behavior and arguably influenced the Wilson administration's decision to introduce significant protective measures for US labor. [28]

This marked a change in the general attitude towards industrial violence, which while polarizing popular opinion, had more often than not been blamed on the workers rather than capital. It was radical workers who were prosecuted for criminal acts as with the Haymarket bombing of 1886 and the violence of the Pullman Strike in 1894. Even when the corporations' "strikebreakers" used firearms against pickets, as in the Chicago streetcar wars of 1903, or when the militia fired on the striking St Louis streetcar drivers in 1900—the police still protected them and the law was seen to be on their side. While industrial violence still flared up, as with the IWW gunfight at Everett in 1916, Standard Oil's use of Pete DeVito's thugs or the extreme violence of Harry Bennet's strong arm "Servicemen" employed by the Ford Corporation in the late 1930s, the attitude of the authorities was generally far less tolerant than in the years before Ludlow. [29]

It is worth noting that during the period of this study, corporate crime was also extended to include public health and consumer responsibilities, often issues which largely affected the poorer members of the population. The best-known example of this is the exposé of the incorporation of rubbish, rats, tubercular lesions, even human remains among other ingredients in the processed meats produced by Chicago's huge meatpacking industry. This horror story was brought to light in Upton Sinclair's *The Jungle* (1906) and led directly to the Pure Food and Drug Act which gave real powers to a federal agency to enforce meaningful safeguards for consumers.

This is generally considered one of the landmark pieces of public health legislation. What is less well known is that, revolutionary as the Act was, in *The Brass Check*, Sinclair relates that the *New York Herald* commissioned a follow-up story, "Packingtown a Year Later" and sent reporters to spend two months undercover. They found conditions worse than ever and were almost certainly bribed to prevent the ensuing scandal, for the *Herald*'s publisher killed the story before publication. What was more, the fines imposed on cosmetic, drug and food companies found to be guilty under the legislation between 1908 and 1911 did not exceed $200. While the adverse publicity was no doubt unwelcome to the guilty parties, the fines as such can hardly be considered a real deterrent.[30]

What was important about the legislation was the precedent that manufacturers could be held criminally liable if their products were found to be faulty, dangerous or misleadingly labeled. This precedent did not prevent a notorious mass-poisoning in 1937. The poisoning followed the discovery of anti-bacterial wonder-drug, Sulphanilamide, which the Massengill Company of Tennessee incorporated into a liquid tonic using an untested glycol derivative as the carrier for the drug. One hundred and five people died of liver and kidney failure after taking the elixir and nearly 250 others were made ill by consuming it. Dr Massengill was fined over $26,000 for mis-labeling, the only crime of which he could be convicted. After a wide-ranging inquest, the Pure Food and Drug Act of 1906 was updated by a law, rushed through Congress in 1938, which among other provisions required manufacturers to show proof of effective and approved product safety tests.[31]

There can be few better examples of the huge changes in the America's attitude to corporations than that illustrated by contrasting the speedy passage of this legislation with the length of time it took to pass the original Pure Food and Drug measure. It had taken over 25 years for the work of the government chemist, Dr Harvey W. Wiley and his so-called "poison squad," to persuade the federal government into action in 1906.[32] Even then, it was more the result of Upton Sinclair's report and novel than the painstaking compilation of evidence by the dogged Wiley. In itself, this change demonstrates not only the increasing power of the media and the consumer throughout the period, but also the increasing attention paid to them by the corporations. It also shows the increasing willingness of the federal government to tackle a huge range of issues relating to workers' rights and consumer safety especially during the bursts of reform which composed the Progressive Era and the New Deal.

It was not only the unintended injuries created by working conditions and products that attracted the attention of the Muckrakers, Progressives and other reformers, but also the environment as a whole. In the initial period of massive industrialization in the late nineteenth century, pollution was seen as an almost inevitable consequence of "progress." During this period, coal-fueled heating and power meant that New York, Los Angeles, Pittsburgh and Chicago and other cities developed such serious air pollution problems that they were later forced to pass clean air ordinances. Air pollution was so bad in the summer of 1928 that New York reported, on some days sunlight was cut by anything up to 50 percent.

In rural areas the situation was often no better. By 1900, over 70 percent of the huge natural forests of the continent had been felled, and replanting was patchy. The wildlife had often been either poisoned or starved through destruction of its habitat. Some species were hunted to near extinction. During this period the last passenger pigeon, Martha, died in captivity and the buffalo nearly suffered the same fate. What was more, the remaining "wilderness" was "tamed" and frequently left scarred by human endeavor to harvest, cultivate, and extract. The result was that from Alaska to Texas, administrations from Grant through to FDR created national parks, designated sites nature reserves and wildlife sanctuaries, and named others as National Monuments.

In spite of these development, it was water pollution which brought the first federal criminal prosecutions. As the story of its enforcement shows, as with all other areas of crime generated by business and industry, the passing of legislation did not mean the end of the problem, but it did at least highlight interest in the issue. The Rivers and Harbors Act of 1899 contained within it a Refuse Act. This was a powerful weapon against water pollution. It forbade any individual, corporation or municipality from the discharging, throwing or dumping of refuse or other matter into any watercourse, tributary or other body of water, on pain of criminal prosecution. The law was, however, honored more in the breach than in obedience. The maximum fine which could be imposed was $2,500 and when the Supreme Court had the opportunity to force home the true power of the legislation, it backed off. In 1921, in a decision which defined the reality of pollution policy, the court upheld the right of New Jersey to dump raw sewage into New York harbor. They claimed, totally justifiably, that the "grave problem of sewage disposal . . . is more likely to be wisely solved by cooperative study and mutual concession . . . than by proceedings in any court."[33]

Nevertheless, waterways would continue to be polluted. The Cuyahoga river oozed its course through northeast Ohio, so polluted with gasoline—then, a useless by-product of kerosene production—and other flammable material that it caught fire some 30 times in the 101 years after its first blaze in 1868. The 1922 report of the Corps of Engineers reported pollution playing havoc with the fish stocks of Gloucester, Massachusetts, "cod capital of the US" as well as Charleston, South Carolina, New Orleans, Portland, Oregon, and Baltimore. In August of that year, the *Philadelphia Ledger* asked how tourists and others could "deliberately go into such black and vile-looking water" as that flowing through the once teeming Delaware river.

The crusade for the criminalization of water pollution did not stop. The next 20 years saw legislation which would criminalize acts from the pollution of fresh and salt water by ships to the pollution of streams by individuals, but as the Izaak

Walton League—a pressure group for clean water, named after the famous English angler—wearily commented, water courses continued to be polluted. They put this down to "short sighted greed and folly that is not even intelligent in its own interests," a statement which could be applied to any of the less savory practices of business in this period, but which the law seemed incapable of rectifying.[34]

Nor was it only the workers, public or the environment which had suffered from the industrialization, commercialization, and incorporation of America. Two days after Christmas Day in 1939, Professor Edwin Sutherland of the University of Indiana gave the presidential address to the American Sociological Society in Philadelphia. His theme would coin a phrase which would become commonplace in the English-speaking world: a theme which would ignite a new mistrust of business. He called his lecture "White Collar Criminality" and defined it as "crime in relation to business," or "crime in the upper or white-collar class, [which, he maintained was] composed of respectable or at least respected business and professional men."[35] Sutherland was arguing that even in 1939, conventional studies of criminality tended to concentrate on what were seen as the "criminal classes." He claimed that this conventional wisdom dictated that the actions of criminals were the result of poverty; lack of opportunity, often combined with other forms of depravation and privation which inspired immoral, if not socio-pathic, behavior.

In his speech, Sutherland cited several of what he called the "suave and deceptive . . . merchant princes and captains of finance" who, he claimed, had inherited the criminal mantle of the nineteenth-century robber barons. In this rogues' gallery Sutherland placed such well-known miscreants as Albert Fall, the central figure of the Teapot Dome scandal. He also included the peculiar Van Sweringen brothers, a pair who shared a room for their entire life and built and then lost a $3 billion empire without ever risking any of their own money. He mentioned the "match king" Ivar Kreuger whose suicide in 1932 revealed fraud and deception on a truly royal level. Alongside him reigned the king of salesmen, "Sunshine Charlie" Mitchell. At the peak of the "wild bull markets" of the 1920s, this eternal optimist's sales targets ranged between $1–2 billion a year although his ambition to "blaze a trail" lost the public billions. Of course, he mentions Samuel Insull, but more interestingly he includes a man called Philip Musica.[36]

Despite his melodic name—which he disguised with a series of aliases, most notably Costa, Johnson and Coster—Italian-American, Musica, was, first, a criminal, and second, a corporate executive. He was a thoroughly unscrupulous and no doubt unpleasant man. Musica falsely accused a business partner of embezzlement, fraud and underage sex in order to make his wife leave the unfortunate man and instead move in with him. Arrested and convicted for fraud, twice, he spent two spells in prison before he was 30. True to form, Musica obtained early release by acting as a police informant and went on, under the assumed name of William Johnson, to serve as a special agent during the Great War—chasing draft dodgers. Over-enthusiastic in this pursuit, he was soon indicted for perjury and

"Johnson" disappeared to re-emerge as Frank Costa, who then went on to far greater crimes.

Three years into Prohibition, Costa's pharmaceutical company, Adelphi, was entitled to buy up to 5,000 gallons of alcohol a month to manufacture its famous hair tonics. These products were in fact sold to bootleggers who then diluted and flavored the "hair tonic" and then shipped it on as high proof booze. When Revenue agents cottoned on to the scam, Costa again changed identities. In his final guise, as Dr Francis Donald Coster, he reached his apogee. He now used the remaining profits from Adelphi to buy the established wholesale pharmaceuticals company, McKesson and Roberts (M and R). Thirteen years later, the respectable Dr Coster headed a company which, the accounts, audited by Price Waterhouse, showed to have a revenue of $174 million, a profit of $3.5 million a year, and assets of over $80 million.

As CEO of this enterprise, he had "earned" a substantial salary, and owned a palatial estate in Connecticut and a 123-ft ocean-going yacht, the *Carolita* which he moored alongside the Vanderbilts and Morgans in Long Island Sound. Moreover, philanthropist that the doctor was, he had founded and then funded a charitable heart hospital. His entry in the 1927 *Who's Who* listed him as a Methodist, born in Washington, DC—rather than a Catholic, born in Naples. It also showed him to be a member of all the most prestigious New York clubs. He even modestly turned down a request by the Republican National Committee in 1937 to run for US President in 1940. The metamorphosis of criminal Musica into businessman Coster was almost complete, but such deception could not last, particularly in the turbulent economic climate of 1930s America. Less than a year later, investigations initiated by his own company's treasurer showed almost all of M and R's assets to be fictitious and the entire business to be fraudulent. Coster was arrested for fraud and released on bail, but days later was exposed as the ex-con and fraudster, Philip Musica. When the US Marshalls called at his house, knowing the game was up, the doctor locked himself in a bathroom and blew his brains out.[37]

In retrospect, Musica's career is important for a variety of reasons. It is significant not so much because he duped so many for so long but more because, like Insull and many to follow, the huge scale of the losses threatened the entire structure of Wall Street. The fallout from Musica's demise demonstrated this as clearly at the end of the 1930s as Enron has in our times. It resulted in deepening the mistrust of business and the financial system in the eyes of the American public during the Depression. In turn, this threat was not so much driven by concern for the money itself, although it was some $19 million, but the confidence in the existing security checks in place. While Musica's scam led to major changes in the auditing processes, it did not alter the perception that there was predilection among many Wall Street bankers for high yielding companies—especially those which would pay high sums to bankers willing to sit on their boards—regardless of the legality of their dealings.

Perhaps this is most clearly demonstrated by the behavior of the celebrity investment analyst Waddill Catchings, who was hired by one of M and R's worried directors as early as 1932. Rather than carrying out a full investigation, Catchings instead took a $5,000 a month consultancy from Musica–Coster. By the end of the decade, when Coster had been disgraced, an article in *Time* insinuated that the "impish" Catchings only threatened to blow the whistle on Musica–Coster when he, himself, was faced with being fired. What was more, even when the scale of the fraud was common knowledge, some Wall Street sources argued that Musica–Coster's actions were, if not legal, then at least responsible and justifiable, even though the man's criminal record was already being splashed all over the newspapers. They claimed that had the company gone bankrupt in the early 1930s— when, according to one of Musica–Coster's suicide notes, he began to fiddle the books—a great deal more small investors would have suffered losses. They argued that the consequences for the market at this early stage of the Depression would have been far worse.[38] To those outside Wall Street, it was seen as the "system" closing ranks and protecting itself and even condoning overt criminal behavior in order make money.

Returning to Sutherland's (1939) lecture, what was equally groundbreaking was that his research seemed to point out that criminal behavior was endemic across the entire spectrum of US corporate activity. He pointed to the criminal records of 70 out of the 200 largest US corporations. He illustrated that the management of these organizations had been convicted of 980 violations—an average 14 per corporation. He went on to detail specific instances. He showed that the meatpacking giants, Armour and Co and Swift and Co had 50 convictions for criminal violations each. The vast car manufacturer, GM had 40 and the retail giants Sears Roebuck and Montgomery Ward had 39 each.

To drive the point home, he showed the scale of such crimes. He demonstrated that the top six of J. Edgar Hoover's Public Enemies in 1938 netted a total haul in total of $130,000. He pointed out that when "The Match King," Ivar Kreuger's fraud was finally unraveled that same year, it was discovered that he alone took investors for $250 million.[39] On the other hand, if it is possible to argue that the "Wall Street classes" condoned and imitated the actions of the "criminal classes," it is equally plausible to turn the argument around and argue that during these years of boom and bust, the criminal classes learned and mimicked the Lords of Wall Street. In terms of their ambitions, their methods and their structure—at the highest levels American crime became incorporated.

With regard to ambition, the one criminal who must stand out is Arnold Rothstein. Son of Abraham Rothstein (Abe the Good), a respected pillar of the New York Jewish community, Arnold started his gambling career running street-corner "craps" games with the loose change his father left on his bedside over the Sabbath. By the mid-1910s he was known as the "Bankroll," a sort of J.P. Morgan for the underworld. He was indicative of the new type of urban gangster emerging in the 1920s. Immaculately turned out and distanced from the thuggery he ordered and inspired, Rothstein appeared as urbane and sophisticated as his Wall Street counterparts—he was also equally ruthless, single-minded and greedy. Specializing in huge stakes gambling, Arnold's ambitions knew few boundaries and even fewer scruples. When he won, he would ruthlessly chase the vanquished man down for the very last cent. When he lost, he might well "welch" on his debt—a habit which probably led to his murder in 1928. Rothstein ordered horses doped, dice rigged, cards marked and men beaten, but he also, to the law and the public at least, appeared legitimate if not anonymous. The most striking example of this invisibility was that Rothstein was almost certainly the brains and the money behind the 1919 Black Sox scam.

In this national scandal, the core of Chicago White Sox, the favorites in baseball's 1919 World Series, were bribed to throw qualifying and final games. Although linked to it, Rothstein was never convicted of any crime related to it. In fact, he was never convicted of any crime at all. What also singled Rothstein out from the herd was his commercial sense. When he got involved in rum running from Europe, he organized his importation business meticulously. The product was of the highest quality, the shipping always on time. He negotiated personally with the European distillers, insuring a good price. He then took care of his distribution network in the US, ensuring immunity from assassination attempts. True to his business background, he remained invisible and sold out, no doubt for a great profit, in the mid-1920s.

If Rothstein was the Morgan of the crime world in this period, Al Capone would have been the Carnegie. Like Rothstein, Capone was ruthless, ambitious, intelligent and brutal. Using these qualities he welded together a criminal empire in Chicago that employed thousands and made millions. But unlike Rothstein, Capone courted the limelight. Just as Carnegie justified his Calvinist/philanthropist/Darwinist take on life, wealth and justice, in the *Gospel of Wealth*, so Capone loved to espouse his idiosyncratic world view. The press was fixated by the millionaire gangster, following his utterances on all subjects from weight loss, to the immorality of the emerging Hollywood elite, to the politics of Prohibition. Capone was considered part thug, part role model, part business guru. Some idea of his status can be gleaned from the idea floated that he should use his underworld contacts to track down the whereabouts of the kidnapped Lindbergh baby. He was serving an 11-year sentence for tax evasion in Alcatraz at the time.

Capone also resembled the robber barons in his business strategy. Perhaps in this respect he most closely resembled Rockefeller rather than Carnegie, not only for his willingness to use strong-arm tactics, but also in his ruthless passion for an integrated business model. Just like Rockefeller, "Scarface" controlled his own means of production, distribution and retail of his product—whether related to booze, prostitution or protection. He was also perfectly at ease with ruthlessly eliminating, if not actually gunning down, any serious competition. What was more, like Standard Oil, he famously controlled those elements which could impede his progress. He would often brag that he "owned" the Chicago police and had the most significant and relevant aldermen, state attorneys, mayors, governors, legislators, congressmen, not to mention voters, in his pocket.

If Capone was the best-known example of the business model for crime in this period, he was certainly not the only one. All the major cities—especially New York and Chicago—had criminal organizations, which, if not as integrated or sizeable as Capone's mob, were equally powerful in their own neighborhoods. Like Capone and his arch enemy Bugsy Moran, they regularly fought turf wars over their gambling, prostitution and, most importantly, booze markets. If the results were rarely as blatant, bloody, daring or well-publicized as Capone's notorious St Valentine's Day attack, it has been argued this was because some gangsters realized that this behavior was wasteful and bloody. What was more, it also attracted the unwanted attentions of the press and often the law as well.

As one Chicago gangster put it, such unprofessional behavior made the crime lords appear like the mobsters were "just a bunch of saps killing each other and giving the cops a laugh."[40] Such a view had a pedigree with the robber barons, for in a similar, if more erudite vein, J.P. Morgan had argued when re-organizing the duplication and unproductive competition in the railroad industry of the last decades of the nineteenth century that such practices were simply business "cannibalism."

Just as Americans in 1900 suspected Trusts existed in all aspects of business, finance and commerce, during the 1930s they were adamant there was a cabal associated with crime—an organization, a governing body, with supreme control across the entire Union regulating the behavior of the various mobs. Businesses were now international; law-keeping was federal—why shouldn't crime be continental? This view was given new credence when, in 1939, following the arrest of the seemingly small-time hoodlum, Abe, "Kid Twist," Reles, it emerged that a highly organized execution squad had operated around the country. Within days the press had christened it "Murder Inc." and used it as evidence that a national crime "syndicate" had evolved. There was much to support this view. When Reles, a hitman for the syndicate, had turned state's evidence, the FBI was able to solve 85 outstanding murders—45 of them in Brooklyn alone. His testimony pointed to at least another additional 400 contracts having been carried out in the years since the syndicate's founding in 1934.

The organization and ruthlessness of Murder Inc. were impressive. In his statements Reles revealed that by paying an annual flat fee of $12,000—and assuming the nod of their fellow members of the criminal elite—any subscribing boss could order any victim, anywhere to be effectively, quietly and anonymously "seen to." In 1941, Reles himself was added to this tally, and the mythology of syndicated crime having its tentacles in all levels of society was further enhanced. The "canary" had been thrown or pushed from the sixth floor window of the Half Moon Hotel on Coney Island where he was under protective custody. As one wag cruelly commented, he was "a canary that could sing, but couldn't fly."

The perception of the ruthlessness, power and reach of the crime syndicate was given a boost when the newspapers revealed that while in the hotel, Reles was always under a guard of at least six uniformed policemen.[41] However, it is also possible to argue that the interaction between crime and business should be seen as altogether more natural, subtle and insidious in America throughout the early decades of the twentieth century. Rather than concentrating on the adoption by criminals of business models, or the corruption of the boardroom, some significant critics argued that it is more important to look at the environment which unfettered *laissez-faire* capitalism created. By the 1930s, in the wake of the Great Crash, the gangsterism of Prohibition and the huge frauds and scandals being regularly exposed, commentators, including the historian Charles Beard, the journalist Walter Lippman and the jurist Murray Gurfein, claimed the existing system of regulation not only created the conditions for the immorality and greed but encouraged "racketeering" at all levels of American society. They maintained that the lack of oversight allowed the sole check in business practice to be the maxim "caveat emptor"—let the buyer beware.

The result was that the New Deal's labor reforms, banking reforms, public utilities reforms, securities reforms, gun controls, and price controls have been seen as being just as important in fighting crime as the increased powers of J. Edgar Hoover's FBI. They not only defined unacceptable behavior and increased policing powers but they also signaled a change in the ethos of the nation towards regulation and the disclosure of information. To New Dealers, these reforms represented the end of the era of the robber baron, for, as FDR himself said, their purpose was for the law in the future to place "the burden of telling the *whole* truth on the seller."[42]

7
PROHIBITIONS

In 1919, the baseball player turned iconic evangelist, Billy Sunday, assured his radio audience of some 10,000 loyal souls that: "The reign of tears is over. The slums will soon be a memory. We will turn our prisons into factories and our jails into storehouses and corncribs. Men will soon walk upright now; women will smile and children will laugh. Hell will be forever rent."[1] This delight was not caused by the end of the recent war, nor did it mark the end of a deadly influenza epidemic. Sunday was not talking of some blissed out vision of the Second Coming or even the hyperbolic campaigning for the election of a new president. It was the result of the passage of the Volstead Act, by which, as a nation, America—or at least the federal government—repudiated alcohol.

If this seems surprising, it was not as if the Reverend Sunday was alone in the optimism of his depiction of an alcohol-free utopia. To the members of the Anti-Saloon League and other dry groups, America was now free to enjoy the benefits of a more sober, healthier, more productive world free from the curse of booze. Fourteen years later, all except for the most diehard Prohibitionists felt that the creation of "God's Dry Kingdom" had been a failure. It had led to an increase in reported drunkenness; it had led to an increase in the prison population and in many urban areas during Prohibition, there were more bars than there had been before. Statistics showed that booze was more fashionable in 1930 than it had been in 1910 and the continuation with what was patently an unenforceable law had made breaking the law a normal part of daily life for a huge number of Americans.

In spite of this manifest failure, many accounts of the 1920s claim that Prohibition defines the decade. Nothing illustrates this better than journalist Harry Philips' brilliant summation of the history of the United States. In 11 immortal words he shows the contempt with which the public held the dry laws—"Columbus, Washington,

Lincoln, Volstead. Two flights up and ask for Gus."[2] In the usual reading of the decade, casual law-breaking went hand in hand with the frenetic partying and reckless speculating—accompanied by the worrying use of credit—followed by even more spending. As if this was not enough, it also had an even darker side. The money to be made from moon-shining, bootlegging and rum running sparked crime on a level never before seen in the US. It spawned characters whose immorality, violence, irreverence and ruthlessness have become legendary in a country already famous for its outlaws and criminals. Considered by many at all levels of American society to be both unenforceable and undesirable, Prohibition has been blamed for blurring even further what was already often a fuzzy distinction between law enforcement and law breaking. Judges and politicians bought booze from known criminals; respectable citizens distilled, bottled and sold "bath tub gin"; police and prohibition agents took huge bribes; small-time hoodlums gained vast criminal empires and through their huge turnover funded an entire network of illegal ancillary industries and laundering operations ranging from transport firms to hitmen.

Yet it should be remembered that Prohibition was itself a crusade, and that however flawed and however unsuccessful that crusade appeared in the 1920s, it had deep roots and an impressive pedigree. It had vocal supporters, in influential areas of US society. Prohibition had been a long time coming and it was by no means the only time that America tried to legislate to preserve the morality of its population. Nor was the "Noble Experiment" the last such experiment. Before the Eighteenth Amendment banned the importing, production, sale or distribution of alcohol, public gambling had come under sustained attack, so much so that by 1914, horse racing was only legal in six states. What was more, the Harrison Act of the same year prohibited the recreational use of most commonly used narcotics. While perhaps less dramatic, these prohibitions outlasted that on alcohol. After the Twenty-First Amendment repealed Prohibition in 1933, Nevada was the only state where most forms of gambling were openly allowed, and the Marijuana Taxation Act of 1937 tried to outlaw cannabis by imposing large fines and lengthy prison sentences on those convicted of possession.

This chapter will investigate three themes associated with these three prohibitions. First, it will examine why these prohibitions were considered necessary. It will look into what drove them; who advocated them, and why the bans were limited to simply alcohol, gambling and narcotics rather than smoking, stock speculation, swearing or other forms of stimulating and seemingly morally questionable behavior. Second, it will investigate how the policing and legislating involved in their being outlawed evolved. It will examine who controlled it, how it was enforced, who it targeted and how effective it really was. Third, and perhaps most significantly, it will look into whether the prevailing view that criminal activity was in fact stimulated rather than controlled by prohibitions, and if so, why they continued—and still continue—for so long.

Turn-of-the-century America was a society in flux. It was an unstable mix of high morals, tradition, and fatalism. This mix was constantly challenged by the self-consciously modern belief in the powers of science, the nation's increasing prosperity, the unstoppable march of "progress," and the potentials contained in the imaginative use of individualism. Poverty, crime, and the social inequalities from which these scourges originated, were viewed as controllable. This, it was argued, could be achieved by two means. It was attainable by strict attention to traditional values of self-reliance, family, thrift, and industry. Alternatively it could be achieved through charity and rational, scientifically based reforms. In America, as in most industrialized societies, it was felt that modernity and its discontents could be managed by a variety of panacea, ranging from improvements in hygiene, diet, and housing to self-restraint, prayer and—in the last resort—by prohibition. Each solution had its advocates, as well as its critics.

The roots of American alcohol prohibition are not particularly difficult to uncover. Alcohol had always played a major part in American life. For many on the early American frontier, whiskey had essentially been a currency. It was a relatively easily manufactured commodity which transformed grain into a product which was as desirable as it was portable, preservable and tradable. At the other end of the alcoholic spectrum, beer, cider and wine had always been seen as safe, staple, thirst quenchers in an age when drinking water supplies might well be contaminated and unpleasant, if not poisonous. In times when life for many was frequently harsh enough to be barely endurable, when communities were scattered and entertainment scarce, booze became the only real, affordable recreation and the saloon, bar or tavern, the only meeting place. There was also a more insidious side to alcohol consumption. In an era when tea and coffee were rare, and consequently expensive, their place was largely taken by intoxicating drinks. It is perhaps indicative that President John Adams would drink hard cider rather than tea or coffee with his breakfast. Alcohol was also connected with the working day. Harvest workers were traditionally entitled to a daily pint of rum throughout much of the first half of the nineteenth century. American workers were in the habit of taking "eleveners" of whiskey in the morning and stopping for a "four o'clock dram" in the afternoon.

All this meant that for one reason or another, by 1830, the average American, over the age of 15, consumed in excess of seven gallons of "absolute" alcohol a year. Nor was this all beer and cider, about two-thirds of the total alcohol drunk was spirits. In our own times, when consumption is on the rise again, the same American consumes less than three gallons.[3] Given this rate of use, it is not coincidence that the main killer of US Army troopers on the frontier during the Plains Wars was alcohol-related illness. Perhaps it should also come as no surprise that it was an American—Benjamin Rush, a signatory to the US Constitution, no less—who was the first physician to diagnose alcoholism as a disease, with a recognizable course, and predictable psychological and physical effects. It should also be no surprise that Dr Rush was one of the first modern advocates of temperance.

At the same time as American alcohol consumption peaked at around 1830, the temperance movement had recruited over one and a half million members—10 percent of the population—dedicated at this stage to moderating the use of alcohol. While the movement cited moral and health reasons for this moderation, they also began appealing to the rising industrialists by claiming that the sober worker was 25 percent more productive than his inebriated equivalent. These crusaders held rallies—often rowdy and ribald affairs, even without the booze. They organized preachy lectures given to huge and attentive crowds. The campaign had remarkable successes and but also suffered some setbacks. Foremost among their checks was the time that the most celebrated of the movement's speakers was caught dead drunk in a bordello. Nevertheless, over the next 30 years the movement achieved considerable, if short-lived, triumphs.

True prohibition started in 1851 in Maine when the state passed a law forbidding the sale of all alcohol. Similar laws followed the next year in Massachusetts, Vermont, the Minnesota Territory, and Rhode Island. By 1855, Michigan, Connecticut, Ohio, Indiana, New Hampshire, Delaware, Illinois, Iowa and New York as well as the provinces of Nova Scotia and New Brunswick were also dry. However, by 1858, the zeal behind what was at this point a northern crusade was diverted into, and diluted by, the movement for the abolition of slavery with the result that those laws which remained on the statute books were more honored in the breach than in observance.[4]

Not that alcohol alone inspired the reformers, because if alcohol seemed to be *an* American vice, gambling was perhaps *the* American vice. The huge fortunes to be made in extractive industries from trapping, to fishing, to mining, in land speculation and in agriculture excited a speculative streak in nineteenth-century America which was perhaps unmatched in any other culture. Early American society lacked many of the sophistications and diversions of the more densely populated, more established and urban regions of western Europe, but significantly the US did not lack the wealth. Add to this the fact that the real money was not to be made in the relatively sophisticated urban regions of the country, but on the frontier where morals differed from other regions and the proclivity for gambling becomes even more understandable. The legend of the exploitation of the West was knitted in with self-reliance, ingenuity, hard-living, resilience and, perhaps above all, luck.

One of the results of this individualism was that the heroes of this region were less constrained by the niceties of high society. On the frontier, the "greenhorn" was less an innocent to be chaperoned, educated, and pitied, than a "sap" or "sucker"—a moving target to be preyed upon. According to legend, the West was egalitarian and the advantage was with those with wit, daring, and luck, not inherited title, wealth, or polish—although many of the more socially advantaged still did remarkably well as both speculators and gamblers. As one veteran resident of a Death Valley mining camp advised—"If you can whack a sixteen-bull team, hit a drill, engineer a wheelbarrow, deal faro [the most popular card game of the nineteenth century in America] or shoot, come right along. Otherwise stay where you are."[5] This was a dog-eat-dog world where fortunes were made and lost with frightening speed, often by means which—if there had been law—would have been illegal. Moving to America, moving to the frontier was in itself a gamble. Thriving there meant accepting that gambling was a part of the life choice that had already been made.

The nineteenth century generated a variety of stock gambling figures. Playing on the fluctuating fortunes of what was a highly mobile society in an era of massive land speculation, the Mississippi Valley steamship gambler of the 1840s became an iconic figure in dime novels of the 1880s. He was prized for his ingenuity in his often autobiographical accounts of his sharp ruses and mannerly scams. When this Mississippi land boom came to an end this figure evolved to become the card sharp of the Wild West, renowned in mythology for being as quick to draw an ace as a six-shooter. Then there were the Forty-niners in California, and the miners in Virginia City, the Comstock, Deadwood, and Tombstone who panned and dug fortunes from the West's rivers and hills. More often than not, this good luck deserted them. Many swiftly lost their claims, stakes and finds to each other and the ubiquitous, predatory, card sharp of legend.

There was also another uniquely American type of gambler—but while planted firmly in the New World, this group drew more on the Old. The slave-holding Southern plantation owners, as well as their wives and then their children with their leisurely rural lifestyle, consciously imitated the glitterati of the English landed gentry. Seeking both role models and pedigree, this so-called Plantocracy sought to resemble the aristocracy in their studied manners, fine clothing, love of exquisitely expensive bloodstock, lavish entertainments and above all reckless gambling. From the birth of the Colonies through to the advent of the cotton economy in the 1830s and beyond, they had played the world-weary gamblers, running up huge debts and winning and losing family fortunes at the tracks, on the tables and beside the rings.[6]

At the other end of the spectrum came the pauper gamblers whose stakes may have been negligible by comparison with the land speculators, gold-strikers and Plantocracy, but their addiction to gambling was no less apparent in the literature of the day. With little to stake, the planters' slaves gambled among themselves, or against equally poor whites. Perhaps they were motivated by the example of their masters. Perhaps they simply sought enough money to buy their freedom. Whatever their motivation, in a curious example of *noblesse oblige*—or perhaps in recognition of their own vices—planters often allowed slaves to keep their winnings. Alongside these impoverished residents, there was the immigrant on the passage to America. These unfortunates became known as a class who could be duped of their worldly goods at the card or dice game on the floor of the steerage decks during the Atlantic crossing. Their downfall could come at the hands of a fellow passenger or the notorious professional gambler. Whichever it was, the lesson was the same—those who would prosper must first realize that the whole idea of "America" was a gamble.

Among these immigrants were those who brought with them new forms of gambling or improvements on the old ones. Different nationalities were associated with different forms of gambling, in turn creating and conforming to national/racial stereotypes. The British brought and developed the bloodstock, knowledge, and inspiration for America's thoroughbred racing and the Italians brought faro. Italians were seen as volatile, violent, excitable and superstitious—prone to complex card games, frequently with violent outcomes. The Irish loved their horses—as well as their drink—and would breed and train the horses, make the odds and just as often provide many of the punters for racing. The Russians and Poles with their melancholia would risk all in the suicidal final flutter. The avaricious and immoral Jews would clean up in any game with their inherent ability with money. The unintelligible, clannish and alien Chinese would simply bet on anything.[7]

While many sought to blame the prevalence of gambling on outsiders, perhaps the most widespread and popular form of gambling was the lottery and this had a healthy all-American pedigree. Not only had four separate lotteries been used to raise $10 million to buy supplies for Washington's Continental Army, but also Benjamin Franklin, George Washington and John Hancock all vocally supported lottery financing as a legitimate way of raising revenue for the early Republic. Thomas Jefferson, an inveterate card, backgammon and lottery player, called state lotteries "a painless tax, paid only by the willing."[8] In 1826, he even had plans to improve his personal finances by selling lottery tickets. He died before he could implement them.

By 1832, the nation had some 420 separate lottery draws, which gave revenues totaling over $60 million. An idea of the scale of this figure can be gathered when it is considered that the entire federal budget at the time made up less than 20 percent of that figure and the price of all tickets combined made up around 3 percent of the nation's entire income. What was more, such fundraising was not limited to government activity. Schools, colleges, churches, and private individuals used lotteries to raise funds. In spite of a long-running campaign by religious groups, spearheaded by the Quakers, by 1850, 24 of the Union's 33 states regularly used lotteries to finance capital projects from road construction to government buildings and other major undertakings. The scope for fraud was enormous. A bogus lottery in the 1830s netted over $400,000 and paid nothing in prizes. In Maine, a lottery organizer kept over $10 million for "expenses" although the total ticket sales were $16 million. Given these high profile frauds it is unsurprising that the efforts of the moralists paid off—although only briefly. By the end of the decade, the lottery was banned in all but three border states, although the need to raise wartime funds led to a resurgence of the lottery as a funding option in the South during the years of the Civil War.[9]

With all these nationalities and classes, all over the nation, regularly gambling it was only a question of time before it attracted the attention of those who charged themselves with preserving the public's morals. By the 1820s, gambling houses were technically illegal in all states except Louisiana. There were also periodic controls placed on various sporting events where betting was liable to take place. For example, by the 1820s, most of the more violent blood sports had been banned in most of the states and this was only partially the result of humane considerations. It was more to do with the fact that the brutality, when combined with money changing hands among the lower classes—who made up the majority of those attending the ratting, bull, and bear baiting—was seen as exciting violence and disorder.

More often than not, such bans merely served to drive betting underground, or create a shift in the sports which attracted the punters. For instance, New England and New York banned horse racing between 1792 and 1821. While this ban was in place there was a notable increase in these regions in both bare knuckle boxing and cock fighting which arguably attracted far higher participation and larger stakes. What was more, the period of prohibition did little to diminish the attraction of the sport. When the race tracks were re-opened in New York, the Union race track on Long Island attracted over 60,000 spectators in 1823 to see the northern horse Eclipse race the southern contender Sir Henry for $20,000 prize money.[10]

The final aspect examined in this section is narcotics. The vast majority of laws prohibiting narcotics were instigated after the turn of the twentieth century. That is not to say that there was no recognizable problem, there was. Opiates were the main narcotic of the pre-Civil War era either mixed in with alcohol as laudanum, drunk without alcohol as "black drop" or eaten or smoked as opium resin. However, if a real starting point for America's modern narcotic problem can be found, it must be the invention of the hypodermic syringe in around 1860—a device designed specifically to administer morphine. In the period before this invention, in terms of the recognition of the scale of usage, the inherent dangers and the control of opiates, America lagged behind Britain. In England, the addictions of such notable figures as Samuel Taylor Coleridge and Thomas de Quincy were highlighted and their dependencies seen as having stunted otherwise promising careers. Such high profile cases resulted in an effort within the British medical establishment to understand the mechanisms of addiction while at the same time distancing themselves from irresponsible prescribing; the result was the 1868 Pharmacy Act. Similar regulation would not be introduced in the US until the 1914 Harrison Act.[11]

America's narcotic problem in the pre-Bellum era was to a large extent unrecognized and as a result unregulated. The effects of smoking opium were for the most part calming and soporific with relatively mild hallucinogenic effects unless the dosage was beyond the norm. Addicts would frequently go unnoticed. What was more, medicinally it was prescribed for an extraordinarily wide range of disorders—everything from anxiety; to muscle spasm; to cholera or as a wormer— with the result that there was no particular class, nationality or occupation particularly associated with its use, or misuse. In an age when bleeding with leeches was still prevalent, opiates—even if they had little actual physical effect other than pain relief—at least did make patients *feel* better. Opiates were, therefore, little short of miracle drugs in an age when the average physician had a year's training or less and in a time before germ theory when herbalism or non-sterile surgery remained the most effective weapons in the doctor's arsenal. The result was that during the early nineteenth century per capita crude opium imports grew steadily and the drug was incorporated into a variety of patent medicines which were subject to few real controls either in terms of delivery, usage or content until the 1906 Pure Food and Drug Act.

By the turn of the twentieth century the situation was markedly different. The Progressive urge—with its moral tone, investigative commissions and rational solutions—sparked a wave of prohibitions which covered all three of the areas. The campaign to outlaw booze had re-emerged in the 1880s when seven states had declared themselves dry and a further 14 had taken serious steps towards prohibition. In large measure this had been the result of the mobilization of a new force of moral guardians—the women of America. By a mixture of displays of public Christian piety and sheer perseverance, women, first in the Mid-West and then across the nation, managed to close bars and harangue politicians to pass prohibitive legislation.

Although largely excluded from the ballot, women's power lay in a potent mixture of radical militancy and irrefutable logic. It was women who would suffer most from the familial breakdown caused by alcohol abuse. It was women that would be left to bring up the children in the event of the unemployment, illness or bereavement which often followed the workingman's flirtation with the saloon. It was women who could understand the real extent of the self-loathing and degradation associated with other women's moral decline through alcohol and it was women who made up the larger part of the nation's evangelical congregations. The result was that the Women's Christian Temperance Union (WCTU) converted the zeal which had accompanied the abolitionist movement into pressure not only for alcohol moderation but also for a range of causes associated with women, from sexual purity, to day care for children, and most importantly female suffrage. Temperance had become a women's issue which was clearly illustrated by the fact that in 1918 booze was illegal in 12 of the 13 states where women had full suffrage. As the *New York Times* put it: "Liquor is going out as women suffrage is coming in."[12]

While women were the main drivers of temperance in the late nineteenth century, by contrast, they were one of the main groups of narcotic addicts. The use of morphine in the Civil War had left a tragic group of up to 400,000 addicts—largely from the Union, since the Confederacy was too poor to afford morphine in any quantity. While these men no doubt recruited others, unlike the image later associated with opiates, the lion's share of addicts was a large reservoir of white, middle-class, middle-aged, rural women. An 1880 survey of those using opiates in Chicago found that women outnumbered men, 3 to 1 and the average age of user was around 46 years old. Similarly an investigation of users in Michigan in 1878 found that over 60 percent were female.[13] One estimate puts these women as representing between 56 and 71 percent of addicts at a time when the rate of opiate addiction was over twice the estimate for the late 1990s.[14]

Perhaps these figures should not be so surprising. This was an age of prurience and chauvinism, where the feminine world was still governed by the strict mores of propriety and obedience and when morphine, as well as codeine and laudanum, was frequently doled out to silence a wide range of "women's problems." Chief among these was the characteristically Victorian problem—created by the increasing frenetic pace of modern life—neurasthenia, or nervous exhaustion, but they included a range of gynecological and psycho-sexual conditions including post-parturient injuries and post-natal depression, as well as nymphomania and masturbation. In addition, there were a group of women—largely prostitutes—who used large, self-administered, doses of opiates in order to interrupt or stop menstruation as a form of contraception.

It is perhaps because due in part to the medical origins of these habits and the fact that these patriots and middle-class women made up such prominent groups of addicts that even though such behavior was regarded as a "vice," the problem was generally medicalized rather criminalized. Essentially, these users were seen largely as victims rather than criminals. What was more, those addicts of the lower orders who chose to use these drugs would no doubt be picked up for other crimes—perhaps prostitution, robbery or vagrancy—so the necessity, at this point, to create a new level of criminal behavior was largely overlooked. Some would argue that it was only when the class of addict and nature of their drug of choice changed that criminalization became necessary, but in reality the situation was more complex than that. While the class of user is important, the overall legislative drivers were actually more complex, they were also reliant on a combination of who it was that sought reform, why they sought it and who benefited.[15]

The first federal anti-opium law was the 1909 Smoking Opium Exclusion Act. This legislation was aimed at opium processed specifically for smoking, a habit largely associated with a group of unpopular non-Americans—the Chinese. China imported over 95 percent of the world's opium and was home to over 16 million regular opium smokers. Since the onset of Chinese emigration to the Pacific regions of the US in the late 1840s, the opium den had been seen as a hazard. Since this form of opiate was seen as having no form of medicinal value and was purely recreational, it attracted opprobrium from a variety of quarters. Missionaries reported that the lethargic legacy of years of opium smoking had contributed to China's political, military, and moral decline. Temperance advocates saw little difference between the inebriation of the drunkard and the stupor of the opium smoker. Moral crusaders argued that Chinese addicts acted as "pushers" and sought out vulnerable victims—frequently teenage girls—who they turned into addicts, if not worse.

The result was that in 1875, at the height of Denis Kearney's violently anti-Chinese crusade, San Francisco—the city with the largest Chinese population on the West Coast—banned public opium dens. Portland, Seattle and the other main cities of the region swiftly followed suit. However, from 1875 until 1909, the private use of opium remained legal, providing the federal government with a revenue stream averaging a million dollars a year via import duties while contributing to the sinister image of the Chinese in the mind of many Americans.[16] In these years of the "Yellow Peril," even the most liberal-minded of Americans began to see more disturbingly insidious forces at work. Opium was seen as just one more way in which the Mongolian Hordes threatened to overthrow white America, because, as Jacob Riis informed his readers in 1890,

> The Chinaman smokes opium as Caucasians smoke tobacco, and apparently with little worse effect upon himself. But woe betide the white victim upon which this pitiless drug gets its grip. Opium destroys the Chinaman far less surely, quickly and completely than it destroys the Caucasian and Americans in particular.[17]

There were also other racial threats associated with narcotics which tied the various different drugs with similarly prevalent images of a variety of nationalities in America over these years. In line with their image as a more industrious, ruthless, and intelligent race, Japanese immigrants were seen as being involved with the opium trade, but as dealers, pushers, and businessmen, rather than like the Chinese, simply as users and addicts. Mexicans, with their indolence and un-American habits, became indelibly linked with the growing, use, and sale of cannabis. As a Texan Senator bluntly argued "All Mexicans are crazy, and this stuff [referring to marijuana] is what makes them crazy." This link was so strong that even the American term for the drug came from the Mexican slang—Mary Jane or Marijuana—and the drive for banning the drug came from New Mexico and Texas, the two states with the highest proportion of Mexicans in their boundaries.[18]

Nevertheless, unsurprisingly, it was those who constituted the most prevalent and numerous "racial threat" in America who had the greatest impact on US perceptions of crime and race. As the new century opened, cocaine was increasingly seen as fueling the newfound confidence and increasing reports of the aggression of the "Negro." While much of this can be put down to simply white prejudice, there was a genuine proclivity among the Southern black males to use the newly discovered drug. Not only did it provide a pleasant detachment from what was frequently an extremely harsh reality, but it was relatively cheap, easily administered (frequently as a powder), hard to detect and, if necessary, easy to conceal.

Cocaine's popularity among this section of the population probably also drew on its energy-giving properties. It was used by the Mississippi River and New Orleans stevedores in the early 1880s, where it enabled them to work long hours in extremes of both heat and cold. There is also evidence that this practice spread, and employers from planters to mine owners frequently encouraged its use among their manual laborers, some even went as far as replacing the traditional whiskey or rum ration with the energizing powder. The radical unionist, William, "Big Bill," Haywood, saw an even more sinister angle to this, claiming that once addicted, workers would stay with the employer in order to insure their supply of the drug.[19]

Like the opiates before it, from its first synthesis in Germany in 1860 and throughout most of the nineteenth century, cocaine had been regarded as something of a wonder drug. Sigmund Freud famously used the drug himself and recommended it for treating conditions as varied as the ubiquitous neurasthenia and asthma. Other physicians found it valuable as an anesthetic for eye surgery, a treatment for gastric conditions and providing some relief from wasting diseases. Along with Bayer's recently patented opiate derivative, "Heroin" (so-called for its "heroic" properties), cocaine was seen as a very effective tool with which to combat alcohol and morphine abuse and addiction. Given its wide range of applications, like the opiates before it, cocaine was included in a bewildering variety of patent medicines. Through elixirs, tonics to soft drinks, including one with the shockingly honest name of "Dope Cola," it was claimed that the wonder drug could cure sinus trouble and blood disorders and also relieve headaches and toothache. According to one source, in one form or another, Americans consumed almost 11 tons of cocaine in 1906 alone.[20] Most importantly for the criminal implications, cocaine was meant to treat "sexual apathy."

In the minds of the turn-of-the-century white readership of the mass-circulation newspapers, it was felt that the average working-class black male did not suffer from "sexual apathy." Far from it, he was seen as sexually voracious, especially when it came to white women. Supercharging the appetites of these libidinous creatures with drugs and adding the frisson of race was the perfect material for a moral panic and it was the *New York Times* which led the charge. According to the newspaper, here was a terrible national threat. The country was undergoing a "cocaine plague" among the most numerous and most threatening of the underclasses of America. Citing medical "experts" and using sensational language, the public was told how the Southern Negro, usually barbaric, when supplied with cocaine by "every Jew peddler in the South," was made little short of a monster. The *Times* reported "nine men [had been] killed in Mississippi on one occasion by crazed cocaine takers, [and a further] five in North Carolina and three [more] in Tennessee." Since emancipation, the Southern black had been viewed as a threat, and increasingly the root of that threat was sexual. No white woman was safe.

Cocaine was a threat greater than any the nation had so far faced because it formed "a hideous bondage from which [unlike slavery] they [these black cocaine addicts] cannot escape by mere proclamation or Civil War." In the years from 1908 to 1914, the *Times* detailed cases of blacks driven so wild by cocaine that "bullets fired into vital parts that would drop a sane man in his tracks fail to check the fiend[s]." It explained how frustrated Southern sheriffs had been forced to increase the caliber of hand guns from .32 to .38 just to have a chance of stopping berserk

"Negro cocaine fiends." The *Times* detailed how as a consequence of this mayhem the sale of cocaine had already been made a felony in many Southern states.[21] This hyperbole was to have huge national and international repercussions. During these years Americans would put their prohibitionist efforts into a campaign which would shape criminality all over the world in which we now live. In order to understand them, it is helpful to look at the influence of one particular activist.

If one single person can be considered the driving force behind this *Times* campaign, it has to be the indomitable Dr Hamilton Wright. Wright was an ambitious Canadian medical researcher specializing in tropical and nervous disorders. However, having married into a wealthy political family, Wright soon realized that he was better suited to the public life and shifted his interests away from medical research and into political lobbying. Through his wife's connections with the upper echelons of the Republican Party, he secured a position on a State Department Opium Commission and quickly rose to become one of the foremost experts on the domestic and international drug control movement. The time was ripe for reform and this commission was to have a major impact. Some historians have argued that this was not because the drug problem in the US was particularly bad, or even that the reformist urge was irresistible—although both hyperbole and the Progressive mood of the times played a part—but, they argue, it more was because the State Department had begun to highlight drug policy as a priority.[22]

While at first glance it may seem curious that the State Department was so interested in narcotics, a closer examination reveals a rational connection. American diplomats realized that opium, morality, and international trade could potentially be beneficially interlinked. The result was that they gave Wright's campaign considerable support. The logic behind the sudden interest was convoluted. It stems back to early twentieth-century diplomacy, where the markets of the decaying empire of China were considered one of the last serious commercial prizes in a world in which all the great colonial gems in Africa and Asia had already been grabbed.

Late to enter the colonization race—at least outside her own continental boundaries—many Americans felt they were not getting their fair share. Having gained Caribbean and Pacific Ocean dependencies in the wake of the Spanish American War, in 1899, the then Secretary of State, John Hay, rather high-handedly demanded what he called an "Open Door" policy on trade with China. Under this agreement the major concessionary powers in China (France, Germany, the United Kingdom, Italy, Russia and, even non-European, Japan) would effectively allow equal access to all Chinese markets for all nations, regardless of the size of the trade concessions the Chinese had already granted. The US was grappling with this effective lock-out from what they saw as potentially limitless markets.

In spite of their public lip service to free trade, rather predictably, the European and Japanese concessionaries ignored the request. As a result, the Americans turned to a strategy of gaining the moral high ground and trying to gain access through gaining popular support in China. Since the trade in opium, led by Britain, was seen as one of the reasons for Chinese decline, American efforts to stamp out the opium trade would, they felt, indicate an unusual degree of sincerity and altruism and hopefully persuade the Chinese that the US was different from the other powers. In essence, the US State Department argued that by advocating the abolition of the opium trade, America would appear more interested in aiding China's battle with narcotics and establishing a true basis of mutually beneficial trade, rather than in feeding off the remains of her decaying empire.

Wright had been one of the American delegates at the 1909 Opium Conference, suitably enough held in Shanghai. At this gathering of all the major powers, the Americans pushed on with their Chinese policy and Wright was in the thick of it. He had personally been instrumental in the Conference's reaching the agreement that all the participating nations would treat the non-medical use of opium via prohibition. On his return he used his considerable influence to make sure that America led, and would continue to lead the way in the pressure for a global criminalization of narcotics use throughout the twentieth century and beyond. Through a mixture of media management, dubious statistics, hyperbole and scare tactics, Wright gained considerable support for the idea that state laws outlawing opium usage or the supply of cocaine were simply not sufficient, what was required was federal legislation. To this end, he sent out questionnaires to law enforcement and prison officers, doctors, and drug companies in order to compile "accurate" statistics on the problem. With this information he lobbied newspapers and congressmen and also put considerable pressure on European governments to control the supplies of opium, cocaine, and Indian hemp coming from their colonial possessions into the United States.

Wright and his colleagues found themselves confronted by a dilemma. When attending a series of narcotics limitation conferences at The Hague between 1912 and 1914, Britain and other colonial powers made it clear that they resented the Americans' moralizing tone. They pointed out that the United States was in no position to preach prohibition to other nations when it had no real, effective, controls at home. The result of this pressure was the relatively unheralded passage of what one of the leading historians of Prohibition memorably referred to as a measure of greater "spiritual malignancy than the Volstead Act"—the 1914 Harrison Act.[23] This Act was highly significant to the development of the criminalization of narcotics in America. Not only did it introduce federal punishments for failure to conform to new requirements for the supply, use, and movement of opiates, cocaine, and marijuana, but as a result of later refinements over the next decade, it effectively criminalized the supply of addicts by doctors. It also set in train the entire framework of modern American drug prohibition.[24]

A previous attempt to introduce similar legislation in 1911, the Foster Bill, had been scuppered by a coalition of drug companies, pharmacists, and doctors resenting the inferences and the interference in their markets by non-experts. By 1914, even their objections were muted and the Act slid through Congress unscathed leaving an admiring Secretary of State, William Jennings Bryan, asking Wright, "How did you manage it?"[25] In keeping with Bryan's incredulity, while most modern texts tend to stress the Harrison Act as being the effective starting point of the US war on drugs, at the time it slipped beneath most of the American public's notice. Some idea of this can be gathered by the fact that although the measure was signed into law by President Woodrow Wilson on December 17, 1914, in spite of the paper's ongoing campaign against narcotics abuse, it was not even reported in the *New York Times* until January 2, 1915. This may seem relatively unimportant given the war being fought in Europe and the holiday nature of the time of year but by contrast the debates surrounding the Volstead Act took up massive amounts of column inches for months before, during, and after it became law. The passage of the Act was the banner headline the day after the Senate overrode Wilson's veto in the same newspaper. As the historian David Musto put it, the question with drugs was one of *how* to outlaw their use, not, as with alcohol, *whether* to ban it.[26]

There were a variety of instructive reasons which each go some way to explain why this fundamental difference existed in the criminalization of the two "vices." In part, it was the result of the seeming anomaly that while a large proportion of Americans condoned moderate drinking, as one expert on opiate addiction put it in 1928, "opium use in any form is regarded by the general public as alone a habit, vice, sign of weak will or dissipation."[27] Once the forces of prohibition had been unleashed on drug taking, the user—however moderate his or her consumption—was regarded as an asocial outcast, a degenerate, and a dangerous criminal. Alcohol had a social function in American society. Some abused it, but it was, and had been, sanctioned by Americans at all levels of society. The Bible even contained references to its manufacture and use. By contrast, opium dens had been seen to be frequented by undesirable Chinese and some weaker members of white society—largely, innocent young girls and weak-willed men. Cocaine was portrayed as a drug for the bestial Negro and the urban poor. The far more numerous mainstream addicts—white, middle-class women; prescription drug and, before the Pure Food and Drug Act of 1906, patent medicine addicts as well as medical practitioners who self-administered their habit—had been more or less invisible until the prohibitionists had highlighted their presence and indicated how, if these Americans could become users, all Americans were at risk.

Once reformers shone their lights into the murky world of narcotics, what they exposed became a warning of the dangers inherent in a whole host of changes taking place in American society at the time. What the public gathered from these highly publicized accounts was that the emerging drug companies, soon to be household names, seemed more than happy to emulate the shocking morals of the Robber Barons, incorporating addictive drugs into their products and resisting legislation which would limit such practices. At the professional and commercial level, these morals were emulated by doctors, pharmacists, and soda-fountain owners who continued the lucrative trade although they knew it to be damaging to their addicted customers and clients. At the lowest end of the social scale, there were the drug dealers who not only fed the vices of their users but used the likes of "janitors, barmen and cabmen . . . [as 'pushers'] to help spread the habit."[28]

These were the years of the rapid urbanization of America. The nation had developed from a rural society in 1865, where vastly more Americans lived and worked in the agrarian sectors, to becoming an urban society where, by 1920, the majority of Americans lived in settlements of 2,500 residents or more. This phenomenon was seen as upsetting, if not removing, America's moral compass. To a variety of groups, from the early twentieth-century rural Progressives of the Country Life Movement, to the Ku Klux Klan of the 1920s, the city was seen as a place of squalor, corruption, and temptation. Cities bred the vice and crime associated with booze and narcotics. Popular perceptions dictated that alcoholics were frequently violent, but always wastrels who were incapable of proper work. Narcotics addicts required money to feed their habits. Between them, whether through promiscuity, immorality, robbery or prostitution, the city offered more varied and lucrative possibilities than rural or small town America could offer. The city also attracted the waifs and strays, the hopeful and the gullible, that were more likely to form easy prey for the pushers, pimps, and dealers already living there.

It is an indication of the changing perception of drug use that in the ground-breaking, best-selling, novel *Porgy* of 1925—later immortalized as George Gershwin's *Porgy and Bess*—the heroine, Bess, is seduced by Sportin' Life, a malevolent "city Negro" who uses cocaine in order to break down her resistance.[29] The prevalence of such interpretations grew as temperance propaganda gave way to prohibition, as the user gave way to the addict, but even so, some groups chose to look at the prevalent opinions from another viewpoint. Since it was illegal to sell alcohol, a small sub-group of Americans took the attitude that they may as well use other illegal substances. These was nothing new in this, earlier experiments with prohibition in the South had led to a shift towards the use of cocaine in the poor blacks of the region. In 1914, the *New York Times* had trumpeted that black Southerners, in many of the states where they were a majority, had "taken to 'sniffing' since being deprived of whisky by prohibition."[30] By the 1920s, this attitude had spread across the nation and into different classes.

As the decade progressed, it became increasingly established in the small, decadent, upper-class "fast set" with money and questionable morals. This elite group of society with its image as self-conscious *avant-garde* trendsetters was willing to question the existing norms and mores. While it could be argued that such super-wealthy hedonists always had found—and always will find—their thrills in more dangerous experiments than those available to or desired by the common herd, in these years of excess, prohibition provided another spur. Both male and female "Jazz Age" thrill-seekers smoked opium and marijuana and used cocaine as they mingled with the underworld in night clubs, cabarets, speakeasies and high class private members' clubs where the booze flowed and the police, often handsomely paid to do so, ignored it. Curiously, while this group certainly attracted far more attention, their antics may actually have served to reduce the urban narcotics problem—at least locally. According to one commentator, in the most infamous of these clubs, the Cotton Club and the Plantation Club, in New York's then highly fashionable Harlem district, the money paid by whites for booze, cocaine, opium, and marijuana led to an increase in price which made these commodities way beyond the reach of the far more numerous local residents' pockets.[31]

If illegal drink and drugs spread through all levels of society during this period, gambling was already prevalent at all levels. There was little new in this. It had permeated all levels of American society since colonial days. While the wealthy colonial planters had often frittered away fortunes on the after dinner gambling tables, their indentured servants had been known to use wagers and lotteries as a way to squirrel away enough to terminate their period of indenture. This had continued with the Plantocracy and their slaves. It appears that although these relationships were often riddled with hypocrisy, at least with respect to gambling, a level of, almost, equality sometimes existed. Some planters allowed servants, and even slaves, to keep their winnings. Others enforced strict, if often hypocritical measures, to outlaw any gambling, punishing it with severe floggings.[32] As the twentieth century opened, industrialization had not really changed this, perhaps all it had changed was there were now wealthier gamblers at the top and poorer ones at the bottom. By 1900, betting was still both a mark of conspicuous consumption for the wealthy—a term coined at the turn of the twentieth century by the sociologist Thorstein Veblen—and of desperation for the poor.

Perhaps inevitably just as social reformers no longer relied on purely religious objections to justify their control of drinking and drug taking, the same was true with gambling. As the new century dawned, as the other vices became associated with sexual promiscuity, prostitution and robbery, so gambling was increasingly associated with other criminal and immoral behavior and the lenient attitude taken towards betting was changing. Gambling "dens," "hells," and "dives" increasingly tended to be cordoned off into one area of the town or city, ostensibly facilitating law-keeping and sparing the city's more sensitive residents inconvenience and unnecessary distress. In reality, they simply concentrated many vices into one area. Gambling was frequently carried out in all-male environments—saloons, clubs, tracks, rings or pits—where the only women, and perhaps some of the men, were liable to be prostitutes. It was rare that drink was not a vital element and, given the company and the lubrication, the atmosphere was hardly likely to elicit exemplary behavior.

What was more, gambling was, as the Muckraker of the slums, Jacob Riis, put it "by instinct and by nature brutal, because it is selfishness in its coldest form."[33] As the twentieth century dawned and America underwent one of its periods of reform, the much publicized excesses of the Gilded Age had made such selfishness repugnant. In the decades either side of 1900 the star of the Progressives was very much in the ascendant. A disparate group made up of largely urban, largely

Christian and largely white reformers, the Progressives advocated civic responsibility, the Social Gospel and rational, scientific reform. Irrational, unChristian and irresponsible, gambling was one of their targets. In 1894, Louisiana finally outlawed lotteries, making state lotteries illegal across the entire Union. By 1900, only the states of Maryland, Kentucky and New York allowed trackside betting at the races. The process of banning gambling dens was started by California, beginning with specific games, spreading through premises, to house banks and finally all players in 1891. By 1910, casinos and other gambling dens were almost universally illegal in America.

As with drinking or drug taking, there was a strong class influence on attitudes to the legitimacy of gambling establishments. Patrician Americans' use of clubs and salons, where gambling and drinking were frequent and accepted, were not the primary target of the prohibitionists' rhetoric. The bulk of condemnation was aimed at the dingy, dirty saloon, selling rot gut and frequented by working men. As one commentator said:

> The country club people will probably go on boozing until the end of time. The best prohibition can hope to accomplish is to save the poor man. It saves him by making drink too expensive for him.[34]

Similarly, the middle-class, white, woman's laudanum or opium habit, or the physician's self-administered cocaine were not the underlying reason for the prohibitionist Harrison Act. That was motivated by poor blacks' use of cocaine and fear that the Chinese opium fiend would push his wares on poor whites. Similarly, and even more strikingly, the majority of gambling regulations were not aimed at those who like Jay Gould or even Arnold Rothstein, men who would gamble hundreds of thousands or even millions of dollars. Regulation of gambling seemed to be aimed at those who would buy lottery tickets or who would place a bet on a favorite horse. Nothing seemed to illustrate this better than the legislation against the "bucket shop."

Imitating their wealthier fellow citizens, many humble urban Americans took to playing the stock market in the final decades of the nineteenth century. Thousands would use small, illegitimate, unregulated, "boiler rooms" and "bucket shops" to speculate on the movement of the securities and futures in companies listed on the New York Stock Exchange. Arguing that since the bucket shops were unregulated and did not actually sell shares and that no certificates changed hands, such speculation was simply gambling. As the *National Police Gazette* put it:

> The spirit of stock gambling is abroad in the land ... The desire to get rich quick without earning it by the sweat of one's brow is a strong incentive to stock gambling ... Did the Vanderbilts, did the Astors ... did one hundred and one other rich men of this country get rich by stock gambling? Answer this question yourself and if you do this truthfully, it will not be "yes."[35]

Unlike the "speculation of this kind [carried out] by competent men" which Supreme Court Justice Oliver Wendell Holmes claimed was a "means of avoiding or mitigating catastrophes, equalizing prices and providing for periods of want," the customers of the bucket shop simply bet for their own profit and should be outlawed.[36] Since there were no universally recognized professional qualifications for brokers, let alone speculators, quite who constituted a "competent man" must have been open to debate. Nevertheless given this distinction, by the 1920s, in time for the greatest bull market up to that point in US history, most of the major urban centers had effectively outlawed such unregulated brokerages.

However, even without the means of the bucket shop, many foreign observers, as well as Americans, still felt that there was a strong link between gambling and the stock market. The mania that grabbed over three million Americans as the stock boom reached a peak in the late 1920s was difficult to differentiate from the fervor of gambling. It certainly appeared so to the old financial elite. This group grudgingly complained that the times were changing when "bootblacks, household servants, and clerks . . . school teachers, seamstresses, barbers, machinists, necktie salesmen, gas fitters, motormen, family cooks, and lexicographers" all had brokerage accounts. They made serious efforts to outlaw such speculation. In February 1928, at the height of the stock bubble, the US Senate Committee on Banking and Currency debated the banning of stock trading. The nation's Senators agreed: "There is no trouble at all in stopping the gambling . . . We have a law against poker gambling, and we can have a law against stock gambling."

The debate hinged on the dilemma which had lain behind the banning of bucket shops. How did legislation preserve the "necessary" and "legitimate" being raised on the open market while outlawing that trading which could be viewed as purely speculative and accumulative? The problem was how to recognize what constituted the illegitimate. As US Senator Earle Mayfield of Texas, fresh from the fight to ban alcohol, informed his fellow Senators, "There are millions of stocks and bonds sold every day by people who do not own them and have no idea of owning them. Purely gambling on the market." Such thinking was not limited to the provincial puritans or even the financially naïve. Virginia Senator, Carter Glass, former Secretary of the Treasury under Wilson, one of the devisors of the Federal Reserve System and co-sponsor of the Glass–Seagal Act, illustrated the problem in terms of stock values. He gave the example of a share which he personally owned. It had nearly halved in value in less than a year. The share had done this without reporting any devastatingly poor accounts or any other rational cause. Given this seemingly randomly generated decline, he asked his fellow Senators: "Now what is that but gambling?"[37] Needless to say, given the devastation caused by the 1929 Crash, over a year later, and the turbulence which has occurred so many times since, the concerned Senators failed in these efforts. Many Americans still sought, and still seek, to isolate the gamblers from the speculators: the criminals from the "competent."

If a small group of Senators failed to isolate "stock gamblers" from businessmen, the same failure was not true of another part of the federal government's attempts to ban another vice. The reasons for the success and failure are enlightening. The Federal Bureau of Narcotics (FBN) under its charismatic, ambitious and driven leader, Harry Anslinger, began an active campaign to make the use, transport, and sale of marijuana a federal offense. Since California had banned its use in 1915, marijuana had been outlawed in a growing number of states, until by 1937 it was outlawed in all the states of the Union. Nevertheless, to most Americans who were even aware of its existence, unlike stock speculation, it was not considered to be a serious problem to the morality or wealth of those who indulged in its use.

Unlike the nation's Senators, the FBN saw such legislation falling directly within their remit and there can be little doubt that there was an element of "empire-building" behind Anslinger's enthusiasm. Unlike the Senators, they could produce direct "scientific" data which showed a direct correlation between usage, addiction, and criminal activity. Like the campaign against alcohol, Anslinger mobilized all media. He showed the correlation between the "killer weed" and sexual license, family breakdown, violence, and insanity. As he told the House Ways and Means Committee in 1936:

> Some people will fly into a delirious rage, and they are temporarily irre-
> sponsible and may commit violent crimes. Other people will laugh uncon-
> trollably. It is impossible to say what the effect will be on any individual.
> [Nevertheless] ... It is dangerous to the mind and body, and particularly
> dangerous to the criminal type, because it releases all of the inhibitions.[38]

With this in mind, unlike the Senators, the opponents of marijuana were committed to outlawing what they saw as a minority practice, not one which had devolved down from the respectable classes. This was a drug whose users largely came from Mexico, or were urban blacks. Like the prohibition on cocaine, Anslinger used this segregated usage as an argument to create a moral panic. Here were small, identifiable, alien groups who were attempting to pollute the American nation. It seemed that this was true since, like the revelers who drank, took cocaine and heroin and, indeed, marijuana, in degenerate Harlem, those whites who used the drug tended to be Bohemian, jazz-loving, *demi-monde* types. Unlike the Senators, Anslinger persisted until Congress passed the Marijuana Taxation Act, in 1937.[39]

Deciding which "vices" should be made illegal is only a part of the influence of such prohibitions on criminalization in the history of modern America. Arguably more important than what was outlawed, or why, is the influence that such legislation itself had on crime. Did prohibiting alcohol improve the quality of life for the ex-drinker and his family? Did it do away with the saloons as hubs of criminal activity? Did legislation proscribing more or less free access to narcotics really prevent the creation of addicts, and the resultant criminal activity? Did banning street games, race track betting, casinos, lotteries and other gambling really stop associated criminal behavior? Or were these prohibitions really just responsible for driving such practices underground, increasing the money available to those willing to indulge those addicted to, or simply requiring, alcohol, drugs or other outlawed "kicks"?

America was not the first modern industrialized state to outlaw booze. By the time the Volstead Act came into force in January 1920, alcohol was illegal in the Soviet Union; in Iceland (where beer remained illegal through until 1989); in Norway and in Finland. It had been prohibited, briefly, the year before, in Hungary under Bela Kun's brutally communist regime and Prince Edward Island in Canada would remain dry right through until 1948. With these other examples in mind, why is it that today prohibition is almost uniquely associated with the United States? Certainly, America was the most populous and the wealthiest of these states, but the essence of the answer must most likely lie with the perceived changes it wrought on US society, most importantly conflation of crime with the Noble Experiment. In this regard, America is seen as unique. Unlike the US, the exclusion of booze in Finland over the same period, for example, is not regarded in the historical memory—at least not in America—with shootouts, corruption, bootlegging and gangsterism. In fact, according to one American correspondent in 1929, throughout the period of the ban, which lasted from 1919 until 1932, a large minority of Finns ignored the legislation in much the same way as their American contemporaries. After ten years as a "Dry" state, Finland's figures for alcohol-related illnesses as well as convictions for drunkenness, violent crime and firearms offenses all grew dramatically, as did the prison population. Bootleggers brought in branded liquor, largely from Germany and Poland and the illegally distilled clear spirit, "Ninety-Six"—so-called because of its hideously high alcohol content—was near ubiquitous in all urban and metropolitan cafés and restaurants.[40]

So why is American Prohibition considered unique? It is perhaps the scale of crime it was seen to unleash. According to one survey taken in 30 US cities, there was a 24 percent increase in the crime rate between 1920 and 1931. The rate of arrests on account of drunkenness rose 41 percent, and arrests for drunken driving increased by over 80 percent. Thefts went up by nearly 10 percent, and assault and battery incidents rose some 13 percent. Before Prohibition, there had only been a little over 4000 federal convicts, of whom less than 3000 were housed in federal prisons. By 1932, the number of federal convicts had increased by 561 percent and the federal prison population had grown by over 350 percent. Moreover, it appeared that it was prohibitions which seemed to lie at the root of this increase, since over two-thirds of all prisoners convicted in 1930 were imprisoned on alcohol and drug-related charges.[41]

Prohibition's influences on crime are varied. It is generally held that the 1920s saw an explosion in gangsterism and that this came about as the result of Prohibition. However there is some dispute as to *which* prohibition it was that caused this. The prohibition of alcohol, it is claimed, gave a much needed shot in the arm to flagging professional, organized crime in the 1920s. One perspective sees the Progressive Era as having removed many of the traditional income streams which had fed large-scale criminal activity, after all, during these years the nation was undergoing one of its periodic spells of reform fervor. The cleaning up of metropolitan and urban government had done away with the bread and butter income of many of the strong-arm gangs who had intimidated and cajoled voters and opponents for the machines in local politics. Wartime crusades against prostitution had also done away with another traditional source of the mobsters' income. When the Progressives instigated what was arguably their final reform—banning alcohol—they revived gangsterism and gave gangsters sufficient capital and income to raise professional crime to a new level. Here was an easily produced, relatively valuable, and easily shippable commodity with a huge market. The profits available to those willing to break the law were huge and these massive profits in turn generated economies of scale and entirely new ways of developing criminal businesses.[42]

Another view sees the roots of crime syndication as going way back before this period, and sees gambling as the engine. In this interpretation it is the clampdown on urban gambling houses in the major cities—most notably Chicago, New York, and New Orleans—which provides the impetus for criminal syndication. When New York introduced anti-gaming legislation in 1867, John, "Old Smoke," Morrissey formed an association of professional gamblers, whose aim was to protect themselves from raids by the authorities. By buying off police and other officials, Morrissey's association managed not only to defend itself from disruptive raids, but their mounting wealth also enabled them to become a significant force in the political activity of the city. By the late 1870s, Morrissey's syndicate was challenging and defeating even the mighty Tammany Hall's power in its previously unassailable strongholds in the city's Fourth and Seventh wards.[43] Similar criminal organizations emerged over the next decade in response to other attempted purges on gambling. The most notorious of these was in New Orleans where a formal system of bribing policemen and politicians at all levels ensured that professional gamblers were left in peace. In Chicago, a syndicate used their financial and organizational muscle to replace a particularly troublesome mayor with a more amenable candidate of their own.[44]

As the historian Mark Haller pointed out, the power of these criminal syndications was such that by the end of the nineteenth century in some cities, "it was not so much that gambling syndicates influenced local political organization; rather, gambling syndicates were [the] local political organizations."[45] Syndicated, organized crime depended on the ability of the criminal "underworld" to have connections with, and protection from, a legitimate "upperworld"—police, lawyers, judges, business leaders, and politicians. Without this complicity the syndicate could never really evolve as criminal entrepreneurs. In this respect the outlawing of both gambling and alcohol provided the catalyst for what historian Humbert S. Nelli called crime's "Great Leap Forward." The lack of a genuine consensus supporting the bans, coupled with the huge market and the massive profits available, meant that those willing to take the risks of producing, importing, shipping, and selling alcohol were able to pay previously unheard amounts to those willing to turn a blind eye, or even facilitate their law breaking. Some prescient opponents of the Volstead Act claimed it would re-introduce an "Old Spoils Evil" reminiscent of the worst days of Tammany's graft.[46]

In fact, in many ways, it turned out to be worse. Bribery reached truly epic proportions. The best example of the spoils available to the ambitious is the tale of George Remus. Within two years of the enacting of the Volstead Act, the Cincinnati-based, German-American bootlegger, Remus, had built up a chain of fake drug stores across the Mid-West. The network employed some 3,000 people selling "medicinal whisky" and he was well on the way to having cornered the American whiskey market. Remus' bonded warehouses were selling "industrial" alcohol by the truck or trainload. What was more, it seemed he was living a charmed life, behaving in an ostentatiously generous fashion. He ran a fleet of cars for his own personal use and held huge parties where the most famous and attractive would rub shoulders with the more brutal of Cincinnati's citizens, as the booze flowed, openly. He once gave 50 women who attended one such party of his a new Pontiac car each, as a parting gift.

All this was done without his actually owning a legitimate business to support such extravagance. It later emerged that he was only able to sustain his imperial-scale business and lifestyle by paying out an estimated $20 million a year—probably half of his annual turnover—as bribes and payoffs. Events would prove that even this was not enough. By the end of May 1922, Remus had been sentenced to a two-year jail sentence and fined $10,000 for bootlegging. More or less unconcerned and confident that his powerful connections would prove sufficiently motivated to quash the charges, he continued to expand his operation while appealing against his sentence. He was over-confident in their abilities and power. By 1924, with all avenues of appeal finally closed, Remus was imprisoned in Atlanta. He ruefully commented later that—"A few men tried to corner the wheat market only to find there is too much wheat in the world. I tried to corner the graft market only to find there is not enough money in the world to buy up all the public officials."[47]

There were a number of reasons for Remus' downfall, but perhaps the most important was that his over-confidence and extravagance meant he came to the attention of Burt Morgan and Sam Collins, respectively the Prohibition directors of Indiana and Kentucky. These two officials were as committed to keeping their states dry as they were persistent, cunning, and incorruptible. They were also highly unusual. Even if the majority of the nation had been committed to the eradication of alcoholic drinks, the task would have been difficult. With support largely concentrated in the South and rural areas of the Mid-West, the 12,000 miles of US coastline plus the lengthy land borders with Canada and Mexico were nearly impossible to police effectively. The forces charged with prohibition were dreadfully under-resourced. Although they might be able to call on coastguard and police forces, at their peak in 1930, less than 3,000 Prohibition agents across the nation were pitted against an estimated 50,000 involved in the illegal booze industry in Michigan alone. In New York City, even the diminutive, but feisty, Mayor, Fiorello La Guardia, realized it was a hopeless task. He claimed it would require 250,000 police to stand a chance of making Prohibition work. What was more, as Remus' tale illustrates, the majority of these agents were hardly committed to catching bootleggers or rum runners. LaGuardia was aware of this when he told Franklin Roosevelt that even if he had the required manpower for interception, he would require a further 250,000 to police the police.[48]

Even when the authorities were genuinely dedicated to enforcing the law, they frequently found themselves hamstrung by what appeared to be legal niceties. The necessity to produce a warrant meant that all but those basest of "blind pigs" (low-end drinking dives) would have been forewarned and all but the most inept smugglers and moonshiners would have paid off the relevant agents. One prose-cuting attorney in Michigan lamented that the system was weighted against the law when he told the court ruefully that "If the [US] Constitution could speak, it would say 'Thou shalt not traffic in intoxicating liquor, but if you do I shall lend my best efforts to prevent its being proved.' "[49] The result was that the most successful Prohibition agents felt that they could only enforce the Volstead Act by breaking or bending the law themselves. As one confessed, he had entrapped bell boys in hotels through claiming he had the mother of all hangovers and pleading with them to get him a hair of the dog. As he explained, "Then a raid followed, the hotel is pinched and the bell-hop arrested—a most glorious achievement for the officials of the great United States."[50]

Another aspect of the problem was summed up when the Seattle policeman turned bootlegger Roy Olmstead was convicted by the use of illegal wiretaps. The Supreme Court ruled that since force was not used, it could not be unreasonable search and seizure, but two of the Justices dissented. One, Oliver Wendell Holmes, saw the problem clearly and argued that, "We have to choose, and for my part I think it is less evil that some criminals should escape than that the government should play an ignoble part [in their conviction]." The other, Louis Brandeis, warned, "Crime is contagious. If the government becomes a lawbreaker it breeds contempt for the law ... It invites anarchy."[51] Some commentators thought anarchy had already been established. The US homicide rate had quadrupled in the first two decades of the twentieth century, and it reached a peak in the 1920s. Some simply saw the gangsterism unleashed by Prohibition behind this, but it was probably more complex than that. What was more, such violent crime as racket-eering engendered tended to be limited to victims from within the bootlegging, gambling or drug communities. For example, when the mobster Hymie Weiss sent a fleet of cars to shoot Capone in the Hawthorne Hotel in 1925, the first car had machine gunners with blanks to disperse "civilians."[52]

It is some measure of how unpopular Prohibition was that figures were frequently cited which "proved" that more were killed in the enforcement of

Prohibition, than by bootleggers. By the end of 1920, one Prohibition agent had been killed enforcing the Prohibition laws. By 1930, official figures claimed that 86 Prohibition agents and over two hundred "civilians" had been killed. These figures were disputed by the *Washington Herald* in 1929, which claimed that the figure for civilians should have been 1,360 killed as well as 1,000 wounded. It was not a coincidence that during these years one of the most popular bumper-stickers read, "Don't shoot me, I am not a bootlegger." Nor was this the only way in which the authorities killed the population through their passion to save them from the demon rum. In order to prevent the use of industrial alcohol to manu-facture booze, as soon as the Volstead Act was passed it was announced that indus-trial alcohol would be "denatured"—in other words, deadly toxins were added. While many made fortunes by removing these toxins, others were less effective and skilled and consequently less fortunate. In 1925, the national toll for people poisoned by alcohol was 4,154 as compared to 1,064 in 1920. In 1926, the *New York World* compared the federal government to the Borgias, so great was their skill at poisoning.[53]

Perhaps the most important way in which Prohibition affected crime was by effectively turning a large section of the populace into criminals. In New York City, federal Prohibition agents arrested 11,000 people for violations of the Volstead Act in 1922 alone. By 1933, 40,000 had been imprisoned nationally and in order to contain the massive increase in prisoners, six new federal prisons were needed. The figures for the growth of bars of one form or another in most urban and metropolitan regions show that the legislation did little to halt alcohol consumption. Surveys revealed that the initial acceptance of the laws was replaced by an increasing irritation, a sense that the Volstead Act was at best unnecessary, if not an infringement of civil liberties. To a growing proportion of the population, those who attempted to enforce the legislation were either corrupt, inept or so sanctimonious their piety kept them out of touch with reality. Alcohol proved to be too well entrenched in the social life of America to be removed by legislation. Despite this, the final president of the 1920s, Herbert Hoover, was a teetotaler. His answer to the obvious failures of what he termed the "Noble Experiment" was to increase the penalties for failure to observe the drinking laws. In spite of complaining about the futility of attempting to legislate alcohol out of America, he signed the Jones Act into law, authorizing first offenders under the Volstead Act to be given up to five years in prison or be fined up to $10,000.

The result was that in these final years of Prohibition the punishments seemed little less than Draconian. Perhaps the most infamous was the case in 1929 of Etta May Miller of Lansing, Michigan. Under the state's last ditch four strikes and out policy, this repeat offender, moonshiner, mother of ten children and grandmother to two, was sentenced in Detroit to life in prison for the possession of a single bottle of gin. Sentencing her, the General Secretary of the Board of Temperance gives some idea of the thinking behind such harsh legislation when he told the court, "Our only regret is that the woman was not sentenced to life imprisonment before her ten children were born. When one has violated the Constitution four times, he or she should be segregated from society to prevent the production of subnormal offspring." Nevertheless, reflecting growing public dissatisfaction with Prohibition, and in spite of this attitude, the governor of Michigan freed her in March 1930, after she had served less than a year.[54]

If the decade of alcohol prohibition made criminals of ordinary people, it also created some extraordinary criminals whose glamorous reputations, flamboyant lifestyles and almost unbelievable wealth were far from ordinary and added to the appeal of such criminal behavior. One such figure stands head and shoulders above the other rum runners and bootleggers of his generation. In the Pantheon of American criminals few have achieved the lasting fame to match that of Al Capone, who has become synonymous with Prohibition, Chicago and gang-sterism. Unapologetically ruthless in his manner and always surrounded by ape-like lackeys, Capone was seen as the archetypal mobster of the 1920s. The exponent of a new and brutal form of urban, hierarchical, organized and integrated crime, he was seen as despicable and bestial by many Americans, but he also had a pecu-liar draw to a large proportion of others. As Capone himself confessed, he supplied a need, and in so doing broke a law. But as he pointed out, it was a law which as the 1920s progressed and his empire grew, had less and less support among the American public. He neglected to mention, or at least played down, the inconve-nient fact that part of his huge turnover was provided by the less acceptable occu-pations of prostitution, protection, and gambling.

Few people represented this time of brash, new money, and brief celebrity better than Capone. In an era when the president famously claimed that "the business of America is business," Capone saw himself as a businessman, the "Rockefeller of Chicago's bootleggers," and one life history of the master racket-eer was sub-titled *The Biography of a Self-Made Man*. It was estimated that Capone made $100 million in 1927 alone and that at his zenith his empire employed over 1,000 people, supplying over 22,000 outlets with booze, with a payroll of $300,000 a week. It was fitting that this businessman was eventually imprisoned, not for murder or racketeering, but for federal income tax evasion.

Few things said more about the new type of gangster than Capone's personal appearance. It was a peculiar mix of ostentation and image management. The gangster was instantly recognizable because of gruesome scars running down the entire side of his face. Those who knew his life history were aware it was the result of three knife slashes on his jaw, neck and face from a drunken customer in his days as a New York bouncer. The image-conscious Capone claimed these wounds had been inflicted while serving his country in the famous "Lost Battalion" in France during the Great War. Either way while he applied talcum powder every day to conceal them, newspapers would often touch up the scars to make them more apparent and Capone's childlike face look more sinister.

Capone was just as fastidious about his clothes. He dressed in flamboyant suits, wore a trademark Fedora hat and ostentatious jewelry studded with diamonds.

What was more, he was as articulate in his underworld patois and trademark drawl, as he was publicity seeking. By the late 1920s, he had become a national media figure and was asked for his opinion on issues ranging from prohibition to the presidency. When he lost weight, reporters pestered him for dieting tips. When he ordered a car, its bullet-proof glass, armor plate, gun loops, v16 engine, 120 mph top speed and $20,000 price tag were almost instantly public knowledge. Not only did Hollywood celebrities—both men and women—vie with each other to be seen with him, but films were made of his life story and stars like James Cagney made their names playing gangsters based on him.

Capone's career clearly demonstrated that the prohibition of alcohol certainly boosted crime. It not only provided a fillip of huge amounts of regular cash for the old-style urban mobs. That income in turn enabled the mobsters to invest in ever faster cars, better weaponry and other benefits of technology. It enabled them to employ more effective lawyers to protect them from prosecution and more effective accountants to bury their profits. It gave them more funds with which to bribe officials and also gave them capital to invest in business diversification—both legal and illegal. Alcohol prohibition fed a sort of symbiosis in the criminal world. Not only could the funds from moon-shining, bootlegging and rum running fund prostitution, labor and protection racketeering as with Capone and his henchmen, but those involved in other prohibited activities, like gambling or narcotics, could use the funds generated by them to enter the booze business.

In the early days of Prohibition, New York's leading criminal fixer, Arnold Rothstein—"the big bankroll," as he was known—used his huge gambling-derived wealth to fund a new style of rum running. He began supplying whole-sale high quality, high priced booze directly from European and Canadian producers, rather than moonshine and "naturalized" industrial alcohol. When the market for these goods became too crowded, and not profitable enough, he shifted to supplying narcotics. Perhaps the last word on this symbiosis of crime should go to a law-keeper. Even during the era of alcohol prohibition, it was not solely the finance generated by the ban which fed criminal activity. As Fiorello LaGuardia—never a great fan of Prohibition—told FDR, the concurrent gambling prohibition took up valuable police manpower since, "We have to use a large part of our police force in the supervision, discovery and apprehension of the gentry who run these lotteries ... [which] if legalized would free these officers for other duties." Perhaps he understood better than many others, the real implications of prohibitions. Perhaps it was more that as a proud Italian-American he realized that immigrants—Jews, Irish and most importantly Italians—were, rightly or wrongly, seen as the leading bootleggers, pimps, racketeers, and drug dealers.

In the end, this increase in crime should perhaps be measured against the, sometimes admittedly limited, benefits the prohibitions brought. The narcotics prohibitions did remove at least some addictive drugs from soft drinks, tonics, and patent medicines. They did reduce the number of registered addicts and made people more aware of the dangers of narcotic abuse. However, with this prohibitive approach the United States set in train a war against drugs which arguably can never be won. Through educating the public the Noble Experiment against alcohol reduced the deaths from alcohol-related illnesses—although, significantly as has been described above, not from alcoholic poisoning itself. It also reduced the nation's overall alcohol consumption and it also, arguably, improved the sanitation, safety and standards of many of the nation's saloons, bars and clubs. The final prohibition of this section was less successful. It is difficult to tell what advantages the gambling prohibitions gave the nation. Of all these morally based campaigns, this was arguably the least successful in this period. As LaGuardia succinctly put it, "Men and women will always gamble. If they don't do it one way, they will do it another." Perhaps this was true of all the prohibitions.[55]

8

SEX CRIME

"Where's Madame?" asked my friend.

"Who wants her?"

This question located Madame in a pretty pink boudoir at the end of the hall, where she was reclining on a sofa reading a novel.

"The gentlemen just came in want you to take a glass of wine" answered the servant.

"I certainly would be ungracious not to accept such an invitation," she replied as the stiff rustling of her skirts declared her getting up. "I hate however," she went on coming into the parlor, "to give up my book. The charming devil of a hero had just escaped from the myrmidons of the law, and—"

We heard a whistle, and the bell rang violently. It was the merest coincidence, but she grasped the situation immediately.

"Gentlemen and ladies," the officer said "consider yourself under arrest."

He threw back his coat and showed his shield. The landlady who had been all smiles, turned to a fury in an instant.

"Devil brute" she almost shrieked and threw her glass of wine over the officer's head . . . As these words were uttered she flashed a glance that contained as many daggers as you would probably find in an Italian whole-sale hardware store. The she swept proudly to the door, rustling and roaring like a silken tornado.

National Police Gazette, "Pulling a Disorderly
House," December 27, 1879

The turn of the twentieth century brought the idea of sex to the forefront in the industrial Western world. In Europe not only were Freud and Krafft-Ebbing embarking on their works on sexual pathology, but the headlines were full of advocates and opponents of birth control; pleas and condemnations of women's suffrage; stories of free love and prurient and celebratory accounts of perversion and pornography. Not only that, but the whole idea of sex and gender was worrying on another, far more philosophical level. At its most extreme it was expressed best, as so many of these "modern" ideas were, in the work of a Viennese Jew—Otto Weininger. Weininger was a young doctoral student at the University of Vienna whose singular lack of success with women bred a curious brand of misogyny which he linked with anti-Semitic self-loathing—making him one of only two Jews mentioned in a favorable light in *Mein Kampf.*

In Weininger's troubled mind—he would kill himself aged just 23 in Beethoven's house—society was undergoing a worrying form of feminization. In his writing, he outlined a world in which human behavior, history and even civilization itself, was modeled either on masculine or feminine characteristics.[1] The female traits of passivity, immorality, and illogicality, which when added to their propensity for irrational action and cruelty, were to his mind increasingly coming to dominate the characteristics of urban, industrial societies. The advent of modernity had submerged the more desirable male features of productivity, chivalry, and rationality which dominated earlier, more noble, times. While Weininger was undoubtedly seen as extreme, he nevertheless gave voice to underlying feelings of unease in the minds of many, all around the world—even in that haven of modernity, the brash, arriviste nation, the United States.

At the same time as Weininger's thesis was published in Leipzig, America was being governed by a president who was undoubtedly the most outspoken advocate of "masculine" virtues among all world leaders. Theodore Roosevelt never ceased in his exhortations towards the strenuous, competitive, life in which everything must be attempted. He was a staunch believer in a hierarchy of races and nations that was founded on principles of active, thrusting, bellicose, virile competition which, although unlikely to have drawn on Weininger's anti-Semitic strands, nevertheless demonstrate at least sympathy with the Austrian's condemnation of the feminization of the modern world. Nor was he alone in this sexualized view of the United States and other societies.

In America, from the Civil War to World War II, the issue of sex was no further from the thinking of the populace than it was in Austria-Hungary, or other European countries. As in many other industrialized nations of the West, women campaigned for, and got the vote. During these years women fought for equal reproductive rights and improved rights at work. Women became ever more vociferous for themselves, their husbands, families and friends, and issues of sex and gender all came to the fore. However, in the United States, the diversity of the nation meant that this development manifested itself in very different problems in different regions of the nation.

As with the attitude taken towards narcotics over this period, the US regulated and governed sexual mores and aberrations with a peculiar mix of prohibition, on the one hand, and a *laissez-faire* indifference, on the other. America was then, as it is now, an idiosyncratic mix of prurience and promiscuity. It is, and was, a nation where the openness and acceptance of pornography and prostitution which rival the most liberal of European attitudes sit uncomfortably with levels of Puritanism and censorship which are almost unmatched anywhere else in the democratic world. In these years in the West, some of the South and a few of the metropolitan regions, the brothel was a part of the daily life of the community. It was regarded as satisfying needs and appetites in the same way as the schoolhouse or saloon. The madam and the working girls were known and pragmatically accepted by the majority of the population of these regions for what they were—hard-working professionals. In other regions of the nation, accusations of sexual impropriety or obscenity were being pursued with such vigor that the people hounded were committing suicide. In these circles, depictions of women's ankles, legs, bellies, breasts, buttocks or—heaven forbid—pubic hair, were simply far too private, too personal, too bestial—perhaps too exciting, to be portrayed, let alone displayed in any form other than "art." Even those depictions that could qualify as art were controlled by rules which kept it within very strict boundaries of propriety.[2]

Nevertheless, despite the best efforts of many different lobbies, sexuality was apparent in American society, it was also, unsurprising, present in American crime. Sex, sexuality, gender and reproduction were all aspects of American society and behavior which the local, state and federal governments, churches and individuals all felt that they had a right and duty to either regulate, control or punish. This study will concentrate on four aspects of sex "crimes" during this period. The first is concerned with the regulation of obscenity and pornography. Second, it will look at what must be termed reproductive crime. The next section will look at the attitudes towards prostitution and the vice industries in the period. Finally, it will analyze what constituted perversions and how such aberrations were dealt with.

It seems that the exposure and control of sexually explicit material have always been spearheaded by a peculiar type of person. White, middle-class, Protestant and male, these people are normally driven by strong religious convictions; they have frequently had an epiphany which has either sparked or crystallized their sense of purpose; they are usually well-educated and articulate, and they are, more often than not, wealthy. Perhaps this is because campaigning on this issue requires both money and status in order to be taken seriously. Perhaps it is because money detaches the moral campaigner from the grim necessities which so often drive the vice industry—poverty, addiction, poor education, and lack of opportunity. Perhaps it simply frees up time to campaign. Whatever the reason, the most notable anti-pornography campaigners of the Gilded Age certainly conformed to this profile—one account of anti-vice campaigners in New York in the period estimated that over a quarter of these men were millionaires or listed on the *Social Register*.[3] It was this group that led to the founding of the Society for the Suppression of Vice in 1873 and launched the campaign which really caught the public imagination, as well as having the most lasting and shocking results.

The Society was founded by a man whose name has become synonymous with puritanical zealotry against vice—Anthony Comstock. Son of a prosperous New England farmer, what Comstock lacked in wealth, he made up for in vigor and sheer, brazen, uncompromising self-righteousness. During the Civil War, the young Comstock was shocked by the profanity, intemperance and crudity of his fellow Union soldiers, and it was arguably this which launched him on his career to clean up America. By the late 1860s, he was working in a lowly position in a dry goods store and campaigning for the Young Men's Christian Association (YMCA) against the circulation of pornographic material among his fellow clerks. When it appeared that the YMCA's efforts at banning this trade through city ordinances had failed, he managed to secure funding for his own campaign to clean up the nation through federal legislation. Comstock's eponymous law targeted pornographers, abortionists and those who sold contraceptives, but by far the most important category were pornographers. It is a measure of Comstock's standing in New York that he, personally, arrested over 100 people in the first two years of his Society and law's existence. Over 60 of those were charged with depositing, mailing or delivering "obscene, lewd or lascivious book[s], pamphlet[s], picture[s], paper[s], print[s] or other publication[s] of an indecent character."[4]

While Comstock was by no means the only campaigner working against the distribution of obscene material at this time, he is certainly the best known, probably the most tireless and arguably the most indicative of his contemporaries. His achievements were impressive. By 1874, "Comstock had seized 194,000 pictures and photographs, 134,000 pounds of books, 14,200 printing plates, 60,300 rubber articles (condoms), 5,500 sets of playing cards, and 31,150 boxes of aphrodisiac pills." By 1880, he claimed he had "substantially suppressed" obscene publications in the US. Twenty-five years later on his own estimation, his Society had been responsible for the prosecution of over 23,000 individuals and the destruction of more than 93 tons of obscene material. In 1913, he bragged to the *Evening World* that his intervention, accusations, and prosecution of individuals led to the suicide, or early death, of some 16 people as well as prosecuting enough people to fill "sixty railcars, holding sixty people in each."[5]

As if these triumphs were not enough, Comstock was responsible for the banning of Margaret Sanger's books on birth control and at one point he even managed to outlaw the sending of anatomy books to medical students via the federal mail. His reputation preceded him. By the 1890s, scared publishers cut out any salacious or obscene passages from their books. They even started using a curious form of self-censorship in which English gave way to other languages in order to avoid crossing Comstock and his legions of vigilant minions. This puritanical zeal went so far that by 1900, some publishers had even replaced the seemingly neutral word "pregnant" with a French equivalent, "enceinte."[6]

Inevitably such prurience led to a backlash. Many Americans felt that Comstock's crusade was sheer hypocrisy. Accusations of double standards dogged him. One of his most infamous examples came about in the mid-1870s, when the charismatic moral guardian and one of the leading preachers of his time, Henry Ward Beecher, was exposed as having had a long-standing affair with his best friend's wife. It created a scandal which quickly made the national press and ammunition for his enemies. What particularly riled Comstock was that an advocate of free love and sexual equality, Victoria Caflin Woodhull, wasted no time in publishing the details of the affair in her journal. Comstock was one of the leading figures who pushed for Woodhull's prosecution and imprisonment, claiming that her crime in publishing the details to the nation far outweighed Beecher's hypocrisy. Unfortunately for Comstock, many influential figures disagreed.

One who was to emerge as an influential opponent of Comstock was the Irish playwright, George Bernard Shaw. Shaw's play, *Mrs Warren's Profession* gave a sympathetic portrait of an impoverished woman driven to prostitution. Comstock condemned Shaw as "an Irish smut dealer" who must have known that his works would "do harm to weak and dishonest people." Unlike many of his American victims, often too shocked and ashamed to fight him, Shaw bit back. He publicly condemned "Comstockery," as the fashion for telling everyone "what is proper for people to read."[7] Shaw had already condemned Comstock in the eyes of many of his fellow Americans. In a brilliantly aimed jab, Shaw had hit at one of Comstock's most deeply buried but deeply held fears, that underlying the modernity of America's cities was a small-town parochialism that would continue to divide the nation through to the present day. Comstockery was, he told them, "the world's standing joke at the expense of the United States. It confirms the deepest suspicions of the Old World that America is a provincial place. A second rate country town."[8]

Comstock also had difficulties with the art world. He had had several tussles over obscene content in art. To the campaigner it was all connected with context. As he put it: "The female form is beautiful—a young girl may be nude in her own room and there is no wrong attached to it; but if a lascivious eye looks through the keyhole, then it is wrong for her to be stripped of her clothing." Extending this idea he told his readers: "Let the nude be kept in its proper place and out of the reach of the rabble."[9] It was this sentiment that launched the typical prosecution of the foremost Fifth Avenue art dealer Edward L. Knoedler for displaying female nudes imported from Paris.[10] Although successful, the case brought him such public opprobrium, he fought shy of tangling with the high art world for some years. However, when telephoned in 1913 about Paul Chabas' *September Morn*, Comstock felt obliged to act, not realizing that he was being duped. The story was convoluted, but informative.

The painting, which had won the gold medal at Paris, showed a naked, pubescent, girl emerging from a lake. The painting had already been the subject of charges of indecency in Chicago, which had been dropped. Its owners, the art dealers Braun and Company, had decided to go down market and had 2,000 lithographic copies made of the painting. On having it rejected for use on a calendar, they found themselves in danger of making a major loss and hired the publicist Harry Reichenbach to get them out of the mess. It was Reichenbach who had phoned Comstock to say that young boys were gawping at a "naughty" painting in the window of a Fourth Avenue art gallery.

Rising to the occasion, the aging zealot tried to have the painting removed and the gallery owner prosecuted. Arguing that there was "Too little morn and too much maid," Comstock was soon left in no doubt about the ways in which the times had changed since his glory days of the 1890s. The judge threw out the case. He could not see the obscenity, instead he claimed that the painting was no more obscene than a "baby's portrait." As if to reinforce this lesson in the changing mores of the nation, Comstock met his most humiliating rebuke when he tried to bring his final prosecution. Attending the International Purity Congress in San Francisco in 1915, he brought a prosecution against window dressers he watched dressing female mannequins in daylight with the public watching. In a display of Western bluntness, the judge threw out the case telling the aging crusader what many Americans already felt—"Mr Comstock, I think you are nuts!"[11] Comstock died days later.

Comstock's death did not put an end to this prurient streak. If the printed word and photograph had excited his attention, his successors were obsessed by the movies. The early years of the 1920s saw a series of headline scandals in Hollywood. The sexual abuse and death of the young model Virginia Rappe at the hands of the comedy star Roscoe "Fatty" Arbuckle; the murder of the bisexual director William Desmond Taylor and the deaths from narcotics abuse of the actors Olive Thomas, Barbara La Marr, Jeanne Eagels, Alma Rubens, and Wallace Reid, highlighted the debauchery of the film industry's emerging capital. What was more, there was an increasingly prevalent trend for films themselves to push the boundaries of "decency" with what appeared to many as increased sexual content and growing depictions of shocking and tasteless behavior. This smut was now no longer limited to the fleshpots of the urban and metropolitan areas, it was now, through the growing network of movie theatres, being transmitted to even the most rural of areas.

In the early 1920s, while many US cities found it possible to create a code and prosecute theatrical or journalistic transgressions, Boston, Philadelphia and Los Angeles all attempted, unsuccessfully, to legislate a coherent code for films. At a state level such measures achieved little. In 1921 alone, over 100 bills were raised in 37 states. The result was that there was a vast discrepancy in what was permissible or illegal across the nation. Some regions would not allow smoking on screen, while others banned any depictions of pregnant women. With an industry which had a national and international appeal, such a state of affairs was highly unsatisfactory to the censors. On the other hand, the Catholic Church was more successful. Initially outraged by a wartime documentary emphasizing the dangers of venereal disease, the Church went on to attempt to cleanse the movie industry and Hollywood in particular. To these religious censors, Hollywood was a "pest hole that infects the entire country with its obscene and lascivious movies."[12]

In the wake of this onslaught and in an effort to retain artistic autonomy and stave off financially damaging censorship, Hollywood attempted to introduce a self-imposed code of production. In 1922, the studios banded together to form the Motion Pictures Producers and Distributors Association. At the head of the Association, as it became known, they installed President Harding's previous campaign manager and former Post Master General, the well-connected lawyer, Will Hays. Through a shrewd mixture of self-censorship, public relations and lobbying, Hays managed to fend off federal film censorship. By the 1930s, Hays had bowed to Catholic-led pressure for films to promote morality rather than simply avoid breaching good taste and his loose "formula" of "do's, don'ts and be carefuls" had to be altered to a full-blown code. By 1934, the Catholic hierarchy was overseeing film standards with its Legion of Decency and sex remained the overwhelming concern. Fully 95 percent of the statements made by the Bishops, who constituted the Legion's board of censors, were concerned with sex rather than crime or violence. Nor were they alone, their congregation shared their concerns. A survey of more than 3 million American Catholics revealed that 40 percent had pledged themselves to boycott immoral movies.[13]

Such pressures could not be ignored. The so-called Production [Hays] Code, introduced in 1930 and amended in 1934 to require film certification, would set the industry standards for the next 30 years. Under the Code, films were expected to outlaw gratuitous depictions of the naked human body and overtly "lustful" behavior—including, famously—perhaps apocryphally, timing on-screen kisses. They were also expected to be pro-active. The Code instructed film makers to promote law-abiding behavior and marital fidelity and prohibit unnecessary depictions of miscegenation, sexual perversions (like homosexuality), prostitution, and adultery. It seemed to be fairly arbitrarily enforced for while Mae West and Groucho Marx found their trademark sexual innuendoes curtailed, Betty Boop's skirt lengthened and Tarzan's mate was covered up, Busby Berkeley seemed able to avoid censorship with his scantily clad beauties dancing suggestively in huge revues. Maybe the movements of the herd provided protection for the individual chorus girl against the predatory censor in Hollywood–Babylon, in the same way it did for wildebeest against the hunter in the Serengeti.

However, during this period, the film industry suffered no high profile prosecutions over transgressions of decency and morality. There was no *September Morn* in Hollywood. Self-censorship worked on that level. Nevertheless, the impact of the Code cannot be over-estimated. The Catholic head of the Production Code Administration until 1954, Joseph Ignatius Breen, had the power to change scenes and alter scripts—and frequently did. For example, the film script of Henry Bellamann's 1940 novel, *King's Row* required vast re-editing after Breen demanded the removal of a nude bathing scene, as well as references to adultery, incest, nymphomania, and homosexuality in order to protect the decency of the people of small-town America from this depiction of the antics of the people of small-town America.[14]

Some of the targets of America's moral guardians were less modern than the movies. Ancient Egyptians had used crocodile dung as a contraceptive suppository, and condoms made of animal intestine were described as protection against venereal disease by Fallopius as early as 1504. Oral contraception, by way of abortion-inducing toxins—including strychnine and mercury—were used in many western countries from the Middle Ages onwards. By the turn of the nineteenth century, all the major forms of barrier contraceptive were already being used. But it was after 1844, when Thomas Hancock in Britain, and Charles Goodyear in America, almost simultaneously discovered the process for the vulcanization of rubber that safe reliable contraception became possible for the masses. By the addition of sulphur, to natural or synthetic rubber, the end product can be made more durable and less sticky, enabling its extrusion into far more lightweight forms than before—making it the perfect material for the manufacture of condoms. The price of condoms dropped from $5 a dozen in the 1860s; in the 1870s they were being advertised in the press at 75c a dozen, or less.[15]

No sooner had reasonably cheap and standard quality condoms become available—after around 1870—than the Comstock Laws imposed penalties of 6 months to 5 years in prison or a fine of $100 to $2,000 for those trying to "sell, lend, or give away or in any manner exhibit . . . any article whatever for the prevention of conception."[16] Within two years of the act, Comstock himself had confiscated and destroyed over 60,000 of what one birth control opponent called these "accessories of evil." To these opponents they were simply "disgusting, beastly, positively wrongful, unnatural and physically injurious."[17] By 1885, some states had taken Comstock's crusade to another level, imposing ever more stringent laws which made even private conversations or other means of transmitting information about contraception offenses which would result in varying terms of imprisonment. Others authorized the searching of private premises for contraceptive material. However, as the new century dawned, these campaigners were fighting a growing number of groups—from feminists and suffragettes, to eugenicists and physicians—who were willing not only to break these laws, but also to proselytize with equal zealotry about the sense in doing so.

Most notable of these was the controversial birth control campaigner, Margaret Sanger. Born in Corning, New York, in 1883, she trained as a public health nurse in the slums of turn-of-the-century New York City. Here she was confronted by the results of poverty, ignorance, and superstition on the lives of women. Treating these women whose lives were ruined by almost unimaginable drudgery compounded by their lack of opportunity and self-determination made Sanger convinced that the only possible way to improve their fate lay in their sexual empowerment. She witnessed the devastating medical, mental, and economic results of almost perpetual cycles of pregnancy. She saw how the constant cycle of child rearing combined with the risks of childbirth in the fetid conditions of the tenements of New York.

The result was that Sanger decided to devote her life to making contraceptive information available to women. Through the *Birth Control Review*, she relentlessly and fearlessly championed the provision of readable, reliable advice on family planning and contraception for all American women. Importing many of her ideas from the contemporary European sexual revolution, relying especially on the support, methods and theories of Marie Stopes in England, Sanger founded the American Birth Control League and opened America's first birth-control clinic in 1921. Within days, it was closed by the police and Sanger was imprisoned for 30 days.

Nevertheless, the importance of Sanger in the birth of modern America does not lie in her criminal record, but more in the ways in which she gradually managed to mobilize opinion behind her. Like many of the women activists of the period, she won through in the end although the possibilities of success initially looked ridiculously unachievable. Like Carrie A. Nation's campaigning for temperance or the continued pressure for women's suffrage, Sanger's implacable persistence seemed to pay off. Alongside her relentless campaigning, she formed pragmatic alliances—as with the politically well-connected eugenicists. She would address any audience she felt might take notice of her message of "planned parenthood," claiming—"to me any aroused group was a good group."[18] She even once famously espoused her views to a gathering of the women of the New Jersey Ku Klux Klan.

Like Carrie A. Nation, she also refused to accept defeat, even when driven into European exile. Instead of abandoning her militant crusade, she continued her campaign from across the Atlantic, concentrating on rallying European support for pressure on the federal government. Sanger's efforts certainly contributed to the legalization of shipping and advertising for contraceptives in 1930. The dissemination of birth control information by doctors was legalized in the United States in 1937 and in that same year North Carolina became the first state to sanction the use of tax dollars to fund birth control. The following year it was estimated that there were more than 300 recognized family planning clinics across the United States. By 1942, this figure had reached over 800.[19] While Sanger's work was crucial, this new liberalization must be seen in the light of the radical social changes wrought by America's Great Depression and, from 1932, the New Deal's attempts to use the crisis to push through legislation which would have been unthinkable in either the Progressive Era or the 1920s.

If the position of contraception had changed over the years of this study, abortion would remain common but illegal throughout the period. One doctor in 1861 claimed he had performed 300 abortions, a lucrative—if illegal—sideline for which he was paid between $10 and $100. For considerably less, a pregnant woman could buy toxic mixtures to induce abortion, and many followed this dangerous course. In 1878, the Board of Health in Michigan estimated that a third of all pregnancies were aborted and the vast majority of these were carried out—always illegally—on "prosperous or otherwise respectable married women." One woman admitted to having to have 21 pregnancies aborted. Her final abortion would prove fatal. For those less wealthy, wishing to retain anonymity, or without access to medical help, even the most reputable newspapers advertised "Infallible French Female Pills," and the like. For $8, a woman could buy a silver probe for relieving "female complaints." This situation remained the case until the 1873 Comstock Law made it a crime to sell, distribute, or own abortion-related products and services, or to publish information on how to obtain them.[20]

Between 1860 and 1890, all except four of the states and territories enacted anti-abortion laws. Nevertheless, in reality, under many circumstances abortion was ignored. Although illegal, most judges and doctors would leave under-3-month abortions unnoted, holding that until the woman noticed the movements of the fetus (the quickening) there was little point in prosecution. Juries tended to be sympathetic to defendants in abortion cases and the conviction rate in many cases was low. On the other hand, abortionists were, as the *National Police Gazette* put it, "wholesale murderers."

The case of New York's most notorious abortionist is informative on many levels. Ann Trow Lohman, who took the suitably Parisian—and therefore risqué—name of Madame Restell, carried out abortions in her impressive house at 148 Greenwich Street—"The Mansion Built on Baby Skulls" as the press luridly called it. Charging $5 for an initial consultation and $100 for the procedure, it was estimated that between her first arrest in 1841 and her suicide in 1878, she earned over a million dollars. By 1870, her annual expenditure on advertising alone was $60,000. This advertising had to be circumspect even before the 1873 laws, but the language was plain enough to those who sought her services. She advertised in the *New York Sun* offering the "strictest confidence on complaints incidental to the female frame" and boasted that her "experience and knowledge in the treatment of cases of female irregularity, [was] such as to require but a few days to effect a perfect cure." Following her arrest by Anthony Comstock in 1878, it was those same newspapers which had taken so much money from Restell in advertising fees that now whipped up public opinion against her to a fever pitch and drove her to slit her own throat in her bath.[21]

Not that contraception was the only aspect of sexual behavior which was outlawed in the late 1800s. In 1858, Dr William Sanger, the resident physician for the New York state charity hospital, on Blackwell Island, drew on no lesser figure than St Augustine of Hippo to show what he argued was the safety-valve effect of the world's oldest profession. The Saint had warned that "suppress prostitution and capricious lusts will overthrow society," and the doctor agreed.[22] Sanger's pragmatism stemmed from a realization that the eradication of prostitution was impossible. He argued that "the lash, the dungeon, the rack and the stake have all been tried and all have proved equally powerless to achieve the object." Instead he advocated a benevolent system of reformation and education in what he called Magdalen Asylums—named after the pious New Testament prostitute, Mary Magdalene. Few others in positions of power shared Sanger's certainty about how to tackle the problem, and as a result the attitude to prostitution would vary as much from one side of the nation to the other as it did across the three-quarters of a century of this study.

In this case it is perhaps worth starting with an examination of the West. The prostitute of the Old West is in many ways as iconic as the cowboy, gunfighter, sheriff or card sharp. The West was a male society, not only in its macho attitudes, but also in its composition. One of the chief characteristics of the region was a dire shortage of women. For example, San Francisco in the 1850s had some 65,000 men to a mere 2,500 women and the result was that prostitution was highly lucrative and largely tolerated. As the male population expanded, so did the number of prostitutes. In the boom town of Leadville, Colorado, in the 1880s, it was estimated that there was one bordello per 148 inhabitants. On the other hand, not all regions of the West can be considered the same. Some communities would not tolerate such vice within their communities. Where the ratio of men to women was more equal, there was less prostitution. Around the familial Mormon society of Salt Lake City, there are no recorded examples of brothels.

Many of the "working women" were immigrants, imported, frequently unwillingly, solely for prostitution. In the eyes of moral crusaders in the West, these sex slaves were more often than not Chinese and Japanese or members of other foreign communities. While much of the sentiment behind this was simply anti-immigrant prejudice, there was some truth to this belief in the more metropolitan areas of the West. It was estimated that in 1860, 85 percent of all the Chinese women in San Francisco were prostitutes, although this figure declined to 21 percent when the region's immigration restrictions bit in the late 1870s.[23] By the Japanese Consul's own estimation, of Seattle's 250 Japanese residents in 1891, 71 were prostitutes, the rest were pimps or gamblers—except 10 who had legitimate work.[24]

Some idea of the attitude towards prostitution, and these oriental sex slaves in particular, can be gathered from the fact that it was not until the 1910s that the openly visible incarceration in the brothels of red light districts was outlawed in Washington State, Oregon, and California. Rather perversely, one of the main opponents of such legislation was the vehemently anti-Asian editor of the *Sacramento Bee*, Valentine Stuart McClatchy. He argued that freeing the sex slaves would cause the "scatteration" of Oriental vices around the city whereas under the existing system they were contained in the Chinatown regions of the cities. In what would prove to be a pattern for such measures in the period as Prohibition and women's suffrage, it was white, middle-class women who united and forced the measures through.[25]

But the "girls" were not always coerced or kidnapped. During the city's boom years, a Denver madam, Mattie Silks, confessed that she "went into the sporting life for business reasons and no other. It was a way in those days for a woman to make money and I made it. I considered myself then, and do now, a businesswoman." Starting as a prostitute in her teens, she was running girls by the age of 19. By her thirties she had worked her way up to owning her own bordello—Jennie's House of Mirrors. She married at the age of 76 when she had already been acknowledged as the "Queen of Denver's Red Light District." When she died at the age of 81, the scale of her funeral indicated that she was not only a wealthy woman, but also judging by those who attended, a respectable woman.[26]

That is not to say that making a living in the sex trade was always so profitable or respectable. As with so many stereotypes of the "Wild West" the good-hearted, beautiful, "soiled dove"—part lover, part businesswoman, part nurse, part mother—of legend is a long way from the all too squalid and sordid truth. In the region's booming mining and cattle towns with huge influxes of cash-rich men who had probably seen no women for months, a working girl would be required to service up to 50 men a day, catering for whatever perversions they desired. The saloon girl or sex slave in her "crib" risked violence, rape and infection on a daily basis. Multiple and botched abortions were an occupational hazard. As the women aged and became less alluring, and all too often more dependent on drink and/or narcotics and perhaps ravaged by syphilis, they would frequently be thrown out on to the street, forced to live off their wits. Some aging prostitutes took to street-walking with all its inherent dangers. Others decided this fate was too much, with the result that 1880s Denver saw the suicides of two or three working girls every week.

Many saw women's influence, even fallen women, as having a stabilizing force on the masculine society of the "Wild West." There are stories of rough miners paying relative fortunes to eat food cooked by women, or simply converse with a "lady." The laws of the Western states largely reflected this curious mixture of adoration and exploitation—initially tolerating or ignoring brothels and prostitutes without regulating them. However, just as this was not true of all regions, it was not the case throughout the entire period. As the region became more settled, increasing numbers of women moved West, "civilizing" the region.

One of the results of this was frequently a moral crusade to clean up their environment. Many of these attempts were short-lived. In the 1870s, in Denver a city ordinance was passed which required prostitutes to wear yellow ribbons on their arms as a mark of shame and the madams were allowed to wear nothing but yellow. The ordinance did not last long, popular pressure meant it was soon rescinded.[27] Its short lifespan is explained by one local politician in nearby Ellsworth, in Kansas. When refusing to outlaw brothels, he explained that:

> If it couldn't be rooted out, the vicious vocation [of prostitution] should be made to contribute to the expense of maintaining law and order . . . The city authorities consider that as long as mankind is depraved and Texas cattle herders exist, there will be demand and necessity for prostitutes . . . [and] it is better for the respectable portion of society to hold prostitutes under restraint of law.[28]

Essentially as with the "Wild West" itself, the legendary era of the ubiquitous saloon girl was as short-lived as it was sanitized. As with other regions of the nation, the problem of prostitution was treated as one of the foremost social problems of the times in one of three ways. Each of these three strategies represented a different strand of social thinking prevalent at the time and can serve to indicate historical events and processes. The first of these strategies was containment or segregation. When the cribs and brothels of San Francisco's notorious Barbary Coast were due to be outlawed in 1913, the newspaper editor, V.S. McClatchy, had cited the Superintendent of the New Orleans police who had maintained that "Immoral women should be compelled to live in certain proscribed districts, and forbidden to scatter at will throughout the residential and business precincts of a city."[29] His choice of city was not arbitrary.

By 1900, most US cities had a "red light district." Some were well known—infamous. New York had its Tenderloin, Chicago had the Levee and San Francisco had the Barbary Coast. One of the last to be established was perhaps the most notorious of all. In 1897, a New Orleans Alderman, Sidney Story, proposed a semi-legal red light district. Storyville, as it became known, was to be contained within 38 city blocks. It was diverse in the services offered. Prices ranged from 25c to $5 and conditions from shuttered "cribs" through gaudy parlors and saloons up to sophisticated mansions with ballrooms. It did not take long for the area to become the city's leading tourist attraction. While many objected, others saw it as entirely in line with the municipal reforms of the time and a rational solution to an unpleasant social problem, very much in keeping with the Progressive spirit of the times. Since it appeared that prostitution could not be eradicated, the thinking went, it was probably best to simply contain it.

There were many advantages which such a system provided. Not only could the forces of law oversee and control the area, but they could also police the prostitutes and punters and contain the moral degeneracy in one area. It was hoped that much of the brawling, fraud and other crimes associated with red light areas could be limited to one area and among people of the kind drawn to such pleasures. In areas outside the "red light" ghetto, decent women could move free from the unwanted attentions of bestial and predatory men. What was more, some feminists believed that freed from the distraction of loose women, the sisterhood would be able to educate men in order that "licentiousness will inevitably shrink and disappear."[30]

There were also, incidental, advantages for the pimps, madams, and prostitutes. The working girls and ancillary folk could police, control, and advertise the area themselves. Some idea of the autonomy of the region can be seen in the face it presented to the public. It developed its own newspaper, *The Mascot*, giving gossip, scandal and local news and a guide—the *Blue Book*—in which madams and prostitutes advertised. As with the premises, the entries in this were varied and indicated the huge variety. The language and content are informative. The girls are described in opaque and polite terms, with attributes like "wit" and "loveliness." Even their profession is blurred by obfuscatory language. According to one advert, a visit to them "could teach more than the pen can describe." But more importantly their nationality and race were also given in a simple code. The discerning punter could look through a "menu" of girls where "w" represented white; "c" was colored; "J" Jewish and "★" meant French. Armed with such information he could avoid embarrassing or offensive encounters in the segregated, Jim Crow, South where miscegenation was by the 1910s a crime in almost half of the nation's states.[31]

Given the Victorian obsession with compartmentalization and hygiene, it is surprising that the second strategy, that of regulation, took so long to come into force. Throughout the period and across the nation, the situation was fluid with regard to regulation. St Louis, Missouri, had passed an ordinance for the inspection of all prostitutes in 1870. It was withdrawn by purity campaigners in 1874 who argued that it simply encouraged immorality. On the other hand, St Paul, Minnesota, introduced mechanisms for the regulation and inspection of brothels in 1870, and the measure withstood five separate purity crusades against it over a 20-year period.

Nor was it simply a case of local authorities who came up against opposition when acting to regulate the sexual hygiene. When the Chicago physician, Dr Denslow Lewis, tried to discuss "the hygiene of the sexual act" at the American Medical Association (AMA) conference of 1899, he was dismissed by Baltimore gynecologist Howard Kelly who stated categorically that—"The discussion of the subject is attended with filth, and we besmirch ourselves by discussing it in public." Nevertheless, the new century brought a slow change in attitude; four years later, the AMA had organized its own committee charged with investigating venereal diseases.[32] A part of this volte-face was due to early twentieth-century advances in understanding of venereal disease with increased knowledge of its epidemiology, prognosis, and prevention which engendered a feeling that cures would soon be available.

In some measure, this improved knowledge can be put down to a new target of moral outrage. At the turn of the century there was growing talk of "syphilis of the innocent," wives and children infected via the "bestial" behavior of their husbands and fathers. This view was especially prevalent among the cosmopolitan middle class who made up the readership of a range of European social novelists like Ibsen, Zola, and Shaw. It was also tied in with the growing move towards the rights of women to sexual, economic, and political equality. This new morality showed that where these rights were absent, vice was prevalent. These views had a slow but sure effect on the vice trade. It was visible in municipal controls. For example, in 1902, in Minneapolis, the city subsidized weekly check-ups, costing $1 a time, which gave "clean" women a certificate and required the infected to cease all sexual activity until they could prove that they were cured. By 1915, this system had been adopted in many of the major cities, including San Francisco, where it had been extended to a free daily check.

Much of this policy of what amounted to decriminalization was the result of the work of the New York dermatologist, Prince A. Morrow. Morrow advocated a policy route which began with inspection and progressed to hospitalization and treatment. Nevertheless, he also advocated the total eradication of prostitution and to this end formed the American Society of Sanitary and Moral Prophylaxis. His aim was "to limit the spread of diseases which have their origin in the Social Evil." He claimed he would achieve this through education and prevention. Straddling the divide between "purity campaigners" with their "birds and bees," dainty, highly moral stance and the venereologists with their "rational modernity" inspired by Freudian liberality, Morrow found a middle ground which found the support of many of the social Progressive heavyweights of the early twentieth century. Figures like Jane Addams supported his educational policy, holding that through books, lectures and articles aimed at women and children, as well as men, it would be possible to point the way to successful marriage as way to eliminate prostitution.[33]

This trend for sex education extended to the stage with the 1913 play *Damaged Goods*, which went on to reach an even wider audience as a silent film in 1914. Eugene Brieux's original illustrated the effects of a syphilitic husband's philandering and was described as "unquestionably the most widely discussed play of a decade," starting a trend for "vice plays." In some quarters this fashion was seen as simple titillation—after all, this was still the age of Comstock.[34] There was the inevitable backlash from moral rights organizations. Leading the charge were religious organizations. Some, in the spirit of these "rational," Taylorist times produced more sophisticated arguments than the usual simple moral condemnations. Typical of these was the argument of the Catholic poet and journalist, (Alfred) Joyce Kilmer. He feared that there was a danger when placing the emphasis on public education rather than simple morality. He maintained that such strategies could backfire and remove "responsibility of sin from the individual and place it on society."[35] Nevertheless there was perhaps an acceptance that there was a relentless move towards acceptance and liberalization in the sex industry which they would have to more or less follow.

Given this seemingly unstoppable progression, other opponents backed the third and final strategy of dealing with vice—simple prohibition. The crusade for the prohibition and criminalization of prostitution drew in the whole gamut of early twentieth-century Progressive reformers. There were the moral up-lifters who felt that the only way to control vice was to outlaw all its manifestations. Others saw it as a racial problem and argued that it was uncontrolled immigration from poor, backward and immoral countries that caused the problem. Others saw poverty and slums as the root cause. Still others held that it was the result of the oppression of women. The problem was approached from the usual progressive starting point—they held a rational investigation. Between 1910 and 1917, some 42 US cities created commissions to investigate prostitution. The result was that starting in Chicago, most major cities argued that they were pretty successful in eliminating segregated red light districts. New York City's reformers claimed that they had reduced the city's population of prostitutes from nearly 15,000 to less than 3,500 between 1912 and 1915. Cities established special courts dedicated to investigating vice cases. There was the Domestic Relations Court in Philadelphia, Chicago had its Morals Court and New York created a specific Women's Court.

Not only did the Progressives reform the way in which they investigated prostitution, but they also moved made a move away from the old system of fining, which it was argued simply increased prostitution since the girls needed more money to pay the charges. Instead the system relied on probation, education and rehabilitation. A typical instance is that of 17-year-old Nellie Roberts who, in 1917, was convicted by a magistrate in Port Jervis, New York, of "travelling around the city and entering saloons and committing acts of prostitution." Nellie was from a poor background with no mother and a drunken, abusive, father. She was committed to the New York State Reformatory for Women at Bedford Hills where she was trained in domestic service, industrial sewing, dressmaking, and a variety of other skills. Through these skills and moral training, reinforced by sanctions, religious instruction, and occasional physical punishment, Nellie was trained to enable her to earn a living without returning to her previous life of vice. In Nellie's case, this was unsuccessful and after a brief spell of employment, she married and started to support her husband through prostitution.[36]

It was not coincidental that Nellie's arrest took place in 1917. When America entered Europe's Great War in April of that year, they launched a concerted effort to make sure that the scourge of prostitution was kept away from US troops. The US Army and Navy strictly enforced a rule that no brothels would be tolerated within 5 miles of training camps, forts and bases. They also erected barbed wire fences and guards patrolled the perimeters of their camps to insure celibacy as much as security. Simultaneously the military launched a high profile campaign against venereal disease. The campaign used catchy slogans and vivid posters. Typical of these was the Commission on Training Camp Activities' billboards which unequivocally claimed that "A German Bullet is Cleaner than a Whore." The language used to describe prostitutes was a key to their new status. They were no longer "fallen women" or "soiled doves" whose morality had been compromised by poverty or corrupted by unscrupulous and perverted men. This was a national emergency. Films were made with titles like "Fit to Fight" and the federal government established a Division of Venereal Disease and a Board of Social Hygiene charged with controlling the spread of sexually transmitted diseases and their carriers, whores. During the war years the already well-supported Progressive crusade to purify the nation reached fever pitch. Storyville and other red light districts were finally closed. Between 1917 and 1920, across the nation some 18,000 prostitutes were detained. Of these, over 15,500 were found to be infected and were taken into detention homes for treatment which could last from two months to a year. Essentially they were imprisoned for this period.[37] Curiously, no servicemen, or any other men, were detained. Perhaps their patriotism had made them immune.[38]

Most of the leading authorities on the history of American prostitution see the federal response to the sex industry as an effective indicator of the nation's moral climate. This is certainly true of the 1920s. After the Progressive crusade against the oldest profession, there was a moral holiday. Also, like civil service reform, bi-metalism, or even immigration restriction, prostitution seemed to have been one of the problems that the Progressives had "resolved." After all, the red light areas had been closed and vast numbers of prostitutes punished, if not rehabilitated. Some historians of organized crime have argued that the prohibition of prostitution, just like that of alcohol, by restricting supply, increased the value and led to syndication of the vice industry in 1920s and 1930s. This was certainly true in metropolitan areas. In spite of his image as a simple, if very effective, boot-legger, Al Capone was deeply involved in a highly lucrative prostitution ring. The extent of the organized prostitution which evolved in these years is readily visible in the 1936 trial of the New York gangster, Lucky Luciano.

This high profile trial revealed Luciano's nation-wide "Prostitution Corporation." It was a highly sophisticated and well-organized enterprise. The so-called Corporation not only had a phone booking department, but it also had facilities to provide legal representation. It did not stop there. It also protected its investments by providing coaching, information and bonds for those caught. What was perhaps even more shocking to the American public than the scale and scope of the operation, were the revelations that it was not only hoodlums and gangsters, pimps and procurers who were involved in the vice industry. Luciano's trial revealed that the mobsters controlled rings of crooked lawyers, judges, police, and informers who extorted money from the women accused of prostitution. The issue of prostitution had developed just like the nation itself. Over the 75 years of this study, it had been industrialized and incorporated and the ideas behind its control had evolved in a similar fashion. Under these progressions, the prostitute was no longer an individual criminal, but a part of an institution and business which needed to be curtailed and regulated. The change is probably best summed up by the historian William E. Leuchtenburg who argued that, "While the Progressive grieved over the fate of the prostitute, the New Dealer would have placed Mrs. Warren's [George Bernard Shaw's infamous prostitute] profession under a code authority."[39] Nevertheless, the world's oldest professionals continued to ply their trade.

The final aspect which it is worth investigating in terms of sex crime is that of perversion. To many, especially in the earlier years of this study, the purpose of sex was simple: it was procreation. From this perspective, prostitution, pornography, and contraception can be seen as morally wrong. So could any form of sex which avoided conception. This might be heterosexual acts such as masturbation or oral or even anal sex. It may have been homosexuality. During this period, the Jewish businessman Leo Frank was lynched, partly on evidence which showed him to be a pervert. Among the prosecution's accusations, they claimed that he had a predi-lection for oral sex. Anglo-Saxon America had always had a strong position on sexual deviance. In the days of the theocracy of New England in the seventeenth century, the crimes of bestiality, adultery, lesbianism, anal intercourse, and masturbation had all carried a death penalty in the various colonies. In the year of Frank's lynching, any such behavior which involved penile penetration of any orifice other than the vagina was labeled "Sodomy" by the state of California which made it a crime that carried a tariff of some 20 years in prison.

Nor was California alone in this sanction. While some states retained the death sentence for such crimes well into the twentieth century, most reduced it to a sentence of imprisonment. Massachusetts shows how these laws changed. In 1835, sodomy was changed from being an act only performed in homosexual sex, to one which applied to anal sex with women as well. The new code also made the maximum penalty 20 years in prison, but no longer with mandatory solitary confinement and hard labor. However, convictions were rare since it required two witnesses and proof of penetration. Some idea of the frequency of sodomy cases can be seen by the statistics for New York City courts. Between 1796 and 1873, they tried a total of 22 cases. These were entirely cases of homosexual buggery and are notable by the way in which prosecutions only normally resulted when there was force used or there was a great disparity between the ages between the accused and their "victims."[40] Two landmark appeals made in the early period of this study both serve to indicate a more tolerant attitude towards homosexuality than may be apparent from a simple glance at the statute books.

In 1873, in the case of *Massachusetts vs. James A Snow*, Willard Smith and James Snow had consensual anal sex. A remorseful Smith later took poison and, on recovering, brought an action against Snow. Snow was found guilty of sodomy. However, on appeal in the Superior Court, under cross-examination Smith revealed that he had committed "acts of a similar nature." A witness testified he had previously "attempted to commit the same offense with him" and that "he had done it with other boys." Added to this it was shown that he only put up a "partial resistance" to Snow. While the District Attorney still upheld the conviction in the lower court, the decision is considered a landmark, establishing as it did at least the idea of consent. The second case took place five years later in the Montana Territory, where a man called "Mahaffey" was found guilty of sodomizing a 14-year-old boy, known simply as "B." It emerged that the pair had had sex several times before at Mahaffey's ranch and that "B" had been paid for the acts. Although Mahaffey was found guilty, this again shows that mitigation was possible and that at least during the early part of the period there was at least some pragmatic tolerance in the way in which the law approached acts of homosexual activity.[41]

In keeping with the Victorian mania for compartmentalism, the 1880s saw increased medicalization of sexuality. This had an impact on a variety of spheres of American life. For example, the 1880 Census listed not only "Defective" and "Dependent" classes but also Deviants as well. Among these classes were "Erotopaths," "Sexual Inverts," and most importantly "Homosexuals," all terms developed in this period. Alongside this improvement in semantics came the belief that if science could define a condition, then perhaps it could treat, or at least contain such perversions. Psychoanalysis, hypnotism, electro-therapy, hydro-therapy, surgery, and other methods were all used at various times to treat a variety of conditions. Each claimed various degrees of success. Where they failed, the law could step in. Again the example of New York is instructive. The figure of 22 arrests for sodomy between 1796 and 1873 had grown dramatically by the end of the 1880s. By the 1890s, nearly every single year of the decade recorded more arrests than those entire 75 years had produced. By the 1910s, the figure averaged 50 a year, and by the 1920s, it had climbed to over 125 in some years. Some of this increase can be seen simply as the result of the Progressive moral urge, but there were also other elements which drove the moral reformers. The Society for the Prevention of Cruelty to Children (SPCC) operated largely in the poorest slums, largely those of the "immigrant colonies" where Italian, Polish, Russian, and other "new" immigrants had made their homes. Since the SPCC initiated between 40 and 90 percent of all sodomy prosecutions in the city, at some level their motives can also be seen as being a reflection of, if not a result of, the simple, all-pervasive, anti-immigrant, bigotry of turn-of-the-century New York.[42]

Like most metropolitan areas during this period, New York was relatively tolerant of gays. Charles Nesbitt, a medical student from South Carolina, stated in 1890 that:

> perverts of both sexes maintained a sort of social setup in New York City, had their places of meeting and had the advantage of police protection for which they could pay ... Many of them were married and lived in homes of their own to all outward appearances with perfect respectability.[43]

Vibrant gay cultures emerged in the Bowery, Harlem, Times Square, and the Village, making New York something of a Mecca for gays. This is borne out by the experience of no less a figure than Horatio Alger, who in 1866 was investigated by a committee of his peers in his post as a minister in Massachusetts for his "unnatural familiarity" with two young boys. He "neither denied nor attempted to extenuate" the charges but simply fled to New York City.[44]

But, like the statistics for prostitution, it is no coincidence that of all the years before 1920, the highest level of arrests for sodomy occurred in 1917. For not only did the campaign to protect the Doughboys from venereal disease focus on prostitution, but also as it grew into a campaign against immorality, it was targeted against deviants. It was an especial fear that hundreds of thousands of young country boys would be subjected to the evil influences of the corrupt denizens of the big cities. This would inevitably arise during the training period and on the transports to Europe when huge numbers of men would be crammed together in camps for extended periods with no women. They would also more than likely be shipped out of the already notorious port areas of major cities. The result was a new moral climate in which the previously taboo subject of homosexuality became a specific fear of the crusaders.

Some idea of the growth in wartime and post-war anti-gay activity can be gathered from the annual arrest statistics for homosexual solicitation in Manhattan. These grew from numbering less than one hundred in 1916 to peak at over 750 in the year 1920. They would average over 500 a year throughout the 1920s. One of the most active groups protecting the troops was New York's influential reform movement, the Committee of Fourteen. Already dedicated to wiping out prostitution, the Committee turned its attention to homosexual activity during the war, setting up surveillance on well-known cruising areas and "hangouts for perverts." Similarly, during the war years and immediately after, Anthony Comstock's Society for the Suppression of Vice (SSV) found a new purpose in spite of Comstock's death in 1915. The SSV gave the NYPD enough information on gay activity in the city to co-ordinate a series of raids on bath houses, and directly assisted in the arrest of over 200 "degenerates" between 1916 and 1921.[45]

In many ways, homosexuals, and the attitudes towards them, were typical of the paradoxes of 1920s America. As George Bernard Shaw had pointed out, this was a country which was in part modern, and in part traditional. For homosexuals, as in the heterosexual community, sexuality in metropolitan regions was slowly brought into the vision of the American public. Gays began to compete with the straight world for cafés, bars and other spaces in the cities. Universally acknowledged gay haunts evolved—it became a standing joke that YMCA really stood for "Why I'm So Gay." Several plays, songs, films and books addressed homosexual and lesbian issues. The psychoanalytical concepts of Freud and the theories of sexuality of Henry Havelock Ellis began to fascinate Americans. Drag Balls became part of the social season in New York. Openly gay communities emerged in many metropolitan areas, attracting mainstream visitors interested in "slumming." One of the favorite haunts for slummers was Harlem, with its vibrant Jazz Age modernity and "otherness." Harlem's blues and jazz venues featured many homosexual and lesbian performers, like Gladys Bentley who always performed dressed as a man. These performers acted as a magnet for similar audiences which many locals tolerated, if not actually sympathizing with them. Alongside Harlem there was equally fashionable Greenwich Village which became another haunt, attracting a Bohemian, liberal type of resident and visitor. Keen to assert their tolerance in the age of Prohibition and bourgeois moral fervor, this population made a show of embracing the local "pansies" and "bull dagger" lesbians.[46]

That is not to say that gay and lesbian culture was always tolerated. Even in New York, a moral backlash was apparent in the late 1920s. In 1927, on Broadway, the lesbian drama, *The Captive*, generated a huge scandal and led to policemen climbing on to the stage during a performance and arresting the entire cast of the play. In the wake of the arrests, New York's popular Tammany Mayor, Al Smith, presided over an anti-gay clampdown in which many of Greenwich Village's drag shows and the city's bath houses were raided, the occupants arrested, and the venues closed down and boarded up. His successor, Fiorella LaGuardia, continued this policy, forcing the drag queens out of the downtown New York districts between 14th and 72nd Streets and closing the clubs and theaters on moral grounds.[47]

Another part of this had to do with reaction to the removal of Prohibition. In many ways Prohibition had helped gay culture. Speakeasies and blind pigs were less choosy and judgmental about their clientele, and more swanky hotels and restaurants, losing money without their alcohol sales, allowed prostitutes and other undesirables to practice their trades in areas from which they would previously have been barred. When the Volstead Act was repealed in 1933, fired by a new Puritanism, the middle classes more or less enthusiastically backed the authorities' clampdown. This was being given additional impetus in New York by a moral crusade being undertaken to drive degenerates out of the city's bars. New ordinances, inspired by FDR's promise not to allow the return of "the saloon in its old form or some modern disguise," gave local authorities the power to close bars.

The situation in New York is again instructive. Here legislation was introduced which permitted the State Liquor Authority to close suspected gay bars purely on the behavior of the clientele. Just as prostitution was driven underground, and to some extent syndicated by the wartime drive to cleanse the nation, so this clampdown on gay life in metropolitan areas led to mob control of gay bars. Syndicated crime liked the high potential profits and was, ironically, more suited to managing such bars than legitimate businesses since it could buy off police—as well as having the will to pay off the relevant authorities to close down the competition.[48]

It is some measure of how homosexuality was regarded that unlike many other groups in this period, gays had no real voice. Those men who spoke out in favor risked having themselves branded degenerates, radicals, effeminate or worse, un-American. Women who spoke out on any issue which did not meet with popular approval such as feminists, pacifists, socialists, were all liable to be seen as all or any of these and be accused of either being nymphomaniacs dedicated to free love, or lesbian man-haters. One of the best instances of this is the image of Emma Goldman. The anarchist free-thinker and pacifist was accused of being both a harlot and a lesbian since as early as the 1890s she had advocated tolerance of same-sex relations as a part of her support for free love.[49] Nevertheless although the term was often used as a slur, in general, lesbianism was less frowned on than gay male relations, largely since women were generally regarded as sexual only in child-bearing fashion and there was a general disbelief in women's same-sex relations being actively sexual in any way. Women living together were often regarded simply as spinsters, too unfortunate to have been chosen for marriage.

In conclusion, it is perhaps worth trying to take some form of overview of the attitudes of the period. In many ways, sexuality and sex crime mirror American industrial and economic development. While it is tempting to take a Whig approach to personal relations and see them as governed by a gradual enlightenment, this is only partially true. It is perhaps equally tempting to look at stasis and crisis as the drivers of sexual tolerance, to hold that where prosperity and optimism reigned, tolerance thrived. When the nation was at war or enduring economic crisis, clampdowns followed. While these models hold true, they do, like all historical models, fit only some of the facts. Homosexuality was tolerated in the 1920s—an era of prosperity, but only for part of the decade. It was frowned on in the Depression era of the 1930s. Also in some regions, the attitude to such perversions never really changed. Smaller towns and religiously based communities saw little alteration in their attitudes, no matter how the economic, political or diplomatic climate changed. However, the outbreak of war in 1941 brought perhaps the greatest surge in homosexual activity in American history, but the post-war prosperity also brought a new level of persecution. Perhaps the situation is simply too complex to be modeled in such a way.

9

POLITICAL CRIME

Scandal, Sleaze, and Corruption

It's awful hard to get people interested in corruption unless they can get some of it.

Will Rogers[1]

Langley's major project, the collection of the daily papers ... consisted of counting and filing news stories according to category ... love scandals, church scandals ... political misdoings with a subhead of crooked elections ... He wanted to fix American life finally in one edition, what he called Collyer's eternally current dateless newspaper, the only newspaper anyone would ever need.

E.L. Doctorow, *Homer and Langley*[2]

In the eyes of Doctorow's fictionalized, eccentric editor, Langley Collyer, scandal and political corruption were endemic in the American society of the 1920s. His encyclopaedic newspaper would detail them along with other typically "American" crimes—lynchings, "gangland rubouts," investment scams and tenement fires. There are various reasons for this. Some might argue that American democracy evolved to favor corruption, with its ever-escalating costs, winner-takes-all mentality and vast spoils system that is wide open to corruption. Others might claim the true, healthy, and open nature of US government is clearly demonstrated by the array of corrupt politicians and scandals that are so frequently brought to light. Whatever view is taken, there can be few other nations which take such a robust attitude to political corruption as the United States. From Colonial times to the present day, American history is peppered with examples of corruption, but one period stands head and shoulders above the others in terms of its corrupt reputation.

With their love of neat divisions, it has become traditional that American historians call the period between 1877 and the turn of the twentieth century, the "Gilded Age." Some would argue that the very compromise, by which the last federal troops were withdrawn from the last recalcitrant former Confederate States in return for the Democrats ceding the Presidential election to the Republicans, was itself a supreme act of corruption. They would claim that the manufacturing of a deal in smoke-filled rooms, without public scrutiny was against the ideals of democracy.[3] It was in these years that America moved from being a purely extractive economy to becoming a major league, modern, mixed economy. This was the time of America's emergence as an industrial power. Nevertheless, Mark Twain's evocative phrase is not the result of the glittering achievements of the period, although there are quite a few. Nor is it the result of the increasing wealth of the period, which was undeniable. It derives its name from the notion that while these years appeared golden, they were in fact simply times symbolized more by an everyday base metal, coated with a very thin, but shiny, veneer of gilt. In other words, in these years, things were not as they appeared.

Deception was the order of the day at all levels of American society, though it was most notably the case in Twain's eponymous story among the "political classes." These were days in which America industrialized and boomed: when vast amounts of capital flooded into the nation and huge fortunes and even bigger possibilities gave rise to unheard-of avarice. These were the times in which the robber barons and political machines conspired to rule the nation with the tacit support and often connivance of the national government. This was the era of the "Great Barbeque" in which spoilsmen, placemen, and middlemen sold their influence locally, regionally and nationally to the highest bidder. It reached to the very top. During these years even the supreme hero of the American Civil War led an administration so tainted by corruption and scandal that his name became shorthand for graft—Grantism. It has been seen as a period of rampant political self-interest, in which politics was motivated by spoils, profit, graft, kickbacks, and corruption. It has been variously described as the era of "excess," of "negation," and "cynicism."

Closer examination reveals not only that the corruption was perhaps not as widespread as it would appear, but also that such corruption was not perhaps as rare as imagined in other periods. There is evidence to support such theories. Since the 1960s there has been a widespread movement in US history to try to rehabilitate the Gilded Age: to show that these years were not quite as stereotypically, or uniquely, rotten as Twain's fellow travelers have argued. To these revisionists, it was not that the Gilded Age wasn't corrupt, it was more that the politicians of these years achieved more, cared more and were more sincere than had been previously argued. It is not difficult to find justifications for these views, even in other years of the period covered by this book. Contrasting the Gilded Age with the first decade of the twentieth century, or the 1920s, reveals that corruption was not limited to the earlier years. William Howard Taft's presidency, perhaps rather unfairly, became known as the era of "Fat Politics," and not only because of the 300-pound bulk of Taft himself. As far as spoilsmen go, especially according to the press of the time, President Warren Gamaliel Harding's so-called "Ohio Gang" were pretty well unequaled in any other period of American history.

Even taking into regard these, more considered, interpretations, there can be little doubt that political corruption in the early years of this study was an epic tale, not only in its depth and scale, but also in its significance—both at the time and since. Modern America has been rocked by huge political scandals, from Watergate to Whitewater, and George W. Bush's presidency has frequently been called the new Gilded Age.[4] No doubt even as this book is being written, there is another scandal about to break.

Nevertheless, few political scandals contain anything new. The mix of ingredients may change, but the ingredients themselves remain the same and in their simplest form they can be reduced to three motives—sex, money, and power. All of these are to be found in abundance in the years of this study and their allure, exposure and, occasional, punishment can be considered distinctly modern, after all, these are the years in which modern America was formed. These are the times of the birth of truly democratic America, when blacks, women and even—in 1924—the supreme victims of American discrimination, the Native Americans, get the vote. These are the years when the modern American economy evolves, when America begins its lasting love affair with technology and finance. These are the times when America becomes an imperial power, on both on her own and other continents. Most tellingly, these are the years when modern temptations proved too much for some American politicians.[5]

Given the centrality of the Gilded Age to any such study of American political corruption, it seems logical that this investigation should concentrate on the engine which drove those years: the quest for money. Venality, financial impropriety, theft, influence peddling, embezzlement, larceny, graft—all formed a central part in Mark Twain's tale. When the heroine of the piece, Laura Hawkins, arrives in Washington, DC, in order to attempt to persuade the government to purchase 75,000 acres in Tennessee from her family, she is treated to a ringside seat overlooking a true orgy of corruption.

What Twain was describing was the result of a combination of the vast forces of capital and industry unleashed by the Civil War, colliding with a lack of effective regulation and watched over by a press growing in power and influence, hungry for the scoop and all too eager to expose corruption wherever they found it. In terms of simple venality, the war itself had escalated corruption in the American capital. The huge demands of what was the first modern "total war" generated mammoth contracts and absorbed vast sums of money. One result was that throughout his time in office, Lincoln was bedevilled by scandals involving military supplies. Newspapers ran story after story of Union soldiers being given sub-standard or over-priced weapons, food, tents, and uniforms as well as exposés of those who were willing to exploit the troops in such a way.

Typical of the deals apparently done by unscrupulous politicians was the 1862 agreement by which a Rhode Island Senator, James Fowler Simmons, influenced contracts for 50,000 breech-loading rifles. In return, Fowler received some $10,000 in cash and $500,000 worth of IOUs from the manufacturers. What makes the case important is not so much the significant amount at stake—which can be put in its true perspective when it is realized that an 1862 dollar is worth about $20 today, in terms of spending power—but more that although Simmons was undeniably linked to the scandal, he resigned before legislation designed to curb just such practices could take effect.[6] Although not the last Senator who was able to avoid scandal in this way, his demise was instructive. As the dawn of the twentieth century neared, an invigorated mass media would hone in on just such cases, allowing for no such escapes. Ironically, in part, this change was the result of technology, in part, it was simply another form of venality.

The advent of linotype and the consequent high speed, high volume presses gave rise to truly mass-circulation newspapers. While these evolved in the nation's metropolises, with the increased use of rail and telegraphy, it also meant that by the 1890s news could travel coast to coast and north to south with a new rapidity. The incessant wars for circulation generated by these competing newspapers meant that national empires of papers were increasingly hungry for scandalous headlines with which to boost their own sales. Examining another wartime case of corruption shows just how much how this change influenced the investigation and punishment of political shenanigans over the 40 years between Simmons' case and the new century.

In the wake of the 1898 conflict with Spain, the nation was horrified to read of its troops once again being supplied with shoddy goods, most notoriously the almost putrefied and inedible "embalmed beef." Unlike Simmons, the supply of this tainted, canned, beef cost the Secretary of War, General Russell A. Alger, his job, even though there was no evidence at all to link him personally to the contracts.[7] What seemed to have brought Alger down was the relentless continuing accusations of his ineptitude by the press. In this they were driven on, rather than put off, by President William McKinley's repeated and solid defense of Alger's abilities. The Hearst-owned *New York Journal* continually took McKinley's ever more desperate defense of Alger as proof of his association with Marcus Alonzo Hanna's, increasingly nepotistic and venal, Republican machine.

In linking Alger to Hanna, the Hearst press was tapping into the rich vein of scandal, mistrust, and hatred which the public had previously largely reserved for big business—the infamous so-called Trusts. Hanna would become the very embodiment of this corrupt tie, and in some ways he even invited this distinction. It was Hanna who famously quipped that "There are two things that are important in politics. The first is money and I can't remember what the second one is."[8] A year later, he went on to prove it, forever changing American politics in the process. As McKinley's campaign manager, Hanna raised the stakes of American political campaigning when he essentially bought the 1896 election by raising an unprecedented $3.5 million from big business to support the Republican candidate.

He did this to ward off the challenge to McKinley's stand pat conservatism posed by the Populist–Democrat alliance and their far more charismatic young candidate, William Jennings Bryan and his supposed threat to the existing financial system. Although the Hearst newspapers vocally championed Bryan, it was essentially the Democrat's measly $700,000 campaign chest which assured his defeat, and did much to implant the persistent idea of Hanna as the "plutocrat" who controlled the McKinley White House. While they could never get any accusation of personal impropriety to stick, Hearst's accusations made sure that Hanna, and most political agents who would follow him, would be seen as the ruthless and nebulous manipulators, exponents of the backroom deal whose sole interests lay with their invisible financial masters.[9]

If press investigation was part of the reason for the exposure of corruption, there was another. It could be argued that more federal corruption was exposed, simply because more corruption was taking place. The money generated by industrialization increased both the scale and rewards which could be gained by taming and maintaining politicians. The best indicator of this must be the railroads: the largest engineering project of the nineteenth century, and arguably the most corrupt. The huge scale of corruption stemmed from the massive federal investment in the rail project. Government land grants, subsidies, and loans meant that there were unprecedented opportunities for skimming, bribery, embezzlement, and kickbacks. Sure enough, within five years of the completion of the trans-continental railroad, more than a dozen—largely Republican—Senators and Representatives were under investigation for corruption.

The railroads, most notably Thomas Durant's fundraising vehicle for the construction of the Union Pacific Railroad, the Credit Mobilier (see Chapter 2), manipulated the federal government shamelessly. They falsified surveys, in order to increase the payments which were made per mile and whose value varied according to the difficulty of the terrain. They doled out "loans" to useful politicians with no request for security or collateral. They gave out vast amounts of stock, or sold them at extremely preferential rates. They paid bribes, sweeteners, and hush money to politicians to assure their co-operation or compliance. When their activities were discovered, the scale of corruption that was uncovered was unparalleled. The investigations included not only the Vice President, Schuyler Colefax, but also his successor in the office, Henry Wilson and a Republican Presidential hopeful, James G. Blaine. Although they were all exonerated in one fashion or another, their careers were permanently tainted.

The completion of the main rail route, and exposure of the Credit Mobilier and associated scams, did not spell the end of railroad corruption. Competitive trans-continental routes, spur lines, regional lines, new north–south connections, and all manner of other rail construction projects continued through into the late 1880s. These served not only to increase the numbers of lobbyists in the capital, but also the competition on the rail routes, as duplication and alternative routes swiftly emerged. Over the next decade, it became apparent that there were huge revenues available to those towns, businesses and industries through proximity to the rail hub, rail head or just a siding. The corruption was by no means one way. While the railroad companies continued to use corrupt methods to improve their chances of selection for construction and freight contracts, many politicians also went in to bat for their local regions. They would pass on sweeteners from constituents eager to "boost" their regions and businesses, more often than not taking their own percentage as and when necessary.

To many politicians, industrialists, and entrepreneurs, both the taking and the giving of bribes became so normal during these years that it was considered a part of the business process. What perhaps summed up the situation best was the justification put forward by one of the Central Pacific Railroad's four governing "Associates," Collis Huntington. When he was asked by the Congressional investigation into the scandal in 1873 why he was in Washington, DC, scattering sweeteners to politicians as if it were going out of fashion, he responded with a disarmingly straightforward logic:

> If you have to pay money [to a politician] to have the right thing done, it is only just and fair to do it . . . If he [the politician] has the power to do great evil and won't do right unless he is bribed to do it, I think . . . it is a man's duty to go up and bribe.[10]

Nor did the exposure of the Credit Mobilier scandal end such unashamed and open admissions of corruption. For example, when in 1909, President Taft appointed Robert W. Archibald to the US Commerce Court, Archibald saw the appointment as a cash cow which he milked for every last drop of money. When struck from the bench and barred from holding any official office, Archibald was unrepentant, arguing that such behavior was usual.[11]

Nevertheless, the Credit Mobilier did have huge repercussions. One of the most oblique, but also arguably subsequently the most important, consequences of the scandal was the loss of a little over $320 by Thomas Nast in the collapse which followed the scandal. The German-born cartoonist was already so outraged by the behavior of the Grant administration, and politicians in general, that this event reinforced him in his conviction as a life-long Democrat. It also confirmed him as one of the most potent forces fighting against corruption over the next years. It was Nast who had drawn the carpetbaggers pillaging in the Reconstruction South, and then drawn them to the attention of the Northern population. Nast would be a key figure in bringing down "Boss" William Marcy Tweed's Tammany empire, largely through his unnerving portrayals in *Harper's Magazine* of the municipal boss as a disturbing leering, menacing, brutal oaf always carrying a money bag. It was Nast who would lead the charge against Hanna, portraying him in the Hearst press as the dollar-suit-wearing father of baby William McKinley.

Nast's experience, and his subsequent targets, demonstrated that the corruption of the Gilded Age was not simply limited to railroads. As the federal government intervened in large-scale projects—be it war or railroad construction—so it required further sources of revenue, which in turn provided greater opportunities for corruption. As the taxation take increased, so did the corruption.

One of the most outstanding, both in scale and implications, was the Whiskey Ring scandal. By the mid-1870s, alcohol duty had become one of the primary sources of federal revenue, with predictable consequences. Centering on Missouri, internal revenue agents were bribed, whiskey production figures were downgraded and the reports generated were falsified to systematically defraud the government of duty. By the time these frauds came to light, the corruption was so widespread it even reached Grant's immediate family. His son, brother, and private secretary were among some 350 arrested.[12] Nevertheless, Grant's administration ran its full term, in spite of what one disgusted politician later identified as "the silver-coinage ring, the Cattle Ring, and whatsoever other rings there may be."[13] Grant's reputation as the hero of the Union also survived, and his tomb in New York remained the greatest tourist attraction until the turn of the twentieth century.

There were those who claimed that his victory had not really benefitted the entire nation. Many in the South during the post-war years of Reconstruction (1865–1877) claimed that they had never experienced more overt corruption. One ex-Union officer's career summed up the extent of venality. When the notorious Henry Clay Warmoth of Illinois retired from the US Army in 1865, like many other ambitious men he went south, but all did not go smoothly. In Texas, he was indicted for embezzlement and theft. Leaving the Lone Star State, penniless, he went to Louisiana where by 1872 he was elected governor in what was, even by the standards of the time, a spectacularly fraudulent election. By the time that the state started impeachment proceedings, it was estimated that through state printing contracts and personal speculation in state bonds, Warmoth had turned his $8,000-a-year salary into over $1 million. He managed to ride out his term before the impeachment vote, marry an heiress and live to a ripe old age. When asked about his behavior, he summed it up with an answer of typical bravado, but also more than a little truth—"Why damn it, everyone is demoralizing down here. Corruption is the fashion. I do not pretend to be honest, but only as honest as anyone in politics."[14]

The sad historical legacy of such carpetbaggers as Warmoth is that most accounts of the post-war South portrayed the entirety of the Republican administrations as corrupt and self-serving. In the short term, this meant that opponents of Republican administrations could play a corruption card, with very little evidence to back their accusations. For example, in Mississippi, the idealistic Republican governor Adelbert Ames was forced to resign when threatened with impeachment on corruption charges by a coalition of the old pre-bellum elites. In spite of the paucity of evidence, his reputation was so shattered that his daughter, Blanche, was still fighting to clear his name in the 1950s when she wrote to future President John F. Kennedy disputing his statement that "no state suffered more from carpetbag rule than Mississippi" and that Adelbert Ames had "raised taxes to fourteen times as high as normal in order to support the extravagance of the Reconstruction government."[15] Although Kennedy subsequently admitted that his account was open to question, his interpretation was by no means unique, and was certainly not the last to draw such a picture.

There were also other long-term consequences. With some notable exceptions mainstream American historians argued that Reconstruction was an episode best forgotten and condoned, if not supported, the systematic practical dismantling of the reforms aimed at racial equality in the region which followed so swiftly on the compromise of 1877. Typical of the argument was the reasoning of another future President, Woodrow Wilson, that

> The white men of the South were aroused by the mere instinct of self-preservation to rid themselves ... of the intolerable burden of govern-ments ... [which were] conducted in the interests of [Northern] adventurers; governments whose incredible debts were incurred that thieves might be enriched, whose increasing loans and taxes went to no public use but into the pockets of party managers and corrupt contractors.[16]

Nor was it only Northerners who were accused of ripping off the defeated South. The term "scalawag" became common during the years of Reconstruction, and would remain in use in histories of the period. Originally referring to a useless pony, it soon came to describe native Southerners who joined in the pillaging of the humiliated region. No one was more indicative of this breed than Franklin Moses. From a prominent family in Charlestown, South Carolina, he was some-thing of Confederate hero, it had been Moses who had raised the rebel flag over Fort Sumter when its US Army garrison had surrendered, essentially sparking the outbreak of Civil War.

His commitment to the Confederate cause did not last beyond the conflict, for no sooner had the South surrendered, than Moses enthusiastically grasped the potential of Reconstruction and joined the Republican Party. As if that volte face was not enough, he was soon organizing the newly enfranchised ex-slaves as a powerbase and he swiftly rose to prominence. As inspector-general of the local militia, he siphoned off funds for equipment to his own personal account. He was then elected to the House of Representatives and from there he went on to become governor of South Carolina. Using his black cronies and his continued control of the state militia, Moses extorted vast sums in what the *New York Times* called "a career of corruption, fee-taking, bribery and robbery, which for extent and audacity is without parallel in the history of any English-speaking people."[17]

Nor was Reconstruction fraud limited to whites. As if to re-affirm their newfound, if albeit brief, moment of political power, blacks too cashed in on the huge opportunities. In 1877, one of the most prominent black Republican Representatives in Congress, Robert Smalls, was convicted of taking a $5,000—nearly $100,000 in today's figures—bribe to buy his vote in Congress.[18] Smalls' case is interesting since his conviction showed less about the dominance of the North over the South, rather, it illustrated the resurgence and re-emergence of the old pre-war elites in the South as Reconstruction drew to a close. Smalls' story is the obverse of that of Moses. A slave on the Charleston waterfront, Smalls had won renown by commandeering a Confederate boat, the *Planter*, laden with arms and delivering it, and himself, to the US Navy blockading the port. For this heroic act, he was made the first black captain of a US Navy ship. His prominence and status made him a prime target for white Democrats, itching to disgrace the new black politicians. When Smalls appealed the charges, they were dropped. This was less to do with the unquestionably dubious nature of the evidence, than a deal made with local Democrats who would be absolved of their part in electoral fraud.

The supreme irony of Smalls' tale is that the deal struck on his behalf so closely mirrored the compromise by which the last Union troops would be withdrawn from the last remaining recalcitrant Southern states. In this deal, made to resolve the stalemate of the 1876 presidential election, the US military retreated north in return for a Republican White House. This thereby effectively sold out any chance of real black power in the Deep South for the best part of another century. Nevertheless the legacy of the Civil War was, at least in the North and West, one of a heroic victory. Perhaps Grant's continued personal popularity rested on his war record. Perhaps it was simply that, as Warmoth suggested, all politicians were regarded as corrupt and as such no one expected him to be anything but tainted. There is certainly much to support this later view in the assessment of Grant's successors. That is not to say that the presidents who followed him were corrupt— far from it.

Rutherford B. Hayes, Chester Arthur and Grover Cleveland all sought to root out corruption. Their target was to clean up the appointment of lucrative public service posts, especially with regard to the massively powerful New York Customs House ring. As if to reinforce this, only months into his administration in 1881, another of Grant's successors, James Garfield, was mortally wounded by the gun of a disaffected office-seeker. Garfield's failure to honor his promise of office—if indeed he had ever made such a promise—was all too indicative of the influence peddling of the period.

It was, however, more a symptom of local and municipal government rather than federal government. The real political "machines," as they were known, evolved in the large metropolitan and urban areas. New York, Chicago, Boston, Philadelphia, Cleveland, New Orleans, San Francisco—it was in the government of these, and other major, cities that the real placemen and spoilsmen, bosses and machines could be found. The reasons for this corruption were varied, but in essence they stemmed from a combination of elements drawing on three inter-related sources. The first was the fundamental failure of government to deal with the squalor of massively expanding cities. These cities had drawn on the colossal increase in economic opportunities, which can be seen as the second element of the equation and the pair of these changes were dependent on the massive growth and change in immigration.

Of all of the machines, the most notorious was Manhattan's Tammany Hall. Center of the Democrat machine in New York, the "Society of St Tammany" had a long pedigree dating back to 1786. However, it was the Irish immigration of the 1840s which really gave it its power base. Despised as Roman Catholics and mocked for their country ways and poverty, refugees from the Irish famine were ostracized and ghetto-ized by the ruling native-born New Yorkers. Unlike many of the previous immigrant groups, having lost their families and fortune through the failure of agriculture, they were reluctant to seek land and move West. Instead they stayed put in the cities, creating powerful constituencies, especially in Boston and New York—cities where there was no longer a property ownership clause excluding the poor from the franchise. Resentful, practical, resourceful and determined to make a better life, the Irish were drawn to urban politics.

The formula was simple: gather in the immigrants, get them, defend them and garner their votes. Tammany's most outspoken boss, George Washington Plunkitt, explained how he got started: "By workin' around the district headquarters and hustling' about the polls on election day ... I got a marketable commodity—one vote."[19] To Plunkitt and other Tammany bosses, politics was a practical pursuit. Unlike the Irish politicians they had left at home, the Tammany bosses were not looking for the heroic, romantic image, such as that which fired the spirit of Home Rulers, Charles Stewart Parnell or John Redmond. They would make their own, Irish, lives, represent their own, Irish, interests, and serve their own, Irish, constituency in the New World. This was politics at its most basic.

Unashamedly pragmatic and self-serving, the bosses sold a service—influence. Tammany was there to fix day-to-day problems. In return for this service, its staff were re-elected year in, year out. That is not to say that Tammany entrusted its elections to anything as fickle as the whims of the electorate. The Tweed Ring, for example, Boss William "Marcy" Tweed's circle of "Forty Thieves" who essentially controlled New York in the 1860s, exercised total control over the ballot box. They did this through a mixture of bribery, violence and a complex and wide-ranging "favor bank" via which they retained power not only over New York's local government, but also strategic use of their own placemen in national politics.

Some idea of the power and methods of Tweed can be seen in his support for New York gubernatorial candidate, John T. Hoffman, in 1868. During this election, the bribery was so conspicuous that there was a Congressional investigation. The report revealed how an election was bought. It showed that the Tammany treasury set aside $1,000 per city electoral district—of which there were 327. In case $327,000 of bribes was not sufficient, there was a huge drive by Tammany to naturalize recent immigrants. Tammany's printing office produced nearly 70,000 certificates of naturalization and validated them by laying on witnesses who would swear to their personal knowledge of the character and eligibility of these new citizens. One such witness signed off 669 sets of naturalization papers. This yielded some 40,000 new voters, of whom it was estimated over 80 percent voted for their Tammany benefactors.

This was just preparation for the big day. On the day of the election, the well-practiced Tammany machine swung into action with its usual techniques. The system revolved around multiple voting. One Tammany worker thought he voted 28 times, although he was not entirely sure of the figure, since he had drunk so much of the free booze Tweed's men had put on, he had lost count of the times he exercised his democratic right. Tweed's men made little effort to disguise this behavior because when other citizens tried to point out the fraud, they were beaten up by Tammany's thugs. Should the multiple votes, thugs or booze not work their electoral magic, there was a final line of insurance. When poll clerks added up the tallies, they were paid out of Tammany funds and told to simply invent totals. As Tweed himself later explained, "The ballots made no result. The counters made the result." The real irony was that although Congress drew up this report detailing these excesses, and went on to draft legislation which was sent to the New York state legislature, who duly passed it, the governor pocket-vetoed it. That governor was the Tammany-elected candidate, Hoffman.[20]

To be able to mount such an expensive campaign demanded a pretty impressive income. It was the future Tammany boss George Washington Plunkitt who succinctly explained how Tammany raised such funds: "My party's in power and its going to undertake a lot of improvements . . . Ain't it perfectly honest to make a profit on my investment and foresight?"[21] The trouble was that not everyone took such a view. When the infamous Tweed Ring was broken in 1871, the boss was arrested on 204 counts of fraud and sentenced to 12 years in prison. He was also required to repay the state some $6.5 million—over $100 million at today's rates.

In his years in charge of Tammany, Tweed had systematically ravaged the state coffers. It was estimated that for each contract awarded through Tammany, the boss and his inner circle received a 20 percent kickback. Rents provided another income stream. The National Guard's armory, on Hester Street, was a single room above a saloon, but it cost the Fifth Regiment $10,000 a year. He also skimmed off money from building projects. Most impressively, the Ring had inflated the cost of a new city courthouse to some $13 million—making it cost the city government nearly twice what the US government would pay the Russian government for the state of Alaska.[22]

While Tweed was brought to justice, it did not spell the end of Tammany's power. It is worth looking at two later bosses, the garrulous but shrewd, Plunkitt, and the wily Richard Crocker. These two simply refined Tweed's techniques. Plunkitt was keen to avoid what he saw as Tweed's "thieving." Rather than having a small circle of powerful cronies, like Tweed, he sought to utilize a wider, favor bank approach. A political fixer, Plunkitt would certainly have fallen foul of today's legislation designed to counter conflicts of interest. However, in times when there was no civil service to speak of, the wily, hard-working Irishman could milk the

12,000 odd jobs at his disposal for all they were worth. He did this well enough to retire and live the last thirty-odd years of his life a very wealthy and highly respected man.

Richard Crocker was rather less fortunate. Growing up as a Tammany tough, earning his keep by repeat voting and intimidating opponents, Crocker was not only a brawler, but a highly astute politician. Emulating Tweed, it was Crocker who took the Tammany machine to its most efficient extreme, tapping the New Immigration of the 1890s for all it was worth. Learning from Plunkitt, Crocker survived a full investigation into Tammany corruption. However, Crocker lived in different times. The reform movement had a new momentum. By 1901, when the papers ran stories of his huge property empire on both sides of the Atlantic, Crocker was ousted from Tammany and left New York to live out the rest of his days in England and Ireland.

What links all three of these "bosses" is their unapologetic approach to city governance. All of them saw the reform movement as both unnecessary and undesirable—and not simply because it threatened their way of life. They saw it as lacking the commitment to the underdog which their own system provided. Plunkitt condemned the reformers as "morning glories" who would soon grow disinterested in the fate of the poorest of New York's citizens By contrast, Tammany was a "mighty oak" which would continue to protect them long after the Progressives, Mugwumps and Muckrakers of the reform movement had moved on to new more fashionable projects. It is perhaps this concentration on private industry, albeit corrupt and self-serving, which is so typical of the period and it is this which pointed the way in which municipal corruption would mutate in the twentieth century.

Tammany was by no means unique, nor was it the most effective or even the most crooked of the machines. It has simply become the best known. A far more impressive crook operated in Chicago throughout the time of all three of the best-known Tammany bosses. From the 1870s until his death in 1907, Michael C. McDonald turned his gambling and vice syndicate into the Democratic machine in Chicago. In many ways, McDonald represents a very different machine. He was very much linked in with active criminals, regulating their practices and skimming off their profits. It was estimated that in order to operate within Chicago, the ambitious criminal needed to pay over some 60 percent of his take to McDonald. What distinguished him from just another criminal was his control over the forces of law and order. From the judiciary to beat-cop, McDonald controlled the system. For example, when he came up against an honest superintendent of police who threatened the smooth running of his organization, he simply had him busted to the rank of captain and then had the vacant position filled with his own man.[23]

Also, unlike the Tammany bosses, McDonald rarely confronted reformers. Perhaps because of his knowledge of the vice industry, he preferred to lie low and ride out their terms in office. Like Plunkitt, he knew the reformers would eventually upset the electorate with their unrealistic objectives and would be replaced when the puritanical urge passed. However, in this patient pragmatism, he has been seen as unique. Many historians and sociologists maintain that the classic political machine gradually disappeared in the early decades of the twentieth century. They argue that this was largely the result of the Progressives' high profile campaigns to clean up municipal politics, as well as a response to growing government welfare and regulation removing much of necessity for the classic social welfare provisions of the nineteenth-century political machine. This, combined with increasing immigration controls, Americanization drives and the rising and widening levels in the provision of state education similarly reduced the need for the political fixer.[24] However, they argue that rather than cleaning up the cities, their demise left a vacuum which was to be filled in many cases by syndicated, organized, crime.[25]

McDonald's model showed that a mutation was already taking place in the larger metropolitan areas. Organized crime utilized revenues from gambling, prostitution, booze, and narcotics to finance their move into city hall. Sometimes it was the gangs who controlled the politicians, other times it was the other way around. A classic example of the first type of symbiosis, what could be termed "mafia and machine," can be found in St Louis, Missouri. In the 1880s and 1890s, wealthy businessman and politician "Colonel" Ed Butler had controlled the city with a classic, if violent, Democratic machine. By the early 1900s, Butler was fighting to control his position, implicated in several shootings and increasingly finding himself without the necessary power to buy his way out.

Ready to step into his shoes were two friends from the Irish slums of downtown St Louis, Thomas, "Snake," Kinney and Tom Egan. By 1910, they had worked their way from sneak thieving, "leg-breaking" and union-busting in the late 1890s to controlling the Democratic machine of the city. This had been achieved partly by Kinney running on the Democratic ticket in the early 1900s and winning, largely by strong-arm intimidation, at the polls. But it was Egan, a brutal tough, who remained the real power. Over the next decades, they used a combination of wide-ranging and liberal bribes backed up by some 400 ultra-violent gang members—known as "Egan's Rats"—to provide enough sufficiently persuasive muscle to essentially give them free rein in the St Louis region. Some idea of the level of immunity which the Rats felt they had bought can be gathered from an interview which Tom Egan gave to the *St Louis Post Dispatch* at the height of his power in 1912. Fully conscious that it would be printed, he told the reporter— "We don't shoot unless we know who is present. If some outsider were there, not bound by the rules of silence, he might tell the police what he saw."[26]

Egan's Rats felt safe knowing that they had bought the local politicians, but in nearby Kansas City, city boss, Thomas J. Prendergast, managed to simply side-step the efforts of reformers and retain control of the city from 1925 through until 1940. Prendergast used a mixture of the traditional machine techniques of graft, kickbacks and placemen, but with a distinctly criminal edge. He personally dealt in prostitution and other vices, but his true nature remained that of political boss rather than gang-ster. By his own admission, Prendergast was the archetypal political fixer, for, as he commented—"I know all the angles of organizing and every man I meet becomes my friend. I know how to select ward captains and I know how to get to the poor [citizen] ...We fill his belly, warm his back and vote him our way."[27]

Some proof of Prendergast's reliance on the "political" rather than "criminal" approach can be seen in the way he dealt with threats. In 1928, former machine employee, "Brother" Johnny Lazia—now the region's racketeering and bootleg-ging boss—went to war on Prendergast for political control of the region. He kidnapped and beat Prendergast workers, but was baffled when the "boss" did not fight back. Instead Prendergast formed an alliance, making Lazia a partner and unofficial Crime Commissioner.[28] This had the effect of neutralizing the threat and at the same time gaining the Irish-American boss the hitherto elusive Italian vote. Similarly, when Lazia was indicted on charges of income tax evasion, it was Prendergast who had the case quashed. However, in keeping with his criminal edge, it was his $600,000-a-year horse racing habit that brought the machine down. In 1939, he was sent to Leavenworth for tax evasion, dying five years later.[29]

Prendergast was by no means the only machine politician who overtly utilized the racketeers. The most glaring example took place in the 1927 Chicago mayoral election, when the particularly corrupt winner, William Hale, "Big Bill," Thompson, famously received the backing of Al Capone. Capone organized a city-wide campaign of brutal intimidation and voter fraud in support of Thompson and his liberal attitude to booze.[30] Capone's support paid off, Thompson was elected with a landslide majority of 80,000. In return, Capone and his bootleggers breathed more easily as the clampdown on booze which had been so ruthlessly imposed by Thompson's reform-minded predecessor was lifted. However, the following year, when Thompson got the notion that he would run for President, he ejected a loudly protesting Capone from Chicago. The well-known gangster, Capone, previously an asset in Chicago was now a liability to the Presidential candidate who needed to show his support for Prohibition, and harassed the rack-eteer into leaving. Tellingly, within months, when his Presidential ambitions failed to materialize, Thompson allowed the gangster to return.[31]

Capone's campaigning for Thompson and Thompson's treatment of Capone illustrate one of the fundamental lessons to be drawn from the advent of truly syndicated crime in the 1920s and 1930s—the emergence of organized, syndi-cated, crime was dependent on the co-operation of politicians. In terms of the most famous gangster city—Chicago—the conclusion is relatively simply: Capone required Thompson's protection in order to operate, or perhaps Thompson required Capone's support in order to get into power. Either way the evidence strongly suggests that crime on such a scale, so overtly organized and widespread, could never have existed without at least the connivance of high-level politicians.

Thompson's regime was arguably the most corrupt American city government of modern times and its ties to organized crime seem undeniable. It would be a remarkable coincidence that it just so happened that during the "amenable" Thompson's spells as mayor, Chicago became the byword the world over for racketeering. Some idea of the extent of corruption can be gathered from two official sources. In 1915, during Thompson's first term in City Hall, the Chicago City Council Committee on Crime had warned of

> [a] "crime trust" with roots running through the police force, the bar, the bondsmen and political officials . . . Instead of punishing the criminal, they protect him. Instead of using the power of the law for protection of society, they use it for their own profit.

By 1929, when Thompson was reaching the middle of his second stint in City Hall, the Illinois Association for Criminal Justice in its *Crime Survey* reported that "crime was organized on a scale and with the resources unprecedented in the history of Chicago . . . leading gangsters were practically immune from punishment . . . due to an unholy alliance between organized crime and politics."[32]

As one of the leading criminal sociologists of the time, John Landasco, claimed in the *Crime Survey*, all municipal politics was "a feudal system based not on law, but on personal loyalties." To Landasco, Chicago was vice-ridden because Mayor Thompson favored a liberal attitude which tolerated prostitution, gambling, and essentially ignored bootlegging, enabling criminal activities to develop as long as sufficient feudal dues were paid to him.[33] To reinforce this, Frank J. Loesch, the head of the Chicago Crime Commission claimed that Capone himself had told him that he gave over $250,000 to Thompson's mayoral fund in 1927. Showing his own power over Loesch, he had also agreed to "have the cops send over squad cars the night before the election [the 1928 mayoral polling day] and jug all the hoodlums." He did, and the violence which had marked out the previous, so-called "Pineapple [slang for a hand grenade] Election" ceased.

What could demonstrate the shift to syndicated crime from bossism better than the city's leading racketeer sitting seemingly relaxed in what was generally known to be his "office," room 430 of the Hotel Lexington, discussing his own crimes of the bribing of the city police with Chicago's supposedly "clean" chief of police. Capone sat with pictures of those he referred to as his heroes—George Washington and Abraham Lincoln—on the wall above his head. His pin-ups— Cleopatra and the actress Theda Bara—were on the opposite wall. As if to reinforce who was really behind this power and immunity, pride of place was occupied by a photograph of his benefactor, "Big Bill" Thompson.[34] Given these stories and the official reports, it would seem that the politicians were turning a blind eye to the criminals. It would appear that they had either been bought off, or that those at the top were making enough from the racketeers to buy off more junior politicians. What further supports the argument that the real power lay with the Chicago politicians was that Capone was eventually indicted for income tax evasion, but neither he, nor the FBI investigators dared, or could, nail Thompson—

even after the electorate tired of the reign of the hoodlums in 1931—and he was replaced by a "reformist" regime in the normal pattern of city elections.

Thompson's career and reputation beg the question, why was he returned to power? It would appear that in spite of his reputation for corruption, and his apparent support for Capone, Thompson was popular. Like Capone, Thompson understood the politics of showmanship, making outrageous comments which were still savvy enough to appeal to the man in the street and which kept the electorate amused and his name in the public mind. What was more, he knew the benefit of commissioning public works. Most of all he knew how to appeal to a disparate electorate in a city where wealth was unevenly divided and on whose streets some 27 languages were used. Nominally Republican, Big Bill drew on a wide electorate and had varied sources of power. He formed a powerful, if fluid, coalition, which at various times contained elements including the minority ethnicities, the newly enfranchised women, the business classes, the wets, the drys, the black vote, and the unions. There can be little doubt that Chicago under Thompson was violent and corrupt, but then it always had been violent and corrupt, even under so-called reformist administrations.

In his connections with the unions Thompson was drawing on an increasingly powerful, and as a result, increasingly corrupt, force. Throughout this period, unions had growing numbers of members, and presented enormous opportunities for skimming off funds from dues, embezzling pension funds and contacts with organized crime and corrupt politicians. Chicago's politicians had a history of turning a blind eye to labor graft—they had to be in on the "racket" in order for it to work. By the time of Big Bill's mayoralty, Chicago had become a byword for this form of racketeering. As the *Chicago Tribune* reported in 1930:

> Organized labor in Chicago stands in peril of being delivered into the hands of gangsters, according to labor leaders . . . Already several unions, rated as the most powerful and active in the city, have been taken over completely by Alphonse (Scarface, Al) Capone and his crew of gangsters.[35]

According to one definition of the origin of the word, the whole concept of racketeering revolved around the eastern metropolitan ward politicians of the late nineteenth century. In this interpretation it stemmed from when the local political boss held a ball to generate campaign funds. The assembled pillars of the business communities, not only handed over their money, they also made a huge noise—"a racket."[36] Whether or not this was the origin, there is no doubt that labor racketeering in the nineteenth century was pretty well exclusive to the bosses. In the wake of the Haymarket bombing, and the emergence of a quiescent form of "acceptable" unionism, any form of labor activism that did not conform to Samuel Gompers' "American," aspirational model would meet with marked hostility. As could be seen in most major strikes of the Gilded Age, in large measure, capital had the law on its side.

The depressions of the last decades of the nineteenth century, coupled with the increasing violence of the labor conflicts of the time—especially in the coal and railroad industries—and a growing sense of a change in the political climate, gave rise to an increased sense of unease among capital. Legitimate forms of law enforcement—the militia and police—were increasingly seen as less than supportive and many felt that some form of insurance was required. Labor "sluggers," as they were known, would be employed by the bosses to break strikes, prevent unionization and generally keep "order" among the workers. Such overt and necessarily public brutality could not be accepted without the connivance or compliance of the establishment. This type of corruption reached its acme in the garment district of New York with Louis "Lepke" Buchalter and his associate Jacob "Gurrah" Shapiro.

By 1900, the New York garment trade produced over 75 percent of the clothing worn by Americans. While highly lucrative for the company bosses, it was poorly paid and—as the Triangle Fire would prove (see Chapter 6)—with intolerable conditions for the employees. The result of this discrepancy was a high level of union activity and an equally active response from the management. Never one to miss a business opportunity, by the mid-1920s New York's criminal fixer Arnold Rothstein had seen the potential of the garment rackets. Rothstein was paid thousands of dollars by the International Ladies Garment Workers Union (ILGWU) which he then distributed to all ranks of the police force as well as to the courts and around Tammany Hall. The object of these payments was to turn a blind eye to Communist agitation and violence in the garment district, which would in turn force garment workers into the Communist Party. Should any agitators be arrested, they would swiftly be freed by "sympathetic" courts. Typically artfully, Rothstein also controlled Buchalter and Shapiro who would invariably be hired by the bosses to put down such disturbances.[37]

Construction was another particularly lucrative trade for the racketeers and their political henchmen. It was ideally suited since a high proportion of the contracts were relatively long in duration and high in value, giving great opportunities for skimming and kickbacks. In addition, there was often a large, frequently casual, workforce which gave opportunities for disappearing dues, taking sweeteners and skimming off the wage bill. In order to successfully achieve these aims, it was necessary to have either the invisibility or the support in high places which only money could buy. In the 1890s, the racketeer Martin B., "Skinny," Madden ruled Chicago's lucrative building trade largely because he had the chairman of Chicago's Civil Service Board in his pocket. His rule lasted right through until 1909 when he was finally convicted of extortion, but even then his connections insured he was only fined $500, and never served a prison sentence.[38]

Nor was Chicago unique. The president of the New York City Board of Building Trades, Sam Parks, was similarly well connected. Working hand in hand with those higher up in Tammany Hall, he was the "typical ward heeler," popular with his constituents who "did not love clean hands less, just full hands more." Parks paralysed New York construction in 1903 with his near total control of the construction unions of the city. Even though he was happy to personally take $200 from the "bosses" to prevent a non-existent strike, it appears he never lost the support of either his political masters or the unions even when sentenced to a spell in Sing Sing for extortion. Both seemed happy to support him and neither worried "how he got his [considerable] pile."[39]

It was only in the 1930s that the cosy relationship between machine politics and racketeering really seemed to break down. It started in New York. As the decade opened, the Seabury Commission was appointed by the ambitious Governor of New York, Franklin Delano Roosevelt, to investigate "the affairs of New York City." In keeping with the mood of the times, it started by looking into the activities of the playboy mayor, Jimmy Walker's scandal-wracked administration. The glamor of Walker's "debonair," open administration was less acceptable to the times of the Depression than it had been to the Roaring Twenties.

Within weeks of opening, Seabury's patient and unrelenting investigations uncovered bribery of public officials from the charismatic ex-mayor down. Seabury showed that almost all the processes in the granting of building zoning were open to bribery and as Walker tried to charm his way out of the accusations, they continued to pile up. Eventually Walker cracked and admitted to over $500,000 of funds in his own accounts. His testimony revealed that on the waterfront and with public transport franchises, as well as a range of other publicly controlled permits, backhanders and graft were normal practice. Inexorably unravelling the layers, Seabury went on to expose corruption as being rife at all levels in the mayor's staff, in the police and in the magistracy.

As the results of Seabury's probings became clear, it emerged that payoffs, kickbacks, graft, and other crimes, were so common that some commentators claimed it was reminiscent of the worst days of Tammany. The mood had changed so much that when in 1935 a grand jury formed to investigate racketeering and gambling in Manhattan sensed that the District Attorney, William C. Dodge, was in the pocket of the racketeers, they barred him from the proceedings and went over his head to the governor. This exceptional display of people power set the tone for the second half of the 1930s and the truly savvy New York politicians now realized that investigation and exposure of organized crime were a better route to power than relying on the feudalism of machine politics.[40] Just as J. Edgar Hoover manipulated popular opinion to garner support for his FBI with his War on Crime, a new generation of political figures emerged from New York's drive to clean up the politics of the city. Leading this move were the diminutive, but feisty, New York mayor, Fiorello La Guardia, and the young, handsome, articulate, Special Prosecutor and later DA, Thomas E. Dewey.

In keeping with the New Deal, resources were allocated at a previously unheard-of level. Dewey had an office staff of 60 and over 60 police officers assigned to his famous "gang-busting" agency, and they got the results. In the 73 cases Dewey brought to court, 72 resulted in convictions. Some were politicians linked to the mob, like James Joseph Hines. Some were lawyers linked to crime, like "Dixie"

Davis. Others were mobsters like "Waxey" Gordon, "Dutch" Schultz and "Lucky" Luciano. All were high profile. These were a new breed of politicians, men who were comfortable using the newspapers, film, and radio to support their war on corruption and in the process drive themselves onto the national political scene. Perhaps they were successful because they personally courted publicity. Perhaps it was more because these efforts were supported by arguably the most astute and media-aware of all American politicians of the generation, Franklin Roosevelt. This was not the Progressive's moralizing liberalism driving the reforms, it was more the New Deal's high profile, pump-priming, pragmatic and partisan politics.

At first glance, the huge increase in federal spending which had sparked the Gilded Age jamboree of graft did not seem to be repeated in the New Deal. Roosevelt managed to present a corruption-free image in spite of the massive increase in the federal budget which his New Deal agencies required. The New Deal saw federal spending double. It jumped from $4.5 billion in 1933 to $9.4 billion in 1939. Federal relief spending grew from nothing in 1932 to $2.2 billion in 1935.[41] Yet remarkably there seemed to be no perceptible rise in overt corruption. There were notorious incidents of skimming, grafting, and embezzling, like the headline-grabbing imprisonment of "Double Dip Dick," Mayor Richard W. Reading of Detroit—which led to the subsequent indictment of some 216 officials at all levels of his administration—but they were not generally as blatant or common as previous scandals.[42]

There is, however, a school of thought which argues that corruption which can be associated with the rise of the federal state is more subtle and far more insidious. A clue to the nature of these accusations can be found in the 1939 passage of the Hatch Act which still governs the rights and responsibilities of federal employees in elections.[43] Some would see little difference between the New Deal of Roosevelt and the old deal of Tammany. Essentially both used patronage to remain in power. The real influence was still to be made out of control of patronage, and directing it to political constituents. Tammany may have bought the votes more openly, but arguably it was not as ambitious in its scope. Several scholars and politicians who have advanced theories along these lines would say that New Deal agencies used money and works project jobs to win votes, especially in areas of the country which could be seen as key marginal regions, which could return Roosevelt's Democrats to power.

There is considerable evidence to support such claims. Supporters of the thesis claimed it would explain why New Deal spending was greater per capita in the less populous states of the West, which had proportionately more Electoral College votes per head and thus returned a greater value in terms of votes per dollar spent. What is more, this explanation clarifies why the states of the South, already 67 percent Democrat, got proportionately less. It explains why from 1933 to 1939, when the average federal spend per head, in the form of loans and other support, was just under $300, Nevada residents received well over $1,000, whereas North Carolinians got less than $150. This line of argument also explains why federal spending increased before elections. This was especially evident in key marginal areas such as Florida and Kentucky where Works Progress Administration (WPA) funding grew in the autumn of 1936.[44]

If the influence of Tammany-style corruption receded in the 1930s as a result of losing authority to higher powers, namely the federal government, it was also superseded "from below" by losing influence to the unions. During the 1930s, American membership of trade unions more than tripled, from 3 million in 1932 to over 10 million by 1940. This surge in membership brought with it a huge boost in political power that in turn was accompanied by a vast increase in dues. This newfound influence would prove too much for some officials, and there was a discernible change in the scale, nature, and sophistication of union corruption. For instance, the Chicago electrical workers' union boss "Umbrella" Mike Boyle made a huge personal fortune from what he called his "great thrift." His caution with money enabled him to save $350,000 off a $35 a week pre-tax salary. Perhaps more realistically, a US Circuit Court of Appeals judge said that the evidence in his 1937 trial, over funding irregularities, indicated he was "a blackmailer, a high-wayman, a betrayer of labor and a leech on commerce."[45]

At its most basic, labor racketeering was no longer predicated on controlling unions to extort money from employers. By the 1930s, racketeers did not simply rely on using muscle to prevent strikes, nor were they only paid to hold down the costs of labor for the bosses. As one union boss would later bluntly tell an interviewer, "Twenty years ago, the employers had all the hoodlums working for them as strikebreakers. Now we've got a few and everybody's screaming."[46] Union bosses now sought power for themselves and perhaps the best example of this is the behavior of the officials in what would become Jimmy Hoffa's Teamster empire. Having grown from 75,000 dues-paying members in 1932, they had nearly 500,000 in 1940. They were now in a position where they could reward "friends" and punish enemies, a situation which was succinctly summed up when Philadelphia Teamster Turk Daniels told a stall holder in the city's Dock Street Market—"I'm putting you out of business because I don't like you, and there's not a thing you can do about it."

It was a sign of what had changed in these times that when Babe Triscaro finished a prison sentence for mob-sponsored intimidation, he did not return to the syndicate and continue his rise up the hierarchy of the mob, but instead became the union official of Teamster local 436 in Cleveland. Unions could now hire the mobsters to do their dirty work, rather than being hired as muscle by them. For example, Hoffa used the local mob to intimidate parking lot attendants into unionizing. If they resisted the union's overtures, the mob would move in and the cars in the lots would be trashed with crow bars and acid in front of the horri-fied attendants, leaving them to explain the damage to their owners.[47] The political clout was no longer solely with the bosses, be they in the workplace or Tammany Hall, it was now more diffuse—and the corruption followed that power.

10

TERRORISTS

Rebels, Radicals and Freedom Fighters, and Criminals with a Cause

Terrorism is a slippery word. It is difficult to define and difficult to distinguish. A simple definition is: violent behavior seeking to induce fear in a community or individual. In this light, terrorism is little more than criminal violence—and indeed, many see it as such. Maybe in order to better understand it, we need a more inclusive definition. The political scientist, Grant Wardlaw, gives a far more complete definition. He sees it as:

> the use or threat of use of violence by an individual, group, whether acting for or in opposition to established authority, when such action is designed to create maximum and/or fear-inducing effects in a target group larger than the immediate victims with the purpose of coercing that group into acceding to the political demands of the perpetrators.[1]

Having established that broad definition of aims, it is also helpful to understand who such terrorists were. One commentator aptly described a terrorist as fitting three simple categories—"crusaders, criminals or crazies."[2] While this is catchy, it is also a truism, since nearly all acts of terrorism are, of course, criminal, but then terrorism attracts truisms—after all "one man's terrorist is another man's freedom fighter" and it is difficult to imagine any nation where such a truism was truer in the late nineteenth and early twentieth centuries than America.

The very roots of America's nationhood stem from rebellion, and some would argue terrorism, and that spirit of rebellion remained present throughout the history of the nation. The period of this study opens with the defeat of another rebellion—the South's short-lived Confederacy. Radicals and rebels, patriots and freedom fighters all play a part in the criminal activity of the three-quarters of a century under scrutiny. They are a disparate group, varied, both in their impact and their aims, united only by the fact that they sought to change American society by violent means. Some were fighting for territory, like the Ponca, others a new political order, like the anarchists. Some, like Leon Csolgosz, aimed to kill individuals, while, given the chance, others like the US Army in the Philippines would have killed thousands.

Some, like Geronimo or Pancho Villa, required the mobilization of significant numbers of the nation's military in order to be brought under control, others were simply arrested by a few police. Some, like the Ku Klux Klan, were later accepted as having legitimate cause for their violent behavior by mainstream America. Others, like the Industrial Workers of the World, would remain terrorists to the majority of Americans well beyond the times of this study. Some were the product of nations at war—later recognized, like the German saboteurs of World War I, or disputed, like the Lakota. Others, like the Molly Maguires, were the product of what they saw as an ongoing internal class war. What they all go to show is that America's democracy was always contested, and they show that the present-day War on Terror is nothing new.

With such diversity, in order to give this section some structure, it is probably best to analyze the objectives rather than the methods of the terrorists in this period. For the purposes of this study, these can roughly be split into four very broad categories. The first of which is probably the most "American," or at least the cause closest to the hearts of Americans—it is that of "patriotic terrorism." That is terrorism inspired by the wish to retain or regain territory within the continental United States. The second is that of the "political terrorist." This group is inspired by a variety of motives. They may be simple objectives like the 8-hour day, or more complex desires which could involve the overthrow of the entire state. Third, there are the foreign threats. Although these may have much in common with the patriots, they can be distinguished by the fact that their allegiance was to an external power rather than a group within US territory. Finally, there are the simple criminal terrorists, those who used terror as a way of extracting money or other goods and commodities simply for their own, or their group's, benefit. As with all the other chapters, this structure means that invariably some elements will be excluded, and others stressed, perhaps, more than some readers would like. It also means that there will be overlap between concepts already discussed in previous—or the final—chapters. Such a format does, however, give the chance to examine four distinct "terrorist" groups in particular—the Ku Klux Klan, the Molly Maguires, German saboteurs, and the Black Hand—and show how they fitted the development of America in their times and affect our understanding of that period.

Terrorism is often seen as the weapon of the disempowered: the last resort of the desperate and the weak. In this reading, it is the action of those who have nothing left to lose, those who will give up their lives or liberty in order to make others aware of their plight. During the birth pangs of modern America there were hordes of disempowered. There were the territorially deprived: those thrown

off their lands by more powerful incomers. There were the economically disempowered: wages slaves working in harsh conditions for little pay. Hand in hand
with that lack of financial muscle went political impotence. Their situation may
well have been the result of their sex, their location, their race, or their nationality.
Many of these unfortunates more or less accepted their lot. Some fought back
against the injustices they perceived, using whatever means possible, including
what many Americans more fortunate than themselves saw as terrorism. Curiously,
one of the most numerous and identifiable groups of these under-classes found
themselves in their unfortunate situation largely as the result of what could be
considered terrorism and yet in spite of their reputation for bestial behavior they
had at the time, to many interpreters today it appears that they very rarely
responded in the same spirit.

In 1861, one in seven people in America was legally defined as being the property of another American. Slavery, that "peculiar institution," had divided the
nation—in many ways physically and geographically, as well as metaphorically—
since the founding of the Republic. It had divided the Continental Congress.
Jefferson had been forced to skirt the issue in the Declaration of Independence.
The founding fathers grappled with how to address slavery when writing the
Constitution. It would create bloodshed and untold misery and it would demand
repeated compromise governing political representation and territory all the while
threatening to divide the nation. When that spirit of compromise ran out in 1861,
it led to war, a war in which more Americans would die than all other conflicts the
nation had fought before or since. That war freed the slaves and united the nation.
It also gave rise to a slew of radical legislation, backed up by Constitutional amendments, which promised to grant a whole new level of civil rights to America's
black population. Unfortunately, most of these high ambitions failed.

The period of Reconstruction, generally taken as running from 1863 to 1877,
is one of the most turbulent in American history. One president, Abraham Lincoln,
was assassinated, another, Andrew Johnson, narrowly escaped impeachment.
Unknown thousands of blacks in the South were lynched, shot, whipped, beaten,
mutilated or otherwise harassed into giving up their newly won rights. Federal
troops and local militias fought running battles with well-armed white supremacists in many of the former Confederate states. Large numbers of these conservatives belonged to the Ku Klux Klan, a shadowy organization largely composed of
former Confederate veterans who were dedicated to preventing what they saw as
the imposition of black civil rights and other federally sponsored reforms in the
Deep South.

The Klan was born as a fraternal society. It was formed to entertain six bored,
ex-Confederate, graduate members in Tennessee in early 1866. However, largely
as a result of its white-only membership, Southern pedigree, and inherent secrecy,
it quickly expanded out of Tennessee into neighboring Alabama and beyond.
Having put together a charter of patriotic and racial principles in 1868, the Klan
quickly spread across the former Confederate states, claiming thousands of

members at all levels of Southern society by the time it was officially disbanded in 1869. As it did so, it morphed into an effective white supremacist organization, dedicated to the prevention of racial integration and reinstatement of the South's pre-Civil War political elites. Most of the leadership were ambitious ex-Confederate officers hungry for a role in the post-war South, men like the first "Imperial Wizard," Nathan Bedford Forrest, or the Freemason and reputed Grand Dragon of Arkansas, Albert Pike. At the lower levels they were men who saw their livelihoods, families, and social status threatened by the reforms being made by Republican interlopers and their Southern lackeys.

The Klan's methods were a simple but effective mixture of pageantry, secrecy, and terror. Riding out in their distinctive costume, largely at night by the light of torches, they would beat, tar and feather and lynch any "uppity niggers" who either spoke out for, or acted for, the equality, education or political rights of Southern blacks. They would also similarly target any whites who worked for such equality—either Northerners who had moved down into the region after the war (carpetbaggers), or their Southern allies (scalawags). They justified their violence under the pretext of the apparent corruption of the post-war Republican regimes imposed on the prostrate South. They coupled this with warnings which played to the visceral fear of black uprising, miscegenation and poor "race etiquette." With these justifications ensuring a large measure of local support, the Klan carried out a campaign of brutal repression on blacks and their supporters, while the large majority of the region's white population either ignored or supported the violence.

Typical of this intimidation was the treatment of Rhoda Ann Childs, a Georgia black married to a black Union veteran and Republican activist. She recounted her treatment by Klansmen in October 1866:

> They bucked me down across a log, stripped my clothes over my head, one of the men standing astride over my neck, and two men holding my legs. In this position I was beaten with a strap until they were tired. Then they turned me parallel with the log, laying my neck on a limb which projected from the log, and one man placing his foot on my neck, beat me again on my hip and thigh. Then I was thrown upon the ground, one of the men stood upon my breast, while two others took hold of my feet and stretched my limbs as far apart as they could, while the man standing on my breast applied the strap to my private parts . . . Then a man, I suppose a Confederate soldier, as he had crutches, fell upon me and ravished me. During the whipping, one of the men ran his pistol into me and said he had "a hell of a mind to pull the trigger [and] . . . swore they meant to kill every black son of a bitch they could find that had ever fought against us."[3]

They induced localized terrors when they were active in a region and many of the local black freedmen were so thoroughly terrorized they took to sleeping in the

rough rather than risk night riders hauling them out of their beds. More importantly, this terror translated into effective political power. Blacks when "Kluxed"
often published statement in local papers denouncing their association with the
Republican Party and civil rights activism. One such change of heart was
published in a Georgia newspaper:

> Anthony Thurster, the negro preacher who was so severely whipped by
> a party of disguised men ... asks that we announce to his white friends
> that from this time forward he will prove himself a better man [and] will
> never again make a political speech, deliver a sermon, or vote a Republican
> ticket.[4]

Overall, the campaign was successful. In Tennessee, the Republicans lost 18,000 of
their majority in the 1868 elections and Louisiana's Republican vote halved while
the state's Democrat vote doubled. More dramatically, by 1870, Kentucky's blacks
were almost entirely disenfranchised. What was even more impressive was the way
in which Southern conservatives capitalized on these local gains. While federal
troops moved into the region and the Klan was declared a terrorist organization,
banned, and 500 leading Klansmen were tried, the organization ultimately
achieved its aims. In response to these setbacks, instead of disbanding, as its leaders
claimed, the organization fractured, becoming a generic term for all Southern
conservative terrorists of the 1870s.

They also diversified their tactics. As well as stepping up the violence—killing,
for example, over 60 black citizens of Colfax, Louisiana, in 1873 and 75 Republican
activists in Vicksburg, Mississippi, the following year—they targeted their violence
more carefully, taking advantage of growing Northern disinterest and well-aimed
propaganda based on tales of Republican corruption which created a national
sympathy with their cause. By 1877, as the last of the federal troops left the South,
it had returned to Democrat rule with many of the pre-war elites returning to
positions of real power. The region was now on course for the effective disenfran-
chising of the vast majority of its black population which would in reality last
until the early 1960s.[5]

At the same time as the Klan were rampaging across the South, there were
other "terrorist" groups fighting for their territory in other regions of the nation.
It was not simply whites who terrorized blacks, for in the vast area of the West,
whites were engaged in an equally brutal struggle with the aboriginal population.
As the Klan was being founded in Tennessee, Colonel Henry Carrington came
across a lost troop of his men and reported to a shocked nation as follows:

> I give you some of the facts as to my men, whose bodies I found just at
> dark ... Eyes torn out and laid on rocks; noses cut off; chins hewn off; teeth
> chopped out; joints of fingers, brains taken out and placed on rocks with
> other members of the body (private parts severed and indecently placed on

the person); entrails taken out and exposed; hands cut off; feet cut off; arms taken out from sockets.[6]

These and other outrages were considered simple terrorism by whites, and led to an escalation in the ferocity of revenge meted out by the white soldiers and civilian posses on such savages—a response which was notably absent among the black populations of the Southern states which the Klan terrorized. A variety of explanations can be raised to explain this apparent discrepancy and they go some way to explaining the history of the two regions in the period. It goes without saying that although in some ways peripheral, both regions are essential to any understanding of the history of this period and the way in which that history was seen over the years of this study. To many among the white population of the nation, the conquest of the West and the "redemption" of the South were both triumphs for the morally, physically, and militarily superior white race, and it is interesting to see how by the end of this study in the one case the terrorists were rehabilitated, and in the other they continued to be condemned.

Throughout most of this period, certainly until the 1930s, there was a widely held consensus among the white American population—North and South—that the blacks in the South, if not elsewhere, had simply not been ready for participation in a democracy in the 1870s, and probably were still unready by the 1930s. In this reading, in the brief period of Reconstruction, during which blacks had real power, the history of the region was marked by decadence, corruption and decline. As the leading political scientist of his day, John W. Burgess, put it in 1902:

> It was the most soul-sickening spectacle that Americans had ever been called upon to behold ... [government not by] the most intelligent and virtuous for the benefit of the governed ... [but by] the most ignorant and vicious for the benefit, the vulgar, materialistic, brutal benefit of the governing set.[7]

There was an increasing suspicion, which gave way to a belief, that during this period Republican rule was essentially a kleptocracy and even the honest reformers had been fundamentally misguided. It stood to reason that in this climate the Klan's actions in overthrowing these idiotic ideals were justified, if not heroic.

This rehabilitation took place not only in the academic sphere—with no less a figure than the future president, political scientist and president of Princeton, Woodrow Wilson, writing a supportive account of the Klan's actions—it was also apparent in the more "popular" genres. From the 1880s onwards, accounts of the heroism of the Klan were fêted in memoirs, newspaper accounts, and biographies. By the turn of the twentieth century, it was celebrated in the best-selling novels of Thomas Dixon, whose triumphant Klan trilogy was adapted for the stage, and went on to become the most popular film to date—David W. Griffith's *Birth of a*

Nation. From the turn of the twentieth century onward, the Klan became more and more visibly acceptable, until, by the mid-1920s, its second manifestation, according to a variety of sources, attracted anywhere from four to ten million members from all walks of life, spread over all states of the Union. At the peak of its popularity, in 1924, to many Americans, the Reconstruction Klan was no longer the terrorist organization of a repressive, but defeated slave power, but a chivalrous and virtuous organization which had fought for the simpler, more glamorous, ordered values of a tragically lost age.

If the Klan's violence came to be seen as justified, the same was not held to be true of the Native Americans. While there was a move to re-assess the treatment of aboriginal Americans, few in the mainstream of American society during the period of this study would have argued that the actions of those Indians who mutilated Carrington's troopers were justifiable. In an age spurred on by the principles of "Manifest Destiny," the racial hierarchies of expansionists like Theodore Roosevelt, or the even missionary zeal of Woodrow Wilson, few paid attention to Helen Hunt Jackson's *A Century of Dishonor* (1881). This work detailed the sad history of broken treaties and broken promises; of land grabs and atrocities committed by "Americans" in their war with the resident populations of the Great Plains and other regions of the West. Hunt sent copies to all incumbent US Congressmen. They were inscribed in red letters on the cover with the evocative words of Benjamin Franklin—"Look upon your hands: they are stained with the blood of your relations." Even her subsequent appointment as Commissioner for Indian Affairs and her best-selling novel, *Ramona* (1884) had little effect when compared with the rehabilitative impact of Thomas Dixon or David W. Griffiths. Far from it. It could not compete with Teddy Roosevelt's triumphant account of the whites' heroic struggle and their unstoppable individualism which civilized the vast emptiness of the West—*The Winning of the West* (1896). Roosevelt's interpretation summed up the view of the vast majority of American society when he wrote that since "[t]he Indians never really had any title to the soil ...This great continent could not have been kept as nothing but a game preserve for squalid savages."

In the last 35 years of the nineteenth century, terrorism was not confined to the disputed areas of the South and the West of the nation. In the Anthracite fields of Pennsylvania, acts of deliberate terrorism were also taking place. Through the 1860s and into the 1870s, mine owners were receiving blood-curdling threats. Sixteen were assassinated, many others—and their subordinates, supporters and spies—were beaten. By 1877, 30 of these terrorists had been brought to justice. The culprits were apparently members of a shadowy group who went by the seemingly innocent-sounding name of the "Molly Maguires." The legacy of the Molly Maguires was just as disputed as that of the Klan, and just as informative of the times.

Throughout the years of the nineteenth century, as America industrialized and capital was king, the Mollys were seen as little other than a violent and radical outgrowth of the Irish terrorism which repeatedly used bombs and assassinations in Britain and Ireland. Drawing on the experiences of one of his operatives, the founder of the eponymous detective agency so often employed to put down violent strikers, Alan Pinkerton, told their story in this light in his *Molly Maguires and the Detectives* (New York, 1877). Their infamy was such that even Sherlock Holmes confronted them in *The Valley of Fear* (London, 1915). It was not until the social leveling of the Great Depression that the ideological climate allowed the Molly Maguires to be seen as anything but an evil terrorist conspiracy born out of the ignorant and brutish nature of the Irish immigrant. As the New Deal freed up trade unionism, there was a move to portray the Mollys in mainstream academia as an understandable organization response to intolerable working conditions. Anthony Bimba's *The Molly Maguires* (New York, 1932) and Walter Coleman's *The Molly Maguire Riots* (Richmond, Virginia, 1936) put forward this view and created the "significant hiatus in the historiography" which has yet to die down.[8]

If the Molly Maguires were a symbol of rehabilitated labor in the 1930s, there was a single "terrorist" act which was considered so atrocious that it killed the largest labor organization and arguably, more than any other single event, set back the American labor organization throughout the period. In 1886, during the most severe economic downturn the nation had yet suffered, workers came out to protest for some sort of relief. In March 1886, the "Great Upheaval" swept the nation and by May that year some 350,000 workers were protesting against layoffs, pay cuts and cuts in hours in marches from one coast to other. By end of the year, there had been some 1400 strikes involving more than 400,000 workers in over 11,000 businesses. The situation was volatile when on the night of May 4th, some 3,000 workers gathered in Chicago's Haymarket Square, in a protest for a universal 8-hour day.

The vast majority belonged to the Knights of Labor, an inclusive, fraternal labor organization. The Knights were fresh from a hard won but significant victory over one of the arch-capitalists of the day, the ruthless, Jay Gould. Its membership was climbing on the back of this and it could claim nearly 750,000 active members, made up of workers of all races in all trades, skilled and unskilled. Alongside the Knights marched an assortment of socialists, anarchists and Marxists. Fearing violence, the police had cordoned off the protest, and they had reason. The atmosphere was even tenser in Chicago than elsewhere, since some days before, at the local McCormack factory, police had killed two strikers. At around 10 pm, as the last speaker finished his rousing oration, the situation worsened, scuffles broke out between workers and the police and bombs were thrown at the police, who in turn opened fire. Seven policemen and three civilians were killed, 59 policemen and more than 200 protestors were wounded.

The Haymarket Massacre, as it became known, immediately drew condemnation in the US from all levels of society. The day after the massacre, the *Chicago Tribune* attacked the bombers, calling them "serpents," "vipers," and "ungrateful hyenas."[9] The leader of the Knights of Labor, Terence Powderly, denounced them.

He and most others were thought to be a small group of anarchists, although one of those arrested for the bombings subsequently rather embarrassingly proved to be Chicago's very first registered Knight of Labor. Powderly referred to the bomb throwers as "a band of cowardly murderers, cut-throats and robbers, who sneak through the country like midnight assassins . . . [They were] human monstrosities not entitled to the sympathy or consideration of any person in the world."[10] When it came to the trial of the eight suspects, it appears that Powderly's words were taken to heart. In a swift trial, all were found guilty, although only one of the suspects had actually been in Haymarket that day—and he was talking on the stage at the time when the bomb went off.[11]

Given the lack of real evidence against the Haymarket "martyrs," it would appear that their sentences were more a result of their politics than their actions. Nor were they alone. Many other radicals would go through a similar experience during these years of industrialization. One of the most notorious groups which underwent this demonization was the Industrial Workers of the World. Founded in 1905, the "Wobblies" as they became known, were immediately controversial. Believing in direct action and "One Big Union" of all workers regardless of trade, sex, ethnicity or race, they drew on a potent amalgam of anarchist, socialist and syndicalist ideas to challenge what they saw as the complacency and obsequiousness of the prevalent "American Unionism" of the all-powerful American Federation of Labor.

This high profile unapologetic and radical activism led to the IWW's ostracism. Much as the Klan became the generic term for conservative violence in the South, so its enemies would implicate the IWW in all acts of labor unrest. Although there were probably never more than 20,000 fee-paying members, wherever there was labor agitation, the Wobblies would be found sabotaging, fomenting treason, and corrupting loyal workers. They were associated with foreign radicalism and violence, like the assassination of the controversial ex-governor of Idaho in 1905. They ran "free speech" rallies in which they advocated class war and they mocked establishment organizations like the Salvation Army. They outspokenly taunted the bosses and their "lackeys" in scurrilous speeches, obscene songs and gleefully insulting cartoons and articles. They provided pickets, moral support and what resources they could afford for most of the nation's highest profile strikes. In short, the IWW became the embodiment of radicalism within its first decade of existence.

However it was only when America went to war, that the Wobblies really became the nation's bogeymen. America declared war in April 1917 with a poorly equipped and woefully small army, and Wilson demanded a huge effort to put the nation on a more war-ready footing. The IWW sensed its moment. Starting with a high profile campaign against the war itself as a capitalist civil war, they then moved on to opposing the draft and then spread fear that they were sabotaging the nation's war effort. They reveled in taunting volunteers, telling the bosses to go and serve in the trenches, and the workers to be "real men," not soldiers. They put their distinctive red and black stickers with their hissing wildcat symbol on war-related machinery, leading to fears of sabotage.

In the popular imagination they put lemon juice and sand in bearings to make them shatter. They put metal spikes in lumber, breaking saws and ruining timber. What was more, when attacked, the IWW fought back—with ferocity—and not just in print. At Everett in Washington State in 1916, they engaged in a gunfight with the local sheriff and his deputies. The debacle ended with the killing and wounding of over 50 people. Three years later they were engaged in another shoot-out, again in Washington State, following an Armistice parade in the lumber town of Centralia, in which the Wobblies killed five members of the American Legion and wounded a further six.

Nevertheless, the Wobblies were not an illegal organization. The crimes of which they were convicted were not ostensibly due to their affiliation with the IWW. But their lack of patriotism and their outspoken support for the Bolshevik regime in Russia meant that, like the anarchist martyrs of Haymarket, they were often treated with little regard for the niceties of the legal system, although it is perhaps their opponents who committed the real crimes. Their "free speech" fights frequently resulted in their forcible expulsion from towns after spells in prison, often accompanied by running the gauntlet of beatings, being hosed down with freezing cold water and other violent abuses. When they organized a strike at a copper mine in Bisbee, Arizona, in 1917, they were freighted out of the town en masse and dumped in the middle of the desert with no water or food. One of the Centralia Wobblies was hunted down and lynched by a posse of vigilantes. That was after he had had his teeth smashed in with a rifle butt and had then been castrated. It is some measure of the way in which the Wobblies were regarded that the coroner at the inquest into his death returned a verdict of suicide.

At least a part of this visceral hatred was the result of the behavior of other radicals, rightly or mistakenly associated with the Wobblies. This was an age of strikes, terrorism and politically motivated violence. The century had opened with the assassination of President McKinley in 1901 by an anarchist, and it appeared it would continue with radical violence. In 1911, during a violent strike by the Iron Workers Union, the two McNamara brothers were convicted of the bombing of the offices of the anti-union *Los Angeles Times*. The explosion had killed 21, and wounded nearly 100 others. Five years later in San Francisco, Tom Mooney was convicted of throwing a bomb into a rally raising funds for America's preparations for war. It killed ten and wounded 40. When the war ended, the strikes began. In February 1919, for nearly a week, the city of Seattle was essentially paralyzed by a general strike. Violent strikes across the nation followed the war in the steel industry, the railroads, public transport, and a whole range of other trades and professions, including actors. In Boston, even the police went out on strike.

As if these were not enough, in June 1919, several well-known conservative figures received letter bombs and a bomber blew himself up planting a bomb on the doorstep of the Attorney General. They were blamed on an anarchist group. Although this led to a clampdown and the arrest and detention of over 10,000 radicals and the deportation of over 500 alien radicals to Russia in the Palmer Raid radical witch hunts of 1919–1920, the violence did not stop. In what, with hindsight, appears like the final blast of the turn-of-the-century anarchists, in September 1920, a bomb concealed in a horse-drawn cart went off outside J.P. Morgan's Wall Street building. Packed with metal bolts, the bomb killed 40 and wounded over 200. Although the *New York Times* saw a "Red plot" in the atrocity, no one was arrested and over the next two decades no further comparable outrages occurred.[12]

Understanding what had sparked the wave of terrorism and industrial and political violence is as difficult to explain as what led to its seemingly sudden end. Economic conditions can account for the Haymarket bombing and the steel strike. The political climate of the war can account for the IWW's behavior, but to attribute the disappearance of this type of industrial and political violence in the 1920s to either political or economic stability is at best simplistic. The relative calm of the 1920s must be seen as a combination of more than just those two elements. Perhaps it was that prosperity brought with it social mobility in the 1920s and improved roads and cheaper cars brought a physical mobility which enabled movement for work. Perhaps it was simply felt that the political and industrial violence of the previous decades was seen not to bring the benefits hoped for. Whatever the reasons, the authorities were not complacent. Throughout the decade, one of the nation's military contingency plans—War Plans White— was drawn up to deal with the consequences of agents provocateur fermenting full-scale revolution on the continental United States.

The recent war had highlighted just such dangers. In late July 1916, 2,000 tons of munitions blew up at the depot at Black Tom Island on the New Jersey water-front. They created an enormous blast which shook the Brooklyn Bridge, burst water mains, blew out plate glass windows in Times Square and peppered the Statue of Liberty with shrapnel. The explosion brought to light a complex sabo-tage network which had attempted to blow up strategic sites as well as transport systems and munitions factories. Also, just like the U-boats on the high seas, these underhanded murderers targeted the crews and cargoes of American and allied shipping. Although Europe was at war, at the time America was still a neutral country. It was in this year that Woodrow Wilson would fight an election on the slogan "He kept us out of the war" and would implore his countrymen to be "impartial in thought, as well as action, must put a curb upon our sentiments, as well as upon every transaction that might be construed as a preference of one party to the struggle before another."

While many Americans thought this was the way in which their government was behaving, it was seen in a totally different light by the Central Powers of Germany and Austria-Hungary. To them, America was anything but impartial. In early 1915, J.P. Morgan had arranged a $50 million loan for the French government and further loans would follow, until by the time of American entry into the war in April 1917 they had loaned them over two and a quarter billion dollars. By contrast, they lent the Central Powers a mere $27 million. What was more, before the explosion at Black Tom, American exports of food, raw materials, munitions and other goods to the Allies totaled over $820 million. By contrast, those to the Central Powers made up a little under $170 million. The Americans also allowed the British to enforce what they termed a naval blockade to control the importing of war materiel and raw materials by the Central Powers. In reality, in the US, this actually amounted to an investigation of shipping manifests and vessels for contraband of all nations, even neutrals, sailing in US waters.[13]

Given this overt support for the Entente, the Germans evolved a complex network of spies, saboteurs and secret agents. In terms of field operations, they achieved some notable successes. Working directly with German Embassy officials in Washington, agents like Horst von der Goltz, Kurt Janke, Paul Koenig, and Franz von Rintelen tried to raise German support for the disruption of the Allies' American supplies. Their agents planted ingenious pencil-sized incendiary bombs—manufactured on an interned German ship in New York—on vessels carrying supplies for the Allies. These almost undetectable devices were timed to go off when the ships were out at sea, making destruction more likely and distancing the saboteurs from the scene. Some idea of how widespread this activity was can be gathered from the following account of one month's discoveries by the US officials:

> Towards the end of April 1915 the S.S. *Cressington Court* caught fire at sea, two bombs were found in the cargo of the S.S. *Lord Erne*, and a bomb was found in the hold of the S.S. *Devon City*. On May 8, 1915, two bombs were discovered in the cargo of the S.S. *Bankdale*. On May 13, 1915, the S.S. *Samland* mysteriously caught fire at sea. On May 21, 1915, a bomb was found on board the S.S. *Anglo-Saxon*. All these ships had sailed from American ports.[14]

They also had some major successes on land—like the explosions at Black Tom; the Hercules, DuPont, munitions plant in Seattle, in May 1915, and the destruction of a munitions repackaging plant at Kingsland, New Jersey, in January 1917. But there were also less visible, and far less quantifiable projects. One was the biological warfare waged from a house in the suburbs of Washington, DC. The aim was to infect the US Army's vital stock of mules and horses with the deadly viruses of anthrax and the equally deadly horse disease, glanders, as they were being shipped to the Western Front from depots on the East coast. The figures for infection are as yet unknown, they probably exceed 100,000 animals. One estimate claimed that German agents had some $30 million at their disposal, although much of this was used to organize strikes and other peaceable industrial disruption to the US war effort.[15] Given this sum, at an organization level, their efforts were in general marked by an amateurish incompetence. Agents left plans and documents lying around and much of their communication was intercepted and decoded by British agents, including the notorious Zimmerman Telegram.[16] Another of these "secret" messages was decoded by the British on December 12, 1914. It read:

> SECRET: The transportation of Japanese troops through Canada must be prevented at all costs, if necessary by blowing up Canadian railways. It would probably be advisable to employ Irish for this purpose in the first instance as it is almost impossible for Germans to enter Canada. You should discuss this matter with the Military Attaché. The strictest secrecy is indispensible.[17]

The telegram is interesting for a couple of reasons, not least because it demonstrates the hostility of Irish, especially Irish-Americans, to the Allies. Although many Irish were fighting for the British army in Flanders and elsewhere, there was a distinct hostility to the Allied cause in the Irish-American community. Many Irish in the US felt that they had been driven from their homeland by British cruelty and imperialism. Now that Britain was fighting for its imperial life, this was the opportunity to press for independence, as demonstrated by the Easter Rising in 1916. In America, alliance with German agents against British targets was regarded by many as a patriotic duty. Irishmen were often less visible, less foreign than Germans. They also had other advantages. In many of the cities of the East coast in particular, unions—including the vital longshore unions—and local political organizations were frequently dominated by the Irish. A good example of this Irish connection can be found in James, "Big Jim," Larkin.

Larkin was an English-born labor organizer of Irish extraction. He left Dublin for the United States in 1914 after being demonized for his part in leading one of the most acrimonious strikes in Irish history. Arriving in New York, he joined the Socialist Party of America and was open about his sympathies for the IWW. After making a particularly impassioned anti-British speech in Philadelphia shortly after his arrival, he was approached by German agents and offered $200 a week to do sabotage work on the waterfront. He refused but organized strikes against the war effort. In later life, Larkin always maintained that he did no actually sabotage work himself, but there is evidence that he was paid large sums of money to supply the German agents with information. He was also of interest to German agents, not least because of his significant address book of radical contacts which could be a valuable aid to them in their anti-British plots. Included among these connections were such radical luminaries as the "Preparedness Bomber"—Tom Mooney; the IWW organizer Big Bill Haywood and the itinerant radical Elizabeth Gurley Flynn. After American entry into the war, he was carefully monitored, arrested for sedition, and acquitted. Increasingly drawn to the Bolshevik regime after the October Revolution in Russia, he was arrested during the Red Scare on a charge of "criminal anarchy" and was sentenced to 5 to 10 years in New York's Sing Sing. He was released in 1922 and returned to Ireland the following year to a hero's welcome.[18]

Unlike Larkin, most of the saboteurs were not punished. One saboteur, Lothar Witzke, was caught and hung in Texas in 1918, but he was a striking exception. At a higher level, in December, 1915, after the discovery of bomb plots by the British, Woodrow Wilson demanded the withdrawal to Berlin of two leading German diplomats in the US. In general, most agents in the country escaped detection, or were arrested outside America, like von Rintelen. Nevertheless, the suspicion that German agents were operating in America was widespread and the fear of saboteurs fed the extreme patriotism of the war years, and the years immediately following with the result that the Attorney General bragged that there was probably no time in the history of the Republic that had seen more rigorous policing. Not only were the police, military intelligence and the increasingly important Justice Department Bureau of Investigation, committed to detection of German agents, slackers, and pacifists but there were also a huge variety of semi-private organizations which emerged, willing to patrol, inspect, and punish any suspects.

The leading group among these was the American Protective League. Founded in Chicago by a successful local businessman, its growth was spectacular, feeding as it did on the fears of sabotage and subversion, and the willingness of "home front warriors" to feel something of the adventure of war. By the end of the war, the League had some 250,000 members in 600 cities, men who investigated suspicious behavior and patrolled their designated region for enemy agents. Frequently this enthusiasm resulted in the arrest and detention of socialists and others who actively opposed the war effort, rather than saboteurs or German agents. It is estimated that over 10 percent of all APL activity was devoted to investigating the IWW. Disbanded in 1919, the APL had become by this point increasingly intrusive and uncontrollable. To the Wilson administration, it was symptomatic of the way in which the genie of "patriotism," so vital to the mobilization of the nation in 1917, had become a menace by 1919. To many in the Wilson cabinet, including initially the Attorney General, A. Mitchell Palmer, it was seen as feeding repression and a frenzied search for subversives. To historians, it is viewed as an unfulfilled force which would propel nativism, division, and dissatisfaction well into the next decade—a climate ideal for the emergence of gangsterism.[19]

If the criminal history of the 1920s is associated with a single individual, that person must be Al Capone, whose name, now as then, is synonymous with gangsterism and organized crime. It is Capone, more than any single figure who sums up the reputation of the ubiquitous and legendary gang leaders of the decade for brutality, ruthlessness and violence. There can be no doubt that part of Capone's authority came from terror: the knowledge that disobedience, incompetence or disloyalty, whether inside or outside his organization would result in ruthless punishment, if not, death. In this, Capone drew on a rich heritage of Italian criminality in the United States and one of the main components of that criminality was that very brutality—genuine terrorism. This abject terror which organized crime inspired in the 200,000-strong Italian community of New York at the turn of the century was meant to have made it one of the most lawless places in America.

According to a range of newspaper accounts, it was sheer terror which prevented Italians from allowing proper policing. The statistics appear to back such conclusions, since it was estimated that a mere 1 in 250 crimes committed was reported to the police. Of those, only 1 in 5 ended in arrest, and of those arrests, 1 in 300 ended in a conviction.[20] However, closer examination of the circumstances of Little Italy would show that this mono-causal explanation is incomplete. The view merely fulfilled a stereotype. There were a variety of reasons for the so-called *omerta*, many of which say more about the theorists and host population, than they tell us about the Italians themselves. Italians did not trust the local police, who rarely spoke Italian and were often equally hostile to both the victims and perpetrators of crime in the region. These police, like many of the other residents of New York, regarded the Italian immigration of the late nineteenth century to be inherently criminal, a view which was propagated by the outstanding criminologist of his day, Caesare Lombroso. An Italian himself, Lombrosco saw the Southern Italians as violent, superstitious, and ignorant, and of course coming from a land of banditry and lawlessness, they were bound to be both used to crime and cowed into a stolid silence when it was perpetrated on them.

Given this climate of opinion, in August 1903, when a wealthy Neapolitan-born construction company boss in Brooklyn paid an extortion note, it would be expected that few would have taken much notice—such things were a common occurrence in the Italian community. However, his son-in-law had gone to the police with enough information to convict two of the gang of extortionists and the ensuing story had all an ambitious newspaper editor could wish for. Resisting threats of death if he went ahead with the prosecution, the builder went to court and the extensive newspaper coverage of the trial which followed fascinated the New York public. In spite of being protected by an extensive police guard, the Neapolitan was obviously terrified in the courtroom, fearing that the extortionists "might blow them [his family] up with dynamite or cut holes in them unexpectedly." Moreover, it appeared that the case was not a one-off. According to newspaper reports, the group were not opportunists, but an organized and ruthless gang—part of a national network of crime—who had "first terrified and then reaped a harvest from hundreds of wealthy Italians . . . doctors, lawyers and businessmen who have received threatening letters . . . [and] have sent the money for fear of incurring the penalty." After the trial, New Yorkers had a new Italian bogeyman to add to the Sicilian *Mafia* and the Neapolitan *Camorra*—the Black Hand.[21]

Although its origins are thought to be Spanish, the Black Hand would now be associated with Italian criminality for the next two decades. The idea behind it was simple. Send a letter with a demand for cash. State how and when the cash should be delivered, and threaten some horrible punishment should the demand be ignored or the police informed. It would be signed with the name "the Black Hand" which would often be accompanied by a hand print, sometimes with a stiletto dagger piercing it. The typical letter was as blunt and sinister as this one sent to a Brooklyn butcher—"You have more money than we have. We know of your wealth and that you are alone in this country. We want $1,000, which you are to put in a loaf of bread and hand to a man who comes to buy meat and pulls out a red handkerchief." Another warned the victim that "not even the dust of your family will exist" should their demands not be met.[22] Some fell victim to the gangs as a result of their fame. The singer Enrico Caruso, in New York for a brief engagement, paid a $2,000 demand, only to be confronted by another for $15,000. Nor were victims or its terrorism limited to Italians, or residents of Italian districts. One German-born Justice of the Peace, living in New Jersey, was sent a lethal letter bomb as retribution for his conviction of several Black Handers.

The sinister sounding name made it memorable in both the Italian community and the outside world. In "Little Italys" across the nation, the case set off a slew of copycat groups. Black Hand letters were regularly used in New Orleans, San Francisco, and Chicago—in fact in all major Italian communities. The press claimed that it was all the work of one, organized, society with networks in the Italian regions of all the country. The scale of this society was meant to be enormous. The *San Francisco Call* claimed that there were 30,000 Black Handers within the organization across the nation. Another source claimed that there had been over 300 Black Hand killings alone in 1907 in Manhattan, and that there were a further four each day. One Chicago article boldly estimated that a third of all the city's Italians were "paying tribute to the Black Hand."[23] In short, the press tended to attribute all Italian on Italian crime to the Black Hand gangs.

There is no doubt that these newspapers overstated the threat of the Black Hand, but it was not only at this time that the importance and significance of the Black Hand were exaggerated. Many historical accounts of the birth of the Mafia have seen the Black Hand as some sort of larval stage in the coalescence of Italian-American criminality into organized crime. In order to be seen as such, it is important to establish that there really was a network of Black Hand societies, all inter-connected, sharing information and helping each other. It seems probable that in reality such a network never existed. Its existence as a unified society was a result of the Yellow Press, for as one commentator put it:

> It is not strange, perhaps, that most Americans believe that a terrible orga-
> nization named the "Black Hand Society" exists in Italy, and is sending its
> members to establish branches for the purpose of plundering the United
> States, since nearly every newspaper in the country conveys that impression
> to its readers . . . Thus the press not only facilitates the commission of crime
> among the Italian ex-convicts, by making it appear that all the evil done by

them is the successful work of a single organization, that aids the individual criminal by leading his ignorant countrymen, upon whom he preys, to believe that he makes his lawless demands on behalf of a powerful society.[24]

While these newspaper accounts almost certainly exaggerated the extent of Black Hand, there is also little doubt that many petty criminals felt that the Black Hand name and symbol were recognizable to all victims, and association with such a "society" gave a certain gravitas and authenticity to their demands. Such a theory is given credence by the example of the second Black Hand demand made to Caruso. The singer went to the police who instructed him to pay and then watched the drop-off site. It was two prominent local Italian businessmen who were discovered collecting the money. These two were hardly the bagmen, the minions, of a huge network of extortionists.[25] They were far more likely to be opportunists, amateurs, who read about the first demand and simply thought they could emulate that success.

Should this theory be true it would appear that just like organized crime as a whole, the Black Hand was more a coincidence of occasional mutual interest—in this case merely a name and a pattern—than a real syndication of the business of crime.[26] While the methods of operation and rituals of many Black Hand groups may well have had much in common with each other, in reality rather than a nationwide network of criminals, Black Hand gangs tended to be parochial in both their outlook and ambitions. Local groups were happy to use the advantages of association, but they tended to jealously guard their own "turf" and co-operation tended to be, at best, rudimentary.

The local and individual nature of Black Hand gangs is backed up by an investigation of the so-called "First Family" of the American Mafia, the Morellos. Claims that the Morello Family were one of the leading Black Hand gangs may well have been true. They certainly used Black Hand methods. Extortion letters were discovered in the ruthless boss Joseph Morello's apartment when he was arrested in 1909, and he certainly negotiated for victims with other gangs, but his main interest was counterfeiting. The negotiation showed the lack of co-operation. It was not done between members of an over-arching secret society, but as one "Man of Honor"—gang leader—and another, and the victim would then be in the debt of the hired negotiator. According to one source, in Morello's case, he acted for a doctor, from the same Sicilian village as himself, who was receiving extortion letters. Once Morello had resolved the issue, all Morello's relatives then expected to receive treatment, for life, for free.[27] Another source claims that Morello set up the entire scam, and had sent the original threats himself.[28] Either way, it does not look like the actions of a national, or even city-wide crime organization—more the criminal opportunism of a local petty gangster.

11

IMMIGRATION AND CRIME

Walking down any reasonably prosperous street in New York in 1900, if you stopped a resident and asked him, or her, what they considered the main problems to be facing the nation, you would probably not find the reply particularly different from what you might expect today. Of course, the economy would loom large, most likely with the behavior of big businesses and taxes—although in the 1900 case, it might be the worries over the "Trusts" and protective tariffs rather than bankers' bonuses and income tax rates which dominated such concerns. Then, as now, crime rates would certainly be a worry, and as with all such surveys the incidence of crime would certainly be perceived as on the rise. There would perhaps be fears about the encroachment into the area of mounting numbers of increasingly violent street gangs and ever more visible prostitution in places where it had not been seen before. They may express a fear of anarchist terrorism. Drink and drugs might well figure. In all, the response would most likely be largely and recognizably similar to the concerns of such a citizen today. One thing which would almost certainly figure, both then as now, would be association of the rising numbers of immigrants with these growing levels of crime.

Nor was this concern entirely unwarranted. In the first decades of the twentieth century, American cities had a higher proportion of immigrants than ever before or since. Overall the foreign-born population peaked during this period, making up nearly 15 percent of the entire nation. Estimates give some boroughs of New York as having up to 90 percent immigrant populations. These so-called "colonies" seemed increasingly like foreign territory. This perception was not entirely the result of the density of population. In these districts not only were the languages and appearance alien to the native-born, but so were the customs, religions, politics, and morals. The vast bulk of these immigrants, although largely European in origin, were from different regions of the continent, from areas which might have well have been Africa or Asia to the now settled Europeans in America. To an increasingly vocal, well-financed and well-connected nativist lobby dedicated to the restriction of European immigration, this was the so-called New Immigration and they were decidedly not the descendants of common ancestors to the older migrants from that continent.

To their opponents, those streams of hopeful immigrants disembarking from the huge passenger vessels in huge numbers every day were not suitable material from which to make Americans. Those arriving were no longer predominantly Germans, Scots, Dutch, Swedes, or even Irish who had come to the nation seeking a better life through thrift, hard work and self-reliance. These were unassimilable Jews from Poland and Russia's Pale of Settlement, or the equally undesirable and downtrodden peasants from Southern Italy, Greece, and the Balkans. These were not distant relatives of residents already in America, coming to settle and raise families, but rather they were economic migrants attracted by the advertising of cynical and grasping steamship and railroad companies. These were the not citizens of advanced nations, used to playing a role, however minor, in the political and economic life of their countries. They would not be bringing necessary skills, enthusiasms, and drive to the United States. These were primitive people who could not possibly add anything valuable to America—this modernizing, industrializing nation. These people would simply scrounge charity, take jobs, threaten the security of the nation, and debase the regions in which they settled. They would also bring their depraved and atavistic ways with them because, as the former superintendent of the US census had put it, these were the "off-scourings" of Europe. They were "beaten men from beaten nations" and "the worst failures in the struggle for existence."[1]

Given that this was the starting point for a significant and vocal proportion of well-placed Americans in their attitude towards the New Immigrants, it is hardly surprising that immigration was associated with crime. This section aims to examine, first, how prevalent and how relevant this connection of immigration and crime really was. Using particular examples, it will look at which crimes were associated with immigration, and which immigrant group was associated with which crime, and why. It will then move on to examine the actual criminalization of the immigration process itself, looking into how it was that simply trying to enter the United States made certain individuals, groups, and even races into criminals and the way in which this criminalization was dealt with, and what this tells us about American society in these years.

The early decades of the twentieth century saw nativists—essentially those dedicated to the interests of the existing residents and hostile to immigrants— deploy a whole range of statistical evidence which they felt demonstrated the irrefutable connections between immigration and crime. There were surveys of prison populations, asylum inmates, and crime statistics which compared the immigrants to the native-born. Using what appeared to be sophisticated statistical formulas, virtually without fail these reports found that, relative to their proportion of the population, the immigrants, and their offspring, contributed more insane, infirm, and criminals to the nation than the native-born. For example, one such report, given to Congress by the "expert eugenics agent," Harry H. Laughlin in 1922, showed that compared with the nation's general population, the Southern and Eastern European immigrant was nearly twice as likely to be found insane. He, or she, was also one and half times as likely to be "criminalistic." When compared with only the "white, native-born, residents of white, native-born, parentage," they were more than three times as commonly insane, and twice as commonly "criminalistic."[2]

What was more, such reports almost invariably claimed to demonstrate that violent crime, drug abuse, drunkenness, burglary—most aspects of criminal behavior—had increased in a simple and direct ratio to the growing numbers of foreign-born residents, especially in the nation's big cities. Some commentators saw this worrying trend simply in racial terms. Even more disturbingly, these die-hard restrictionists claimed that these "racial" criminal proclivities were less alterable and more fixed, than crimes which resulted from simple lack of opportunity—poverty or ignorance. Unlike previous immigrant groups whose misfortunes had led them into crime, these "New" immigrants did not seem to adjust to American morals as they resided in a democracy and their opportunities, status, and wealth increased. As the Immigration Restriction League concluded in 1910:

> A considerable proportion of immigrants now coming are from races and countries, or parts of countries, which have not progressed, but have been backward, downtrodden, and relatively useless for centuries. If these immigrants "have not had opportunities," it is because their races have not made the opportunities; for they have had all the time that any other races have had.[3]

As one critic of the race theorists put it, there was among these "Nordic Supremacists"

> [a] general idea that an increase of crime in America is due to [the] degeneration of the national stock (Nordic) which in its turn is due to intermixture with disharmonic and inferior races (Alpines and Mediterraneans from Southern and Eastern Europe).

Not only did this mean that the immigrants bred these criminal traits in their own communities, but they also—in mixing with the resident population—threatened to corrupt the entire nation's racial character. The New Immigration

> was destroying initiative, ability, ambition, ideals, independence, resourcefulness, public spirit, and capacity for self-government—qualities peculiarly characteristic of their Nordic origin . . . [Paramount among these was] their

respect for law and detestation of crime. [For] law observance amounted almost to a passion with our American forefathers.

To these committed race theorists, American society demonstrated the results of this racial corruption, degeneracy and dilution. The decline in standards was clearly visible in

> yellow journalism, [the] disintegration of parental authority, the waning of school discipline, the exaggeration of sex (including cigarette smoking by women and short skirts), addiction to sports, [in growing levels of] inebriety and the drug habit, [the] growth of political corruption, [the] coddling of criminals, and an increasing disrespect for law.[4]

While most nativists agreed that the influence of these new-style immigrants was undesirable, they did not necessarily agree that *all* immigrants were all *equally* undesirable. For example, while it was generally accepted that the Southern and Eastern European migrants were racially inferior, it was not entirely clear what this actually meant or how it would manifest itself. To some, this meant that their criminality was largely the result of ignorance. Taken to its logical conclusion, this meant that immigrants would have neither the ambition, nor the ability to master complex or large-scale crimes. Their criminal behavior would be the result of constant and irresistible temptation: they would commit crimes largely because of either opportunity or poverty.

While this may have been an irritant, it did mean that, as one report put it, the "native criminal exhibits in general a greater tendency to commit more serious crimes than the immigrant."[5] It appeared that even in crime, many of the race theorists were anxious to prove the superiority of the Nordic races. To other opponents of the New Immigration, such views over-looked the inherent bestial, criminal nature of many of these immigrants. According to New York's Police Commissioner, Theodore Bingham, immigrants had a penchant, a predisposition, for crime, America was playing home to all the "predatory criminals of all nations . . . the Armenian Hunchakist, the Neapolitan Camorra, the Sicilian Mafia, the Chinese Tongs and other . . . scum of the earth."[6] In short, immigration was seen as being associated with almost all types of criminal behavior.

Throughout the period certain crimes were associated with certain immigrant groups. The various stereotypical views of different races, religions or groups were often applied—backed up with greater or lesser levels of evidence—to their criminal activities. For example, it was held to be the Chinese who established the growing number of opium dens in the sleazier regions of almost all the major cities of the nation. As one commentator remarked in 1883, it was "a poor town nowadays that has not a Chinese laundry . . . and nearly every town has its opium lay-out."[7] Since the Chinese were considered indolent, decadent, feckless, hedonistic, and ignorant, the soporific and debilitating effects of the drug were seen as both appealing to their nature and creating their inherent characteristics—even though the smoking of the drug had been introduced to them relatively recently by Europeans. In spite of the overt racial typecasting that was the basis of such opinions, there was evidence to support the claims since it has been estimated that during the period of this study a minimum of 20 percent, and probably far more, of America's Chinese regularly used opium.[8]

On the other hand, on the West coast in particular, the Japanese, often simply by reason of their oriental origins, were also frequently seen as being involved in the narcotics trade. However, since in the nativist mind the Japanese were seen as better motivated, more acute and more acquisitive, it was often argued that the Japanese "pushed" and smuggled the opium, making money, while the Chinese simply consumed it and slid further into characteristic decadence. As a narcotics agent in the Pacific Northwest put it—"The Chinese are the worst violators of the [Harrison] Narcotics Law—the Japs next. The Chinese use the most narcotics of any nationality—usually they smoke it. The Japs use the least, but they do tend to sell it."[9] Such a comment seems to have ignored the evidence that the vast majority of opium dens, across the nation were Chinese-owned, Chinese-run and used Chinese products, and that—in spite of their near identical appearance to many nativists—the interaction between the Chinese and Japanese communities was, at best, limited.

Similarly, it was argued that it was the wily Japanese who imported the Chinese, Korean and Filipino women who made up the "China Marys" of so many Western brothels. There was some truth to these claims, at least initially, however, the group which received the blame was usually the group which was most resented in the region in question. For example, before the mass emigration of Japanese to Hawaii and America in the 1890s, the problem of Asian prostitution was blamed solely on the Chinese. Similarly, in New York, even in the 1900s, there were few Japanese but a well-established Chinese community. By contrast, in Seattle, both nationalities were relatively numerous. Consequently, in the 1910s, in Seattle the Japanese were blamed for much of the vice problem, since Chinese immigration had been halted in 1882, whereas Japanese "picture brides" could continue to enter the country until 1924.[10] Whichever group was blamed, nationally there was a strong tie between Asians and prostitution.

There were two strong justifications for such a view. First, there was a traditional acceptance of concubines and sexual slavery in both Chinese and other Asian cultures.[11] Even more compelling was the huge discrepancy between male and female immigrants in Chinese American society. By 1890, it was estimated that there were 22 Chinese men to each Chinese woman in San Francisco, the city where half of the nation's Chinese lived.[12] Coupled with anti-miscegenation laws which forbade Chinese–white marriages, there was a correspondingly massive demand for scarce Chinese women by Chinese men. This was visible in the "Yellow Slavery" of the nation's Chinatowns. One estimate in 1871 claimed that 61 percent of all Chinese women in America were prostitutes, although there is perhaps reason to think that the figure may actually have been considerably higher.[13]

As if these blighted areas of America's cities were not enough, as anti-Chinese agitation grew in the late 1870s and early 1880s, an even more worrying trend emerged with a rash of newspaper and magazine reports. These "first-hand" accounts showed that the "Chinaman" not only enslaved his own women, but also acted as a predatory menace for any young white girls who happened to stray into his path. In a series of articles, the link between opium smoking and prostitution was highlighted. Giddy, innocent, young white girls were lured first into opium addiction and then into prostitution in order to feed their habit.[14] Nor was it only the Chinese who were associated with this diabolical trade. By the first decade of the twentieth century according to a growing number of salacious and sensational sources, the panic induced by this so-called White Slavery had reached the level of an epidemic.

Just as the anti-Chinese rhetoric had coincided with rising hostility to Chinese migration, this surge in moral outrage drew on the growing hostility to the New Immigration. Nothing shows this more clearly than the article which launched this movement. It appeared in *McClure's* magazine in 1909, as over one million European immigrants a year were arriving at the ports of the east coast. The author, George Kibbe Turner set the tone with his depictions of the denizens of the "racial slums of Europe" arriving at bustling, overcrowded, Ellis Island dragging poor and innocent country girls with them to satisfy the needs of jaded and perverted city men. He then went on to describe the selling of these unfortunates to their compatriots with the connivance, nod and winks of the "debauched" politicians of the urban machines.

It would have been clear to contemporary readers that the sellers were most probably Jewish, and the politicians Irish, Catholics. Turner had tapped potent nativist sources attacking these two groups, and he further expanded his potential audience by warning that the procurers were probably, even as he wrote, trawling the Italian ice cream parlor, the "German skating rink" and "fruit stores run largely by foreigners" for fresh victims. Parents, siblings, reformers, and moral guardians were outraged, as was the President. William Howard Taft immediately released $50,000 to combat the trade and Representative William Richardson of Alabama promised the nation that there were no limits to the federal government's commitment to "regulate the morals of the state."[15]

While much of this fear has been seen as the result of the quintessential "moral panic"—the over-reaction to a threat by a society driven by panic—it does illustrate many of the concerns of the time. The connections between "foreigners," abduction, and sexual perversion had always troubled the American nativist mind—and rather handily at the same time provided lucrative best-sellers. Italians, and Sicilians in particular, had always been associated with kidnapping. This was sometimes associated with ransom. At other times it was simply enslavement either for labor, sex or begging.[16] It was not only the foreigners who entered the country who posed a threat. There had long been a morbid dread of wild savages capturing white women, enslaving, torturing, raping, and killing them and their husbands and children on the frontier.[17]

These fears also included "Americans" who had foreign beliefs, like the sex-starved celibate Catholic priests who were the villains in many best-selling "true accounts" of the horrors taking place within closed orders in America. These often fabricated and extraordinary popular documents detailed the illicit and perverted sexual liaisons between the priests and the novices and initiates of the orders. What made them even more horrific to nineteenth-century audiences was that the priests then insisted on the burying of the aborted offspring within the confines of convents, often with the collusion of equally un-American and depraved nuns. The most famous of these accounts was the salacious and entirely fabricated *Awful Disclosures by Maria Monk of the Hotel Dieu Nunnery of Montreal* (New York, 1836) which set the scene with an abused nun touring the nation with tales of her abuse at the hands of a whole legion of priests. Not only was this book a bestseller throughout the 1840s, its story line was regularly plundered and re-animated by other abused young novices. On their "escape" from their tormenters, they often found themselves adopted and used by anti-Catholic groups well into the 1930s and beyond.[18]

However, the emerging threat which Turner saw was on an entirely new scale. The nation had more immigrants and resident foreigners than at any other time in its history. This not only meant that there were more potential procurers, handlers, pimps, and perverts, but it also meant that concealing and transporting the unfortunate women had never been easier. The career of the psychopathic murderer, burglar, rapist, brothel owner, and white slaver Joseph Silver clearly shows this. Born Joseph Lis in Poland, he traveled the late Victorian, Anglo-Saxon, world from London to New York to Cape Town, as well as extensively in Latin America, living off abusing, trading and shipping women for prostitution. His criminal activities illustrate that even if it was not as widespread as some claimed, there really was a very sophisticated white slavery network, and also that it was truly international.[19]

What makes Joseph Silver all the more relevant to any study of immigration and crime is the fact that he was Jewish. Jews played a central role in the narratives of the white slave scare and other criminal activity of the times. In part, this was a result of simple numbers. Jews from Poland, Austria-Hungary, Russia and the Ottoman territories made up a major part of the New Immigration. There were a number of reasons for this Diaspora which are highly significant to this study and make Jews an ideal illustration of the undercurrents of contemporary attitudes towards immigration and crime: The image of Jewish criminal aliens serves to illustrate both the changes and the constants of this period. Not least of these is that the prejudice they encountered in the US was a mix which was in part predicated on views which traveled across to America with other Europeans, and partly the result of the fillip to the emerging "scientific racism" which opposition to the New Immigration provided. In order to understand these, it is important to have at least some knowledge of the currents which drove this massive Jewish exodus.

The huge upsurge in Jewish emigration was largely the result of the relaxation by the 1890s in much of the legislation which had previously bound these often impoverished and poorly educated would-be emigrants to their homelands. In cases where these restrictions remained, they were ignored or were not enforced as the authorities saw a way of ridding themselves of what was seen as an increasingly troublesome population. To some extent this animosity was justified. The poverty and persecution of the Jews had given them little love for the autocrats of these regions and over the years they came to be associated with political radicalism—especially socialism and anarchism. Rarely considered full citizens of their host nations, they were increasingly seen by those governments as more of a nuisance than an asset. What was more, they produced little revenue, and even if they could provide cannon fodder for the huge conscript European armies—Russia at this point had a 25-year conscription policy and would field an army of some 5 million in 1914—they were still seen as unreliable at best, and troublesome and treasonous at worst.

Nor was it simply the authorities who wanted them to leave. Often the impetus for emigration came from the Jews themselves. When Jews had been directly or indirectly implicated in acts of violence and terrorism, the usual low, background, level of persecution flared up into brutal violence. Even those Jews who stayed within the law, or avoided the attention of the violent anti-Semites, were subjected to limitations on the trades they could enter. Traditionally, Jews were unable to own property or land, with the result that they were often forced into jobs in which their wit was their capital. Many led lives of dreary squalor, or subsisted through such trades as tailoring, rendering, peddling or other trades. The more fortunate, or intelligent, became associated with banking, money changing and accountancy—frequently leading to accusations of usury and sharp practice, especially when the business ventures they funded failed, or the economy slumped.

In addition, as an alien population, Jews were only allowed to live within defined areas—the ghettoes of cities and shtetls of the countryside constraints which severely limited both opportunity and ambition. As the period progressed, many of these restrictions were lifted or reduced in severity and a Jewish middle class of industrialists, manufacturers, and entrepreneurs emerged in regions of Germany, Austria-Hungary and, even, to a lesser extent, Russia. Nevertheless as the prosecution and persecution of Alfred Dreyfus for alleged spying so clearly showed, even in democratic France, Jews still found themselves treated as, at best, second-class citizens, and more usually clannish, dishonest, self-serving, undesirable, and unreliable alien arrivistes. For them the opportunities and freedoms of America seemed simply fantastic and in many of the Jewish communities of Eastern Europe, the advertising of steamship and railroad companies selling passage to the New World found many of their most eager customers.

To some extent, even some of the most liberal of Europeans, while fighting for improvement in the political and economic conditions of the Jews, still felt that they brought some of their troubles upon themselves. Enlightened Europeans argued that traditional Jewish religious superstitions had played some part in their isolation—with such practices as their insistence on kosher food and strict hygiene laws leading to a voluntary segregation which had served to exaggerate their "other-ness." Superstition also added potent weapons to the armory of the anti-Semites. There were age-old accusations that Jews were "Christ-killers" and, as a result, the natural enemies of Christians. Coupled with this, they were also periodically accused of participating in bloody rituals at Passover which involved the sacrifice and bloodletting of Christian children—the so-called Blood Libel. By the turn of the twentieth century, the pattern was all too familiar. A young Christian child would go missing, or a body would be discovered, and the Jewish community would suffer the consequences. This was most destructively exemplified at Kishinev, in what is now Romania, but was then a part of the Russian Empire. Here, in 1903, over seven hundred of the Jewish community were either killed or wounded and the Jewish quarter of the town was razed to the ground.[20]

It is estimated that over two and a half million Eastern European Jews settled in America in the period 1890–1924 and although there were certainly less frequent or violent instances of anti-Semitism in the United States than in Europe, much of the old prejudice followed them over the Atlantic. Alongside a general mistrust of them as immigrants, the Jews encountered specific prejudices which it was held adapted them perfectly to the white slave trade. They were seen as having no respect for authority—be that the family, police, or the government—which, it was held, made them the perfect operatives at all levels of the international prostitution racket. Their greed was seen as making them wicked and venal, suiting them to crimes of fraud and deception as well as the necessary simple actions of basic cruelty and immorality against defenseless women. There were the accusations of clannishness which, just like the allegations made against the Chinese, led to suspicions that Jews lived in a criminal underworld of their own.

In this *demi-monde*, it was argued, the Jews protected each other and organized criminal networks which fed the conviction that they ran the white slave trade and other illicit activities. Over years of migration from Europe, they had established a network which gave them international ties, enabling them to almost effortlessly source, ship, work, and distribute girls with efficiency, secrecy, and safety anywhere in the world.[21] Nor was it simply the white slave trade which Jewish organizations dominated. For example, in the 1870s, the German-Jewish immigrant, Fredericka, "Marm," Mandelbaum arguably ran the most sophisticated criminal organization of nineteenth-century America.

Her million-dollar New York crime empire was founded on fencing stolen goods, but she also provided a range of criminal services to her acquaintances which would foreshadow those associated with the syndicates which were not meant to have emerged until the 1920s and 1930s. Marm's little empire took on such tasks as posting bail for those she was associated with. Alongside this she kept a team of high quality lawyers on retainer—initially at her own expense, although she would be reimbursed. She also provided a service to re-model stolen goods and in many cases acted as a pawn-broker. Like many organized crime networks which would later evolve, Marm relied on an inner core of extended familial relations in order to maintain absolute security at the highest level of the organization. While this could have given rise to her organization being seen as an example of Jewish clannishness, a major part of her success actually lay in her unusual ability to transcend racial, class, and gender boundaries.[22]

Nevertheless, it is a sign of the changing currents of American opinion that after Mandelbaum's empire was hurriedly dismantled in the 1880s, there is no record of her criminal activity being put down to her Jewish roots. Some 30 years later, the same religious/racial "tolerance" would not be true. As the views of the hierarchies of eugenicists and other "scientific" nativists began to gain popularity, they were increasingly applied in the analysis of criminal propensity. When this was combined with hostility to the New Immigration and the latent imported background anti-Semitism, it swiftly fed detectable views that Jewish criminality was not only shaped by the Jews' background and previous experience, but that they showed a natural inclination for crime which exceeded that of other immigrant groups.

In 1908, New York's Commissioner of Police, Theodore Bingham, claimed in the *North American Review* that while Jews made up only a quarter of the city's population, they made up half of the convicted criminals. He maintained that they excelled at every criminal activity from insurance fraud and arson to highway robbery, but most especially pick-pocketing.[23] Moreover, in the same year, a far more influential survey—conducted by the famous Dillingham Immigration Committee—found that "Hebrews" topped a list of the 21 leading alien "races" for two out of four categories of criminals incarcerated in the US. Unsurprisingly, the statistics showed what nativists had long suspected, that there were more Jews in US prisons than any of the other races. This was not only the case for the "crimes against chastity"—presumably including white slavery—but also the "gainful crime" which Marm Mandelbaum so exemplified.[24]

What many of these statistical studies also seemed to indicate was that the criminal ambitions of the immigrant tended to increase, rather than decline, with the second generation, reinforcing the idea of the immutability of such trends through race.[25] Perhaps no one exemplified this surge in second generation criminal vigor better than the son of a New York businessman, Abraham Rothstein. Rothstein had emigrated from Europe in the 1870s and prospered in New York's East Side Jewish community. By the early twentieth century he was a highly respected local figure, a key member of his synagogue and something of a philanthropist—known as in the Jewish community as "Abe the Good." His son, Arnold, was arguably more successful, but the route he took was far less benign, and far less respectable.

Arnold Rothstein was perhaps the most successful criminal of his generation. Born in New York in 1882, from an early age, the younger Rothstein showed an aptitude for mathematics and wayward behavior. Starting off by stealing change from his father's pockets and using it to finance his "craps" games on the street, as a young adult, he became the "highest roller" of his generation. Although essentially remaining at heart a gambler, Rothstein became involved in any criminal activity which he felt would pay. He went on to become the ultimate criminal fixer—taking a fee to put criminals in touch with each other, rectifying problems or organizing meetings. By the 1920s, he was arranging and financing huge stakes poker games and betting tens, if not hundreds, of thousands on them. He planned, rigged and made books at most major race tracks. During Prohibition, he ran a whisky importation business that had directly negotiated monopolies for the American trade with many of the Scottish distilleries—shipping, landing and distributing huge quantities on the East coast. Throughout his career, he maintained good contacts with legitimate business and he paid off policemen and politicians at the highest level. Most notoriously it was strongly suspected that it was Rothstein, the Big Bankroll, who financed the Black Sox World Series fix of 1919. AR, as he was known, even bet over $500,000 on Herbert Hoover's victory in 1928. Unfortunately, he was murdered by an unpaid creditor before he could collect.

In many ways Rothstein typified a new type of criminal. Urban, urbane and professional, he appeared to be the respectable family man, although his long-suffering wife frequently threatened to leave him. What was more, if only because he was never caught, he was considered semi-legitimate. Elegantly and unostentatiously dressed, with gracious manners he dealt with, and indeed controlled, some of the most notorious sociopaths and thugs of his day, including the sadistic Monk Eastman and the corrupt and brutal cop, Charlie Becker—who remains the only US policeman to meet his death on the electric chair. Not only was Rothstein novel in his appearance and demeanor, his habits were unusual for his day. He operated semi-openly from Lindy's Restaurant, on Broadway. Here he issued orders to his subordinates, met with associates such as Tammany boss, Charley Murphy, and negotiated with other underworld figures like Legs Diamond and Waxey Gordon. These names were significant, showing that Rothstein's circle of contacts and connections was wide-ranging and that unlike many crime lords before him, he was catholic in his acquaintances: Rothstein did not limit his business associates to simply those from his own community.[26]

One of the features of late nineteenth- and early twentieth-century gangs which troubled criminologists and nativists alike was their racial homogeneity. To these observers it was the clannishness which prompted and encouraged disregard for the morals and mores of the host population. Nevertheless, their violence, while often aimed at those within their own community was also frequently prone to spill out into the wider community as different groups tried to muscle in on each other's territories. New York, Chicago, New Orleans, and Boston, and most other major cities, had criminal histories dominated by inter-ethnic criminal turf wars. These were most frequently between the Irish and the Italians, but sometimes involving Jews, or even the Chinese and Japanese. Rothstein did away with this. He would happily mix and utilize figures from the Irish, Italian, and other communities as long as they were best suited to carry out the job in hand. Traditionally it had been assumed that immigrants could trust no one other than their own relatives, or at least near neighbors. For example, Rothstein's near contemporary, Zelig Zvi Lefkowitz, known as "Big Jack Zelig," hired only Russian Jews for the trusted positions of the gang he inherited from Monk Eastman.

Using this structure, Big Jack built up a mob which came to dominate New York's underworld in the closing years of the first decade of the twentieth century. The casually brutal Zelig made his name partly by terrorizing his own community, but he also gained prestige by showing little regard for the seemingly all-powerful Tammany machine, even personally and publicly beating up the half-brother of Tammany boss, Big Tim Sullivan. Ironically, the thinking behind this reliance on kith and kin seemed to be borne out by the circumstances surrounding both his own death and the fate of his most notorious henchmen. When Zelig took on the contract for the murder of the small-time gambler, Herman Rosenthal, he also became involved directly with the Irish-controlled City Hall and their influence over a totally corrupt police force. It was Rothstein who had originally been instructed by Big Tim Sullivan to "get that stupid son of a bitch [Rosenthal] out of town." When Rosenthal refused to leave, it was Rothstein who hired Zelig. When the case came to light, the cosmopolitan Rothstein walked away. The result was different for the more parochial Zelig. The contract led directly to his murder, and the subsequent execution of his four henchmen.[27]

In spite of the obvious violence which surrounded the deaths of Rothstein, Zelig and their henchmen, it was neither the Jews, nor the Irish, who had the reputation for being the most ruthless of all the new immigrants. Chicago's arrests statistics for the years 1905 to 1908 show that per capita, out of a group of the 20 largest immigrant communities, the vast majority of homicides were committed by the city's Italians. They were nearly one and a half times higher than the next group, the Lithuanians. What was more, nearly 40 percent of all violent crime reported to be committed by immigrants in New York during the year to April 1908, were carried out by Italians. The next largest group was the Austrians who committed less than 20 percent.[28] Reports variously described Italians as "assassins, blackmailers and thieves." They were seen as "vermin" who were as likely to use the knives they always carried for stabbing an enemy as cutting up their bread. The police chief, Theodore Bingham, estimated that New York had some 3,000 Italian desperadoes—"as many ferocious and desperate men as ever gathered in a modern city in time of peace—medieval criminals who must be dealt with under modern law."[29]

Many Americans did not feel that they needed such statistical evidence to be sure of the Italians' proclivity for violence, it was just apparent in what the papers reported. It seemed that every day there were Italians charged with violent robberies, stabbings or threatening blackmail or extortion. Nevertheless in the last decade of the nineteenth century, there seemed to be a change in the nature of these crimes. For years, newspapers had circulated stories of growing numbers of murders and other outrages being committed by shadowy secret Italian societies, but it was in August 1890 that "evidence" emerged of a transformation in the nature of Italian crime. It seemed that the Italians in most major cities were no longer satisfied with carrying out opportunistic crime within their own communities, but were well on the way to establishing a network of criminal organizations which challenged the Jewish criminal web in scale and scope.

The transformation in perception was in large measure sparked by the murder of Peter Hennessy—the incorruptible and popular, good-looking, young Irish dare-devil chief of police in New Orleans. Hennessey's death was held to be connected with his investigation of a war between rival Italian gangs for control of fruit shipping on the New Orleans waterfront. In the wake of Hennessey's murder, the city was caught up in a near-hysterical anti-Italian rage, whipped up and added to by the mayor who was fearful of growing Italian influence in local politics. When nine Sicilian suspects were found not guilty of Hennessey's murder, the situation exploded with the largest mass lynching in American history. Eleven Italians were hunted down and either hung or shot by a furious mob.[30] Arguably, this hysteria never really disappeared and it brought with it a new word for the American popular vocabulary—"Mafia." Mafia scare stories emerged in most major cities in the 1890s. Denver, Milwaukee, Boston, and San Francisco suffered Mafia scares, and Chicago and New York, with their large Italian populations, rapidly became viewed as Mafia hubs.

Although it has been argued that the Mafia evolved from the peculiar, poverty-induced codes of banditry and an inherent loathing of civil authority associated with tax-farmed peasants in the wilds of Sicily, in many ways, the growth of the Mafia mirrored the image Americans had of their own society in this period. As the organization grew in scale and sophistication, it was argued that this growth marked the disappearance of the Italian clannishness and overt violence, which had up until then limited their criminal activity in America. These traits were replaced by a subtle incorporation and the emergence of a new integrated form of crime—organized or syndicated crime. On the urban "frontiers" of cities like Chicago, St Louis, Detroit, Kansas City and New York, the immigrant—and most notably the Italian immigrant—used crime as a method of gaining a leg up on what the sociologist Daniel Bell has memorably called "a queer ladder of social mobility."[31] In a decade of conspicuous consumption, crime enabled immigrants to buy the accoutrements of, if not actual, "respectability."

Unlike Jewish involvement in the white slave trade, or the Chinese opium networks, the Mafia retains its association with Italian-Americans through to the present day. In part, this is because of its continued glamorous-yet-violent image in popular fiction and film, but it is also associated with its roots. Some have argued that the Mafia has been entangled with everyday, legitimate, American life since its main source of business, Prohibition, was making crime a part of the lives of almost all Americans. Not only did the "Noble Experiment" make a vast proportion of the adult population law breakers, but it also meant that most people knew someone who broke the law, regularly. Moreover, most Americans had a strong opinion about whether the sale of liquor should continue to be illegal.

Although the actual term "Mafia" lay largely dormant until it re-emerged with the Kefauver and McClellan Senate investigations of the 1950s, there were other stereotypes which abounded in the association of organized crime with the Italians. Not the least of these was the assumption that to those who supported the outlawing of alcohol, the bootleggers, rum-runners and speakeasy owners were by their nature foreign—their values were un-American. It was almost natural that in a large section of the popular imagination, the Italian-American—whether native-born or immigrant—was ideally suited to this trade, perhaps better than many of his fellow immigrants. Foreign in his brutality, lawlessness, and clannishness, he was also like most Catholics, "religiously" opposed to Prohibition. As one criminologist would later put it—"organized crime [came] to represent popular rebellion against the Protestant ethic (witness Prohibition which gave the Mafia its start)."[32]

The emergence of syndicated crime in the 1920s and 1930s seemed to bear this out. Through violence, ruthlessness, and intimidation the Italians gradually took over the urban criminal underworlds. In this, they were aided by existing gangs and criminal networks, like Big Joe Collisimo's proto-syndicate in Chicago, but this expansion was mostly the result of the power granted by the accumulation of the vast sums of money made available through Prohibition. A new generation of Italian-Americans like Johnny Torrio, Charles "Lucky" Luciano, Frank Costello (born Francesco Castiglia), Vito Genovese, Frank Nitti and, most notably, Al Capone, came to dominate the urban underworlds of the nation's metropolises with syndicates which more closely resembled the vertically integrated businesses of the robber barons than the street gangs of the 1900s.[33]

Moreover, it appeared that the Italians were able to defeat all-comers for their position as supreme gangsters of the era. Capone's St Valentine's Day Massacre saw off Dion O'Banion's Northside threat to his criminal realm in Chicago, just as Luciano took over Dutch Schultz's empire in New York. Where the Italians could not defeat competitors, they reached agreements, as with Luciano's lucrative pact with Bugsy Segal and Meyer Lansky. Nor did they squander these advantages. Even when the goose of Prohibition had stopped laying the golden eggs—with repeal in 1933—Italian crime syndicates had apparently already diversified in order to protect their turf. They controlled labor racketeering, narcotics, prostitution, numbers rackets, and all manner of other lucrative criminal activities. It appeared that just as the Irish had used a "natural ability" for politics—and its subversion—as a route to power and acceptance in American society, so in the minds of many native-born Americans, the Italians had almost monopolized violent crime, or at least the threat of it.[34]

Although many immigrants were associated with crime and criminal behavior, it was and still remains notoriously difficult for the authorities to either prove the veracity of this link, or to rectify the problem. Essentially there were two strategies available with which to control immigrant crime. The government could either refuse admission to those whom they suspected would carry out criminal activity once in the United States, or it could deport those convicted of crimes carried out while resident in America. Given the massive rise in immigration and the growing consensus for its limitation in the early twentieth century, it is hardly surprising that it was in this period that the immigration strategies used today were really laid out. It is during these years that America first seriously experimented with both individual and mass exclusions as well as deportations.

In his annual address to Congress in 1905, President Theodore Roosevelt recommended that the United States should expand their exclusion of "insane, idiotic and pauper immigrants . . . [To include] all people of bad character, the incompetent, the lazy, the vicious, and physically unfit, defective and degenerate." Perhaps more interestingly, he also stated it would be his aim to keep out "every man of anarchistic tendencies, [as well as] all violent and disorderly people."[35] In some ways this is hardly surprising. Roosevelt had assumed the presidency on the assassination of William McKinley, in 1901 and the nation had been involved in trying to find some way of controlling alien radicals and other criminals ever since.

Over 30 years before Roosevelt, President Ulysses S. Grant had argued that the Union was being threatened by another undesirable group—the Chinese—and a year later the process of their exclusion had begun with the Page Act of 1875. This law outlawed the "involuntary immigration" of laborers and the importation of women for the "purposes of prostitution." Unsurprisingly, given their persistent association with prostitution—as detailed above—this legislation has historically been seen as being aimed at the migration to America of Chinese women. What also linked it to Chinese immigration was an increasingly pervasive fear that coolies could be replacing the recently liberated blacks—a trade in which American citizens had been banned from participating since 1862. By 1882, any doubt over the target of such legislation was laid to rest when federal law extended exclusion to include virtually all Chinese immigrants.

Under the 1882 Act, any Chinese of the banned classes, and this applied to the vast majority of them—excluding a handful of merchants and missionaries—found to have illegally emigrated to the United States would first be imprisoned for a year and then deported. The Act was effective. In 1882, nearly 40,000 Chinese entered the United States. The following year the number admitted had dropped to around 8,000. By 1901, this figure was down to around 2,500 immigrants and by 1940, it totaled a little under 650.[36] The era of mass exclusion had begun. Essentially this had the effect of turning those who attempted to enter the country without permission into criminals, purely by the nature of their ethnic background—a phenomenon challenged in a series of Supreme Court decisions in the late nineteenth and early twentieth centuries. Further, since the demand for entry into the US did not halt with exclusion, it also created an entire new criminal industry—people smuggling.

While the figures for this illegal trade are understandably nebulous, some idea of the scale can be gathered from the report of the 1901 House Committee on Immigration. The Committee was told that as many as 20,000 Chinese were illegally entering the US each year through the notoriously porous land borders with Canada and Mexico. On the ground, the figures were less daunting. In 1907, some 503 Chinese were arrested as illegal aliens. Of these, 366 were deported.[37] That is not to say that then, as now, the vast majority of these "illegals" entered, worked and resided in America undetected and unmolested. In part, this was down to the ingenious and often ruthless efforts of people smugglers, operating an entire industry shipping hopeful Chinese migrants into America, coaching them in ways to avoid detection and fabricating the necessary documents and life histories.

By 1900, there was a thriving industry in producing illegal documentation for so-called "paper sons"—immigrants posing as close family members of Chinese residents and therefore legally allowed to reside in the US. The widespread nature of this tactic is shown by the figures which came to light as a result of a 1956 amnesty of illegal Chinese residents in America. It revealed that although the Exclusion Acts had been repealed in 1943, some 19,000 Chinese admitted to having used this course to gain admission. Nevertheless, as early as 1901, one federal judge claimed that each Chinese woman resident when the Exclusion laws were first passed in 1882 would have needed to have at least 500 offspring in order for there to be so many Chinese legally entitled to residency.[38]

In 1917, this criminalization by race was expanded beyond the Chinese to include most Asians—excluding the colonized Filipinos and the Japanese who had negotiated a separate agreement in 1907. By 1924, it included the Japanese and it had also been extended to limit many of the less desirable southern and eastern European nations. This was achieved by reducing their numbers to fractions of their previous multitudes through the imposition of strict quota limits on those granted visas in their home countries without which entry to the US was denied. In this respect, the 1924 Immigration Act was far more modern than the 1882 Exclusion Act and it required a modern bureaucracy to enforce it. Asian immigrants were readily detectable and equally easy to exclude. What was more, while America's immigration restrictions had been limited to the mentally retarded, persons with "dangerous and loathsome contagious diseases," the "feebleminded" and insane, detection and exclusion were also relatively simple.

When these excluded classes were extended to include paupers, contract laborers, polygamists, and prostitutes, it became more difficult, but the problem was of an individual scale. The inclusion of a whole swathe of European immigrants, often physically indistinguishable from those Europeans who could legally enter, made the problem far more difficult. It relied in great measure on a system of "remote control" by which American Embassy staff vetted prospective immigrants in order to ascertain their suitability for emigration in their own countries, granting or withholding visas accordingly. In order for this system to work, it was necessary to establish some form of identification and verification system. With this in mind, in 1917, passports were introduced, initially as a wartime measure, but swiftly made permanent at the end of the war. There were serious implications which stemmed from this increased border security. It shifted much of the emphasis for control back to the emigrant's home country. If the migrant did not have the relevant paperwork, he or she would not be allowed to enter the US and would be returned to their point of embarkation.

While this system was relevant and effective for the limited number of ports able to handle the large trans-Atlantic ships, it highlighted the realization that it was now America's land borders which formed the real threat for large numbers of illegal immigrants. This threat was limited in part by the existing naturalization arrangements which the US had with Canada. Canada's points-based system allowed Europeans to enter and reside as long as they could provide necessary skills or trades. Once resident in Canada for five years, they could legally enter the US. This proved a popular way for immigrants to overcome the quotas—legally. The popularity of this route is demonstrated by the fact that non-Canadian-born migrants entering the US from Canada went from making up a fifth of those crossing the border to over a half in the period from 1925 to 1930. Nevertheless there were still nearly 6000 illegal immigrants caught trying to cross the border over the same period, and in the 1930s this would rise to 8000.[39]

These figures were considerably less than those for the US southern border with Mexico. During the last five years of the 1920s Mexicans caught illegally entering America jumped from under 2000 a year in 1925 to over 15,000 in 1929. On crossing the Canadian border, migrants were met by procedures carried out by civilian staff with the efficiency and consideration most Americans would expect when crossing borders themselves. Unlike this, on the Mexican border, the process involved a paramilitary Border Patrol who subjected would-be immigrants to an in-line de-lousing, bathing and routine medical inspections. What was more, much of this inspection was carried out on naked immigrants whose hair was shorn and clothes were fumigated. The assumptions behind this contrast were obvious. Poor, illiterate peasant Mexicans, like poor, ill-educated, Jews or Italians, were not only racially, politically and morally inferior, but as a result would be far more liable to commit crimes, therefore the border needed to be more effectively policed than the border with "European" Canada.[40]

By the early 1930s, the Immigration Service was apprehending three times as many suspected illegal aliens on the southern border as on the northern—even though both nations were exempt from quotas. By the late 1920s, the Mexican, Central and Latin American in many ways became the archetypal criminal immigrant. Like almost all immigrant groups, Mexicans were associated with crimes which were both specific to them, and ubiquitous in the immigrant communities. They committed the crimes associated with poverty, ignorance, and opportunism so common in all the immigrant colonies. Like the southern Italians and Sicilian peasants, many Americans saw Mexican history as one of unmitigated exploitation by first European masters and then homebred tyrants, with the result that the populace emerged superstitious, violent, bandits, who would rather rob than work. Like the Irish, Russians, and Poles, they could only see politics change as being achieved through violence and terrorism. Like Jews, the more educated Mexicans were seen as cliquish, mercenary, and devious. Like the Chinese, they were associated with drugs—not opium, but cannabis, which became so synonymous with Mexicans that it was known throughout the US as marijuana, from its Mexican nickname.

Although unrestricted by quotas, like the Chinese before them, the Mexicans became criminals largely as a result of simply being resident in America. Some idea of the Mexican as law-breaker can be gathered from the behavior of government officers in the 1930s. On assuming office in 1930, Secretary of Labor, William N. Doak announced that there were some 400,000 illegal aliens in the country. He claimed that these foreigners were taking "American" jobs and he instigated a campaign to rid the nation of these "parasites." When the Depression really started to bite, with one in four Americans out of work, the pressure on foreigners to return home grew. Mexicans made up the prime targets for these nativist activists. There were highly publicized raids staged by the US Immigration Service, beginning in 1930.

Concentrating on California and the South-west, the raids caused up to half a million "illegals" to leave the US by 1935. In San Antonio in 1930, some 3000 Mexicans were gathered at the main rail station and sent across the border. Before the year was out, they were followed by another 2000. The Mexican population of Texas was cut by a third over these years. In 1931, the LAPD surrounded a park in downtown Los Angeles and detained 400 Mexican men, women and children who were then deported. Like Texas, the Mexican population of the city was estimated to have dropped by a third as the authorities demanded that Mexicans who had lived in the region for years, if not decades, prove their right to residence. Between 1930 and 1939, over 82,000 Mexicans were deported from America, making up over half of all of those deported, although they constituted less than 1 percent of the nation's population.[41] Some were deported. Others simply found the atmosphere so oppressive that they left of their own accord. Still others, children of illegal immigrants, born in the US and thus entitled to residence, could not produce the relevant documentation and were forced to leave.

In large measure, this pressure for Mexican exclusion was simply economic. It stemmed from the fear that in economic depression those who were in the nation by the sufferance of the native population should be expelled to allow the economy to recover. Alongside them there was also a small proportion of those deported who were actually convicted criminals, Mexican-Americans serving time in US prisons. In return for a commutation of sentence, these undesirables agreed to return to Mexico, even though they were American citizens. Other American citizens were simply rounded up along with aliens and transported back to Mexico. Procedures were ignored, warrants rarely produced and violence frequently flared in these round-ups. While more or less sanctioned by the federal government, this often draconian behavior by Immigration and Naturalization agents, often accompanied by National Guardsmen and American Legionnaires was, in the case of citizens, unconstitutional. In the case of aliens, its position is less clear, for as non-citizens they did not fall within the remit of the Constitution. Arguably, in this instance the immigrants were the victims of crime, rather than the perpetrators.[42]

Nevertheless, it is interesting to note that in spite of the differences in magnitude, duration, and after-effects between these deportations and those of the more notorious Palmer Raids of 1920, there was less outcry at the time and since. Perhaps this was the result of simple racism, after all, the victims of Palmer's Raids were largely Europeans. Perhaps people's indignation was dulled by the economic straits of the time. Perhaps it simply goes to justify the social worker and immigrants' rights activist, Edith Abbot's contention that nativists would always feel that the current source of immigrants was the most bestial, undesirable and criminal, that "the most recent 'wave of immigration,' whatever the nationality, is less desirable than the old ones, [and] that all newcomers should be regarded with an attitude of suspicion."[43]

NOTES

Introduction

1 Timothy J. Gilfoyle, *A Pickpocket's Tale: The Underworld of Nineteenth-Century New York* (New York, 2006), and Charles van Onselen, *The Fox and the Flies: The Secret Life of a Grotesque Master Criminal* (London, 2007).
2 Figures taken from Daniel Burton-Rose (Ed.) *The Celling of America* (Monroe, ME, 1998), pp. 246–247.
3 See Federal Trade Commission, *Identity Fraud Report* (McClean, Virginia, 2003), p. 10 and Federal Trade Commission, *Identity Fraud Report* (McClean, Virginia, 2009), p. 7.

1 The Crimes of the Century

1 *Harper's Magazine* 155 (August, 1927): 337.
2 Maurice Urstein, *Leopold and Loeb: A Psychiatric-Psychological Study* (Chicago, 1924), cited in Paula S. Fass, "Making and Remaking an Event: The Leopold and Loeb Case in American Culture," *The Journal of American History* 80, 3 (Dec., 1993): 919.
3 For biographical details of James Gordon Bennett, see James L. Crouthamel, *Bennett's New York Herald and the Rise of the Popular Press* (Syracuse, New York, 1989). Quotation taken from the New York *Courier and Enquirer*, August 6, 1830.
4 See *National Police Gazette*, December 1, 1866. For a history and analysis of the magazine, see Guy Reel, *The National Police Gazette and the Making of the Modern American Man, 1879–1906* (New York, 2006).
5 See Daniel Stashower, *The Beautiful Cigar Girl: Mary Rogers, Edgar Allen Poe and the Invention of Murder* (New York, 2006).
6 *New York Times*, July 26, 1865.
7 *The Indiana Progress*, August 24, 1871.
8 See, for example, *The Defiance Democrat* (Ohio), March 5, 1877; *The Fort Wayne Sentinel* (Indiana), March 7, 1877 and *The Globe* (Atchison, Kansas), August 21, 1880.
9 Henry M. Hunt, *The Crime of the Century* (Chicago, 1889), reproduced in full at http://ia341221.us.archive.org/0/items/crimeofcenturyor00huntiala/crimeofcenturyor-00huntiala.pdf.
10 See the *Pittsburgh Post*, October 16, 1889.

11 *Oakland Tribune*, July 30, 1895.

12 Two of the best accounts of white violence against Reconstruction can be found in George C. Rable, *But There Was No Peace: The Role of Violence in the Politics of Reconstruction* (rev. ed. Athens, GA, 2007) and Allen Trelease, *White Terror: The Ku Klux Klan Conspiracy and Southern Reconstruction* (New York, 1971).

13 For details of the case, see Richard Gambino, *Vendetta* (Garden City, New York, 1977).

14 The implications, commentaries, and repercussions of McKinley's assassination are superbly covered in Eric Rauchway, *Murdering McKinley* (New York, 2003).

15 The trial and its implications are extensively covered by J. Anthony Lukas, *Big Trouble* (New York, 1998).

16 Some idea of the public fears behind, and importance attached to, the McNamara case can be found in the *New York Times* review (July 9, 1913) of *The Masked War*, the story as told by Detective Burns who brought the brothers to trial. W. W. Robinson, *Bombs and Bribery* (Los Angeles, 1969) is a good full-length account of the McNamara case. For the Mooney trial, see Ron Christenson, *Political Trials in History: From Antiquity to the Present* (New Brunswick, NJ, 1991), pp. 300–302.

17 Vanzetti, cited in Philip Sheldon Foner, *History of the Labor Movement in the United States*, vol. 10 (New York, 1991), p. 227. There is a vast literature on the Sacco–Vanzetti case. The most recent notable book is an analysis of the original documents, background and historiography by Richard Newby (Ed.), *Kill Now, Talk Forever: Debating Sacco and Vanzetti* (Bloomington, IN, 2007).

18 As Hoover put it in 1919, in a memo to a subordinate, Garvey "has been particularly active among radical elements in New York City in agitating the Negro movement. Unfortunately, however, he has not yet violated any federal law whereby he could be proceeded against on the grounds of being an undesirable alien." Colin Grant, *Negro with a Hat: The Rise and Fall of Marcus Garvey and His Dream of Mother Africa* (Oxford, 2008), p. 155.

19 *Santa Fe New Mexican*, June 21, 1923.

20 The best account of the case remains Dan T. Carter, *Scottsboro: A Tragedy of the American South* (Baton Rouge, LA, 1969).

21 For details of the agitation and propaganda associated with the case in the 1930s, see Hugh T. Murray, "Changing America and the Changing Image of Scottsboro," *Phylon* 38: 1 (1977): 82–85 and James A. Miller, Susan D. Pennybacker, and Eve Rosenhaft, "Mother Ada Wright and the International Campaign to Free the Scottsboro Boys, 1931–1934," *The American Historical Review* 106, 2 (Apr., 2001): 387–430.

22 Taken from Don Mankiewicz, *Trial* (New York, 1962), p. 163.

23 See Charles Ponzi, *The Rise of Mr Ponzi* (New York, 1937).

24 See the *Boston Post*, May 22, 1912.

25 See the *Boston Traveller*, *Boston American* and *New York Times*, July 30, 1920.

26 The case of Celia Cooney is very well covered in Stephen Duncombe and Andrew Mattson, *The Bobbed Haired Bandit* (New York, 2006).

27 James McKinley, "After Lincoln, the Deluge," *Playboy* (February, 1976): 188.

28 See Joseph L. Holmes, "Crime and the Press," *Journal of Criminal Law and Criminology* 20 (May, 1929): 9–59.

29 See Mick Sinclair, *San Francisco: A Cultural and Literary History* (San Francisco, 2002), pp. 120–122.

30 Charles Merz, "Bigger and Better Murders," *Harper's Magazine* 155 (August, 1927): 337 and 343.

31 The Leopold and Loeb case has always excited great interest, especially immediately after trial in the late 1920s and after Nathan Leopold's release in 1956. Perhaps the most thorough examination of the case can be found in Hal Higdon, *Crime of the Century: The Leopold & Loeb Case* (New York, 1975). For the implications of the case, see Fass, op. cit.

32 The celebrity of the case is detailed in the *New York Times,* January 23, 1907. For details of the crime, see *Washington Post*, June 27 and July 6, 1906.

33 A good flavor of the reporting of Stanford White's murder can be found in Allen Churchill, *Park Row: A Vivid Recreation of Turn of the Century Newspaper Days* (New York, 1931), pp. 241–247.

34 Lawrence M. Friedman, *Crime and Punishment in American History* (New York, 1993), p. 398. For a detailed account of the case, see Michael MacDonald Mooney, *Evelyn Nesbitt and Stanford White: Love and Death in the Gilded Age* (New York, 1976). For a fictionalized account, see E.L. Doctorow, *Ragtime* (New York, 1974).

35 See *Washington Post*, July 8, 1906.

36 *Washington Post*, August 10, 1906.

37 See John William Ward, "The Meaning of Lindbergh's Flight," *American Quarterly* 10 (Spring, 1958): 3–16.

38 For details of the jump in sales and the interest generated in the case, see Helen McGill Hughes, "The Lindbergh Case: A Study of Human Interest and Politics," *The American Journal of Sociology* 42, 1 (July, 1936): 35.

39 For some idea of the hyperbole involved, the international fame and longevity of interest in the Lindbergh Case, see "A Hard Case," *Time*, March 18, 2005.

40 Jim Fisher, *The Lindbergh Case* (New Brunswick, NJ, 1987), p. 270.

41 For the details of the almost daily breaking news surrounding the case, see Lloyd Gardner, *The Case That Never Dies: The Lindbergh Kidnapping* (New Brunswick, NJ, 2004).

42 *Daily Mirror*, May 12, 1932.

43 See Stephen Fox, *Blood and Power: Organized Crime in Twentieth Century America* (New York, 1989).

44 For details, see Gilman M. Ostrander, *The Prohibition Movement in California, 1848–1933* (Berkeley, CA, 1957), p. 173.

45 One of the most influential, best written and entertaining accounts can be found in Samuel Hopkins Adams, *Revelry: A Novel* (New York, 1926), which did for the Harding administration what *The Jungle* did for the meatpacking industry. One of the worst, most salacious and controversial accounts can be found in Gaston Bullock Means, *The Strange Death of President Harding* (New York, 1930).

46 Judge Kenshaw Mountain Landis, cited in *New York Times*, August 4, 1921.

47 *Chicago Herald and Examiner*, September 9, 1920.

48 The authoritative account remains Eliot Asinof, *Eight Men Out: The Black Sox and the 1919 World Series* (New York, 1963).

49 For details, see George Benson, *Political Corruption in America* (Lexington, MA, 1978), pp. 99–100, and *New York Times*, February 12, 1927 and December 30, 1931.

50 For an overview, see Kim Long, *The Almanac of Political Corruption, Scandals and Dirty Politics* (New York, 2007), pp. 146–149.

51 Cited in Margaret Leslie Davis, *Dark Side of Fortune: Triumph and Scandal in the Life of Oil Tycoon Edward L Doheny* (Berkeley, CA, 1998), p. 162.

52 *New York Herald Tribune*, March 3, 1932.

53 See, for example, Bryan Burrough, *Public Enemies: America's Greatest Crime Wave and the Birth of the FBI, 1933–34* (New York, 2004).

54 Quotation cited in Roger A. Bruns, *The Bandit Kings: From Jesse James to Pretty Boy Floyd* (New York, 1995), p. 238. For an aged but sophisticated analysis of the distinction between these forms of lawlessness, see Eric Hobsbawm, *Primitive Rebels: Studies in Archaic Forms of Social Movement in the 19th and 20th Centuries* (Manchester, 1959), pp. 30–56.

55 Cited in Richard G. Powers, *G-Men: Hoover's FBI in American Popular Culture* (Carbondale, IL, 1983), p. 15.

56 Fred D. Pasley, *Al Capone: The Biography of a Self-Made Man* (New York, 1931). See Michael Woodiwiss, *Organized Crime and American Power* (Toronto, 2001), p. 229.

57 *New York Times*, July 13, 1933.

58 For a good description of Hoover's ruthless ambition, see Ovid Demaris, *The Director: An Oral Biography of J. Edgar Hoover* (New York, 1975), pp. 132–135.
59 Attorney General Homer Cummings laid out his plans for the agency clearly in a speech reported in the *New York Times*, September 12, 1933.
60 This forms a part of the thesis put forward in Claire Bond Potter, *The War on Crime: Bandits, G-Men and the Politics of Mass Culture* (Oxford, 1998).
61 The fullest account of the shootings, their aftermath and the various theories surrounding them is probably Robert Unger, *The Union Station Massacre* (Kansas City, 1977).
62 On June 17, 1932, Congress passed the Lindbergh Law, named after baby Charles, making kidnapping across state lines a federal felony. For details of its actual and perceived impact, see Ernest K. Alix, *Ransom Kidnapping in America, 1874–1974: The Creation of a Capital Crime* (Carbondale, IL, 1978), pp. 123–124.
63 *Literary Digest*, March 12, 1932.
64 For a good overview of Hoover's influence and career, see Joseph L. Schott, *No Left Turns: The FBI in Peace and War* (Westport, CT, 1975).
65 Cited in Alfred R. Lindesmith, "Organized Crime," *Annals of the American Academy of Political and Social Science*, 217 (Sept., 1941): 119. The Chicago Crime Commission was founded in 1919 by concerned businessmen, lawyers and bankers in an attempt to deal with the "10,000 professional criminals" who ran the criminal activities within the city. For details, see Klaus von Lampe, "Not a Process of Enlightenment: The Conceptual History of Organized Crime in Germany and the United States of America," *Forum on Crime and Society* 1, 2 (December, 2001): 104.
66 For a racy account of the entire gory Murder Inc. saga, written by an Associated Press reporter and an Assistant DA who were both investigating the case at the time, see Sid Feder and Burton B. Turkus, *Murder Inc.: The Story of the Syndicate* (New York, 1951).
67 The workings of Murder Inc. are well described in Paul R. Kavieff, *The Life and Times of Lepke Buchalter: America's Most Ruthless Labor Racketeer* (Fort Lee, NJ, 2006), pp. 69–84.
68 For a good historical assessment of the role of violence in US history, see Michael Belsile (Ed.), *Lethal Imagination: Violence and Brutality in American History* (New York, 1999), pp. 1–16.

2 Crime and the West

1 Heather Cox Richardson, *West from Appomattox: The Reconstruction of America After the Civil War* (New Haven, CT, 2007), p. 4.
2 This argument that violence, whether criminal or not, was the motor for Western expansion and that it has driven US history since the inception of the nation, is most comprehensively covered in Richard Slotkin's trilogy *Regeneration Through Violence* (New York, 1973); *Fatal Environment* (New York, 1985), and *Gunfighter Nation* (New York, 1992)
3 Robert Warshow, "Movie Chronicle: The Westerner," *Partisan Review* 21 (1954): 190–203.
4 Stewart L. Udall et al., "How the West Got Wild: American Media and Frontier Violence: A Roundtable," *Western Historical Quarterly* 31, 3 (Autumn, 2000): 292–295.
5 Frederick Jackson Turner, *The Significance of the Frontier in American History* (Chicago, 1893).
6 Michael Bellesiles' prize-winning *Arming America: The Origins of a National Gun Culture* (New York, 2000) argued that gun ownership in the US was never as prevalent as many had thought. These findings had what the historian Michael Kammen called "inescapable policy implications." On close scrutiny by a panel of academics and other interested parties, his reasoning, methodology, and citations were alleged to be questionable and, as a result, in some quarters his arguments have been refuted.

7 See Robert R. Dykstra, "Body Counts and Murder Rates: The Contested Statistics of Western Violence," *Reviews in American History* 31, 4 (December, 2003): 554–563 and his "To Live and Die in Dodge City: Body Counts, Law and Order, and the Case of Kansas Versus Gill," in Michael Bellesiles (Ed.), *Lethal Imagination: Violence and Brutality in American History* (New York, 1999), p. 211.

8 Richard White, *It's Your Misfortune and None of My Own* (Norman, OK, 1985), pp. 331–332. See Roger D. McGrath, *Gunfighters, Highwaymen and Vigilantes: Violence on the Frontier* (Berkeley, CA, 1984), pp. 253–255. For an attack on this statistical fallacy of small numbers, see Dykstra, op. cit., pp. 213–215 and 223–224.

9 Udall et al., op. cit., p. 279.

10 See Richard White, *It's Your Misfortune*, and William S.E. Coleman, *Voices of Wounded Knee* (Lincoln, NE, 2000).

11 For a good analysis of the massacre, see Chip Colwell-Chanthaphonh, "The 'Camp Grant Massacre' in the Historical Imagination," a paper given at the Arizona History Convention, Tempe, Arizona, April 25–26, 2003, and reproduced at www.cdarc.org/pdf/camp_grant.pdf.

12 *San Francisco Bulletin*, May 15, 1874, cited in William B. Secrest, *California Desperadoes* (Sanger, CA, 2000), p. 146.

13 See Roger Daniels (Ed.), *Anti-Chinese Violence in North America* (New York, 1978), and John R. Wunder, "Anti-Chinese Violence in the American West, 1850–1910," in John McLaren, Hamar Foster, and Chet Orloff (Eds.), *Law for the Elephant, Law for the Beaver: Essays in the Legal History of the American West* (Pasadena, CA, 1992).

14 See Eric Hobsbawm, *Primitive Rebels* (New York, 1965), pp. 13–29 and Richard White, "Outlaw Gangs of the Middle Border: American Social Bandits," *Western Historical Quarterly*, 12, 4 (Oct., 1981): 387–408. For an example of the contemporary take on the phenomenon, see the description of the Younger brothers in "Honor Among Thieves," *National Police Gazette*, November 4, 1881.

15 For a first-hand account of Native American popular support for bandit outlaws, see Morris E. Opeller, *Apache Odyssey* (Lincoln, NE, 2002), p. 54. The issue of racially based social banditry is well covered in Rodolfo Rocha, "The Influence of the Mexican Revolution on the Mexico-Texas Border, 1910–1916," unpublished PhD thesis, Texas Tech. University, 1981.

16 The oath of Quantrill's Raiders cited in David Thelen, *Paths of Resistance* (Oxford, 1986), p. 71.

17 For details of the activities of Quantrill's Raiders, see Richard S. Brownlee, *Gray Ghosts of the Confederacy* (Baton Rouge, LA, 1958), pp. 241–246. For James' own account of his brutalization at the hands of the federal government, see *New York Times*, July 20, 1875.

18 Homer Croy, *Jesse James Was My Neighbor* (New York, 1949), pp. 82–86.

19 *Kansas City Times*, September 27, 1872.

20 *Kansas City Times*, October 15, 1872.

21 Cox Richardson, op. cit., p. 223.

22 Nat Love, *The Life and Adventures of Nat Love* (Los Angeles, 1907), p. 163.

23 Quotations taken from William A. Settle, *Jesse James Was His Name* (Columbia, MO, 1967), pp. 71 and 81.

24 See *National Police Gazette*, December 6, 1879.

25 A good example of the ludicrous lengths to which the Jesse James myth went can be found in "The Bandit's Boast" in which "The Much-Killed Jesse James Writes to the Police Gazette." The *National Police Gazette* ironically published this on April 1, 1882.

26 Richard White, "Outlaw Gangs of the Middle Border," p. 404.

27 "Eccentric Tantrums," *National Police Gazette*, May 21, 1881.

28 See Richard Slotkin, *Gunfighter Nation* (Norman, OK, 1998).

29 For an assessment of the impact of the railroads, see Sarah H. Gordon, *Passage to Union: How the Railroads Transformed American Life, 1829–1929* (Chicago, 1996).

30 Figures taken from Richard White, *It's Your Misfortune*, pp. 247–249.

31 For details of the investigation, see W. Allan. Wilbur, "The Credit Mobilier Scandal, 1873," in Arthur M. Schlesinger, Jr., and Roger Bruns, *Congress Investigates: A Documented History, 1792–1974* (New York, 1975).
32 One of the best assessments of the results of the scandal remains E. Ray McCartney, *The Crisis of 1873* (Minneapolis, 1935).
33 All figures taken from Richard Rayner, *The Associates: Four Capitalists who Created California* (New York, 2008), pp. 159–162.
34 Carey McWilliams, cited in ibid., pp. 164–165. For the best contemporary account of the behavior of the railroads in the West, see Frank Norris, *The Octopus: A Tale of California* (New York, 1901). A good analysis of the nature, consequences and history of railroad corruption in this region is available in William Deverell, *Railroad Crossing: Californians and the Railroad, 1850–1910* (Berkeley, CA, 1996).
35 See Terry Beers (Ed.), *Gunfight at Mussel Slough: Evolution of a Western Myth* (Berkeley, CA, 2004).

3 Hate Crime

1 *Chicago Tribune*, May 1, 1899.
2 Perhaps the fullest account of the atrocities committed that night can be found in the *Charleston News and Courier*, April 24, 1899.
3 Some idea of the complexities involved in the ideas behind defining and explaining hate crime as a concept can be gleaned from Donald P. Green, Laurence H. McFalls and Jennifer K. Smith, "Hate Crime: An Emergent Research Agenda," *Annual Review of Sociology* 27 (2001): 479–504.
4 For a discussion of the issues involved in modern hate crime legislation, see James B. Jacobs and Kimberly Potter, *Hate Crimes: Criminal Law and Identity Politics* (New York, 1998), especially pp. 3–10.
5 James E. Cutler, *Lynch Law* (New York, 1905), p. 1.
6 From 1885 onwards, the *Tribune* recorded more blacks each year and by 1890 it reported lynching to be predominantly performed on blacks, in the South. Figures extrapolated from the *Congressional Record*, February 26th, 1948, p. 1793. "White" in this case means "non-Negro" and so would include Mexicans, Native Americans and southern Europeans, who would normally be considered outside such a definition. See also Christopher Waldrep, *Lynching in America: A History in Documents* (New York, 2006), p. 115.
7 For first-hand accounts, see *Chicago Tribune*, July 28 to August 6, 1919. The most detailed account of the Chicago riots can be found in William Tuttle, *Race Riot: Chicago in the Red Summer of 1919* (Urbana, IL, 1970).
8 For readable accounts of Sundown Towns and other forms of enforced segregation in the period see Elliot Jaspin, *Buried in Bitter Waters: The Hidden History of Racial Cleansing in America* (New York, 2007) and James W. Loewen, *Sundown Towns: A Hidden Dimension of American Racism* (New York, 2005). An interesting "case study" of one such ethnic cleansing can be found in Jacqueline Froelich and David Zimmerman, "Total Eclipse: The Destruction of the African American Community of Harrison, Arkansas, in 1905 and 1909," *Arkansas Historical Quarterly* 58 (Summer, 1999): 131–159.
9 For the evolution of anti-Chinese sentiment in California, see Jean Phaelzer, *Driven Out: The Forgotten War Against Chinese Americans* (New York, 2007).
10 Cited in Philip Perlmutter, *Legacy of Hate: A Short History of Ethnic, Religious and Racial Prejudice in America* (Armonk, New York, 1999), pp. 122–123.
11 Perhaps one of the best discussions of the causes of lynching in the Deep South can be found in E.M. Beck and Stewart E. Tolnay, "Violence Toward African Americans in the Era of the White Lynch Mob," in Darnell F. Hawkins (Ed.), *Ethnicity, Race and Crime: Perspectives Across Time and Place* (New York, 1995), pp. 121–144.

12 Figures taken from Ida B. Wells, *Southern Horrors: Lynch Law in All its Phases* (New York, 1892); James Elbert Cutler, "Proposed Remedies for Lynching," *The Yale Review* 13, 2 (Aug., 1904): 194–212; W. Fitzhugh Bundage (Ed.), *Under Sentence of Death: Lynching in the South* (Chapel Hill, NC, 1997), pp. 291–294 and Steven Hahn, *A Nation Under Our Feet: Black Political Struggles in the Rural South from Slavery to the Great Migration* (Cambridge, MA, 2003), pp. 426–428.

13 Walter F. White, "I Investigate Lynchings," *American Mercury* 16, 61 (January, 1929): 78.

14 See Walter White, *Rope and Faggot: A Biography of Judge Lynch* (New York, 1929), pp. 227–269.

15 See *New York Times*, June 8, 1903 and Douglas A. Blackmon, *Slavery By Another Name: The Re-Enslavement of Black Americans from the Civil War to World War II* (New York, 2008), pp. 198–200.

16 William D. Carrigan and Clive Webb, "The Lynching of Persons of Mexican Origin or Descent in the United States, 1848 to 1928," *Journal of Social History* 37, 2 (2003): 411–438.

17 A good first-hand account of the destruction can be found in Robert A. Hill, *The Marcus Garvey and Universal Negro Improvement Association Papers*, vol. 1 (Berkeley, CA, 1983), pp. 216–218. The most comprehensive analysis must be Harper Barnes, *Never Been Such a Time: The 1917 Race Riot That Sparked the Civil Rights Movement* (New York, 2008).

18 For a comprehensive and concise account of the Red Summer's riots, see Walter Rucker and James Nathaniel Upton (Eds.), *Encyclopedia of American Race Riots* (Westport, CT, 2006), pp. 550–554.

19 NAACP leader, Walter White writing in *The Nation*, June 29, 1921.

20 The accusation that Filipinos, and blacks, were in the mob was made in the *Bellingham Herald* of September 5, 1907. For an analysis of the riot, see Gerald N. Hallberg, "Bellingham, Washington's Anti-Hindu Riot," in James A. Halseth and Bruce A. Glasrud (Eds.), *The Northwest Mosaic: Minority Conflicts in Pacific Northwest History* (Boulder, CO, 1977), pp. 140–155. For the context, see Kristofer Allerfeldt, "Race and Restriction: Anti-Asian Immigration Pressures in the Pacific North-West of America during the Progressive Era, 1885–1924," *History* 88 (2003): 53–73.

21 For a gruesome account of the massacre, see Margaret I. Carrington's memoir, *Absaraka (Ab-Sa-Ra-Ka) Home of the Crows* (Chicago, 1950), pp. 332–335.

22 Cited in Stanley F. Horn, *The Invisible Empire: The Story of the Ku Klux Klan 1866–1871* (Boston, 1939), p. 393.

23 See William G. Shepherd, "How I Put Over the Klan," *Collier's* LXXXII (July 14, 1928): 6–7, 32, 34–35, and Mark Calney, "D.W. Griffith and 'The Birth of a Monster': How the Confederacy Revived the KKK and Created Hollywood," *The American Almanac*, January 11, 1993, and Richard Wright, *Native Son* (New York, 1940).

24 For details of the Frank case, see Steve Oney, *And the Dead Shall Rise* (New York, 2003).

25 Jane Addams, "Respect for Law," *The Independent* vol. 3, no. 2718 (January 3, 1901): 18–20.

26 Cited in Glenda E. Gilmore, "Gender and 'Origins of the New South,' C. Vann Woodward's 'Origins of the New South, 1877–1913: A Fifty-Year Retrospective,'" *Journal of Southern History* 67, 4 (Nov., 2001): 776.

27 Ben Tillman, "The Black Peril," (1907), cited in William Chace and Peter Collier (Eds.), *Justice Denied: The Black Man in White America* (New York, 1970), p. 182.

28 Quotation taken from Ida B. Wells-Barnett, op. cit., p. 3. For an analysis of her opinions, see Christopher Waldrep, "Word and Deed: The Language of Lynching, 1820–1953," in Michael E. Bellesiles (Ed.), *Lethal Imagination: Violence and Brutality in American History* (New York, 1999), pp. 244–245.

29 Figures taken from Richard A. Buckelew, *Racial Violence in Arkansas: Lynchings and Mob Rule, 1860–1930* (Ph.D. dissertation, University of Arkansas, 1999).

30 Cited in Gunnar Myrdal, *An American Dilemma* (New York, 1944), pp. 560–561.

31 For details, see George W. Hufsmith, *The Wyoming Lynching of Cattle Kate, 1889* (Glendo, WY, 1993).

32 See Estelle B. Freedman, "'Uncontrolled Desires': The Response to the Sexual Psychopath, 1920–1960," *Journal of American History* 74, 1 (Jun., 1987): 83–106, and Jeffrey Melnick, *Black-Jewish Relations on Trial: Leo Frank and Jim Conley in the New South* (Jackson, MS, 2000) p. 71.

33 Cited in Michael Bronski, "The Return of the Repressed: Leo Frank Through the Eyes of Oscar Micheaux," *Shofar: An Interdisciplinary Journal of Jewish Studies* 23, 4 (Summer 2005): 36.

34 See Melvyn Stokes, *DW Griffith's Birth of a Nation: A History of the Most Controversial Motion Picture of All Time* (Oxford, 2007), pp. 232–235 and Wyn Craig Wade, *The Fiery Cross: The Ku Klux Klan in America* (New York, 1987), pp. 144–145.

35 For details of the Dennis Kearney's Sand Lot movement, see Jerome A. Hart, *In Our Second Century: From an Editor's Note-book* (San Francisco, 1931), pp. 52–63.

36 Figures taken from William J.H. Traynor, "The Policy and Power of the APA," *North American Review* (June, 1896): 666.

37 The best account of the Ludlow war and the tensions building up to it can be found in Thomas G. Andrews, *Killing for Coal: America's Deadliest Labor War* (Cambridge, MA, 2008).

38 One of the best of many analyses of the historiography of the Prager lynching can be found in E. A. Schwartz, "The Lynching of Robert Prager, the United Mine Workers, and the Problems of Patriotism in 1918," *Journal of Illinois History* 5 (Winter, 2002): 283–308.

39 Figures extrapolated from Maurine and Henry Beasley and Holly R. Shulman, *The Eleanor Roosevelt Encyclopedia* (Westport, CT, 2001), p. 29 and the *Congressional Record*, February 26, 1948, p. 1793.

40 For a list of these proposals see *Hearings before the Committee on the Judiciary of the House of Representatives on H. R. 41*, 80th Congress, 2nd Sess. (1948): 185.

41 For a complete discussion of this issue, see William D. Ford, "Constitutionality of Proposed Federal Anti-Lynching Legislation," *Virginia Law Review* 34, 8 (Nov., 1948): 944–953.

42 Cited in Ida B. Wells-Barnett, op. cit., p. 7.

43 The *Atlanta Georgian*, August 15, 1915.

44 James E. Cutler, *Lynch Law* (New York, 1905), p. 77.

45 *New York Times*, June 10, 1905.

46 For examples of studies of the development of anti-lynching consciousness, see Christopher Waldrep, "War of Words: The Controversy over the Definition of Lynching, 1899–1940," *Journal of Southern History* 66, 1 (Feb., 2000): 75–100, and Judith L. Stephens, "Racial Violence and Representation: Performance Strategies in Lynching Dramas of the 1920s," *African American Review* 33, 4 (1999): 655.

47 See Amy MacKenzie, "Walter White on Lynching," *The Interracial Review* 9, 9 (Sept., 1936): 134–135.

48 See Melissa Stein, "Walter White, Scientific Racism, and the NAACP Anti-Lynching Campaign," paper presented at the annual meeting of the 94th Annual Convention of the Association for the Study of African American Life and History, Cincinnati, Ohio, Sept. 30, 2009.

49 Committee on Interracial Cooperation, *Lynchings and What They Mean* (Atlanta, GA, 1931), p. 43.

50 Cole Blease, cited in Arthur Raper, *The Tragedy of Lynching* (Chapel Hill, NC, 1933), p. 293.

51 A good detailed account of the political intrigue surrounding the Costigan–Wagner Bill can be found in Isabelle Whelan, "The Politics of Federal Anti-lynching Legislation in the New Deal Era," unpublished MA Dissertation, School of Advanced Studies, London, 2007.

52 David M. Kennedy, "How FDR Lost the Struggle to Enact an Antilynching Bill," *Journal of Blacks in Higher Education* 25 (Autumn, 1999): 121.

4 Policing and Imprisonment

1 Eric Monkkonen, *Crime, Justice, History* (Columbus, 2002); David R. Johnson, *American Law Enforcement* (Wheeling, Ill., 1981); Richard Wade, "Violence in cities" in Roger Lane, *Riot, Race, Tumult* (Westport, 1978) and Paul Keve, *Prisons and the American Conscience* (Carbondale, 1991).
2 The importance of internal migration in American culture of this era is often overlooked. It is dealt with in Eric Rauchway, *Blessed Among Nations* (New York, 2006).
3 Eric H. Monkkonen, *Police in Urban America, 1860–1920* (Cambridge, 1980), pp. 65–69, gives an excellent analysis of the research up to that date.
4 See Paul A. Gilje, "The Crowd in American History," *American Transcendental Quarterly* 17, 3 (Sept., 2003): 138.
5 Charles Loring Brace, "The Life of the Street Rats," in *The Dangerous Classes of New York and Twenty Years Among Them* (New York, 1872), cited in David M. Scobey et al., *Empire City: The Making and Meaning of the New York City Landscape* (Philadelphia, PA, 2003), p. 148.
6 Cited in Monkkonen, op. cit., p. 45. For the contrasts between the US and British urban policing models, see Wilbur R. Miller, *Cops and Bobbies: Police Authority in New York and London, 1830–1870* (Columbus, OH, 1999).
7 For details of the Orange Riots, see Lisa Keller, *The Triumph of Order: Democracy and Public Space in New York and London* (New York, 2008), pp. 165–170.
8 For an analysis of this change in relation to the police, see David Bayley, *Patterns of Policing: A Comparative International Analysis* (New Brunswick, NJ, 1990) especially p. 34. For a more in-depth account, see Allen Steinberg, *The Transformation of Criminal Justice, Philadelphia, 1800–1880* (Chapel Hill, NC, 1989).
9 For details of this function, see Monkkonen, op. cit., pp. 86–128.
10 Quotation taken from George McWatters, *Knots Untied: A Narrative of Marvellous Experiences Among All Classes* (New York, 1871), pp. 648–649.
11 His work was published in the groundbreaking Alphonse Bertillon, *Photography: With an Appendix on Anthropometrical Classification and Identification* (Paris, 1890). For an example of how it was disseminated in the press, see Alphonse Bertillon, "The Bertillon System of Identification," *Forum* 2, 3 (May, 1891): 335. For a monograph-length study of Bertillon, see Valerie Petit-Kearney, *Alphonse Bertillon: Father of Scientific Criminal Investigation* (San Diego, CA, 2002).
12 Alexander von Hoffman, "An Officer of the Neighborhood: A Boston Patrolman on the Beat in 1895," *Journal of Social History* 26, 2 (Winter, 1992): 309–330.
13 For a full account of Charles Becker's career, the corruption of the era and his final demise, see Mike Dash, *Satan's Circus* (New York, 2007).
14 See Eugene J. Watts, "St Louis Police Recruits in the Twentieth Century," *Criminology* 19, 77 (Mar., 2006): 105–106.
15 For details of Becker's background, induction, and early career, see Dash, op. cit., pp. 21–43.
16 For lively and evocative details of police corruption, see Luc Sante, *Low Life: Drinking, Drugging, Whoring, Murder, Corruption, Vice and Miscellaneous Mayhem in Old New York* (London, 1991), pp. 236–250.
17 Details of Williams' career can be found in David R. Johnson, *American Law Enforcement: A History* (St Louis, MO, 1981), pp. 55–60.
18 For the full Lexow Committee report, see New York State Senate, *Report and Proceedings of the Senate Committee Appointed to Investigate the Police Department of the City of New York* (New York, 1895). For details of the Lexow Committee's findings, see *New York Times*, June 6, 1894. A report on Williams' death and the value of his estate can be found in the *New York Times*, January 30, 1918.

19 For a thorough assessment of Roosevelt's career as President of the Police Board, see Jay Stuart Berman, *Police Administration and Progressive Reform: Theodore Roosevelt as Police Commissioner of New York* (Westport, CT, 1987), and H. Paul Jeffers, *Commissioner Roosevelt: The Story of Theodore Roosevelt and the New York City Police, 1895–1897* (New York, 1996).

20 Figures taken from Robert C. Wadman and William T. Allison, *To Protect and Serve* (Upper Saddle River, NJ, 2004), p. 75.

21 See Leonard F. Fuld, *Police Administration* (New York, 1909). For a précis of his long career, see his obituary in the *New York Times*, September 1, 1965.

22 For the background to Haager's appointment, see Tracy Campbell, "Machine Politics, Police Corruption, and the Persistence of Vote Fraud: The Case of the Louisville, Kentucky, Election of 1905," *Journal of Policy History* 15, 3 (2003): 269–300. For Haagar's policies, see J.H. Haager, "The Automobile as Police Department Adjunct," cited in Bryan Vila and Cynthia Morris, *The Role of Police in American Society: A Documentary History* (Westport, CT, 1999), pp. 82–84.

23 Morton O. Childress, *Louisville Division of Police: History and Personnel* (Nashville, TN, 2002), p. 71.

24 See Thomas J. Deakin, *Police Professionalism* (Springfield, IL, 1988), p. 85.

25 William Penn, "The Frame of the Government of the Province of Pennsylvania in America," cited in Jean R. Soderland (Ed.), *William Penn and the Founding of Pennsylvania: A Documentary History* (Philadelphia, PA, 1982), p. 121.

26 For details of the founding principles of the ill-fated Newgate Prison, see the account of the founder and first warder of Newgate Prison, Thomas Eddy, *An Account of the State Prison or Penitentiary House in the City of New York* (New York, 1801), see especially pp. 38–39 for details of the night rooms. For details of the day-to-day running and riots of the Pennsylvania system prisons in general, and the riots in Newgate, see Orlando F. Lewis, *The Development of American Prisons and Prison Customs, 1776–1845* (Albany, NY, 1922), pp. 43–63.

27 A good analysis of the two systems can be found in John W. Roberts, *Reform and Retribution* (Lanham, MD, 1996), pp. 32–46.

28 Wines, cited in Larry E. Sullivan, *The Prison Reform Movement* (Boston, 1990), pp. 18–19.

29 See, for example, Harry Elmer Barnes, *The Story of Punishment* (Boston, 1930) which argues that since there is no evidence that punishment works, a psychological approach is not only more humane, but more effective. Figures taken from Norval Morris and David J. Rothman, *The Oxford History of the Prison* (Oxford, 1998), p. 159.

30 C.P. Farrell (Ed.), *The Works of Robert G. Ingersoll*, vol. 11 (New York, 1900), pp. 497–498.

31 For the details of the campaigns to outlaw prison labor, see Blake McKelvey, "The Prison Labor Problem: 1875–1900," *Journal of Criminal Law and Criminology* 25, 2 (Jul.–Aug., 1934): 254–270.

32 See Mark T. Carleton, *Politics and Punishment: The History of the Louisiana State Penitentiary* (Baton Rouge, LA, 1971), pp. 20–59.

33 This quote is taken from the most comprehensive study: Mathew J. Mancini, *One Dies, Get Another: Convict Leasing in the American South, 1866–1928* (Columbia, SC, 1996), pp. 2–3. A good overview can be found in Douglas A. Blackmon, *Slavery by Another Name* (New York, 2008), pp. 52–58.

34 Kate Richards O'Hare, *In Prison* (New York, 1923), p. 68.

35 For an assessment of O'Hare's position as a Muckraker, see Sally M. Miller, *From Prairie to Prison: The Life of Social Activist Kate Richards O'Hare* (Columbia, MO, 1993).

36 Joseph F. Fishman, *Crucibles of Crime* (New York, 1923), p. 121.

37 For examples, see *New York Times*, June 9, 1922 or Joseph F. Fishman, *Sex in Prison: Revealing Sex Conditions in America's Prisons* (New York, 1934).

38 Figures taken from Paul W. Keve, *Prisons and the American Conscience: A History of US Federal Corrections* (Carbondale, IL, 1991).

39 Rhodri Jeffreys-Jones, *The FBI: A History* (New Haven, CT, 2007).

40 Jefferys-Jones' thesis ignores the brief spell of activity in the Spanish American War, and the presidential bodyguard duties.
41 Figures taken from Athan Theodoris et al. (Eds), *The FBI* (Phoenix, AZ, 1999), p. 4.

5 Conmen, Swindlers, and Dupes

1 "Political Notes: Capric Candidate," *Time Magazine*, October 17, 1932.
2 Brinkley, cited in Gerald Carson, *The Roguish World of Doctor Brinkley* (New York, 1960), p. 35.
3 Eric S. Juhnke, *Quacks and Crusaders: The Fabulous Careers of John R Brinkley, Norman Baker and Harry Hoxsey* (Lawrence, KS, 2002), and R. Alton Lee, *The Bizarre Careers of John R Brinkley* (Lexington, KY, 2002).
4 Edgar Allen Poe, *Diddling: Considered as One of the Exact Sciences* (New York, 1850).
5 For details of Thompson's technique and final arrest, see *New York Herald*, July 7, 1848.
6 Herman Melville, *The Confidence-Man: His Masquerade* (New York, 1857). See also Johannes Dietrich Bergmann, "The Original Confidence Man: The Development of the American Confidence Man in the Sources and Backgrounds of Herman Melville's *The Confidence-Man: His Masquerade*," unpublished Ph.D. dissertation, University of Connecticut, 1968.
7 See Tom Quirk, "The Confidence-Man," in Janet Gabler-Hover and Robert Sattelmeyer (Eds.), *American History Through Literature, 1820–1870* (Andover, 2006), Charles Dickens, *Martin Chuzzlewit* (rev. ed., London, 1994), pp. 339–342 and Steven Watts, "Through a Glass Eye, Darkly: James Fenimore Cooper as Social Critic," *Journal of the Early Republic* 13, 1 (Spring, 1993): 55–74.
8 For details, see W.A. Croffut, *American Procession, 1855–1914* (New York, 1931), pp. 236–255.
9 See Stephen Hyde and Geno Zanetti (Eds.), *Players: Con Men, Hustlers, Gamblers and Scam Artists* (New York, 2002), p. 128, and Marcus Klein, *Easterns, Westerns, and Private Eyes: American Matters, 1870–1900* (Madison, WI, 1994), p. 170.
10 Richard Rayner, *Drake's Fortune: The Fabulous True Story of the World's Greatest Confidence Artist* (New York, 2002), pp. 123–126.
11 See George Devol, *Forty Years a Gambler on the Mississippi* (Cincinnati, OH, 1887).
12 Ernest C. Cotterill, cited in the *New York Times*, November 13, 1913.
13 A huge amount of information on scams and their perpetrators is to be found in Jay R. Nash, *Hustlers and Conmen: An Anecdotal History of the Confidence Man and his Games* (New York, 1976). The tale of Sokolowski can be found on page 98.
14 The most entertaining account of Engel's career can be found in *Time*, July 4, 1949.
15 See Jay R. Nash, op. cit., p. 97.
16 See *New York Times*, May 20, 1922.
17 For this and other aphorisms of this, most famous of grifters, see Joseph Weil, *"Yellow Kid" Weil* (Chicago, 1948). For background, see "American Credulity," *The Outlook*, vol. 96 (December, 1910).
18 For a contemporary view of this phenomenon, see John K. Barnes, "Harvest Time for the Get-Rich-Quick Promoter," *World's Work* 34 (October 1917): 157.
19 See Edward J. Balleisen, "Private Cops on the Fraud Beat: The Limits of American Business Self-Regulation, 1895–1932," *Business History Review* 83 (Spring, 2009): 114.
20 See Kenneth Scott and David R. Johnson, *Counterfeiting in Colonial America* (rev. ed., Philadelphia, PA, 2000), p. 8.
21 The political economist, William Graham Sumner, writing in 1896, cited in Stephen Mihm, *A Nation of Counterfeiters: Capitalists, Con Men, and the Making of the United States* (Cambridge, MA, 2007), p. 360.
22 *New York Times*, May 26, 1862.
23 Stephen Mihm, *A Nation of Counterfeiters: Capitalists, Con Men, and the Making of the United States* (Cambridge, MA, 2007), p. 325.

24 For good contemporary examples of the Secret Service's successes and the methods of counterfeiters, see *National Police Gazette*, November 26, 1867 and November 6, 1880 and *New York Times*, October 31, 1880. For a detailed overview, see David R. Johnson, *Illegal Tender: Counterfeiting and the Secret Service in Nineteenth-Century America* (Washington, DC, 1998).

25 See Lyn Glaser, *Counterfeiting in America: The History of an American Way to Wealth* (Philadelphia, PA, 1960), pp. 105–107.

26 See Thomas Craughwell, *Stealing Lincoln's Body* (Cambridge, MA, 2007).

27 For details of these events, see *New York Times*, April 21, 1896 and Stephen Mihm, op. cit., pp. 361–374.

28 See *National Police Gazette*, November 6, 1880 and *New York Times*, June 6, 1882.

29 *National Police Gazette*, June 26, 1880.

30 See *New York Times*, January 21, 1906.

31 For details of the case, see Raymond T. Kuwahara, Robert B. Skinner, and Robert B. Skinner, "Nickel Coinage in the United States: The History of a Common Contact Allergen," *Western Journal of Medicine* 175, 2 (August, 2001): 112–114.

32 See Kathleen Chamberlain, "Capitalism, Counterfeiting, and Literary Representation: The Case of Lizzie Borden," *Primary Sources & Original Works* 4, 3 (1997): 175–192.

33 For details of this theory, in relation to Guiseppe Morello's activities in the 1910s, see Mike Dash, *The First Family* (London, 2009), pp. 183–206.

34 Virginia Statute, 1645, cited in Kenneth Scott, "Counterfeiting in Colonial Virginia," *Virginia Magazine of History and Biography* 61, 1 (Jan., 1953): 3.

35 For the growth of counterfeit tickets, see "Fleecing the L," *National Police Gazette*, July 19, 1884.

36 William N. Blake, *An Excursion Through the United States and Canada* (London, 1824), p. 176.

6 Business and Financial Crime

1 Cited in Roy P. Basler (Ed.), *The Collected Works of Abraham Lincoln*, vol. VII (New Brunswick, NJ, 1953), pp. 259–260.

2 Cited in Archer H. Shaw (Ed.), *The Lincoln Encyclopedia* (New York, 1950), p. 40.

3 For details of the activities of the Pujo Committee, see Arthur M. Schlesinger, Jnr. and Roger Bruns (Eds.), *Congress Investigates, 1792–1974* (New York, 1975), pp. 169–196.

4 For a good biography of Alger, see Gary Scharnhorst and Jack Bales, *The Lost Life of Horatio Alger, Jr.* (Bloomington, IN, 1985).

5 Andrew Carnegie, *The Gospel of Wealth* (New York, 1889), p. 89.

6 *The Nation*, March 8, 1933.

7 Figures taken from Joseph H. Davis, "An Improved Annual Chronology of U.S. Business Cycles since the 1790s," *Journal of Economic History* 66, 1 (March, 2006): 103–121.

8 Figures and quotation taken from David M. Scobey, *Empire City* (Philadelphia, PA, 2002), pp. 76–78.

9 Cited in Scott B. MacDonald and Jane E. Hughes, *Separating People from their Money* (New Brunswick, NJ, 2007), p. 45.

10 Cornelius Vanderbilt, cited in Matthew Josephson, *The Robber Barons* (New York, 1934), p. 72. The best account of the affair remains Kenneth D. Ackerman, *The Gold Ring* (New York, 1988).

11 Thomas W. Lawson, *Frenzied Finance* (New York, 1905), p. viii.

12 See Jerry W. Markham, *A Financial History of the United States*, vol. 1 (Armonk, NY, 2001), pp. 18–20.

13 Liaquat Ahamed, *Lords of Finance: 1929, The Great Depression, and the Bankers Who Broke the World* (New York, 2009), pp. 438–441.

14 Figures taken from Harold L. Platt, *The Electrical City* (Chicago, 1991), p. 272.

15 The best account of the Insull battle in the context of the New Deal's political ambitions can be found in Amity Schlaes, *The Forgotten Man: A New History of the Great Depression* (New York, 2007).

16 See Forrest McDonald, *Insull* (New York, 1962), pp. 335–336.

17 For details of the Insull case, see MacDonald and Hughes, op. cit., pp. 101–119; David Skeel, *Icarus in the Boardroom* (Oxford, 2005), pp. 75–106, and Charles D. Ellis and James R. Vertin, *Wall Street People*, vol. 2 (New York, 2003), pp. 166–173.

18 Figures taken from Hugh T. Rockoff, "Great Fortunes of the Gilded Age," *NBER Working Paper* No. 14555 (December, 2008). Available at SSRN: http://ssrn.com/abstract=1327228.

19 Henry Demarest Lloyd, "Wealth against Commonwealth," in Richard and Beatrice Hofstadter (Eds.), *Great Issues in American History*, vol. III (New York, 1982), p. 96.

20 Cited in Roger E. Meiners et al., *The Legal Environment of Business* (Andover, 2008), p. 626.

21 See Theodore Roosevelt, "Justice and Popular Rule: Essays, Addresses, and Public Statements Relating to the Progressive Movement, 1910–1916," in *The Works of Theodore Roosevelt, Memorial Edition*, vol. XIX (New York, 1925), pp. 136–139.

22 Cited in Irvin G. Wyllie, "Social Darwinism and the Businessman," *Proceedings of the American Philosophical Society* 103, 5 (1959): 632.

23 Published first in the *Atlantic Monthly* in 1881, it is cited in Henry Damarest Lloyd, *Lords of Industry* (New York, 1910), p. 15.

24 A readable account of Ida Tarbell's crusade against Standard Oil can be found in Steve Weinberg, *Taking on the Trust* (New York, 2008).

25 Cited in Alex Hunter (Ed.), *Monopoly and Competition: Selected Readings* (Harmondsworth, 1969), p. 163. For a contemporary analysis of Harlan's comments, see *New York Tribune*, May 16, 1911.

26 The full horrors and implications of the Triangle disaster are covered in David von Drehle, *Triangle: The Fire that Changed America* (New York, 2003).

27 Rockefeller, cited in the *New York Times*, April 1, 1915.

28 For details, see Priscilla Long, *Where the Sun Never Shines: A History of America's Bloody Coal Industry* (New York, 1989) and Thomas G. Andrews, *Killing for Coal: America's Deadliest Labor War* (Cambridge, MA, 2008).

29 For details of industrial violence and the response it evoked, see Stephen Norwood, *Strikebreakers and Intimidation: Mercenaries and Masculinity in 20th Century America* (Chapel Hill, NC, 2002).

30 See Marc T. Law, "How Do Regulators Regulate? Enforcement of the Pure Food and Drugs Act, 1907–38," *Journal of Law, Economics, and Organization* 22, 2 (2006): 459–489.

31 See Paul M. Wax, "Elixirs, Diluents, and the Passage of the 1938 Federal Food, Drug and Cosmetic Act," *History of Medicine* 122, 6 (March, 1995): 456–461.

32 See C. C. Regier, "The Struggle for Federal Food and Drugs Legislation," *Law and Contemporary Problems* 1, 3 (1933): 15.

33 New York versus the New Jersey and Passaic Valley Sewage Commissioners, cited in Patricia Wouters (Ed.), *International Water Law: Selected Writings of Professor Charles B. Bourne*, vol. 1 (1998), p. 120.

34 Cited in the *New York Times*, June 21, 1938.

35 Edwin H. Sutherland, "White-Collar Criminality," *American Sociological Review* 5, 1 (Feb., 1940): 1.

36 For interesting, often contemporary, accounts of many of these figures, see Charles D. Ellis and James R. Vertin, *Wall Street People*, 2 vols (New York, 2003).

37 See Brett Messing et al., *The Forewarned Investor* (Franklin Lakes, NJ, 2006), pp. 75–80, and Paul M. Clikeman, *Called to Account: Fourteen Frauds That Shaped the American Accounting Profession* (New York, 2008), pp. 30–34.

38 See *Time*, January 9, 1939.

39 See Sutherland, op. cit., pp. 3 and 5.

40 Quote taken from Michael Woodiwiss, *Gangster Capitalism* (New York, 2005), p. 52.

41 The most racy and informative account of the case remains that of Brooklyn Assistant DA, Burton B. Turkus who was involved in the investigation. See Burton B. Turkus and Sid Feder, *Murder Inc: The Story of the Syndicate* (New York, 1951).

42 For a full discussion of this view of regulation, see Michael Woodiwiss, op. cit., pp. 57–67.

7 Prohibitions

1 Cited in Larry Englemann, *Intemperance* (New York, 1970), p. xi.

2 Cited in Sean Dennis Cashman, *Prohibition: The Lie of the Land* (New York, 1981), p. 18.

3 For details of American drinking habits, see Mark E. Lender and James K. Martin, *Drinking in America: A History* (New York, 1987). For a sophisticated and readable account of the early temperance movement, see James A. Morone, *Hellfire Nation: The Politics of Sin in American History* (New Haven, CT, 2003), pp. 281–317.

4 See John Kobler, *Ardent Spirits: The Rise and Fall of Prohibition* (New York, 1973).

5 Quotation taken from Henry Chafetz, *Play the Devil: A History of Gambling in the United States from 1492 to 1950* (New York, 1960), p. 115.

6 For an example of the Southern aristocratic penchant for gambling, see T. H. Breen, "Horses and Gentlemen: The Cultural Significance of Gambling among the Gentry of Virginia," *The William and Mary Quarterly* 34, 2 (Apr., 1977): 239–257.

7 For an original and comprehensive analysis of gambling in nineteenth-century America, see Ann Fabian, *Card Sharps and Bucket Shops: Gambling in Nineteenth-Century America* (New York, 1999).

8 Jefferson, cited in William N. Thompson, *Legalized Gambling: A Reference Handbook* (Santa Barbara, CA, 1997), pp. 8–9.

9 See Charles T. Clotfelter and Philip J. Cook, *Selling Hope: State Lotteries in America* (Cambridge, MA, 1989), p. 20. For a detailed analysis of lotteries, see John Samuel Ezell, *Fortune's Merry Wheel: The Lottery in America* (Cambridge, MA, 1960).

10 For details of spectator sports in pre-Bellum America, see Elliott Gorn and Warren Goldstein, *A Brief History of American Sports* (Champaign, IL, 2004), pp. 47–152.

11 See Virginia Berridge and Griffith Edwards, *Opium and the People: Opiate Use in Nineteenth-Century England* (London, 1982) and David T. Courtwright, *Dark Paradise: Opiate Addiction in America before 1940* (Cambridge, MA, 1972).

12 *New York Times*, September 29, 1918.

13 Figures taken from Charles Edward Terry and Mildred Pellens, *The Opium Problem* (New York, 1928), p. 13.

14 Figures taken from Humberto Fernandez, *Heroin* (New York, 1998), p. 20.

15 See David T. Courtwright, op. cit., pp. 35–60.

16 See Eric C. Schneider, *Smack: Heroin and the American City* (Philadelphia, PA, 2008), pp. 2–5.

17 Jacob A. Riis, *How the Other Half Lives: Studies Among the Tenements of New York* (New York, 1890), p. 76.

18 Quotation taken from Charles Whitebread, "The History of the Non-Medical Use of Drugs in the United States," a speech to the California Judges Association 1995 annual conference and reproduced in full at http://www.druglibrary.org/schaffer/History/whiteb1.htm.

19 For details of cocaine in the working population, see Joseph F. Spillane, *Cocaine: From Medical Marvel to Modern Menace in the United States, 1884–1920* (Baltimore, MD, 1999), pp. 90–96.

20 See Jill Jonnes, *Hep-Cats, Narcs and Pipe Dreams: A History of America's Romance with Illegal Drugs* (Baltimore, MD, 1996), pp. 19–21. The consumption figure is taken from

Joel L. Phillips and Ronald D. Wynne, *Cocaine: The Mystique and the Reality* (New York, 1980), p. 56.

21 The most important, and most cited article, remains the *New York Times*, "Negro Cocaine Fiends: New Southern Menace," February 11, 1914. For details of the *New York Times* campaign and citation of quotes used, see Doris M. Provine, *Unequal Under Law: Race in the War on Drugs* (Chicago, 2007), pp. 76–82.

22 One of the best analyses of this view can be found in David R. Bewley-Taylor, *The United States and International Drug Control, 1909–1997* (London, 1999), pp. 18–27.

23 Norman H. Clark, *Deliver Us From Evil: An Interpretation of American Prohibition* (New York, 1976), p. 222.

24 For an analysis of the debate over, the structure of and the immediate implications of the Harrison Act, see David F. Musto, *The American Disease: Origins of Narcotic Control* (Oxford, 1999), pp. 54–65.

25 Ibid., pp. 58–63. Quotation on p. 59.

26 Ibid., p. 65.

27 Charles E. Terry and Mildred Pellens, *The Opium Problem* (New York, 1928), pp. 1–2.

28 Quotation taken from interview with a New York prison physician and cited in John C. Burnham, *Bad Habits: Drinking, Smoking, Taking Drugs, Gambling, Sexual Misbehavior and Swearing in American History* (New York, 1993), p. 117.

29 See Duboise Heyward, *Porgy* (New York, 1925).

30 *New York Times*, February 11, 1914.

31 See Kathleen Drowne, *Spirits of Defiance: National Prohibition and Jazz Age Literature, 1920–1933* (Columbus, OH, 2006), especially pp. 144–146.

32 For an idea of the scale of gambling among the slaves of the South, see Jeff Forret, *Race Relations at the Margins: Slaves and Poor Whites in the Antebellum Southern Countryside* (Baton Rouge, LA, 2006), pp. 56–62.

33 Jacob Riis, "Gambling Mania," *Century* 73 (1907): 926.

34 Colonel Patrick H. Callahan, cited in Andrew Sinclair, *Prohibition: The Era of Excess* (Boston, 1962), p. 220.

35 *National Police Gazette*, February 12, 1881.

36 Cited in Ann Fabian, op. cit., p. 199.

37 Quotations taken from Liaquat Ahamed, *Lords of Finance: 1929, the Great Depression, and the Bankers Who Broke the World* (New York, 2009), pp. 214–217.

38 Anslinger, cited in the *Washington Post*, November 23, 1936.

39 For a very brief overview of the issues involved in the campaign, see Erich Goode and Nachman Ben-Yehuda, *Moral Panics: The Social Construction of Deviance* (Oxford, 1994), pp. 16–18. For a very full account of the issues, characters involved in, and progress of, the outlawing processes, see Richard J. Bonnie and Charles H. Whitebread II, *The Marijuana Conviction: A History of Marijuana Prohibition in the United States* (New York, 1999).

40 Rheta Childe Dorr, "The Other Prohibition Country: The Facts about Finland's Noble Experiment," *Harper's Magazine* (September, 1929): 495–504.

41 Statistics taken and extrapolated from Bureau of Investigation, *Uniform Crime Reports* vol. 2: 1 (Washington, DC, 1931), and David E. Kyvig, *Law, Alcohol, and Order: Perspectives on National Prohibition* (Westport, CT, 1985).

42 This view is best espoused in Humbert S. Nelli, *The Business of Crime: Italians and Syndicate Crime in the United States* (Chicago, 1981).

43 See Henry Chafetz, op. cit., pp. 290–293.

44 See Virgil W. Peterson, *Barbarians in Our Midst: A History of Chicago Crime and Politics* (Boston, 1952), pp. 84–91.

45 Mark Haller, "The Changing Structure of American Gambling in the Twentieth Century," *Journal of Social Issues* 35, 3 (Summer, 1979): 88.

46 See *New York Times*, October 16, 1919.

47 Remus, cited in Edward Behr, *Prohibition: Thirteen Years that Changed America* (New York, 1996), p. 102.
48 See Michael A. Lerner, *Dry Manhattan: Prohibition in New York City* (Cambridge, MA, 2007), p. 234.
49 Robert Toms, cited in Larry Engelmann, *Intemperance: The Lost War Against Liquor* (New York, 1979), p. 130.
50 Cited in Michael Woodiwiss, *Crime Crusades and Corruption: Prohibitions in the United States, 1900–1987* (London, 1988), p. 20.
51 Quotations taken from *New York Times*, June 5, 1928. For details of the Olmstead case, see Norman H. Clark, *The Dry Years: Prohibition and Social Change in Washington* (Seattle, 1988), pp. 161–184.
52 This claim was made by Frederick Lewis Allen, *Only Yesterday* (New York, 1929), pp. 185–186.
53 Figures taken from Andrew Sinclair, *Prohibition: The Era of Excess* (London, 1962), p. 10. See also the *New York World*, August 9, 1926.
54 See *New York Times*, January 1, 1929; *Chicago Tribune*, November 24, 1929, and March 12, 1930, and Ernest Sutherland Bates, "From Temperance to Wheelerism," *Commonweal* 11, 24 (April, 1930): 682.
55 LaGuardia quotations taken from Herbert Asbury, *The Great Illusion: An Informal History of Prohibition* (New York, 1950), p. 210.

8 Sex Crime

1 Otto Weininger, *Geschlecht und Charakter: Eine prinzipielle Untersuchung* [Sex and Character: An Investigation of Fundamental Principles] (Leipzig, 1903).
2 For a very good appraisal of what constituted the acceptable and unacceptable in Gilded Age society, see M. H. Dunlop, *Gilded City: Scandal and Sensation in Turn-of-the-Century New York* (New York, 2001), especially p. 45.
3 Barbara M. Hobson, *Uneasy Virtue: The Politics of Prostitution and the American Reform Tradition* (New York, 1987), pp. 85–87.
4 Taken from Section 148 of the "Comstock" Act, 1874, cited in Nicola Beisel, *Imperiled Innocents: Anthony Comstock and Family Reproduction in Victorian America* (Princeton, NJ, 1997), p. 39.
5 Figures taken from an interview given to the *New York Times*, September 28, 1905. Quote taken from the *New York Sun*, July 6, 2005.
6 The best full-length biography of Comstock is probably Anna Bates, *Weeder in the Garden of the Lord: Anthony Comstock's Life and Career* (Lanham, MD, 1995).
7 G.B. Shaw in the *New York Times*, September 26, 1905.
8 *New York Times*, September 26, 1905.
9 Comstock, cited in Heywood Broun and Margaret Leech, *Anthony Comstock: Roundsman of the Lord* (New York, 1927), pp. 224–225.
10 The story is reported best in the New York *Evening Telegram*, November 16, 1887, which also took the trouble to publish sketches of many of the art works on its front page.
11 See *New York Times*, July 19, 1915.
12 Quote taken from Leonard J. Leff and Jerold Simmons, *The Dame in the Kimono: Hollywood, Censorship, and the Production Code* (Lexington, KY, 2001), p. xiv. See also Frank Walsh, *Sin and Censorship: The Catholic Church and the Motion Picture Industry* (New Haven, CT, 1996).
13 Figures taken from John D'Emilio and Estelle B. Freedman, *Intimate Matters: A History of Sexuality in America* (Chicago, 1997), pp. 281–282.
14 For details of the negotiations, see Rudy Behlmer, *Inside Warner Bros. (1935–1951)* (New York, 1985), pp. 135–141.

15 See Vern L. Bullough, "A Brief Note on Rubber Technology: The Diaphragm and the Condom," *Technology and Culture* 22 (January, 1981): 104–111.

16 The Act for the Suppression of Trade in, and Circulation of Obscene Literature and Articles of Immoral Use, 1873, cited in Janet Farrell Brodie, *Contraception and Abortion in Nineteenth-Century America* (New York, 1997), p. 256.

17 Figures and quotations taken from James A. Morone, *Hellfire Nation: The Politics of Sin in American History* (New Haven, CT, 2003), p. 251.

18 See Margaret Sanger, *An Autobiography* (New York, 1938), p. 366.

19 Figures taken from John D'Emilio and Estelle B. Freedman, op. cit., p. 244.

20 Ibid., pp. 63–65.

21 See Carroll Smith-Rosenburg, *Disorderly Conduct: Visions of Gender in Victorian America* (New York, 1985), p. 226, and Clifford Browder, *The Wickedest Woman in New Town: Madame Restell the Abortionist* (Hamden, CT, 1988).

22 William W. Sanger, *The History of Prostitution* (New York, 1858), p. 91.

23 Figures taken from Harriet Sigerman, *Land of Many Hands: Women in the American West* (New York, 1997), p. 66.

24 Figures taken from Kristofer Allerfeldt, *Race, Radicalism, Religion and Restriction* (Westport, CT, 2003), p. 171.

25 See *The Sacramento Bee*, 30 January; 6 February; 8 February, 1913 and Suzanne Lebsock, "Women and American Politics, 1880–1920," in Louise A. Tilly and Patricia Garin (Eds.), *Women, Politics and Change* (New York, 1990), p. 35.

26 Cited in Sigerman, op. cit., pp. 139–140, and Vardis Fisher and Opal Laurel Holmes, *Gold Rushes and Mining Camps of the Early American West* (Caldwell, ID, 1968), pp. 208–209.

27 See Fisher and Holmes, op. cit., p. 203.

28 Cited in the *Topeka Commonwealth*, July 1, 1873.

29 *The Sacramento Bee*, January 18, 1913.

30 Quotation taken from *Woman's Journal*, June 17, 1893, pp. 186–187. See also Neil Larry Shumsky, "Tacit Acceptance: Respectable Americans and Segregated Prostitution, 1870–1910," *Journal of Social History* 19, 4 (Summer, 1986): 665–679.

31 See Pamela D. Arceneaux, "Guidebooks to Sin: The Blue Books of Storyville," *Louisiana History: The Journal of the Louisiana Historical Association* 28, 4 (Autumn, 1987): 397–405.

32 Cited in John C. Burnham, "The Progressive Era Revolution in American Attitudes Toward Sex," *Journal of American History* 59, 4 (March, 1973): 886.

33 For a good short biography of Morrow, see Vern L. Bullough, *Science in the Bedroom: A History of Sex Research* (New York, 1994), pp. 100–106. For details of Morrow's educational ideas and campaigns, see Bryan Strong, "Ideas of the Early Sex Education Movement in America, 1890–1920," *History of Education Quarterly* 12 (1972): 129–161.

34 For details of the reception of the play, see Katie N. Johnson, "Damaged Goods: Sex Hysteria and the Prostitute Fatale," *Theatre Survey* 44, 1 (2003): 43–67.

35 Joyce Kilmer, "The Drama as an Instrument of Sex Education," *Journal of the Society of Sanitary and Moral Prophylaxis* 5 (April, 1914): 54–55.

36 Details taken from Ruth M. Alexander, *The Girl Problem: Female Sexual Delinquency in New York, 1900–1930* (Ithaca, NY, 1995), pp. 11–13, 75–77 and 145–146.

37 For details of these changes, see Roy Lubove, "The Progressives and the Prostitute," *Historian* 24 (May, 1962): 308–330. Statistics taken from Allan M. Brandt, *No Magic Bullet: A Social History of Venereal Disease in the United States Since 1880* (Oxford, 1985), pp. 91–93, and Ruth Rosen, *The Lost Sisterhood: Prostitution in America, 1900–1918* (Baltimore, MD, 1982), pp. 34–35.

38 It was rare for prostitutes' customers to be prosecuted at any point in the period of this study. Famously, New York's Committee of Fourteen, dedicated as they were to stamping out vice in the city attempted to prosecute "Johns" in 1920, sparking vigorous debate. The experiment is detailed in Thomas C. Mackey, *Pursuing Johns: Criminal Law*

Reform, Defending Character and New York City's Committee of Fourteen, 1920–1930 (Columbus, OH, 2005).

39 Cited in Mark Thomas Connelly, *The Response to Prostitution in the Progressive Era* (Chapel Hill, NC, 1980), p. 153.

40 See Michael Lynch's study, "New York Sodomy, 1796–1873," cited in D'Emilio and Freedman, op. cit., p. 123.

41 See Jonathan N. Katz, *Gay American History: Lesbians and Gay Men in the USA, A Documentary History* (New York, 1976), pp. 34–36.

42 Figures taken from George Chauncey, *Gay New York: The Making of the Gay Male World, 1890–1940* (London, 1995), p. 140.

43 Cited in Leila J. Rupp, *A Desired Past: A Short History of Same-Sex Love in America* (Chicago, 1999), p. 78.

44 Quoted in Richard M. Huber, *The American Idea of Success* (New York, 1971), pp. 45–46.

45 See Chauncey, op. cit., pp. 139–141.

46 For a good fictionalized account of gay New York in the Prohibition era, see Blair Niles, *Strange Brother* (New York, 1931).

47 See Clayton R. Koppes, "Review: A Golden Age in Gay Gotham," *Reviews in American History* 24, 2 (June, 1996): 304–309.

48 See Chauncey, op. cit., pp. 335–354.

49 See Emma Goldman, *Living My Life* (New York, 1934), especially pp. 555–556.

9 Political Crime

1 Will Rogers, *Weekly Articles*, April 22, 1928.

2 E.L. Doctorow, *Homer and Langley* (New York, 2009), pp. 48–49.

3 The term "Gilded Age" has its origins in Mark Twain and Charles Dudley Warner, *The Gilded Age: A Tale of Today* (Hartford, CT, 1874).

4 For examples of headlines putting forward this idea, see *New York Times*, October 20, 2002, July, 15 and 16, 2007, and *Christian Science Monitor*, March 6, 2006.

5 For an assessment of the changing scale, nature and response to corruption, see Edward L. Glaeser and Claudia Goldin, "Corruption and Reform: An Introduction," *National Bureau Working Paper 1074* (Cambridge, MA, 2004).

6 See Anne M. Butler and Wendy Wolff, *United States Senate Election, Expulsion and Censure Cases, 1793–1990* (Washington, DC, 1995), pp. 115–116.

7 See *New York Times*, February 21, 1899.

8 Cited in William Safire, *Safire's Political Dictionary* (Oxford, 2008), p. 237.

9 Most famously, they failed in their Senate investigation of charges of bribery in 1898, which relied on transcripts of intercepted telephone calls. See *New York Times*, November 1, 1898.

10 Cited in J. Bradford Delong et al., "Financial Crisis in the 1890s and 1990s: Must History Repeat?" *Brookings Papers on Economic Activity* 1999: 2 (1999): 268.

11 For details of the case, see Harold Chase (Ed.), *Biographical Dictionary of the Federal Judiciary* (Detroit, 1976), p. 9.

12 The most informed and complete account remains that of the former supervisor of the internal revenue, General John MacDonald, *Secrets of the Great Whiskey Ring* (Chicago, 1880).

13 Cited in Mark Wahlgreen Summers, *Party Games: Getting, Keeping and Using Power in Gilded Age Politics* (Chapel Hill, NC, 2004), p. 64.

14 Quotation taken from Richard N. Current, *Three Carpetbagging Governors* (Baton Rouge, LA, 1967), p. 63. Details of Warmoth's career can also be found in Chester G. Hearn, *The Impeachment of Andrew Jackson* (Jefferson, NC, 2000), pp. 218–220. Warmoth's own side of the story can be found in Henry Clay Warmoth, *War, Politics, and Reconstruction: Stormy Days in Louisiana* (New York, 1930).

15 John F. Kennedy, *Profiles in Courage* (New York, 1956), p. 163.
16 Thomas Woodrow Wilson, *A History of the American People*, vol. 5 (New York, 1908), p. 58.
17 See *New York Times*, December 26, 1878.
18 For details of the case, see Eric Foner (Ed.), *Freedom's Lawmakers: A Directory of Black Officeholders During Reconstruction* (Baton Rouge, LA, 1996), p. 63. For Smalls' career, see also Edward A. Miller, *Gullah Statesman: Robert Smalls from Slavery to Congress* (Chapel Hill, NC, rev. ed., 2009).
19 George Washington Plunkitt, "How to Become a Statesman," in William L. Riordon, *Plunkitt of Tammany Hall: A Series of Very Plain Talks on Very Practical Politics* (New York, 1905), pp. 8–9.
20 For details, see Oliver E. Allen, *The Tiger: The Rise and Fall of Tammany Hall* (Reading, MA, 1993), pp. 103–105.
21 George Washington Plunkitt, "Honest Graft and Dishonest Graft," in Riordon, op. cit., p. 3.
22 For details of these and other scams, see *New York Times*, July 21, 1870.
23 See Richard C. Lindberg, *The Gambler King of Clark Street: Michael C. McDonald and the Rise of Chicago's Democratic Machine* (Carbondale, IL, 2009).
24 For the historiography and an analysis of the arguments raised by this section, see George C.S. Benson, *Political Corruption in America* (Lexington, MA, 1978), pp. 90–113.
25 This argument is perhaps made most cogently in Michael Woodiwiss, *Organized Crime and American Power* (Toronto, 2001), pp. 170–226.
26 *St Louis Post Dispatch*, January 21, 1912. For details of the St Louis machine, see Daniel Waugh, *Egan's Rats: The Untold Story of the Prohibition-Era Gang That Ruled St Louis* (Nashville, TN, 2007).
27 Quotation cited in Alfred Sternberg, *The Bosses* (New York, 1972), p. 341.
28 Prendergast was by no means the only machine politician who utilized the overt gangster. Most famously, in the 1927 Chicago mayoral election, the winner, William Hale, "Big Bill," Thompson, famously received the backing of Al Capone. See below.
29 For details of the Kansas City machine, see Frank R. Hayde, *The Mafia and the Machine: The Story of the Kansas City Mob* (Fort Lee, NJ, 2007).
30 For details of Capone's aid to Thompson's 1927 campaign, see The Illinois Association for Criminal Justice, *The Illinois Crime Survey* (Chicago, 1929), p. 902.
31 See Michael Woodiwiss, *Crime Crusades and Corruption: Prohibitions in the United States, 1920–1987* (London, 1988), p. 74, and Michael Green and Melvin G. Holli (Eds.), *The Mayors* (Carbondale, IL, 1992), pp. 61–80.
32 Quotations taken from Virgil W. Peterson, *The Barbarians in Our Midst: A History of Chicago Crime and Politics* (Boston, 1952), pp. 90–91 and The Illinois Association for Criminal Justice, *The Illinois Crime Survey* (Chicago, 1929), p. 1091.
33 See The Illinois Association for Criminal Justice, op. cit., p. 1027.
34 See John Kobler, *Capone: The Life and World of Al Capone* (New York, 1992), pp. 15–17.
35 *Chicago Tribune*, April 20, 1930.
36 Eric Partridge, *A Dictionary of the Underworld* (New York, 1950), pp. 551–552.
37 See Jenna Weissman Joselit, *Our Gang: Jewish Crime and the New York Jewish Community, 1900–1940* (Bloomington, IN, 1983).
38 See *New York Times*, May 30, 1909.
39 Quotes taken from Hayes Robbins, "The New York Building Trades Paralysis of 1903," *American Journal of Sociology* 9, 6 (May, 1904): 757. For more on Sam Parks, see Philip S. Foner, *The Policies and Practices of the American Federation of Labor, 1900–1909*, vol. 3 (New York, 1973), p. 150.
40 Mary M. Stolberg, *Fighting Organized Crime: Politics, Justice, and the Legacy of Thomas E. Dewey* (Boston, 1995).
41 Figures taken from John Joseph Wallis, "The Political Economy of New Deal Fiscal Federalism," *Economic Inquiry* 29 (1991): 139.

42 See *Time*, May 6, 1940.

43 For the historical context of the Hatch Act, see Dorothy Ganfield Fowler, "Precursors of the Hatch Act," *Mississippi Valley Historical Review* 47, 2 (Sep., 1960): 247–262.

44 See Gavin Wright, "The Political Economy of New Deal Spending: An Econometric Analysis," *Review of Economics and Statistics* 59 (February, 1974): 35. The most comprehensive historiography and argument for this case can be found in Jim Powell, *FDR's Folly* (New York, 2003), especially pp. 89–104. A comprehensive statistical refutation of these arguments can be found in Robert K. Fleck, "Voter Influence and Big Policy Change: The Positive Political Economy of the New Deal," *Journal of Political Economy* 116, 1 (2008): 1–5.

45 *Time*, February 1, 1937.

46 Jimmy Hoffa in 1959, cited in Michael Woodiwiss, *Organized Crime and American Power* (Toronto, 2001), p. 163.

47 Teamster's details taken from Stephen Fox, *Blood and Power* (New York, 1989), pp. 201–202.

10 Terrorists

1 Grant Wardlaw, *Political Terrorism: Theory, Tactics and Countermeasures* (Cambridge, 1982), p. 16.

2 Taken from the title of Frederick J. Hacker, *Crusaders, Criminals or Crazies: Terror and Terrorism in Our Time* (New York, 1978).

3 Taken from the *Loyal Georgian*, October 13, 1866, cited in Lisa Cardin, "Sexualized Racism/Gendered Violence: Trauma and the Body Politic in the Reconstruction South," unpublished PhD, New Haven, 2003, pp. 95–96.

4 Taken from Wyn Craig Wade, *The Fiery Cross: The Ku Klux Klan in America* (New York, 1987), p. 72.

5 Perhaps the best account of how the South won the peace can be found in Nicholas Lemann, *Redemption: The Last Battle of the Civil War* (New York, 2006).

6 Quoted in Ralph K. Andrist, *The Long Death: The Last Days of the Plains Indian* (Oklahoma, 1968), p. 122.

7 John W. Burgess, *Reconstruction and the Constitution* (New York, 1902), p. xvii.

8 See Kevin Kenny, *Making Sense of the Molly Maguires* (Oxford, 1998), pp. 3–12.

9 *Chicago Tribune*, May 5, 1886.

10 Cited in Eric L. Hirsch, *Urban Revolt: Ethnic Politics in the Nineteenth-Century Chicago Labor Movement* (Berkeley, CA, 1990), p. 75.

11 See Howard Zinn, *A People's History of the United States* (New York, 1996), p. 265 and subsequent pages for a discussion of the evidence against the convicted. See also James Green, *Death in the Haymarket: A Story of Chicago, the First Labor Movement, and the Bombing that Divided Gilded Age America* (New York, 2006).

12 See Mike Davis, *Buda's Wagon* (New York, 2007), pp. 1–3.

13 A comprehensive analysis of the American supplying of the Entente can be found in Hew Strachan, *The First World War, Volume One: To Arms* (Oxford, 2003), pp. 941–990. See Eric W. Osborne, *Britain's Economic Blockade of Germany, 1914–1919* (New York, 2004).

14 Henry Landau, *The Enemy Within: The Inside Story of German Sabotage in America* (New York, 1937), pp. 36–37.

15 Ibid., p. 4.

16 For details, see Franz von Rintelen, *The Dark Invader* (New York, 1933) and Emanuel V. Voska and Will Irwin, *Spy and Counterspy* (New York, 1940).

17 Cited in Jules Witcover, *Sabotage at Black Tom: Imperial Germany's Secret War in America, 1914–1917* (Chapel Hill, NC, 1989), p. 67.

18 Emmet O'Connor, "James Larkin in the United States, 1914–23," *Journal of Contemporary History* 37, 2 (Apr., 2002): 183–196.

19 The best account of the impact of One Hundred Percentism and the build-up to the 1920s remains John Higham, *Strangers in the Land: Patterns of American Nativism, 1860–1925* (New Brunswick, NJ, 1955), especially pp. 194–233.

20 See *New York Times*, March 3, 1907, and Mike Dash, *The First Family: Terror, Extortion and the Birth of the American Mafia* (New York, 2009), pp. 76–77.

21 Quotations taken from the *Brooklyn Eagle* and the *New York Herald*, cited in Thomas Monroe Pitkin, *The Black Hand: A Chapter in Ethnic Crime* (New York, 1977), p. 16.

22 Quotations taken from Carl Sifakis, *The Encyclopedia of American Crime* (New York, 1982), p. 79 and Dash, op. cit., p. 77.

23 See Dash, op. cit., p. 79 and Sifakis, op. cit., p. 79.

24 Gaetano D'Amato, "The 'Black Hand' Myth," *North American Review* 187, 629 (Apr., 1908): 543, 548.

25 For details of the Caruso threat, see Pitkin, op. cit., p. 138.

26 See Robert Lombardo, *The Black Hand: Organized Crime and the Social Construction of Deviance in Chicago* (Chicago, 2009).

27 See David Critchley, *The Origin of Organized Crime in America: The New York City Mafia, 1891–1931* (New York, 2009), pp. 30–32.

28 See Dash, op. cit., pp. 170–171.

11 Immigration and Crime

1 Cited in Francis Amasa Walker, "Restriction of Immigration," *Atlantic Monthly* 77 (1896): 823.

 2 Joseph M. Gillman, "Statistics and the Immigration Problem," *American Journal of Sociology* 30, 1 (July, 1924): 41.

 3 US Congress, "Senate, Statements and Recommendations Submitted by Societies and Organizations Interested in the Subject of Immigration, Reports of the U.S. Commission on Immigration," *Senate Document, 764*, 61st Congress, 3rd Session (Washington DC, 1911), p. 107.

 4 Quotations taken from Kate Holladay Claghorn, "Review of Crime, Degeneracy and Immigration by David A. Orebaugh," *Journal of the American Institute of Criminal Law and Criminology* 21, 2 (Aug., 1930): 312.

 5 Gino C. Speranza, "Crime and Immigration (Report of Committee G, of the Institute)," *Journal of the American Institute of Criminal Law and Criminology* 4, 4 (Nov., 1913): 526.

 6 See Theodore Bingham, "Foreign Criminals in New York," *North American Review* 188, 634 (Sept., 1908): 384 and 387, and David M. Reimers, *Unwelcome Strangers: American Identity and the Turn against Immigration* (New York, 1998), p. 15.

 7 Allen S. Williams, *The Demon of the Orient and His Satellite Fiends of the Joints* (New York, 1883), pp. 59–61.

 8 For a readable and well-informed account of opium use in the Gilded Age, see Timothy J. Gilfoyle, *A Pickpocket's Tale: The Underworld of Nineteenth Century New York* (New York, 2006), pp. 81–88 in particular.

 9 Quote taken from Kristofer Allerfeldt, *Race, Radicalism, Religion and Restriction* (Westport, CT, 2002), p. 172.

10 See Yujio Ichioka, "Ameyuki-san: Japanese Prostitutes in Nineteenth-Century America," *Ameriasian Journal* 4, 1 (1977): 1–21.

11 For an historical overview of the position of women in Chinese society, see Patricia Buckley Ebrey, *Women and the Family in Chinese History* (New York, 2003), pp. 1–9.

12 Figures taken from Brian Donovan, *White Slave Crusades: Race, Gender and Anti-Vice Activism, 1887–1917* (Chicago, 2006), p. 112.

13 See Mildred Crowl Martin, *Chinatown's Angry Angel: The Story of Donaldina Cameron* (Palo Alto, CA, 1977), p. 43.
14 See, for example, J. W. Alexander, "American Opium Smokers—Interior of a New York Opium Den," *Harper's Weekly*, 8 October, 1881, and Frank Yeager, "New York City— The Opium Dens in Pell and Mott Streets—How the Opium Habit Is Developed," *Frank Leslie's Illustrated Newspaper*, May 19, 1883.
15 George Kibbe Turner, "The Daughters of the Poor: A Plain Survey of the Development of New York as a Leading Center of the White Slave Trade of the World Under Tammany Hall," *McClure's* 34 (November, 1909): 45–61. See also James A. Morone, *Hellfire Nation: The Politics of Sin in American History* (New Haven, CT, 2003), pp. 260–268.
16 For details of the Italians, see "Concerning Kidnappers," *National Police Gazette*, November 15, 1879.
17 A detailed and scholarly account of the experiences of victims on the Western frontier from 1835 to 1885 can be found in Gregory and Susan Michno, *A Fate Worse than Death* (Caldwell, ID, 2007).
18 See Kristofer Allerfeldt, *Race, Radicalism, Religion and Restriction* (Westport, CT, 2002), pp. 36–41.
19 For a superbly researched biography of the gruesome but fascinating Silver, see Charles Van Onselen, *The Fox and the Flies* (London, 2007).
20 A contemporary account of conditions for Jews within Russia with special attention to the Kishinev pogrom and reaction to it in America can be found in Michael Davitt, *Within the Pale: The True Story of Anti-Semitic Persecution in Russia* (Philadelphia, PA, 1903).
21 For details of Jewish involvement in the white slave trade, see Edward J. Bristow, *Prostitution and Prejudice* (New York, 1983), pp. 11–46.
22 The best account of Mandelbaum's influence and career can be found in Rona L. Holub, "Fredericka 'Marm' Mandelbaum, 'Queen of Fences,'" unpublished PhD thesis, Columbia University, 2007.
23 See David M. Reimers, *Unwelcome Strangers: American Identity and the Turn against Immigration* (New York, 1998), p. 15.
24 US Senate, *Report of the* [Dillingham] *Immigration Commission: Immigration and Crime* (Washington, DC, 1911), p. 181.
25 See, for example, Carl Kelsey, "Immigration and Crime," *Annals of the American Academy of Political and Social Science* 125 (May, 1926): 170–171.
26 Although there are many other accounts of Arnold Rothstein, many written very recently, they all draw heavily on Donald Henderson Clarke, *In the Reign of Rothstein* (New York, 1929).
27 A detailed account of Zelig's life and times can be found in Rose Keefe, *The Starker: Big Jack Zelig, The Becker-Rosenthal Case and the Advent of the Jewish Gangster* (Nashville, TN, 2008). Quotation taken from ibid., p. 188.
28 Statistics taken from the US Senate, *Report of the* [Dillingham] *Immigration Commission: Immigration and Crime* (Washington, DC, 1911), pp. 121 and 155. For an example of anti-Italian sentiment, see Appleton Morgan, "What Shall We Do with the Dago?" *Popular Science Monthly* 38 (December, 1890): 172–179.
29 Quotations taken from Edward Alsworth Ross, *The Old World in the New* (New York, 1914), p. 111.
30 For details of the killing and its aftermath, see Richard Gambino, *Vendetta* (New York, 1977). See also John E. Coxe, "The New Orleans Mafia Incident," *Louisiana Historical Quarterly* 20 (1937): 1067–1110, and John S. Kendall, "Who Killa de Chief?" *Louisiana Historical Quarterly* 22 (1939): 492–530 and "Blood on the Banquette," *Louisiana Historical Quarterly* 22 (1939): 819–856.
31 Taken from Daniel Bell, "Crime as an American Way of Life," *The Antioch Review* 13: 2 (Summer, 1953): 131–154.

32 Patricia McBroom, "Rethinking Crime," *Science News* 90, 16 (Oct. 15, 1966): 306.

33 For a contemporary view of the evolution of gangs into business, see James C .Young, "Crime Gangs Organized as Big Business," *New York Times*, April 4, 1926.

34 For a full investigation of these views, see James M. O'Kane, *The Crooked Ladder: Gangsters, Ethnicity and the American Dream* (New Brunswick, NJ, 1992), pp. 79–111.

35 Theodore Roosevelt, cited in Daniel Kanstroom, *Deportation Nation: Outsiders in American History* (Cambridge, MA, 2007), pp. 131–132.

36 Figures taken from Helen Chen, "Chinese Immigration into the United States: An Analysis of Changes in Policies," unpublished PhD thesis, Brandies University, 1980, p. 174.

37 Figures taken from Madeleine Y. Hsu, *Dreaming of Gold, Dreaming of Home: Transnationalism and Migration between the United States and South China, 1882–1943* (Palo Alto, CA, 2000), p. 207.

38 Figures taken from Emily Ryo, "Through the Back Door: Applying Theories of Legal Compliance to Illegal Immigration during the Chinese Exclusion Era," *Law & Social Inquiry* 31, 1 (Winter, 2006): 109–110. The judges' comments are cited in Hsu, op. cit., p. 75.

39 See May Ngai, *Impossible Subjects: Illegal Aliens and the Making of Modern America* (Princeton, NJ, 2004), pp. 66–67.

40 For an example of American views on Mexicans, see Frederick Starr, "The Mexican People," *Journal of International Relations* 11, 1 (July, 1920): 7–26.

41 See Abraham Hoffman, *Unwanted Mexican Americans in the Great Depression: Repatriation Pressures, 1929–1939* (Tucson, AZ, 1974).

42 Francisco E. Balderrama and Raymond Rodríguez, *Decade of Betrayal: Mexican Repatriation in the 1930s* (Albuquerque, NM, 2006).

43 Cited in National Commission on Law Observance and Enforcement, *Report No. 10: Crime and the Foreign Born* (Washington, DC, 1931), p. 23.

INDEX